BARNES & NOBLE
ILLUSTRATED
GUIDE TO

SITES OF THE
AMERICAN
REVOLUTION

by
Diane Ney

Consultant
John Buchanan

Concept and Design by
Richard J. Berenson

Produced by
Berenson Design & Books, Ltd.
New York

This book is dedicated to the thousands of ordinary men and women who hazarded their lives, their fortunes, and their sacred honor for the revolutionary ideal of individual liberty and to the National Park Service, which maintains and preserves America's Revolutionary War battlefields, monuments, and historic sites for future generations.

For information address:
Barnes & Noble
122 Fifth Avenue
New York, NY 10011
212-633-4000

Barnes & Noble and colophon are registered trademarks.

Library of Congress Cataloging-in-Publication Data
is available on request.

ISBN 0-7607-5095-5

First Printing

BARNES
& NOBLE
BOOKS
NEW YORK

The Barnes & Noble Illustrated Guide to Sites of the American Revolution is a fascinating guide to the many battlefields, museums, and sites that memorialize the war. By visiting these places, readers will discover—or rediscover— the bravery of the thousands of ordinary individuals who fought so strongly for their beliefs, and they can explore the sites on which history was made and America born.

Not every Revolutionary War site is included, since many merely have signposts denoting battlements and battlefields that are lost beneath urban sprawl. But within these pages, readers will find those sites and collections that are most worth exploring—places where the visitor can come away with some sense of what life was like for a participant in the war, or for a loved one waiting at home.

Included also are sections on the achievements of some of the people whom many history books have forgotten— women, African Americans, and Native Americans—as well as discussions on the Continental Army, the weaponry of the Revolution, and the founding of the navy and marines.

While every effort has been made to ensure the accuracy of the information contained in these pages, readers would be well advised to call the sites they wish to visit, as hours and admission fees are subject to change.

Contents

★ Site of Revolutionary War Battlefield

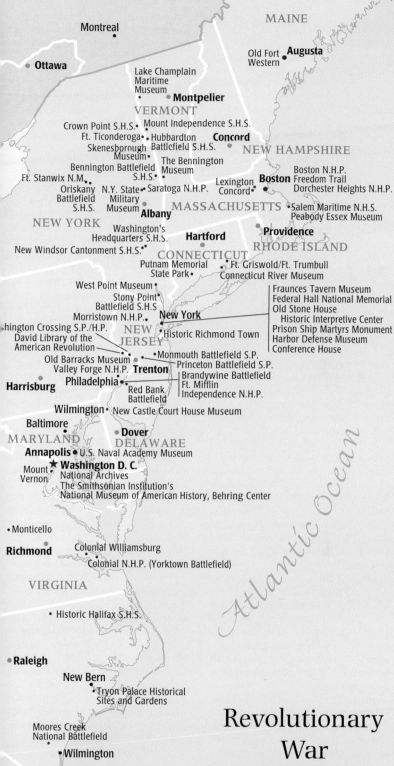

Montreal

MAINE

Ottawa

Old Fort Western • **Augusta**

Lake Champlain Maritime Museum

Montpelier

VERMONT

Crown Point S.H.S. • Mount Independence S.H.S.
Ft. Ticonderoga • Hubbardton
Skenesborough Battlefield S.H.S. **Concord**
Museum
Bennington Battlefield **The Bennington**
Museum

NEW HAMPSHIRE

Boston N.H.P.
Freedom Trail
Dorchester Heights N.H.P.

Ft. Stanwix N.M.
Oriskany N.Y. State Lexington **Boston**
Battlefield Military Saratoga N.H.P. Concord
S.H.S. Museum

Salem Maritime N.H.S.
Peabody Essex Museum

MASSACHUSETTS

NEW YORK **Albany**

Washington's
Headquarters S.H.S.

Hartford

Providence

New Windsor Cantonment S.H.S.

CONNECTICUT

RHODE ISLAND

Putnam Memorial
State Park

Ft. Griswold/Ft. Trumbull
Connecticut River Museum

West Point Museum

Fraunces Tavern Museum
Federal Hall National Memorial
Old Stone House
Historic Interpretive Center
Prison Ship Martyrs Monument
Harbor Defense Museum
Conference House

Stony Point
Battlefield S.H.S
Morristown N.H.P.

New York

...hington Crossing S.P./H.P.
David Library of the
American Revolution

**NEW
JERSEY**

Historic Richmond Town

Old Barracks Museum
Valley Forge N.H.P.

Trenton

Monmouth Battlefield S.P.
Princeton Battlefield S.P.
Brandywine Battlefield
Ft. Mifflin
Independence N.H.P.

Harrisburg
Philadelphia

Red Bank
Battlefield

Wilmington

New Castle Court House Museum

Baltimore

MARYLAND

Dover

DELAWARE

Annapolis

U.S. Naval Academy Museum

Mount
Vernon

★ **Washington D. C.**
National Archives
The Smithsonian Institution's
National Museum of American History, Behring Center

• Monticello

Richmond

Colonial Williamsburg

Colonial N.H.P. (Yorktown Battlefield)

VIRGINIA

• Historic Halifax S.H.S.

Raleigh

New Bern
• Tryon Palace Historical
Sites and Gardens

Moores Creek
National Battlefield

Wilmington

Atlantic Ocean

Revolutionary War Battlefields, Historic Sites, and Museums in the Guide

Connecticut River Museum

This museum chronicles the river's impact through exhibits on the maritime, economic, and cultural history of the Connecticut River Valley, which stretches from Canada to Long Island Sound.

Located in the charming New England town of Essex and housed in an 1878 steamboat warehouse, the museum doesn't have a lot of Revolutionary War artifacts, but what it has is choice—namely a working model of David Bushnell's submarine *American Turtle*.

Bushnell and the *Turtle*

The basic principle of a submersible watercraft was first put forth in 1578 by William Bourne, a British mathematician, who wrote, "It is possible to make a ship or boat that may go under the water unto the bottom, and so come up again at your pleasure. . . . Anything that sinketh is heavier than the proportion of so much water, and if it be lighter than the magnitude of so much water, then it swimmeth or appeareth above the water."

A Dutch inventor, Cornelius van Drebel, is thought to have actually built the first submarine, in the early 1600s. Subsequently, more than a dozen types of submarines were patented in England alone during the early 1700s. But apparently no one thought to use the submarine as a military weapon until David Bushnell.

Raised on a Connecticut farm, Bushnell did not have the money to enroll at Yale College until 1771, when he was 31 years old. While at Yale, Bushnell experimented with exploding gunpowder underwater and, during his final school vacation, used his own funds to construct an underwater bomb and the submarine to deliver it.

Bushnell was an engineering officer during the Revolution. On the recommendation of Governor Jonathan Trumbull of Connecticut, he was given an audience with George Washington, to whom he proposed using his submarine to explode a British ship.

Washington, who would later describe Bushnell as "a man of great Mechanical powers—fertile of invention—and a master in execution," hadn't much faith in the project's succeeding but gave Bushnell the go-ahead. One supporting factor may have been that Bushnell financed the operation himself, and, indeed, never received any compensation for any of his efforts.

Between May and July of 1776, British commander General Thomas Gage received reports from a spy that an American device was being built "that would effectively destroy the Royal Navy," but the British weren't able to find out exactly what the device was.

In July 1776, Admiral Lord Richard Howe arrived in New York with 150 ships, the largest expeditionary force England had ever launched. In late August, the Americans lost the battle for Long Island; and on September 3, Congress passed a resolution that Washington's forces retreat from the city of New York if it could not be held, rather than have it destroyed in battle. Into this desperate situation stepped David Bushnell and his *American Turtle*.

On the night of September 6, the *Turtle* was launched into New York Harbor with the mission to blow up Lord Howe's flagship, H.M.S. *Eagle*. The *Turtle* was to have been operated by Bushnell's brother Ezra; but Ezra, according to differing accounts, had either fallen very ill the day before or had died. In either case, he wasn't available, and a last-minute substitute was found in Ezra Lee.

After paddling two and a half hours to get himself into position beneath the *Eagle*, Lee found he couldn't attach the explosive device to the ship's bottom. For years after, it was thought that the *Eagle* was copper-bottomed and the screwing device couldn't penetrate the copper. But Stephen Howarth in his history of the United States Navy writes that records show the *Eagle* did not have a copper bottom at that time. "All that prevented [the attaching of the bomb] was that Bushnell had not allowed for Newton's third law of dynamics—that a given force has an equal and opposite reaction. With nothing to support *Turtle* underneath, the harder Lee turned the drill, the harder he pushed himself away from the *Eagle*."

After repeated attempts, Lee admitted defeat, steered the *Turtle* away from the British fleet, and released the mine, which exploded in the East River. Several similar attempts were made by Bushnell but also proved unsuccessful. The *American Turtle* was finally captured by the British during transport and destroyed.

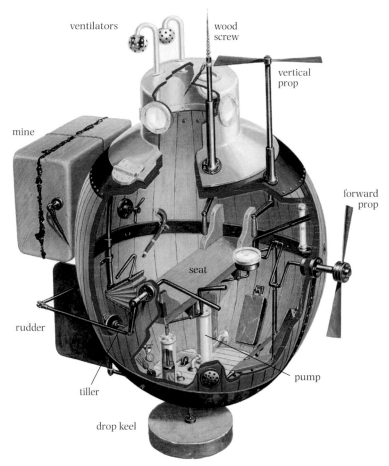

ventilators   wood screw

vertical prop

mine

forward prop

seat

rudder

pump

tiller

drop keel

This modern rendering *of* Turtle *is based on Bushnell's own written description, and is more accurate than an often reproduced 1875 drawing. This drawing does not show the ballast tanks. To submerge, the operator simply flooded water into the craft until it was negatively buoyant. This left the operator knee-deep in water. A hand pump was used to remove the water for returning to the surface.*

In January 1778, Bushnell was called upon again to use his fertile inventor's mind, this time to disrupt the British line of supply ships heading into Philadelphia.

He came up with the idea of mines—kegs loaded with powder that would explode upon bumping against another object. These were set floating down the Delaware River and immediately caused great alarm among the British on land and sea, who feared that the kegs were something akin to Trojan horses, "filled with armed rebels, who were to issue forth in the dead of the night, as did the Grecians of old from their wooden horse at the siege of Troy, and take the city by surprise."

British troops on shore and seamen aboard ships began shooting anything floating by. Most of the kegs were destroyed, along with large logs, floating branches, and fish that just happened to be in the wrong place at the wrong time.

In 1785, Thomas Jefferson wrote

George Washington from Paris, asking for his recollections of Bushnell and his submarine. Washington admitted to Jefferson he didn't have much faith in the apparatus, but "I then thought and still think that it was an effort of genius." Bushnell, responding to Jefferson's interest, sent him a detailed description of his "Submarine Vessel." He also noted that he would have experimented further and perfected the Turtle but for lack of money. It's tempting to speculate the impact a fleet of submarines would have had on the war, had funding been made available.

In 1795, Bushnell settled in Georgia, where he began teaching at Franklin College and practicing medicine under the name Dr. David Bush.

Visiting the Museum

The museum is in the process of creating a new exhibit showcasing its working replica of the *American Turtle*. This exhibit, which will include information on the building of the submarine and its expedition into New York Harbor and on the life of David Bushnell, is expected to open in 2005.

The working replica is an extraordinary piece of craftsmanship, built according to Bushnell's specifications. Launched during the 1976 American Bicentennial, it was taken out into the Connecticut River, where its maneuverability and ability to submerge were proven. Looking at the replica, it's apparent that this was a prototype of simplicity and efficiency. The *Turtle* got its name from the fact that it looked like two tortoise shells banded together. The submarine was made of several large pieces of oak held together with iron bands to help withstand water pressure. The seams were caulked, and the whole device was smeared with tar to prevent water from seeping in. Its hull measured seven and a half feet by six feet, and it was maneuvered by a rudder and vertical and horizontal propellers. The *Turtle* could stay down as long as 30 minutes. To descend, the operator let water into a ballast tank; to ascend, he pumped water out.

In his detailed description to Jefferson, Bushnell described how "the navigator rows with one hand, & steers with the other . . . [The submarine] had two oars, of about 12 inches in length, & 4 or 5 in width, shaped like the arms of a windmill . . . and were worked by means of a winch (or crank) and with hard labour, the machine might be impelled at the rate of 3 nots an hour for a short time. Seven hundred pounds of lead were fixed on the bottom for ballast, and two hundred weight of it was so contrived, as to let it go in case the pumps choaked, so that you could rise at the surface of the water." There was also a screw that was used to drill through the wooden bottom of a target vessel and attach a line that brought the bomb, with a timing device, against the vessel.

The museum also has a small model of the *Oliver Cromwell*, a Connecticut navy ship that was constructed in the building still standing across from the museum, though the building no longer houses the shipbuilding operation it did in 1776. Seamen who sailed aboard the *Cromwell* had to sign an agreement similar to those used by other state navies, which dictated in part that they "Do hereby severally Acknowledge ourselves Inlisted on Bord the Armed Ship belonging to the Free State of Connecticut under Command of Capt Wm Coit . . . in Defence of the Rights & Liberties of the United States of North America in General & of Connecticut in Particular subject to Do the Duties of our Respective Places on bord and Obey the Commands of all the Officers Superior to us. . . ." The *Cromwell*, whose longest cannon was an 18-pounder, was captured in 1779.

There's also information about the role the Connecticut River Valley played in the construction of two frigates for the Continental Navy—the *Trumbull* and the *Bourbon*, both built by John Cotton in Chatham, Connecticut. The *Trumbull* was launched in September 1776 and captured in August 1781 off the Delaware Capes. Little is known about the Bourbon other than that construction was begun in 1779 and she was sold before she was completed in 1783. The Connecticut River was too shallow for the ships, and they had to be carried across the bar at the mouth of the river.

Connecticut supplied a large share of American privateers during the war, with ships from Connecticut ports capturing 80 vessels in one year, as noted in an exhibit. Another exhibit displays samples of shipbuilding tools.

The museum is planning a new exhibit in 2005 on Silas Dean, a Connecticut native who preceded Benjamin Franklin as Congress's representative to France during the war.

Visitor Information

860-767-8269

www.ctrivermuseum.org

Hours: Tuesday through Sunday, 10 a.m. until 5 p.m.; closed on Easter, Thanksgiving Day, December 25, and January 1.

Admission: Moderate charge, with reduced rates for seniors and for children six years and older.

Accessibility: The museum is handicapped accessible.

Special Events: Guided hikes, lectures, and educational programs are held throughout the year. Consult the Web site for schedule.

Getting There: From I-95, take exit 69 to state route 9. Go north on route 9 to exit 3 (Essex) and follow signs to the Historic Waterfront. From the north, take I-91 to exit 22S onto state route 9. Go south on route 9 to exit 3 (Essex) and follow signs to the Historic Waterfront. The museum is at 67 Main Street in Essex.

Fort Griswold Battlefield State Park and Fort Trumbull State Park

The last known military action in the North took place at Fort Griswold, where the Battle of Groton Heights began as a valiant defense of the port of New London, Connecticut, and ended in a notorious massacre of untrained militia as young as 10 years old.

Benedict Arnold, though he had no actual part in the massacre, will always be branded as the commander in charge who lost control of his men. Added to his firing of the town of New London, the Fort Griswold massacre for generations following the war erased any credit due for Arnold's brave assault on Quebec and his determined valor at Lake Champlain.

There have been numerous accounts of the atrocity, and from this distance it's impossible to know the absolute truth of what occurred, but the accepted truth is that New Jersey Loyalists under British command bayoneted and shot unarmed men who had surrendered. Savagery was not unheard of in the Revolutionary War; but coming as this did just a month before the war effectively came to a close at Yorktown, it rankled for years and set the tone for later encounters against the British during the War of 1812.

Fort Griswold remains one of the best extant remains of a Revolutionary War fort in the country, with almost all the original earthworks and stone walls. The facilities at Fort Trumbull have undergone a 25-million-dollar facelift in the last six years.

The Battle of Groton Heights

In the summer of 1781, a Loyalist newspaper referred to New London as "the most detestable nest of pirates on the continent." Salem, Massachusetts, may have taken issue with that charge, as it considered itself quite a detestable nest of pirates, or privateers, too. Since the start of the war, both towns—and several others—had taken delight in their privateers capturing British merchant ships. By 1781, the shipping rates of British insurance firms had reached 23 percent, and British merchants and financiers were pressuring the government to find a solution or risk a ruined economy.

It was also in the summer of 1781 that George Washington and his French allies began their incredible march from New York to Yorktown, Virginia. Sir Henry Clinton, now in his fourth year as British commander in chief, knew about the march and sought ways to delay or disrupt it.

Around this time a New London privateer captured a ship transporting the personal effects of a number of British officers, and the knowledge that these would now be sold on the open market rankled.

Into this complex picture stepped Brigadier General Benedict Arnold, patriot turned Tory and regretted son of the town of Norwich, just 12 miles from New London. Arnold suggested to Clinton that he could take a small contingent of men, catch an onshore breeze, sail into New London Harbor on the Thames

East of the river on Groton Heights, Fort Griswold commands the harbor and the surrounding countryside. Originally a deep trench surrounded the fort on three sides. The lower walls were faced with stone and topped with a barrier of cedar pickets projecting outward. Above this was an earthen wall with openings for cannons. A tunnel-like passageway led to a covered ditch that ended at the southwest battery (upper right).

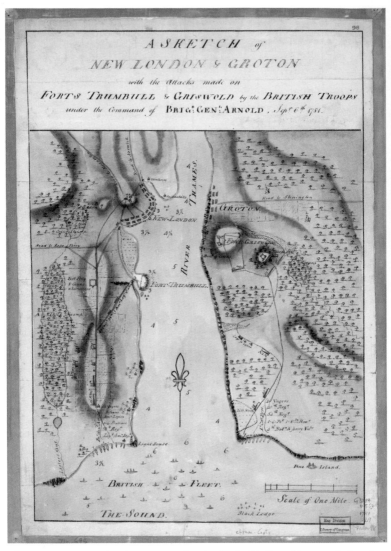

A SKETCH of NEW LONDON & GROTON with the attacks made on FORTS TRUMBULL & GRISWOLD by the BRITISH TROOPS under the Command of BRIG: GEN: ARNOLD, Sep: 6th 1781.

This contemporary sketch map, created and published by Daniel Lyman, depicts the attacks made on Forts Trumbull and Griswold by the British troops under the command of Brigadier General Benedict Arnold on September 6, 1781.

River, disable Forts Griswold and Trumbull, destroy the privateer fleet and New London's warehouses, return to his ships in time to catch an offshore breeze, and skedaddle back to New York. His would be a surgical raid that would catch the residents unaware, destroy a thriving privateering business, and force George Washington to look over his shoulder and perhaps send some of his troops back to New England.

But on September 6, when Arnold and his ships arrived, the wind changed unexpectedly and Arnold found himself stuck in the mouth of the harbor. Rather than play sitting duck, Arnold disembarked his men, sending 800 up the east bank of the river under Lieutenant Colonel Edmund Eyre to attack Fort Griswold and another 800 along the west bank to attack Fort Trumbull and New London.

Before disembarking, however,

Arnold played a clever trick on the local militia. As it was morning, he knew that his ships had been spotted, so he waited for the two cannon shots signaling that the forts were under attack. As soon as these were fired, Arnold fired a third shot. Three shots was the signal a privateer was returning to port with a prize—cause for celebration, not alarm. This ruse delayed the arrival of defenders at both forts and contributed to the disorganization in their ranks.

Also contributing was the fact that these men were not regular militia. The oldest was in his 60s, the youngest 10. Two were African American. These were ordinary citizens, some of whom had served at one time or another in the state or county militia but were certainly not trained soldiers. This band of local defenders was setting itself against seasoned British troops, Tory soldiers from New Jersey's 3rd Battalion, and a smattering of foot jägers—the elite Hessian sharpshooters of the British army.

The two forts—Fort Trumbull on the west side of the river at New London and Fort Griswold on the east side on the heights at Groton—had been built between 1777 and 1779 by the local citizens working in relays. In designing Trumbull, the assumption had been that attackers would come by water, so the three earthen ramparts, built on three acres of a rocky point called Mamacock, were facing east, south, and north. The land side had no rampart. Fort Griswold, on the other hand, was very much a secure four-sided fort, plus it had the advantage of being on the heights.

Arnold marched into New London and set fire to the town, destroying 143 buildings and leaving 100 families homeless. The remainder of his contingent attacked Fort Trumbull, which had only about 45 defenders. Their commander, Captain Adam Shapley, wisely ordered his men to fire a volley, spike their guns (spiking a muzzle-loading gun meant driving a spike into the vent, the small hole through which the charge is ignited, to render the gun useless), and evacuate to Fort Griswold to join their confederates.

With this addition, Fort Griswold faced the British force of 800 with about 165 defenders, under the command of Colonel William Ledyard. When Lieutenant Colonel Eyre demanded Ledyard surrender, Ledyard is said to have replied, "Let the consequences be what they may, we will not surrender."

Following a volley that killed a large number of British, another demand for surrender was made, and again Ledyard refused. Meanwhile, two things were happening elsewhere. Benedict Arnold had scaled the hill outside New London and, seeing how well situated Fort Griswold was, sent word to call off the attack. The order came too late. About the same time, the New Jersey Loyalists were arriving at the fort with the artillery, which had been held up in the marshes below.

A Terrible Massacre

A few of the later accounts stated that at some point during the battle the halyard was hit and the fort's flag dropped. Though it was quickly raised again, the British may have taken this as a sign of surrender. They rushed to enter the fort, at which point they were repulsed and many killed. If this is true, their thinking the Americans acted dishonorably might provide some reason for their subsequent actions.

In any event, once Ledyard saw the artillery arriving, he knew the fort couldn't hold out and he did signal surrender, ordering his men to lay down their arms. The battle had lasted 40 minutes.

By this time, the British commander, Eyre, had been mortally wounded, and his second in command, Major William Montgomery, had been killed. Here again accounts vary. One of the British commanders, perhaps a Major Bromfield, himself wounded, pushed his way into the fort, yelling, "Who commands here?" Ledyard approached him, saying, "I did, sir, and now you do," and handed over his sword.

The American version of the story has the major taking Ledyard's sword and repeatedly running him through with it. As Ledyard lay dying, one of his officers grabbed the sword and killed the major, after which the British troops attacked, bayoneting and shooting the unarmed men.

The British version, written by Benedict Arnold, makes no mention of this. In his report to Clinton dated September 8, Arnold wrote, "Our loss, though very considerable, is very short of the enemy's who lost most of their officers, among whom was their commander, Colonel Ledyard. Eighty-five men were found dead in Fort Griswold, and 60 wounded, most of them mortally."

Two Spies

Benedict Arnold wasn't the only spy to fight in the Battle of Groton Heights. One of the defenders of Fort Griswold was a Captain David Gray. A Massachusetts Yankee and veteran of Fort Ticonderoga, Gray was one of the most successful American spies of the war. Since early in 1780, he had been feeding useless information to the British, sometimes to Sir Henry Clinton himself, while reporting intelligence on British movements and plans to George Washington. By a stroke of bad luck, Gray stopped in New London to give written intelligence to Colonel Ledyard at the time of the battle. Gray joined in the fight, but escaped, before the fort was taken.

He also stated that the firing of residences in New London was an accident, the result of an unknown store of powder exploding.

Rufus Avery, one of the few survivors to be taken prisoner to New York, described the battle in his journal. He didn't see the attack on Ledyard, but he did see the carnage afterward. He was bayoneted three times and stumbled to a magazine near where lay many of the dead and wounded. Avery noted that it was only the fact that "the ground and everything [was] wet with human blood" that kept the magazine from exploding from errant gunfire.

Some 30 of the less wounded were put in a wagon for transport to the ships. Prisoners expected to survive were valuable commodities, as they could be traded for British prisoners. Descending the steep hill from Groton Heights, the wagon got away from its handlers and crashed into a tree at the foot of the hill. Now suffering even more horribly, those who survived the crash were taken to the nearby house of Ebenezer Avery, who himself was among the wounded, and left there all night with no medical attention or even water to drink. Next day, Avery and the others were taken on board the British ships.

At the conclusion of his report to Clinton, Arnold noted, "The officers and troops in general behaved with the greatest intrepidity and firmness."

The day after the battle, at a church service, there was only one male. All the other males of the congregation had been killed or captured.

*A **bronze tablet** memorializes the spot where British major William Montgomery fell during the battle. The defender aiming a spear at Montgomery is Jordan Freeman, an African American.*

Visiting Fort Trumbull Park

This is the third Fort Trumbull constructed on this site. The three forts have served a variety of purposes, among them a Revolutionary War fort, the first Coast Guard Academy, a merchant marine officers school, a branch of the University of Connecticut, and, lastly, the Naval Undersea Warfare Center, which closed in 1996. The current fort, built sometime between 1839 and 1852, is a restoration of Fort Trumbull as it was in the 1800s.

The Visitor Center, located in the state park at 90 Walbach Street in New London, shows a 10-minute surround-sound video on the history of the fort, from the Revolutionary War to modern times. Exiting the theater, visitors see a large diorama of the Thames River, showing the movements of British and American troops on September 6. A chronological exhibit then takes visitors through the history of the three forts, using touch-screen interactive displays, 3-D models, graphics, and text panels.

Visitors can walk out onto the fort's ramparts for a spectacular view of New London Harbor and Long Island Sound. There are also two Rodman cannons and an artillery crew on display.

A water-taxi service between Fort Trumbull and Fort Griswold begins the summer of 2004.

Visiting Fort Griswold Battlefield State Park

The centerpiece of this 16-acre park is the fort itself, with its original earthworks and stone walls that, through time, have been worn down to about three feet in height.

Visitors begin at the Monument House Museum, which has a model of the fort as it was in 1781, exhibits on the battle and on life in Groton at the time, and artifacts that include powder horns, muskets, clothing from the 18th century, and Colonel Ledyard's sword.

There are also books containing the names of the defenders of the fort, each with a brief biological sketch, which visitors are welcome to print out.

The fort itself has a tablet marking the spot where Colonel Ledyard fell, a plaque noting where the British commander Montgomery was killed, and another plaque listing the names of the defenders.

Nearby is the Groton Battle Monument obelisk, dedicated in 1830. In celebration of the 1881 centennial, the top was enclosed and the monument was increased to a height of 134 feet. There are 166 steps to the top, from which there's a beautiful view of the fort below and the surrounding towns.

Also nearby is the Ebenezer Avery House, administered by the Avery Memorial Association. It was here that the wounded were brought and left the night of the battle. The house originally stood on the banks of the Thames River. In 1971, to ensure its preservation, the house was dismantled and recreated on this site.

Visitor Information

860-444-7591 or 860-449-6877
www.dep.state.ct.us/stateparks/
    parks/fort_trumbull.htm
www.dep.state.ct.us/stateparks/
    parks/fort_griswold.htm
www.fortfriends.org

Hours: Fort Trumbull grounds are open 8 a.m. until sunset, year-round. The fort and Visitor Center are open Wednesday through Sunday, 9 a.m. until 4 p.m., from late May through Columbus Day. The fort is closed between the Columbus Day and Memorial Day weekends.

Fort Griswold grounds are open 8 a.m. until sunset, year-round. The fort, museum, and monument are open daily from Memorial Day until Labor Day and weekends from Labor Day until Columbus Day, 10 a.m. until 5 p.m. The Ebenezer Avery House is open June through August on weekends and holiday Mondays, 1 p.m. until 5 p.m.

Admission: There is no admission to the park area at either fort. Fort Trumbull and its Visitor Center have a moderate charge. Connecticut residents 65 and older may obtain a Charter Oak Pass for free admission to all state parks. There is no admission fee for Fort Griswold. A donation is welcome at the Ebenezer Avery House.

Accessibility: Fort Trumbull and its Visitor Center are handicapped accessible, as are the park area and walkways. Fort Griswold and the obelisk are not accessible, but the Monument House Museum is.

Getting There: To Fort Trumbull from I-95 northbound, take exit 83 to downtown New London. Go straight at the light on Huntington Street. Turn right on Jay Street and continue as it becomes Truman Street. Turn left on Blinman Street and continue straight ahead as it becomes Howard Street. Turn left on Walbach Street, then right on East Street. The park entrance is on the left.

To Fort Trumbull from I-95 southbound, take exit 84S to downtown New London. At the end of the ramp, merge onto Eugene O'Neill Drive. Turn left at Tilley Street, then right on Bank Street. At Howard Street turn left. Turn left on Walbach Street, then right on East Street. The park entrance is on the left.

To Fort Griswold from I-95 northbound toward Groton, take the second exit after the Gold Star Bridge, onto the Clarence B. Sharp Highway. Follow signs to Fort Griswold.

To Fort Griswold from I-91 southbound, take exit 22 onto state route 9. Go south to the end of route 9 and take I-95 northbound. Then follow directions above.

Gravestone Inscriptions

The dead from the Battle of Groton Heights are buried in several places in New London and Groton. Many of their tombstones are very expressive of the anger and despair felt by the survivors. Those interested in reading all the tombstone inscriptions should check out www.revwar.com/ftgriswold/graves.html. Some include religious verses; others poetry; still others the simple emotions of a searing pain. Elnathan Perkins, volunteer: "In Memory of Mr. Elnathan Perkins who was Slain at Fort Griswould Septr 6th 1781 in the 64th year of his Age/ Ye British Power that boast aloud of your Great Lenity/ Behold my fate when at your feet I and three Sons must Die."

Colonel William Ledyard is buried in a cemetery named for him in Groton, where a monument was erected in 1854 by the state of Connecticut.

Putnam Memorial State Park

This lovely state park honors Connecticut's own General Israel Putnam and the several thousand men under his command who were quartered near Redding during the winter of 1778–79.

In November 1778, Washington directed that his Northern Army build their winter bases in what became the form of an arc from New Jersey to Connecticut, creating a three-quarter ring around the more than 25,000 British in New York. From Redding, Putnam and his three brigades had to be prepared to move west if the British attacked the Hudson Highlands or southwest to defend the Connecticut coastal towns.

Visitors to the historic sections of the park gain a sense of the deprivations suffered by those quartered here, and through their interest honor the memory of those Patriots.

History of the Encampment

By the winter of 1778, Boston had been lost and won, New York City lost, Philadelphia lost by the Patriots and then relinquished by the British. Saratoga had been won, prompting France to enter the war as America's ally. The Hessians had been surprised at Trenton; Washington had won at Princeton and held the field at Monmouth. Although Savannah was lost in late December, things were looking up, and the Continental Army had reason to be proud of itself.

Yet there were still problems with pay distribution and delivery of supplies, and these were especially felt in winter encampments such as the one established here. Records show 1500 of Putnam's men had no shoes and 400 no coats or blankets.

In late November 1778, General Israel Putnam, a commander at the Siege of Boston and the Battle of Long Island, was ordered to winter his troops in Redding, Connecticut. These troops consisted of two Connecticut brigades, one New Hampshire brigade, and one additional regiment. Also here were some 200 free African Americans and a number of Native Americans, plus a large number of wives and camp followers.

When the troops arrived, they were given the task of building three campgrounds on the northern edge of Redding. Heavy rains in mid-December slowed the building process. In late December, a terrible winter storm brought construction to a halt. Though most of the men were in huts, reportedly some had to endure the storm in tents.

Whether in huts or tents, everyone was enduring insufficient supplies of food. One of the soldiers later recalled, "We went in our old Continental line of starving and freezing. We now and then got a little bad bread and salt beef . . . I believe chiefly horse beef, for it was generally thought to be such at the time."

Putnam and his senior officers were quartered in houses in the town, which may be why they didn't sense the growing unrest among some of the men. On December 30 a group of men in one of the Connecticut brigades mutinied in protest over the lack of supplies and overdue pay. When they threatened to march on the State Assembly in Hartford with their demands, Putnam confronted them. He reminded them of their commitment to the Patriot cause, and ordered them back to their huts.

Given the deprivations and misery the men suffered, it's incredible that by the beginning of March, only 200 men had deserted the Connecticut brigades.

With the coming of spring, exercise drills were incorporated into the daily routine to prepare the troops for the summer campaigns. From March until May, troops left here to take up their duties, some in northern Vermont and others in the Hudson Highlands. Before leaving, they burned all the structures—numbering about 100—to prevent the British from using them.

Visiting the Encampment Site

Putnam Memorial State Park, established in 1886 as Connecticut's first state park, was officially recognized by the state for its historical and archaeological importance in 2001. As a result, a four million dollar restoration of the park, its Visitor Center, points of interest, and signage is expected to be completed in the spring of 2005.

A map of the encampment that includes information on the campgrounds and the soldiers is available at the fieldstone museum building. Artifacts discovered during archaeological digs are displayed here, among them building tools, cannonballs, and personal items that belonged to the soldiers.

The area behind the museum is thought to be the site of one of the campgrounds. More than 100 piles of stones mark the location of the huts. A log cabin near the piles is an early-20th-century attempt to reconstruct a hut using a written description from one of the soldiers' journals, as described in the brochure. The 14-by-16-foot huts were built of logs, with mud filling the cracks between. Each had a fieldstone chimney for heating and cooking for its group of 12 soldiers or eight officers.

The soldiers were allotted one 16-foot strip of land per hut from which they had to garner building materials and firewood. The strips were guarded fiercely, especially when wood became less plentiful as the surrounding area was stripped of resources.

West of a stone-lined pit that is traditionally identified as the powder magazine is a reconstructed Officers' Barracks. Situated on Overlook Hill, the original barracks would have enabled officers to keep an eye on the huts below. Those who perished are remembered in the Cemetery, where the headstone is inscribed "In Memory of the Unknown Heroes Buried Here." Exactly how many died that winter is unknown, but there were 15 recorded deaths.

Near the Cemetery is the Monument, dedicated in 1888 to those who lived and died here. The 42-foot-high obelisk is topped with a large granite ball inscribed with the names of the senior officers who served here and a eulogy for their troops.

A more distinctively individual monument stands at the main entrance off route 107: a statue of Israel Putnam depicting him in what came to be known as the ride down Put's Hill.

In February 1779, Putnam was almost captured by a raiding party of British soldiers at the house where he was staying. Jumping into the saddle, Old Put, as he was called, steered his horse down a flight of stone steps (or a steep cliff, depending on which version of the story is being told) while the British fired rather than dared to follow. Though such a ride might have seemed a risky gamble for a 60-year-old at that time, it was business as usual for Putnam, who was a vigorous, indefatigable leader. A little more than three years earlier, Putnam had ridden 100 miles through the Connecticut countryside spreading the news of Concord and Lexington.

Israel Putnam's famous ride down Put's Hill, depicted in a 19th-century engraving.

Some historians tend to dismiss Putnam as a well-meaning bungler when it came to battle tactics, and his decisions at the Battle of Long Island apparently contributed to the Patriots' disastrous defeat. Yet Putnam should also be remembered as a committed Patriot who put his life and all he had on the line for the cause.

The cannons flanking the entrance are from the Civil War, as are the stacked cannonballs.

A reconstructed log Guardhouse inside the entrance gates is thought to be similar to the one built for the encampment.

The 232-acre park is open for hiking, fishing, picnicking, and field sports year-round. Visitors interested in taking the three-quarter-mile self-guided tour should enter the park from state route 58, rather than through the main gates off state route 107.

Visitor Information

203-938-2285

dep.state.ct.us/stateparks/ (click on Find a Park, then choose Putnam)

Hours: The park is open year-round, 8 a.m. until sunset. The museum is open Memorial Day through Columbus Day, 11 a.m. until 5 p.m. daily.

Admission: Free.

Accessibility: The museum is accessible. Parts of the trails may require assistance.

Special Events: Reenactments of the encampment are held every June.

Getting There: The park is located about 5 miles southeast of Danbury, at the junction of state routes 58 and 107.

National Archives

The Declaration of Independence, the Constitution, and the Bill of Rights are on display at the U.S. National Archives in Washington, D.C., in a newly renovated exhibition—*Charters of Freedom*—that opened in September 2003. It's part of an ambitious new design called The National Archives Experience. Charters of Freedom will eventually be joined by Public Vaults, an interactive and display exhibition that explores the history of records, from parchment to electronic, and provides computer access to thousands of archived documents. Also planned are the William G. McGowan Theater, a special Exhibition Gallery, and a Learning Center. The entire Experience is expected to be completed by 2005, with Public Vaults and the McGowan Theater opening in 2004.

History of the Archives

The National Archives is the permanent collection of historical documents related to the establishment and administration of the United States government, dating back to 1774. The government agency that oversees the collection is the National Archives and Records Administration (NARA), a nationwide network with 33 facilities.

Housed in these 33 facilities are approximately 26 million cubic feet of original textual and nontextual materials; 93,000 films; five and a half million maps, charts, and architectural drawings; 207,000 sound and video recordings; 18 million aerial photographs; 35 million still pictures and posters, and three and a half billion electronic records. Of these billions of records, only three are on permanent display.

Thomas Jefferson is thought to have been the first to officially express concern about preservation of government records, and plans for national archives were considered as early as 1810. Plans were finally brought to fruition in the 1930s, with the completion of the National Archives.

The Archives was built on the site of what had been Washington's Central Market and an underground waterway called Tiber Creek. To ensure stability in the marshy soil, 8575 piles were driven 21 feet into the ground. When the cornerstone was laid in 1933, it contained, among other items, copies of the Constitution and the Declaration of Independence.

The originals, meanwhile, had endured more than 200 years of adventurous travels. Tradition has it that the Declaration, once signed, was kept in the offices of Charles Thomson, secretary of the Continental Congress, in Philadelphia, and that during the war it traveled with the Congress, often one step ahead of the British army.

In 1790, Thomas Jefferson, as the first Secretary of State, was put in charge of "all records, books and papers" of the new government, including the Declaration of Independence and, presumably, the Constitution, soon to be joined by the Bill of Rights.

At this point, the documents were traveling with the Department of State from Philadelphia to New York and finally to Washington, D.C. When the British set parts of the city afire during the War of 1812, the documents were put in linen bags and carted to an unused gristmill in Leesburg, Virginia, where they stayed until the British had vacated the area.

For the next 30 years or so, they were transferred from one building to another in the capital city as the State Department changed locations in an ever-growing bureaucracy. At one point, the Declaration, along with George Washington's commission as commander in chief, was mounted in a single frame and hung in a hallway—directly opposite a window letting in lots of bright sunlight. Eventually people noticed that the Declaration was fading, and it was placed in an exhibit cabinet in the State Department library. Finally its condition was so alarming that in 1894 it was taken from the display and placed in a steel case.

On September 21, 1921, an executive order was issued transferring the Constitution and the Declaration of Independence to the Library of Congress. The next day, the Librarian of Congress transported the documents in his Model T Ford from the State Department to his office safe, where they remained three years before being put on display in the library in 1924. Except for a brief sojourn during World War II to the vaults at Fort Knox, they remained at the Library of Congress until 1952.

On December 13, 1952, the documents were transported from the Library of Congress to the National Archives in an armored Marine Corps personnel carrier accompa-

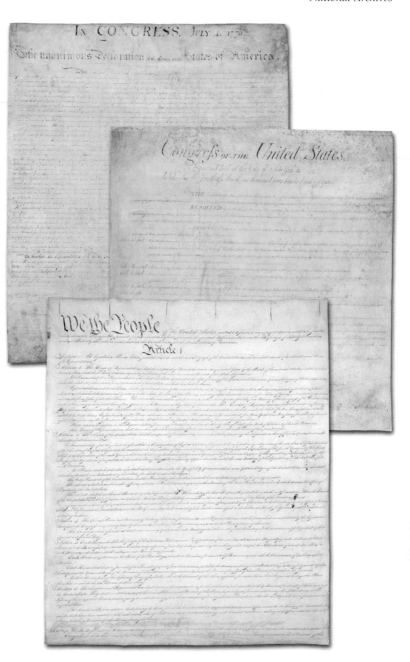

***The Declaration of Independence**, the Constitution, and the Bill of Rights were written using iron-gall ink, as were Leonardo da Vinci's notebooks, Johann Sebastian Bach's compositions, and thousands of other cherished items. Iron-gall ink was valued by the ancients and well into the 19th century because of its staying power, and only in modern times have preservationists discovered its corrosive effect on paper and parchment. Ongoing research continues at major institutions worldwide, including the National Archives, to offset this corrosive element and preserve the world's treasured documents.*

nied by ceremonial troops from all the services, two tanks, four servicemen with submachine guns, and a motorcycle escort. There the documents, which had been placed in glass encasements filled with helium gas, were displayed in the building's rotunda.

The renovation of the display area, completed in 2003, included new encasements filled with argon gas and restoration of Barry Faulkner's murals above the documents on the east and west walls.

Visiting the National Archives

Entry to the newly renovated exhibit area is through a belowground entrance on Constitution Avenue, and then through a series of passageways leading to the rotunda, with its 75-foot half-domed ceiling and neoclassical interior.

Faulkner's beautifully restored murals (originally completed in 1936) dominate the walls. Measuring 13 feet by 36 feet, they depict Thomas Jefferson submitting the Declaration of Independence to John Hancock (*Declaration of Independence*) and James Madison submitting the Constitution to George Washington (*The Constitution*). The regally clad George Washington brings to mind that the Senate originally wanted the President's official title to be His Highness the President of the United States of America and Protector of their Liberties. Fortunately the House's idea to call him or her simply the President of the United States prevailed.

On either side of the Charters of Freedom are cases with displays depicting events leading up to the founding of the United States and events that evolved from that founding. Among these documents are the 1775 proclamation by King George III "Suppressing Rebellion and Sedition," the "Agreement of Secrecy" signed by the Continental Congress in 1775, the Articles of Confederation, and the Louisiana Purchase.

The Declaration of Independence, not surprisingly, is barely readable, but John Hancock's signature can still be made out. All four pages of the Constitution remain legible, as does the Bill of Rights.

At the end of each day, the encasements holding the documents are secured in a vault.

At the formal transferal ceremony in December 1952, President Harry Truman said, "We are enshrining these documents for future ages." In America, that means continuing to make them accessible to the average citizen. One is an inspired "expression of the American mind" as Thomas Jefferson called it, one a reflection of the American genius for compromise, and the last a statement of basic freedoms. Combined they become an eloquent articulation of the American Revolution's legacy to succeeding generations.

Visitor Information

202-501-5000
www.archives.gov

Hours: The Rotunda is open 10 a.m. until 5:30 p.m. from the day after Labor Day through March 31 (except December 25), and from 10 a.m. until 7 p.m. from April 1 through the Friday before Memorial Day weekend, then from 10 a.m. until 9 p.m. from Memorial Day weekend through Labor Day.

Admission: Free.

Accessibility: Those with special needs should use the entrance on Pennsylvania Avenue. Handicapped-designated parking is available in a small lot on 9th Street between Constitution Avenue and Pennsylvania Avenue, on a first-come first-served basis.

Special Events: Events will be scheduled to celebrate the openings of the remaining sections of The National Archives Experience.

Getting There: The National Archives is located at 7th Street and Constitution Avenue NW.

By car: From Virginia, take I-395 into the city onto 14th Street. Proceed north on 14th Street to Constitution Avenue and turn east (right) to 7th Street. From Maryland, take I-495 (the Beltway) to U.S. 50 west and follow route 50 into the city, where it becomes New York Avenue, then go south on 7th Street to Constitution Avenue. In the city, take Pennsylvania Avenue from the west or Maryland Avenue from the east. Parking is extremely limited in this area and public transportation is strongly recommended.

By subway: The Archives/Navy Memorial stop (yellow and green lines) is across from the Archives' Pennsylvania Avenue entrance.

By bus: The 30s bus route stops at the corner of 7th Street and Pennsylvania Avenue and at the corner of 7th Street and Constitution Avenue.

Genealogy at the Archives

For those interested in tracing an ancestor who may have fought in the Revolutionary War, the National Archives has veterans' records dating back to 1775. Before coming to the Archives, it's best to check out the NARA Web site at www.archives.gov regarding researching veterans records.

Revolutionary War Weaponry

Small Arms

Muskets, fowlers, carbines, rifles, and fusils (short muskets)—Continental soldiers carried a variety of firearms in the early years of the war. Many arms were brought from home, since most colonials were required to serve in their state and local militias.

Single-shot flintlock muskets were by far the most common weapon for those living in the eastern colonies, while rifles, being far more accurate, were preferred on the frontier. Muskets were effective in the massive firing of an army, but a rifle provided better defense in individual fighting and better assurance of a meal when hunting.

The British Brown Bess musket or a similar model was the primary weapon issued to the infantry once the army was organized and the Continental war machine got into full gear. American gunsmiths used the Brown Bess as their model for mass production. Later in the war, the French Charleville musket would also be used in large numbers.

Traditional infantry combat in the 1770s consisted of two lines of soldiers firing controlled volleys at each other across an open space. Quantity, not quality, of firing was the focus, and thus speed was more important than accuracy.

British infantrymen were trained to accomplish twelve distinct loading and firing procedures in a matter of seconds. After 1777 and the issue of von Steuben's infantry manual and drilling procedures, Continental infantries began to acquire the same type of firing efficiency.

Continental officers and cavalrymen carried pistols, such as the British Cavalry model.

Edged Weapons

The bayonet charge was typically the climax of 18th-century battle. Once the musket barrel had become clogged with powder residue, the cartridge box empty, and the line of infantry irregular from fallen soldiers, it was time to use the musket as a handle for the bayonet locked into a socket on the right side of the barrel.

A line of British soldiers advancing with sunlight reflecting off their steel 16-inch-long bayonets was enough to send the Continental Army into a panicked retreat. It wasn't until well into the war that the Continentals had enough training and experience to hold their own in vicious hand-to-hand bayonet fighting.

Continental soldiers preferred tomahawks, hunting knives, and daggers, while their officers carried swords or sabers.

Artillery

Artillery for both sides consisted of a smooth-bore, muzzle-loading gun. Within this classification, however, was a huge variety: These were 1-, 2, 3-, 4-, 6-, 9-, 12-, 24-, and 32-pounder cannons (indicating the weight of the ball fired), 4 1/2, 5 1/2, 8, 10, 13, and 16 inches, according to the size of the bore. And 3 1/2- and 8-inch howitzers were made of iron or brass.

Field cannons could weigh as much as 3200 pounds, requiring twelve horses to haul them into position. Garrison cannons were longer, but had less mobility and were used mainly to defend forts and defensive enclosures. Both field and garrison cannons had flat trajectories.

Howitzers and the shorter mortars had high trajectories and were used to lob shells over the walls of a fort. Their trajectory was only a few hundred feet, compared to the 1200-foot trajectory of a field cannon.

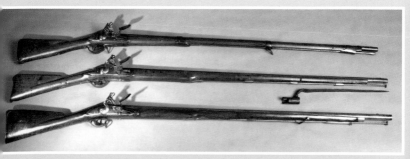

French, American, and English muskets on display at Valley Forge National Historical Park. The flintlock musket represented the most advanced technological weapon of the 18th century. Muskets were smooth-bored single-shot muzzle-loading weapons. The standard rate of fire for infantrymen was three shots per minute.

The Smithsonian Institution's National Museum of American History, Behring Center

The *Philadelphia*, a gunboat from the 1776 Battle of Valcour Island, is the centerpiece of the Revolutionary War artifacts displayed in the National Museum of American History, Behring Center (NMAH) in Washington, D.C. Also on view here of Revolutionary War interest are a reconstructed home from the period, an impressive collection of ship models, and several firearms.

The NMAH is part of the Smithsonian Institution, the largest museum complex in the world. Englishman James Smithson, for whom the institution is named, bequeathed 500,000 dollars in his will for the establishment of an institution in America whose purpose was the "increase and diffusion of knowledge." In 2000, philanthropist Kenneth E. Behring donated 80 million dollars to the NMAH, after which the name was changed to the National Museum of American History, Behring Center. Behring's donation is partially funding a major renovation of the building, as well as providing money for new exhibitions.

Revolutionary War Artifacts

The museum has three floors of exhibitions, plus a lower level with a food court and museum store. In general, exhibitions on the first floor relate to commerce, those on the second floor to communal life and family, and those on the third floor to politics, the military, and popular culture. The museum will be undergoing renovations for the next several years, and exhibitions may be moved or closed as necessary.

The *American Maritime Enterprise* exhibition on the first floor encompasses 300 years of America's ocean and river commercial enterprise. Featured is a large collection of ship models, among which are beautifully detailed examples of vessels from the colonial period, such as sloops and schooners, and several Revolutionary War–era vessels, including the *London* (1772), the *Rhodes* (1782), and the *Oliver Cromwell* (1777). The *Cromwell* was part of the state navy of Connecticut (11 of the 13 states had their own navies) and was captured in 1779, but not before it had seized two British ships.

The Smithsonian Online

The Smithsonian Institution provides excellent Web sites to complement visits to its museums. The Museum of American History, Behring Center's main Web site has basic information about the museum's facilities and its exhibitions, including those highlighted above. A virtual tour of items not on display in the museum is offered at historywired.si.edu. This site is truly a gem, with a photograph, detailed information about the item, and links to related items and history. Among the Revolutionary War–related artifacts are George Washington's sword and a Continental banknote.

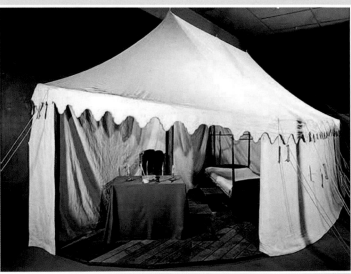

One artifact displayed on the Web site is General Washington's linen sleeping tent. It would also have been used for dining and for meetings with his staff.

There's also a larger tabletop model of the *Brilliant*, a merchant ship commandeered when she landed in Liverpool in 1775, because of the outbreak of hostilities in New England. Converted to a ship in the Royal Navy two years later, she was lost in the Arctic in 1798.

A nearby replica of a colonial warehouse in a small Virginia port displays various tools, a ledger table, and barrels whose staves are held together with entwined wood.

Within These Walls . . . on the second floor, showcases 200 years of American history within one house—an 18th-century two-and-a-half-story, timber-framed structure built in Ipswich, Massachusetts. It was dismantled, then reassembled in the museum in 1966, eventually to become the centerpiece of this exhibition. Five periods of American history—colonial, Revolutionary War, pre–Civil War, Industrial Revolution, and World War II—are explored through the personal lives of the five families who lived here.

The house was built for Abraham Choate in the 1760s, when Ipswich was one of the busiest ports in the colonies. The Choates were part of a growing middle class whose lifestyle was influenced by English styles and customs. Choate, a gentleman merchant, could afford a larger-than-normal house for his wife and eight children. Most people in the colonial era lived in small one-to-three-room houses, ranging from 320 square feet to around 800 square feet. This house was 2300 square feet and included such niceties as a parlor with imported wallpaper and elegant furnishings.

Artifacts displayed from this period include a doll from England, a porcelain teapot from China, and a clay marble. Marbles date back to ancient times, and were often used to teach children mathematics. By the 1700s, glass marbles were being produced in Venice, Italy, but the English and their colonies favored wooden ones.

Also displayed is a Betty lamp, sometimes called a fat lamp because its fuel was animal fat. The name Betty comes from either the German word "besser," mean-

ing better, or from the archaic English word "bettings," meaning kindling. The Betty lamp improved on earlier designs by decreasing smoke residue and preventing drippings. Variations of the Betty lamp were used in America until well into the 1800s.

At the time the Choates sold the house, in 1772, the Stamp Act of 1765 had already riled the colonies into minor acts of rebellion, and the Boston Tea Party would soon cross the line into more overt hostility. In 1774 the town of Ipswich passed a resolution stating, "If any Person shall have so much Effrontery and Hardness as to offer any Tea for sale in this Town . . . he shall be deemed an Enemy of the Town."

A year later, the Battle of Bunker Hill was fought 30 miles away in Boston. In 1777 a veteran of Bunker Hill, Abraham Dodge, bought this house and lived here with his wife, Bethiah, and their African American slave, Chance. It's not known what happened to Chance once slavery was outlawed in Massachusetts in 1783. In 1789, three years after

*A **Continental Army** uniform coat worn by Brigadier General Peter Gansevoort, Jr., during his command of Fort Stanwix, New York, in 1777.*

Washington, D.C.

Dodge's death, his wife was forced to sell the house because of debts accumulated during the war.

Displays include implements possibly used by Chance in maintaining the house and grounds, and a rare Revolutionary War uniform used by a general in a New York regiment.

The **Hands-on History** room, nearby, is a fascinating experience for children five and older and their adult escorts. Docents invite small visitors to try on colonial costumes and learn about colonial life.

First Ladies: Political Role and Public Image, also on the second floor, is one of the museum's most popular, with its display of inaugural gowns. There is a small but charming display on Martha Washington, known as Lady Washington while her husband was in office simply because no other title had yet been settled on. One of Mrs. Washington's gowns is displayed, as well as a traveling trunk she used when visiting the general during the war. There is also a replica of an account Mrs. Washington kept of her travel expenses that includes at the bottom the honest qualifier "Errors Excepted."

Not to be missed on this floor is Horatio Greenough's statue of George Washington. Stationed next to the escalators, this 1840 classic revival rendition

of Washington in toga and sandals takes its pose from an ancient Greek statue of Zeus. Greenough, one of America's first internationally recognized artists, was commissioned by Congress in 1832 to create a statue of Washington that would sit in the Capitol rotunda. His completed piece met with such controversy, as well as derision, that it now serves mainly as a curiosity—but an impressive curiosity, with dimensions of roughly 11 feet by 9 feet by 6 feet, and certainly one of the rare opportunities to see the commander in chief rendered in marble and seminude.

The Price of Freedom, a new permanent 18,000-square-foot exhibition, opens on the third floor in November 2004. It will examine pivotal military events in American history, from the French and Indian War through the Cold War. Interactive media stations and artifacts, such as George Washington's commission from Congress to be commander in chief of the Continental Army, will be included.

One of the focal points of the

The Gunboat
Philadelphia,
rescued from the depths of Lake Champlain, still has the cannonball that sank it embedded in its side. The boat was armed with a 12-pounder bow gun, a 6-pounder broadside gun, and a half-pounder swivel gun.

exhibition will be the gunboat *Philadelphia*, the oldest existing American fighting vessel, with a detailed display illustrating how these "gondolas" of the Continental Navy were built and operated. The *Philadelphia* was part of a fleet of 15 vessels that Benedict Arnold commanded in the Battle of Valcour Island, also called the Battle of Lake Champlain (*see* Lake Champlain Maritime Museum). The 53-foot-by-15-foot boat was discovered in 1935 in Valcour Bay with its main battery intact and its mainmast standing erect only about 10 feet below the water's surface. Still embedded in its hull is the 24-pounder cannonball that sank it.

Visitors will be able to view the vessel from below—to better understand its shape and design—and from above, to see the 12-pounder bow gun that still had shot in its muzzle when discovered, the 6-pounder broadside gun, a half-pounder swivel gun, and a replicated cookstove with a recovered frying pan and kettle. A small model of the ship will be accompanied by an illustrated explanation of how it was constructed. Dozens of artifacts found with the vessel—including shipwright's tools, deadeyes, swivel and rigging hooks, and musket parts—will be displayed, as well as the original payroll, with the names of the crew. In his report of the battle, Arnold wrote, "The Philada was hulled in so many Places that She Sank, About One hour after the engagement was over."

Also included in the exhibition will be items from the Smithsonian's outstanding firearms collection, among them Revolutionary War pieces such as a Brown Bess, a British trade musket, and a French musket. The French musket was considered by some an improvement over the more commonly used Brown Bess because it was easier to clean and supposedly handled more smoothly.

Other Revolution-era pieces displayed will be the double-barreled holster pistols carried by Brigadier General Daniel Roberdeau. Roberdeau, a member of the Second Continental Congress, took an army into the wilds of western Pennsylvania to establish a mining operation for production of much-needed lead, which operation was eventually sabotaged by Loyalists. Roberdeau also fitted out two highly successful privateers and then donated his share of the resulting prize money to Congress.

The American Presidency: A Glorious Burden, which explores the office, the men who have held it, and their impact on history, has small displays on George Washington, John Adams, and Thomas Jefferson. Among the pieces is Washington's uniform, said to be the one he wore when he surrendered his commission in 1783.

Visitor Information
202-357-2700
americanhistory.si.edu
Hours: Daily 10 a.m. until 5:30 p.m.; closed December 25. The Information Center, in the Smithsonian building known as the Castle, is open from 9 a.m. until 5:30 p.m.
Admission: Free.
Accessibility: The museum is handicapped accessible.
Special Events: There are many public events scheduled throughout the year, the largest of which is the Folklife Festival held every June and July. For specific information, consult the museum's Web site.
Getting There: The museum is located at 14th Street and Constitution Avenue, NW.

From Virginia, take I-395 into Washington, D.C., and onto 14th Street. Proceed north on 14th Street to Independence Avenue and the Mall. From Maryland, take I-495 (the Beltway) to U.S. 50 west and follow route 50 into the city, where it becomes New York Avenue, then south on 7th Street to Constitution Avenue and the Mall.

Parking is extremely limited in this area. There are 2-hour parking spots on the Mall, and small parking lots at the Washington Monument and the Jefferson Memorial, also with 2-hour parking. Parking is available for longer periods along Ohio Drive between the Lincoln and Jefferson Memorials.

The museum can be reached by subway, getting off at the Smithsonian Station (orange and blue lines), which exits at 12th Street and Jefferson Drive NW onto the Mall, two blocks from the museum.

The 30s bus route has stops at 7th and at 9th streets on the Mall, and at 15th and Pennsylvania Avenue, from which you turn right if you're traveling east, left if you're traveling west. Walk one block on 15th Street to Constitution Avenue and then left one half block on Constitution Avenue.

New Castle Court House Museum

The charming town of New Castle, Delaware, with its brick sidewalks and cobblestone streets, evokes the colonial and Revolutionary War period not only in its graceful architecture but also in the determined preservation of its unique character.

Like a prized jewel, New Castle spent its earliest years being exchanged between European powers, then had to contend with another foreign power—Philadelphia—before declaring its independence in 1776.

A tour of New Castle includes at least ten 18th-century structures, the most impressive being the New Castle Court House, now a museum exhibiting a fine collection of artifacts and portraiture.

New Castle's History

New Castle began not as a town but as a fort, established by the Netherlands in 1651 after Swedes landed near what is now Wilmington in 1638 and built their own fort. The Dutch fort was seized by the Swedes in 1654 but was reclaimed by a Dutch fleet from New Amsterdam in 1655. Soon after, England came into possession of the settlement through treaty and named it New Castle, probably for Newcastle upon Tyne. The Dutch got it back in 1673, and then the English took it again the next year. Presumably, at this point the town's sign painter retired an exhausted but wealthy man.

Enter William Penn in 1682 with, in effect, the deed to what is now Pennsylvania in one hand and the deed to the Delaware River Valley in the other. Pennsylvania was a grant from King Charles II, the Delaware River Valley a grant from the king's brother the Duke of York. However, the more liberal residents of the three lower counties—which now make up Delaware—chafed under the strict regulations of Pennsylvania's Quaker legislature. In 1701 they appealed to William Penn to be allowed to establish their own autonomous government, and Penn granted their request. The Assembly of the Lower Counties met in the New Castle Court House, and though they were still under the authority of Penn himself, they had a great deal more freedom to suit their own needs in their own ways.

The coming of the Revolution brought complete independence to Delaware. On June 15, 1776, the assembly voted to separate from Great Britain and from Pennsylvania and to become the autonomous state of Delaware. Though not a leader in the move toward independence, Delaware was known to support it. John Adams, discussing support for independence in May 1776, wrote a friend, "The Delaware government, generally, is of the same opinion with the best Americans, very orthodox in their faith and very exemplary in their practice."

For the most part, Delaware was not a field of battle during the war, though there was one engagement, the Battle of Cooch's Bridge in 1777. However, a Revolutionary War military historian has written, "It is just here that one fact in the struggle for American Independence should have specific notice. From 1776 before Boston and through the entire war, the states of Maryland and Delaware were represented on nearly every battlefield. Although

The prosecution and defense sat together at this table in the colonial courtroom, facing the three-judge bench in this criminal court.

their troops were few in numbers, they were distinguished for valor." Nearly 4000 men from Delaware fought in the war.

Delaware was the fourth state to adopt a state constitution, on September 10, 1776, and the first state to ratify the U.S. Constitution, on December 7, 1787.

Visiting the Museum

Visitors arriving at the court house will notice two things right away. First are the four flags flying from the balcony above the entrance. These are the flags of the Netherlands, Sweden, Great Britain, and the United States—honoring Delaware's multicultural history.

Second is the comely cupola atop the building, reminiscent of that atop Independence Hall in Philadelphia. There is some evidence that the buildings were designed by the same man, which seems likely considering that the Pennsylvania legislature approved the funds for both buildings at the same time. This cupola has served as the geographic center of the 12-mile circle that constitutes Delaware's northern boundary with Pennsylvania since 1732.

On the court house's first floor is the colonial court as it looked during the colonial and Revolutionary War period. This is an English common law court, with a dock for the accused and one table where the defense and prosecution sat together, facing the three-judge bench. An artifacts case displays items from the 1600s through the 1800s, including ceramics, glassware, and other 17th- and 18th-century artifacts.

The colonial assembly met on the second floor. The court house served as the first capitol building of the state of Delaware until May 1777, when the capital was moved to

Dover, an inland town thought to be more secure from British ships along the Delaware River. Here in the Assembly Room visitors can put faces to names, with portraits of Continental Congressman John Dickinson and signers of the Declaration of Independence George Read and Thomas McKean, among others. Here also is the original chair where these presidents of the assembly and those that followed them sat.

Other rooms on the second floor include an office of the court from the early 1800s, and space for changing exhibits.

Visitor Information

302-323-4453

www.destatemuseums.org/
Information/Museums/ncch/
nc_courthouse.shtml

Hours: Tuesday through Saturday from 10 a.m. until 3:30 p.m., Sunday from 1:30 p.m. until 4:30 p.m.; closed Mondays and state holidays

Admission: Free, but donations are accepted.

Accessibility: The first floor of the Court House is handicapped accessible.

Special Events: Special activities are held throughout the year at the Court House and in New Castle. These include A Day in Old New Castle on the third Saturday in May, with celebrations on Separation Day (the first Saturday in June), the Fourth of July, and Christmas Candlelight tours the second Saturday in December.

Getting There: Take I-95 to exit 5A, state route 141 south, and continue past the route 13 and 40 overpass. At the intersection of state routes 9 and 273, turn left onto route 9 north; bear right at the next light onto Delaware Street and into New Castle.

Fort Morris State Historic Site

Fort Morris was one of the last Patriot posts to fall in the Revolutionary War. Built to defend Georgia's coastal ports and deter invasion from the south, Fort Morris and its defenders proved resilient against attacks from land and sea. It was only after Savannah fell and Britain brought an overwhelming force to bear on the small fort and its coastal town of Sunbury that Fort Morris surrendered.

Visitors today can stand within the earthwork remains of the fort, the only Revolutionary War fort still intact in the state of Georgia, and marvel at the fortitude of the Patriots who held off the British army from within these walls.

Early History of the Area

Fort Morris was built soon after the Second Continental Congress voted for independence in the summer of 1776. Georgia, which had absented itself from the First Continental Congress, by 1776 had somewhat reluctantly joined the other colonies in calling for a break from the mother country. Since Georgia was the last of the original 13 colonies established in America, it hadn't had time to build up the kind of resentment against Britain that burned in the other colonies.

Established by royal charter in 1732, Georgia began as the utopian vision of a British army general, James Edward Oglethorpe, whose intention was to provide a second chance for those needing one, such as debtors languishing in British prisons. Named Georgia in honor of Oglethorpe's benefactor, King George II, the colony was intended to be a model of morality and sobriety. Rum and slavery were outlawed and land holdings were limited to 500 acres for each individual. In less than two years, these rules were set aside and Georgia was on its way to being a prosperous southern colony whose wealth was based on large plantations maintained with slave labor.

The town of Sunbury—which no longer exists—was founded in the 1750s, and by the early 1770s it was rivaling Savannah as a major coastal port. Two of Georgia's three signers of the Declaration of Independence—Lyman Hall and Button Gwinnett—lived in Sunbury, which may be one of the reasons Fort Morris was located here. The other reason was that it was an excellent location from which to defend Georgia's middle coast.

The Attacks on Fort Morris

The first attempt on the fort by the British was made in November 1778. The month before, Sir Henry Clinton had decided that Florida's British and Loyalist forces and Seminole Indians would be part of the army securing Georgia. These forces, led by Lieutenant Colonel Lewis Fuser, were part of a larger contingent moving north.

In fact, the British attack on Fort Morris was something of a diversionary tactic. Brigadier General Augustine Prevost, commander of the British forces, was ordered by Clinton to move toward Savannah. Prevost, ever mindful of the needs of a large army, ordered his brother, Major James Mark Prevost, to raid the Midway and Newbury settlements for cattle. Fuser's attack on the fort was meant to distract defending forces who might otherwise rush to the aid of Midway or Newbury.

On November 25, Fuser surrounded Fort Morris and sent the following message to the commander of the fort, Colonel John McIntosh: "Sir, You cannot be ignorant that four armies are in motion to reduce this province. . . . The resistance you can or intend to make will only bring destruction upon this country. On the contrary, if you will deliver me the fort which you command, lay down your arms, and remain neuter until the fate of America is determined, you shall, as well as all the inhabitants of this parish, remain in peaceable possession of your property. Your answer, which I expect in an hour's time, will determine the fate of this country, whether it is to be laid in ashes, or remain as above proposed." Fuser added a postscript: "Since this letter was closed, some of your people have been firing scattering shot about the line. I am to inform you that if a stop is not put to such irregular proceedings, I shall burn a house for every shot so fired."

Colonel McIntosh replied, "Sir, We acknowledge we are not ignorant that your army is in motion to endeavour to reduce this State. . . . We have no property compared with the object we contend for that we value a rush, and would rather perish in a vigorous defence than accept your proposals. We, sir, are fighting the battles of America, and therefore disdain to remain neutral till its fate is determined. As to surrendering the fort, receive this laconic reply,

'Come and take it!' Major Lane, whom I send with this letter, is directed to satisfy you with respect to the irregular, loose firing mentioned on the back of your letter."

Following this polite exchange, Fuser likely rethought his strategy, probably realizing that since his was primarily a diversionary tactic, it would make better sense to rejoin the main force rather than be delayed here in a protracted battle. He withdrew.

But the British came back. After Savannah fell in December 1778, a force of 2000 British troops again surrounded Fort Morris, this time bombarding it with heavy artillery. The 200 defenders inside couldn't hold out against such an attack and surrendered the fort on January 9, 1779. The fort was renamed Fort George and remained in British hands throughout the war.

The town of Sunbury became a military prison for Patriot officers. During the War of 1812, the fort was reinforced and called Fort Defiance, and it was later used by Confederate forces early in the Civil War.

Visiting Fort Morris

Located on a low bluff on the Medway River, about 20 miles south of Savannah, this star fort provides an excellent view of the surrounding area. Standing at the northeast corner of the fort's earthworks, looking out over the river toward St. Catherine's Sound, visitors can understand the strategic importance the fort had during the war.

An engaging 11-minute audiovisual program in the Visitor Center enlarges on the fort's strategic importance and on the stand taken by Colonel McIntosh. *Sunbury Sleeps* also tells the history of the town before and during the Revolutionary War.

The center's museum includes artifacts from Sunbury's colonial days and a diorama of Fort Morris as it would have been at the time of the attacks. There are also a 4-pounder cannon, a Brown Bess musket, and a reproduction of the uniform of a Continental Army artillery officer.

A brochure with a map of the walking trail around the fort explains in detail how the fort was constructed of earth and wood, as were almost all forts built prior to the 1880s, and that it was much larger than the earthworks indicate. There's also information about the palisades (sharpened poles stuck into the ground at an angle) that were planted in the bottom of the moat encircling the fort.

The blacksmith shop near the Visitor Center offers demonstrations during the spring and summer, and cannon and musket demonstrations are given at special events throughout the year.

For those who would like a small taste of what the area was like during the Revolution, there is a very peaceful and lovely nature trail along the nearby salt marsh that is home to birds, fiddler crabs, alligators, deer, and raccoons.

Visitor Information

912-884-5999

gastateparks.org/info/ftmorris/

Hours: Open from 9 a.m. until 5 p.m., Tuesday through Saturday, and 9:30 a.m. until 5:30 p.m. on Sunday. Closed Monday (except legal holidays), Thanksgiving, December 25, and January 1.

Admission: Minimal charge.

Accessibility: The museum is accessible. The walking tour path is accessible, but not completely smooth and may pose a problem for some.

Special Events: For Memorial Day and Labor Day commemorations there are musket and cannon firings; Independence Day Colonial Faire includes firings, plus colonial games and music; and the annual Freedom's Flame Candlelight Tour takes visitors on a lantern tour while costumed interpreters tell the story of Sunbury and of Fort Morris.

Getting There: Take I-95 south to exit 76, then take Island Parkway east and turn left on Fort Morris Road.

George Rogers Clark National Historical Park

"Who knows what fortune will do for us? Great things have been affected by a few men well conducted. Perhaps we may be fortunate. We have this consolation: that our cause is just, and that our cuntrey will be grateful. . . ."

These lines, written by George Rogers Clark in February 1779 as he set out to capture the town of Vincennes from the British, seem to encapsulate Clark's moral philosophy. Great things were always possible, especially if the cause was just and those supporting that cause were organized and disciplined.

George Rogers Clark was only 23 when the war started—one of the young men to whom the mantle of leadership would pass in the early days of the new nation. Over the course of five years, his successes in the Northwest Territories would expand the American horizon to the center of the continent and beyond.

The War on the Frontier

Clark was born in Albemarle County, Virginia, the second son of a farming family. To the west of the Clark farm was the frontier—so thick with trees it was said a squirrel could hop branches from Virginia to the Mississippi River and never touch ground.

Clark's older brother Jonathan would become a general in the Continental Army, and his younger brother William would later win fame for his expedition across the continent with Meriwether Lewis.

In 1772 Clark became a surveyor. Surveying the frontier—lands west of the Appalachian Mountains—opened up the western territory and all its possibilities to Clark. In the years preceding the war, he moved to present-day Kentucky, then part of Virginia, where he became a leader among the settlers.

The British, who opposed further expansion by settlers into the territory, were headquartered at Fort Detroit. By 1777 the fort's commander, Lieutenant Governor Henry Hamilton, was encouraging Britain's Native American allies to raid and destroy settlements in present-day Kentucky, Ohio, Indiana, and Illinois. (*See* New York, Old Fort Niagara for further information about British and Native American alliances during the war.) The raids were so destructive that by late summer of 1777 there were only three settlements left in Kentucky. Part of the impetus for the raids was likely the bounty paid by Hamilton for each scalp brought to him, earning him the label of "hair buyer."

Clark called a meeting of representatives from the remaining settlements at Harrodsburg, Kentucky (*see* Kentucky, Old Fort Harrod State Park), to decide what to do about the decimating attacks. The settlers voted to send a delegation headed by Clark to the Virginia governor, Patrick Henry, to request recognition and protection as a separate county of the state.

Clark had other ideas. By this time an experienced Indian fighter, he realized that the only lasting protection would come from taking the offensive, defeating the British and subduing the Native Americans. Accordingly, he devised a campaign that included capturing key British forts. In late summer of 1777, he wrote to Governor Henry proposing an expedition to capture Fort Kaskaskia along the Mississippi River in present-day Illinois.

Kaskaskia was a French settlement that had been lost to the British in the French and Indian War. Its inhabitants were mainly French Catholics who had no love for their lieutenant governor in Detroit or his king, but who also "are entirely against the American cause," wrote Clark, "and look on us as notorious rebels that ought to be subdued at any rate; but I don't doubt that after being acquainted with the cause they would become good friends to it."

George Rogers Clark

Since Kaskaskia supplied the Native American tribes with goods and trade, capturing the town would lead to Indian submission, Clark asserted. In addition, "If it was in our possession it would distress the garrison at Detroit for provisions, it would fling the command of the two great rivers [the Ohio and the Mississippi] into our hands, which would enable us to get supplies of goods from the Spaniards [who held everything west of the Mississippi], and to carry on a trade with the Indians."

Clark followed up his letter by traveling to Virginia and meeting with the governor and the General Assembly, convincing them to give him the money and authority to raise an army. Ostensibly Clark was under orders to protect the Kentucky frontier, but his primary and secret orders were to capture the British forts at Kaskaskia, Cahokia, and Vincennes. Clark's agenda considered those as stepping-stones to the capture of Fort Detroit.

The Forts Are Won

In the spring of 1778, Clark and about 150 Virginia volunteers came down the Ohio River to Corn Island, across from present-day Louisville, Kentucky. Here Clark trained the men, who had been promised 300 acres of land for their services, for several weeks. In late June, volunteers from Kentucky and Tennessee joined Clark's forces, which he divided into four companies. The last week in June this small army headed down the Ohio River.

Clark's boats came first to the mouth of the Wabash River, which would lead them to Vincennes, but Clark kept going. He had decided to take Kaskaskia first, saving the larger Fort Sackville at Vincennes for later. While still on the Ohio, they were overtaken by a man in a canoe. He was delivering a dispatch from Fort Pitt (present-day Pittsburgh) telling Clark that France had officially become America's ally in the war.

Clark moored his boats at Fort Massac, an abandoned British fort. He and his men cached their belongings nearby and set out on foot overland to Kaskaskia. After getting lost and eating nothing but berries found in patches along the trail, they came within sight of Kaskaskia and its fort, Fort Gage, the evening of the Fourth of July.

Clark decided on a night attack, but there was little of an attack quality involved. The gates of the fort were unguarded and the French commander, Philippe de Rocheblave, was in bed.

De Rocheblave was not happy in his work. The past few months he had been writing letters of complaint to Quebec, asking that he be replaced by an English officer. He hadn't been paid in months and he resented having to spend his own money buying gifts for the leaders of the local tribes.

At midnight he and his wife were awakened by two men standing in their bedroom doorway telling them they were now prisoners of America. Clark's forces secured the rest of the town by scaring it half to death, charging through the streets howling like an army of 1000. This was part of Clark's plan for winning over the population. Clark had decided that "the greater the shock I could give them at first, the more sensibly would they feel my lenity and become more valuable friends."

His ploy worked. The local priest, Father Pierre Gibault, begged Clark for mercy, especially for the women and children. Clark responded by asking, "Did they suppose . . . that we would . . . make war on the women and children or the church?" He told them that "as the king of France had joined the Americans . . . [t]hey were at liberty to take what side they pleased, without any dread of losing their property or having their families destroyed [and that] all religions would be tolerated in America. . . . They retired, and, in a few minutes, the scene was changed . . . to that of joy in the extreme—the bells ringing, the church crowded, returning thanks."

Things began to move very quickly now. The residents of Kaskaskia took an oath of allegiance to the United States. Cahokia quickly followed suit. When Clark made a feint about sending for an army to capture Vincennes, Father Gibault and the town doctor interceded, traveled to Vincennes, and at the end of July brought back the news that Vincennes would welcome the Americans.

With the three forts now in American hands, Clark set about making peace with the surrounding Native American tribes. In August he held a conference with representatives of dozens of tribes. The conference lasted five weeks, at the end of which he had agreements for peace.

After a bold 180-mile midwinter march from Kaskaskia to retake Sackville, Clark and his men reached Vincennes on February 23, 1779. He created the impression of an overwhelming force, and after a brief fight Colonel Henry Hamilton agreed to surrender. Looking around as he presented his sword to Clark, Hamilton is said to have exclaimed, "Colonel Clark, where is your army?"

The British Arrive

Lieutenant Governor Hamilton learned of Clark's campaign in mid-August. On October 6 he left Detroit with his force of British Regulars, about 70 French militia, 60 Native Americans, and one 6-pounder cannon.

Hamilton and his men traversed the western end of Lake Erie to the mouth of the Maumee River, then made a nine-mile portage to the Wabash, which they reached on November 9. Hamilton was gaining men as he went along and by now had about 500.

On December 17 he arrived in Vincennes, where word of his mighty force had preceded him. The townspeople immediately surrendered. Captain Leonard Helm and the three men Clark had left behind to guard Fort Sackville were "determined to act brave," Helm wrote in a letter to Clark. But their untenable position, Hamilton's assurances they would be treated humanely, and a request from the townspeople (now once again loyal to the British) that there be no fighting that might endanger the town, convinced Helm to surrender the fort.

Hamilton could have marched on and likely taken Kaskaskia, but he decided to spend the winter at Fort Sackville, repairing the fortifications, which had fallen into disrepair, and giving his Regulars a chance to rest from their strenuous journey from Detroit. Sure that Clark wouldn't be foolish enough to chance a winter march with his small army, Hamilton dispersed the majority of his militia and Indian fighters, keeping only a small force at Vincennes.

Vincennes Regained

Clark had been greatly aided in his campaign by a Spanish merchant named Francis Vigo, who had furnished Clark and his men with supplies from his St. Louis store and given Clark money to pay for goods from others. On December 18, the day after Helm surrendered Fort Sackville, Vigo, not knowing what had happened, set out from St. Louis for Vincennes.

Captured and questioned by Hamilton, Vigo told him about Clark's army at Kaskaskia, but he downplayed what Hamilton might have heard about Clark's efficiency by emphasizing that it had "no discipline or regularity." Hamilton, also playing it cagey, told Vigo that a large army would be attacking Kaskaskia in the spring, probably in the hopes that this news would reach Clark and he and his army would leave before then.

Vigo took an oath that he wouldn't give any information to the Americans on his way back to St. Louis. In order not to break his oath, he returned to St. Louis before going to Kaskaskia to inform Clark about happenings in Vincennes.

Clark's options were few. He had less than 200 men, almost half of them French volunteers whose reliability was in question. He could wait until spring and hope that by then he could get more volunteers from the western settlements, he could retreat to Spanish St. Louis and give up without a fight, or he could attack Fort Sackville now.

On February 5, 1779, Clark and his men set out for Fort Sackville, across flooded country that at times had the men almost up to their shoulders in icy water and at other times had them slogging through freezing rain. On February 23, Clark and his weary army arrived within a few miles of Vincennes, where they encountered some duck hunters from the town. Concerned he would lose the element of surprise if he let the hunters go, but not wanting to alienate the townspeople by taking the hunters prisoner, he sent a letter. "Being now within two Miles of Your Village with My Army, determined to take your fort this night and not being willing to surprise you, I take this step to request of such of you as are true citizens and willing to enjoy the liberty I bring you, to remain still in your houses."

The townspeople stayed in their houses, while Clark's army surrounded the fort and opened fire. After two days of fight, Hamilton was convinced that he couldn't win this battle and could only ensure the death of his men if he continued. On February 25 he and his men marched out of the fort and surrendered their arms.

Though the British had been vanquished in the northern part of the frontier, Clark was never able to muster enough of an army to capture Detroit. Still, by firmly establishing American control of the western frontier, he helped make the case for the Americans' acquiring the territory from Great Britain at the end of the war. In 1787, Congress established the "Territory Northwest of the River Ohio," which later came to be the states of Ohio, Indiana, Illinois, Michigan, Wisconsin, and parts of Minnesota.

Clark continued to work and live in the territories after the war, but he lost all his land to debt and was impoverished by 1808 when he became partially paralyzed in a fall and had one of his legs amputated. The state of Virginia gave him a sword and a 400-dollar-a-year pension. Clark died in 1818.

Visiting the Clark Historic Site

This 26-acre enclave in downtown Vincennes is dominated by the gracefully colonnaded Revival-style granite-and-marble memorial to Clark that stands in what is thought to have been the southeast corner of Fort Sackville.

Inside the massive structure, a bronze statue of George Rogers Clark stands on a marble pedestal surrounded by seven murals on Belgian linen depicting scenes from Clark's campaign and the expansion of the United States into the territories. The memorial was dedicated by President Franklin D. Roosevelt in 1936.

Near the memorial is a statue honoring Francis Vigo. A statue to Father Pierre Gibault stands near the Visitor Center.

At that center, visitors can see a 30-minute video, *Longknives*, on the Clark campaign. There is a small museum with artifacts from the period and a diorama depicting the four groups of people in Vincennes in the 1770s—a Frenchman, a Shawnee warrior, an American frontiersman, and a British soldier from the 8th Afoot Regiment. There is also quite a bit of interesting information about the French culture of Vincennes's early inhabitants.

Visitor Information

812-882-1776, x 110
www.nps.gov/gero
Hours: The Visitor Center is open daily year-round from 9 a.m. until 5 p.m. The memorial is open daily from 9 a.m. until 4:45 p.m. Note that Vincennes, and most of Indiana, does not observe daylight saving time. The park is closed Thanksgiving, December 25, and January 1.
Admission: Moderate charge for adults, children under 16 free.
Accessibility: The Visitor Center is accessible, the interior of the memorial is not.
Special Events: One of the Midwest's most celebrated Revolutionary War reenactments, called the Rendezvous, is held at the Clark Historic Site every Memorial Day weekend. The event attracts close to 500 reenactors and some 35,000 visitors. Besides reenactments, there are demonstrations of arts and crafts and colonial-period entertainment.
Getting There: George Rogers Clark National Historical Park is located in Vincennes, on the Wabash River, approximately 50 miles north of Evansville and 55 miles south of Terre Haute, Indiana. Take U.S. route 41 from either of those cities or U.S. 50 from the east and west, and use the 6th Street exit off either, then follow the signs to the park.

Native Americans in the Revolution

The War of Independence was as much a civil war for Native Americans as it was for their European American counterparts. The Native Americans, however, were fighting for possession of their lands.

Some tribes had previously been driven from their eastern territories to the western frontiers, only to find themselves being threatened with new waves of settlers moving farther west. These settlers gave little thought to the rights of those currently living in and cultivating the region.

The British, to their credit, attempted to hold back western migration, but with only partial success. During the French and Indian War, the majority of Native Americans sided with the British, and for their loyalty were left in peace to create thriving communities. Others in the South and on the frontiers lived more traditionally but no less peaceably with the colonials.

In return the British endeavored to enforce a 1763 agreement that limited western expansion into Indian lands. But the British were far away, and the new waves of Europeans and the poorer populations of the larger colonies were pushing at the boundaries set by the British.

At the beginning of the Revolutionary War there were an estimated 250,000 Native Americans living in the colonies and along the frontiers of present-day Ohio, Illinois, and Kentucky.

Those in the south included the Cherokees, Creeks, Choctaws, and Chickasaws; along the western frontier, the Delawares, Shawnees, and Wyandots; and in the Northeast and Mid-Atlantic regions, the Senecas, Mingos, Munsees, and, most dominant, the Six Nations of the Iroquois Confederation.

With the coming of the war, Native Americans were given a stark choice—side with their traditional allies, the British, or with their neighbors and sometime friends.

At first both sides encouraged Native Americans to remain neutral. Soon after Lexington and Concord, the Continental Congress sent a message to the Iroquois Nations, urging them to stay out of the fight.

In the South, the Creeks and Cherokees met to discuss their options and wrote a formal message to the British and Patriot representatives in their region: "We thought that all the English people were as one people but now we hear that they have a difference amongst themselves. It is our desire that they drop their disputes and not spoil one another."

The white people could not settle their differences, and by the summer of 1775 the British government began to enlist its agents to approach the Indians as possible allies.

By 1777 most Native Americans had chosen sides, the majority of them going with the British. In the Northeast and Mid-Atlantic regions, tribes fought in strategic battles led by British Regulars or Loyalist regiments. In the frontier regions of the southern states of Virginia, the Carolinas, and Georgia, Indians were mainly fighting a battle against settlers infringing on their land, with the war as background.

At the Battle of Oriskany in 1777, Iroquois fought each other, a civil war that fatally weakened the confederation. The Iroquois also joined with the Loyalists for a series of raids in the western frontiers of New York and Pennsylvania in 1778 and 1779. What became known as the Wyoming Valley massacre in Pennsylvania and the Cherry Valley massacre in New York prompted a major campaign by the Continental Army and militia.

After the final battle of that campaign the Indians retreated to the safety of Fort Niagara on Lake Ontario, while the Patriots moved into New York, destroying an estimated 40 Iroquois towns and hundreds of acres of crops and orchards.

Following George Rogers Clark's defeat of the Delawares on the Northwest frontier, they signed a treaty at Fort Pitt in 1778, the first treaty ever made by the United States government with an Indian tribe.

The treaty with the Delawares was short-lived. Successive raids by them culminated in the Battle of Blue Licks.

The Treaty of Paris extended the western boundaries of the new nation to the Mississippi, across broad expanses of Native American land. The United States government treated those who had fought with the Patriots no better than it did those who had sided with the British, parceling out their land to settlers eager to stretch across the continent. The ferocious military battles between the army and Native Americans during and after the war wouldn't end until 1890 at Wounded Knee, South Dakota.

Blue Licks Battlefield State Resort Park

What is often referred to as the last battle of the Revolutionary War was actually one of the first battles of the Indian wars that followed. The Battle of Blue Licks, northeast of Lexington, Kentucky, was the result of retaliatory actions on the part of Native Americans and settlers—a vicious cycle where each action elicited a deadly reaction.

The British understood how strongly Americans coveted the land west of the Alleghenies. The land was "free" (not deeded to any white man), the game plentiful, and there were bountiful forests providing timber for building. During the war, the British manipulated the animosity Native Americans felt toward the white interlopers pushing into their territory. Although the Indian presence had considerably diminished since the French and Indian War, tribes were encouraged to fight alongside British companies such as Butler's Rangers (*see* New York, Oriskany Battlefield State Historic Site) to rid the territory of settlers supported by Patriot militias.

The Battle of Blue Licks

Early in 1782, a company of Pennsylvania militia slaughtered a group of Delaware Indians who were part of a Moravian mission. Several of the Indians were scalped and the others were hacked to death with tomahawks. A survivor wrote, "They began to sing hymns and spoke words of encouragement and consolation one to another until they were slain."

This vicious massacre incensed other Delawares, who joined with the Shawnees and Wyandots in an attack, late in June, on a militia force led by Colonial William Crawford. Crawford was captured, tortured, and burned to death. Joining with the Indians in the attack was a white man named Simon Girty, renowned in the territories as a brutal and canny fighter. It is said, though, that Girty tried to save Crawford, or at least to give him a swift and less horrific death.

Raised by Indians, Girty tried living among the settlers once he reached adulthood, but was ostracized because of his Native American upbringing. At the beginning of the Revolutionary War, Girty was an emissary between several of the tribes and the Continental Army, but an incident in which Indian women and children were brutally murdered sent him back to his Indian friends and their allies, the British.

In August of 1782, Girty and a force of Delawares, Wyandots, and Shawnees joined with Butler's Rangers in an attempt to capture Bryan's Station, 40 miles northeast of Lexington, Kentucky, then part of the state of Virginia. On the morning of August 16, settlers inside the compound at Bryan's Station heard musket fire and discovered it was several Wyandots on the edges of the forest to the rear of the fort shooting and trying to draw out the men inside. More than 300 Indians and 50 Butler's Rangers, led by Captain William Caldwell, lay in hiding, ready to attack.

The settlers didn't fall into the trap. Two men burst out of the compound on horseback, riding to Lexington for help. In the meantime, the settlers pretended nothing was amiss, fearing if the British-led forces realized the settlers knew they were there, they would attack rather than continuing to try to draw the Kentuckians out into the open. At one point, when the water supply inside the fort was running low, the girls and women left the compound's safety and casually walked to the spring outside, filling large containers with water before returning to the fort.

Finally the Indians and British tired of waiting and attacked. Well into the next day they kept up their fire, but Bryan's Station was too strongly built and defended. In the end, the British-led forces destroyed crops, slaughtered livestock, burned a few cabins, and left.

On August 18, three groups of Kentucky militia—182 men—had gathered at Bryan's Station. They were led by Colonel John Todd, Lieutenant Colonel Stephen Trigg, and Lieutenant Colonel Daniel Boone, renowned frontiersman and explorer. There was also a Major Hugh McGary, whose family had been killed by Indians a year earlier and who was driven to kill every Indian he could find. Though he was thought to be a bit unstable, he was also known to be a fierce fighter. At an officers' council that evening, McGary urged the militia to wait for reinforcements, but the others were concerned the Indians and their British allies would get too far ahead and escape across the Ohio River. Returning to his men after the meeting, McGary was teased for his timidity, and the unspoken charge of cowardice hung in the air.

The next day the Kentuckians set off in pursuit, following the attackers to a ford of the Licking River at the lower Blue Licks. Licks were so called because that was where animals went to lick the saline, brackish earth near springs. At this point Daniel Boone became cautious. Their quarry, he felt, had been too easily tracked. He sensed a trap, thinking the Indians by now would have the superior placement on the other side above the ford, and he urged the Kentuckians to wait for reinforcements.

McGary, still brooding from the accusations of timidity, spurred his horse into the river, yelling, "All who are not cowards, follow me!" As the men scrambled to catch up, their leaders reluctantly followed.

Boone was right. It was an ambush. The British and Indian forces were hidden by two wooded ravines on a crest of a hill above the ford. Though the Kentuckians had time to form themselves into three columns, within minutes more than a third were killed or captured. Those who were captured were tortured and killed. Among the dead were Colonel Todd, Lieutenant Colonel Trigg, and Daniel Boone's son, Israel. Boone escaped, but not before hiding the body of his dead son, to prevent its being mutilated. McGary also escaped.

In retaliation, George Rogers Clark, commander of Patriot forces in the territories (*see* Indiana, George Rogers Clark National Historical Park), led his forces in the destruction of six Indian villages.

Visiting the Park

Though Blue Licks is a beautiful state park, with picnic areas and a playground, respect has been paid to the tragic battle that was fought here, with a well-preserved battlefield, a monument, and a fine museum.

At the Pioneer Museum, visitors can see an eight-minute video relating the story of the battle and

---

What's in the Name?

The park originally got its resort title from its pre–Civil War history, when visitors sought the curative powers of the mineral springs nearby. The Arlington, a 670-foot, three-story luxury hotel, welcomed visitors from the wealthiest families in the South, who, after spending the day in tub baths, would enjoy lavish dinners in the dining room and dances in the fancy ballroom. After the Arlington burned down in 1862, the Blue Licks water retained its restorative power, but it was being bottled and sent elsewhere. The wealthy found other places to go. Today, this is again a resort, with a lodge and cottages.

Daniel Boone was one of the Kentucky militiamen who barely escaped the ambush at Blue Licks. The event is reenacted every August at the site.

putting it in the context of the early settlements in the area. Information about the ancient Buffalo Trace—the road created by buffalo on their way to the salty banks of the springs—explains the importance of this trail in bringing Native Americans and later settlers to the region. McGary led his men up the trace to face their attackers, and remnants of the road can be found on the battlefield. Signage along the trace points out the braided pattern created by the buffalo.

The museum displays pioneer artifacts, including firearms and a surveyor's compass similar to that used by Clark and Boone.

There's also fascinating information about what pioneers went through to obtain salt, as necessary to their survival as guns and shelter. Search parties frequently went out looking for salt licks. Once the basic ingredient was found, the process to make usable salt was incredibly long and tedious. Stone-and-mud furnaces several feet deep and 12 to 15 feet long, gallons of water (approximately 840 gallons to make one bushel of salt), and stacks of wood to keep the furnaces fired were required, necessitating hours and hours of work.

A brochure has a map of the park, which includes a burial site and a monument to the fallen. Days after the battle, when the bodies of the slain were being retrieved, those who could be identified were taken back to their families for burial; the others were buried here in a mass grave. The Daughters of the Ameri-can Revolution placed a headstone on the burial site in 1935.

The 32-foot granite obelisk monument pays tribute to those who fought and died here, with the names of the officers inscribed on the front.

Visitor Information

859-289-5507 or 800-443-7008
parks.ky.gov/bluelick.htm

Hours: The park, battlefield, burial site, and monument can be visited year-round. The museum is open from April through October, Sunday through Thursday, from 9 a.m. until 5 p.m.; Friday and Saturday, from 9 a.m. until 6 p.m.; November through March, Thursday through Saturday, from 9 a.m. until 5 p.m.; closed Thanksgiving Day, December 25, and January 1.

Admission: There's a minimal admission fee for adults for the Pioneer Museum.

Accessibility: The first floor of the museum, where the video is shown and most of the Revolutionary War artifacts are displayed, is accessible.

Special Events: From April through October there are daily interpretive talks on subjects ranging from pioneer dress to 18th-century weapons. There is a Reenactment Celebration in August. Guided tours of the battlefield are given daily in season.

Getting There: Blue Licks is located 48 miles northeast of Lexington, on U.S. 68.

Old Fort Harrod State Park

Despite the 1763 British law forbidding expansion into the western territories, pioneers found their way into the verdant lands west of the Alleghenies. The earliest-known settlement was established by James Harrod in 1774 at what is now Harrodsburg, Kentucky.

Today visitors can experience what frontier life was like during the war years at Old Fort Harrod State Park, where a realistic re-creation of the fort and its surroundings evokes the optimism and determination of Kentucky's founders.

History of the Fort

James Harrod, a Pennsylvania-born frontiersman known for his marksmanship and his leadership skills, headed west from the Monongahela Valley of Pennsylvania in the late spring of 1774 with 32 men, dugout canoes to get through the spring floods, and a large supply of "jerky, cornmeal, oats, flour, and coffee."

By June they had reached the Salt River, where they made camp and began laying out the first town established in Kentucky, which they called Harrodsburg. Soon, however, Daniel Boone brought word that the men were needed to defend Virginia against an Indian uprising.

Once the uprising was settled, Harrod and the others returned to the settlement, in March 1775, this time bringing their families. They began to build cabins, but by September they realized the site they had chosen was not going to work, mainly because of an uncertain water supply.

The site was moved to the south, and instead of a town, the men began building a fort. The 264-square-foot compound had 12-inch-thick walls, seven cabins, blockhouses, a large spring providing ample water, and a schoolhouse. The fort became a haven for nearby settlers throughout the war, when Kentucky was under frequent Indian attack. George Rogers Clark settled here in the summer of 1775, and led the way in having Kentucky made a county of Virginia in 1776, at which time Harrodsburg became the county seat.

While here, Clark formulated plans for his Northwest Campaign (*see* Indiana, George Rogers Clark National Historical Park), and established Kentucky's first jail. Among those Clark imprisoned here was

Henry Hamilton, the British lieutenant governor of Canada known as a "hair buyer" among Native Americans for the bounty he paid on Patriot scalps.

Following the war, the fort was considered unnecessary and dismantled, but the town of Harrodsburg continued to prosper. In 1793, James Harrod disappeared while searching for a silver mine. Relatives claimed he was lured from Harrodsburg with false tales of the mine and murdered by a man against whom he was scheduled to testify in a court case. Harrod's body was never found.

Visiting the Park

This is a fascinating place to visit any time of the year, but even more so between April and October when it becomes a living-history museum.

Craftspeople in period costumes demonstrate what are now considered crafts but were then survival skills, such as woodworking, broom making, tinsmithing, weaving and dyeing, and blacksmithing.

The George Rogers Clark Block House displays five maps used by Clark during his Northwest campaign, along with a number of original period pieces, such as a saddlebag, a trunk, and several Betty lamps (*see* Washington, D.C., Smithsonian's National Museum of American History).

Other sites in the compound include the James Harrod Block House and six other homes that exhibit period and reproduced furnishings reflecting the pioneer

experience, as well as a pioneer schoolhouse and a pioneer cemetery. Of particular interest are the Earliest Settlers Cabin, which displays the tools used in making household items such as brooms and soap, and the Bryant Station Cabin, which is a memorial to the brave women who left the safety of the fort to fetch water when it was surrounded by Indians (*see* Blue Licks Battlefield State Park). The Lincoln Marriage Temple is the log cabin where Abraham Lincoln's parents were married. The Lincolns were actually married in Springfield, Kentucky, and the cabin was later moved here.

The Mansion Museum, built in 1813, with additions in 1836, displays one of the finest gun collections in the country. The McIntosh Gun Collection has pistols such as the Prescott Navy revolver .38-caliber, the Allen & Thurber pepperbox six-shot .31-caliber Model 1845 Winchester, and the Colt New Model pistol .6-caliber patent 1862. Among its carbines are a Spencer breechload .50-caliber repeater Model 1855, a Cosmopolitan breech-load lever-action .50-caliber, and an Allen & Wheelock .44-caliber repeater.

In the mansion's Pioneer Room, visitors can see portraits of James Harrod, Daniel Boone, and George Rogers Clark. In the enclosed upstairs porch there are exhibits of Native American artifacts and pioneer tools.

Next to the museum is the Federal Monument, dedicated in 1934 in a ceremony attended by President Franklin D. Roosevelt. The monument honors George Rogers Clark and the pioneering settlers who founded Kentucky.

Visitor Information
859-734-3314
www.oldfortharrod.com

Hours: The fort is open from 8 a.m. until 5 p.m., mid-March through October; and from 8 a.m. until 4:30 p.m., November through mid-March. During the outdoor drama season (see below) the fort is open from 8 a.m. until 8 p.m. The fort is closed Thanksgiving Day and Christmas week through January 1.

Admission: There is a moderate admission fee; under 6 years of age admitted free.

Accessibility: The fort and first floor of the museum are accessible; the cabins are not.

Special Events: An outdoor drama, *Daniel Boone—The Man and The Legend,* is performed from mid-June through mid-August in an amphitheater behind the fort. Information is available at www.boonedrama.com. Guided hikes, lectures, and educational programs are held throughout the year. Consult the Web site for schedule.

Getting There: The park is 32 miles southwest of Lexington at 100 South College Street (U.S. 68) in Harrodsburg. From Lexington, follow U.S. 68 south to Harrodsburg. From the Blue Grass Parkway, take exit 69 and go south on U.S. 127 to U.S. 68. From the south take U.S. 127 (Cumberland Parkway exit 62) north to U.S. 68 in Harrodsburg.

Old Fort Western

This National Historic Landmark is the oldest surviving wooden fort in the country. Located in the center of the city of Augusta, it commemorates the community's history from colonial times to the 1840s. Its Revolutionary War exhibits focus on the fort's service as a staging area for Benedict Arnold's invasion of Canada in 1775.

History of the Fort

The Kennebec Proprietors, a Boston land company with a claim to the Kennebec River valley, built the fort in 1754. Sailing vessels requiring deep draft could go no farther, so supplies, military matériel, and trade goods were loaded onto bateaux—flat-bottomed shallow-draft vessels propelled by oars. They could then be transported 17 miles upriver to Fort Halifax, then Massachusetts's northernmost outpost, since Maine was part of Massachusetts until 1820.

From 1754 until 1766, Captain James Howard commanded a Massachusetts provincial garrison here. During the French and Indian War, the fort served primarily as a vital link in the supply route for the British to Fort Halifax. After the war, Captain Howard bought the fort and the area surrounding it. From 1763 until 1812, the Howard family operated a retail business, S&W Howard, that sent local lumber to Boston and the West Indies and brought goods from the outer world to local settlers.

Hasty Boat Building

For a few days in September 1775 the fort was a beehive of activity, as Benedict Arnold and his 1100 men waited here for the boats that would carry them on the Kennebec River in the first stage of their invasion of Canada.

Once the invasion plans were set, George Washington placed an order with Reuben Coburn, a boat maker living south of Fort Western, for 200 bateaux. Reuben was told he had two weeks to complete the job, for which he was to hire 10 carpenters. Coburn was at a disadvantage. He hadn't enough time or men to do the job, and not enough seasoned wood for the boats. The green pine wood he had to use for many of the bateaux was still heavy with moisture. As it dried, it would shrink; and as it shrank, the boat's seams would pull apart.

When Arnold arrived and discovered the problems with the boats, he ordered some to be replaced and others recaulked. Since more men than were needed had volunteered for the invasion, Arnold selected his troops and organized them into companies for traveling the 350 miles to Quebec.

After Arnold and his men departed on September 27, activity at the fort settled back into its former routine. The fort saw no more military-related action during the war, but continued in its role as a supply station and trading center.

Once the war was over, more settlers came to the area and the lum-

ber trade increased. What had been a steady enterprise became a thriving trade between the locals, Boston, New Foundland, and the West Indies. One of Howard's sons captained family-owned sloops between here and Boston, carrying the family's goods.

After the fort passed out of the Howard family in the 19th century, it was used for housing. In 1922 a local newspaper publisher and his son bought the fort, financed its restoration, and donated it to the city of Augusta.

Visiting the Fort

Visitors start with an orientation in the north blockhouse that includes a talk about the fort and its history, complemented by interpretive panels. Depending upon the program schedule, visitors either join a guided tour or take self-guided tours where they can meet with costumed staff in the principal exhibit areas.

These exhibits include a military display on the parade ground and in the south blockhouse, a store exhibit in the original storehouse section of the main house, and an eight-room house exhibit in the original barracks section of the main house.

The main house is a 100-foot-long by 32-foot-wide two-story log structure built in 1754. Used for military purposes initially, its north end had been converted to residential space by the time Arnold arrived here in 1775, and the south end was where the Howard store was located.

Visitors can browse the store's selection of local, English, and West Indian goods, just as shoppers would have from colonial times to the mid-1800s. Ceramics, tableware, pocketknives, factory-made textiles, copperplates, tongs, fishhooks, and a wide variety of other goods chronicle America's changing consumerism in its earliest days.

At the military exhibit, which covers the French and Indian War and Arnold's stay here during the Revolutionary War, visitors can try their hand at drilling, enjoy firing demonstrations, or learn how to present arms. Cooking, weaving, and crafts demonstrations are given at the main house.

The eight-room house exhibit includes 15 pieces of furniture that were here in the 1790s. This exhibit is particularly interesting in contrasting how people lived in colonial times through the 1790s with how they live today.

Visitor Information

207-626-2385

www.oldfortwestern.org

Hours: Memorial Day weekend through July 3, 1 p.m. until 4 p.m. daily. July 4 through Labor Day, 10 a.m. until 4 p.m. Monday through Friday and 1 p.m. until 4 p.m. on weekends. Labor Day until Columbus Day, 1 p.m. until 4 p.m. on weekends only. November through May, 1 p.m. until 3 p.m. the first Sunday of every month.

Admission: There is a moderate fee; children under 6 free.

Accessibility: Those requiring special accommodations should call two weeks in advance. Every effort will be made to meet specific needs.

Special Events: In 2004, many events related to the 250th anniversary are being held throughout the year. In addition, the fort's usual schedule of special events includes hands-on programs every Sunday afternoon in July and August, Maple Syrup Day in March, nature walks, talks, special tours, and occasional canoe, kayak, jet boat, or bateau excursions on the river.

Getting There: Take I-95 to Augusta and then follow the signs to Downtown, River Front, City Center, and Old Fort Western. Park in the city hall parking lot just behind Old Fort Western and enter through the main gate off Cony Street.

U.S. Naval Academy Museum

The United States Naval Academy Museum in Annapolis exists for the display and preservation of naval artifacts and as an educational tool and resource for the Academy's midshipmen, the latter in recognition of the Academy's motto *Ex Scientia Tridens*—From Knowledge, Sea Power.

The museum's extensive resources include ship models, particularly the Rogers Ship Model Collection, flags, swords, firearms, medals, sculptures, paintings, prints, rare books, photographs, ship instruments and gear, and personal memorabilia. Among its Revolutionary War–related items are a flintlock pistol, swords, and various John Paul Jones artifacts.

The genesis of the U.S. Naval Academy Museum was a collection established in 1845 at the New York Navy Yard's Naval School Lyceum. By the time of the Civil War, the collection had grown to include objects brought back from exploring and surveying expeditions, as well as from diplomatic missions, and trophies of war.

When the Naval School Lyceum was disbanded in 1888, its impressive collection was transferred to the Academy, as was an extensive collection of naval objects from the Boston Naval Library and Institute in 1921. At first housed in a room over the mess hall and later displayed in Bancroft Hall, the collection finally was given its permanent home in 1939. In 1970 the museum building was formally dedicated to the memory of Commodore Edward Preble, an early leader in officer education and a veteran of the Revolutionary War.

The museum has several exhibit galleries—the Gallery of Ship Models, the Main Hall, and two additional galleries featuring changing exhibits.

Outstanding Ship Models

The Ship Model Gallery, located on the lower deck, displays the Rogers Ship Model Collection, one of the most valuable collections of its type in the world. Included in this collection are 108 ship and boat models dating from 1650 to 1850.

Colonel Henry Huddleston Rogers began buying these elaborate models around 1916. Over the next 16 years, he amassed an exceptional selection of ships, paying an average price of about 5000 dollars for each. For a time, part of his collection was at the Metropolitan Museum of Art in New York. When Colonel Rogers died in 1935, he bequeathed the collection to the Academy.

Almost every rate (ships were rated according to the number of guns they carried) and type of warship built between the mid-17th and mid-19th centuries is represented. These exquisitely detailed models—called dockyard models because they were constructed at the major dockyards of Europe's leading naval powers—are made from hardwoods, such as boxwood and pear wood, at a general scale of one inch to four feet. Twelve of the Rogers models are displayed in original 17th- and 18th- century cabinets, which are as valuable as the ships they contain. Breathtaking in its scope and the elaborate authenticity of its models, the Rogers Collection is an excellent primer for understanding the kinds

The Bonhomme Richard, captained by John Paul Jones, fought and captured the British ships Serapis, *carrying 50 guns, and the* Countess of Scarborough, *with 22 guns.*

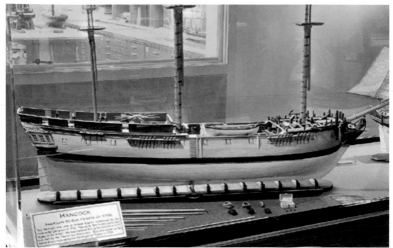

Captured after a 39-hour chase, the Hancock *was refitted and renamed* Iris. *Sailing under the British flag, she was acclaimed "the finest and fastest frigate in the world."*

of ships the fledgling Continental Navy set itself against in the War for Independence.

Modern models of ships, not part of the Rogers Collection, are also displayed here. Several of these ships were used by the Continental and state navies of the Revolutionary War, among them John Paul Jones's 42-gun *Bonhomme Richard; Fair American,* a 14-gun privateer brig that was captured and incorporated into the British Navy in 1782; and *Hancock,* one of the 13 frigates authorized by Congress for the Continental Navy.

The 34-gun *Hancock,* with its figurehead of patriot John Hancock, was captured by the British after a 39-hour chase in 1777, then by the French in 1781, and was finally blown up by the British in the French port of Toulon in 1793. When the *Hancock* was in the hands of the British, her owners boasted she was "the finest and fastest frigate in the world."

On one side of this gallery is a glass-enclosed model-preservation area, which allows visitors to see how these works of art are constructed and repaired.

Also on this level is the museum's Bone Model Display—models crafted from animal bones, with human or horsehair used for the rigging, in the 1700s and 1800s by prisoners of war. Originally painstakingly constructed from ration scraps, some of the later bone models included parts made of whalebone and ivory. The majority of known surviving bone models, such as those in the museum's collection (one of the largest in the world), were made by French prisoners of war held in Britain during the Napoleonic Wars, between 1799 and 1815. One story tells of a prisoner held at Dover Castle who was so involved with the creation of his model that, even though hostilities had ended, he refused to be repatriated, staying at the castle to finish the model. By the time he'd finished it, hostilities had resumed and he was a prisoner again.

The Main Hall

In the entrance foyer is a large portrait of Abraham Whipple, a hero of the Continental Navy whose exploits began with the *Gaspee* Affair in 1772. The *Gaspee* was a British sloop sent to Narragansett Bay, Rhode Island, to harass local smugglers. The smugglers didn't take kindly to this interference, nor did the locals, who found themselves equally harassed by the ship's crew, who stole cattle and cut fruit trees for firewood.

When the *Gaspee* ran aground, eight longboats, under the command of Abraham Whipple, set out to burn the sitting duck where it lay, off a point of land then called Namquit Point, now called Gaspee Point. As the longboats approached the sloop, a sentry on board called out, "Who goes there?" to which Whipple replied, "I am the sheriff of the county of Kent, God damn you! I have got a warrant to apprehend you, God damn you! So, surrender, God damn you!" Sensing hostility, the British put up a fight but were overpowered, and the sloop was destroyed. Whipple later served with distinction as a commodore in the Continental Navy.

The uniform he wears in his portrait is an authentic Continental Navy uniform. Uniforms were mandated by the Marine Committee in 1776 for both the Continental Navy and the Continental Marines. Marine officers all wore the same uniform, which included a green coat faced with white, white waistcoat and britches edged with green, and black garters. Naval officers wore the same basic uniform—blue cloth with red lapels, stand-up collar, blue britches, and red waistcoat—with variations according to rank.

Many of the Revolutionary War artifacts in the Main Hall pertain to John Paul Jones, among them a cuirass, which is akin to a breastplate, worn by Jones, and a sextant thought to have belonged to him. The museum also has in its collection correspondence written by Jones that can be viewed by appointment. Also available for viewing by appointment are pieces of Revolutionary War ships.

There is a bust of Commodore John Barry in the foyer. Other artifacts include a flintlock pistol, a flintlock swivel gun used for repelling boarders during battle, a pine tree three-shilling note, a nautical lamp, and several swords.

The museum's additional exhibition spaces include "100 Years and forward . . . ," which chronicles the history of the navy and marine corps, beginning with the Spanish-American War of 1898. The Beverley R. Robinson Collection—with 6000 woodcuts, etchings, line engravings, mezzotints, aquatints, and lithographs of naval scenes—covers naval history from 1514 through World War II. The Malcolm Storer Naval Medals Collection has more than 1000 commemorative coin-medals dating from 254 B.C. to 1936. The U.S. Navy Trophy Flag Collection contains more than 700 historic American and captured foreign flags, including the "Don't Give Up the Ship" flag from the Battle of Lake Erie. There are also changing exhibits.

In the next several years, the museum will be undergoing renovations of its exhibit areas to better combine art, artifacts, models, text, and audiovisual presentations.

John Paul Jones

Across the yard from the museum is the Naval Academy Chapel, in whose crypt is the sarcophagus containing the remains of John Paul Jones, the most celebrated hero of the Continental Navy. Other com-

manders of that navy, especially John Barry, were considered as brave and able as Jones, but none was as flamboyant nor had the luck to take part in a naval battle as famous as that of the Battle of Flamborough Head, considered by some the greatest sea battle of its time.

In 1779, a few months before the battle, John Adams had written, "Jones has art, and secrecy, and aspires very high. . . . Eccentricities and irregularities are to be expected from him." Though not welcomed in an established navy, eccentricities and irregularities could be accommodated and even beneficial to a hardscrabble navy just getting its sea legs. How many others would have taken to sea in refitted ships with ill-trained crews to challenge the greatest sea power of the age?

Though John Barry is considered by some the father of the American Navy, history has bestowed more glory on John Paul Jones, in part because he courted it, but also

John Paul Jones's flamboyance made him a legend even before the Revolution was over.

because of his grit, daring, and dogged determination. "I wish to have no Connection with any Ship that does not sail fast," he declared early in his career, "for I intend to go in harm's way."

Jones was born just John Paul in 1747, the son of a gardener on a Scottish estate. At the age of 13 he went to sea as an apprentice on board a merchant ship, and by 21 he was a captain. In 1773 he was accused of killing a man on board another ship he was commanding.

Warned that his life was in danger, Paul went into hiding and after almost two years turned up in Virginia with a new name—John Paul Jones. Two years later, he was commissioned an officer in the Continental Navy and appointed first lieutenant of the *Alfred*, the first Continental warship to fly the national flag.

Promoted to command of the *Alfred*, Jones captured a number of prizes that yielded much-needed supplies for the army. Next, Jones was appointed captain of the *Ranger* and assigned the task of bringing the news of Burgoyne's surrender at Saratoga to Benjamin Franklin in Paris.

Another ship arrived first, but Jones, ever ambitious, courted favor with the American delegation, hoping for a better command. He was especially popular with the ladies, so that even John Adams's hardheaded Yankee wife, Abigail, was enamored. "He is small of stature, well proportioned, soft in his speech, easy in his address, polite in his manners, vastly civil, understands all the etiquette of a lady's toilette as perfectly as he does the mast, sails and rigging of his ship."

After cancellation of a planned invasion of England in which Jones would have served under the Marquis de Lafayette, Jones was given command of the *Ranger* in 1778 and instructed by Franklin to "proceed . . . in the manner you shall judge best for distressing the enemies of the United States, consistent with the laws of war, and the terms of your commission."

Jones more than fulfilled his commission. He raided British seaports, which had not been done since 1667, and terrorized the British populace through its press, who printed dire predictions of imminent invasions by marauding colonial savages.

Returning to Paris, Jones was given command of a fleet. A sorry fleet, to be sure, but one that would prove up to the task through the sheer grit of its commander. Jones's flagship was an old 40-gun French East Indian merchant ship renamed the *Bonhomme Richard* in honor of Franklin's pen name (Poor Richard) in French. Its crew numbered 380, 60 of whom were Americans and the rest were of eight other nationalities, including some British.

There were also three French navy ships, two French privateers and the *Alliance*, commanded by Frenchman named Pierre Landa who would later be judged insan a court of law. Landais had made an honorary citizen of achusetts and, considering the only American in co refused to take orders f Scotsman Jones.

Once on Brittany's s the privateers left the their trade. One of the

In an attempt to board the Serapis, *John Paul Jones managed to lock the two ships together. The* Bonhomme Richard *was afire and the water in the hold was rising. When the British captain asked for surrender Jones's memorable reply was, "I have not yet begun to fight!" A grenade from the* Richard *exploded ammunition on board the* Serapis *and after three and a half hours of battle, the* Serapis *struck its flag. Jones and his crew later boarded the British ship and saw the* Richard *sink.*

got lost and another broke her tiller, leaving Jones and the *Bonhomme Richard* with the frigate *Pallas*. The position of Landais and the *Alliance* was unknown.

"I have not yet begun to fight!"

On September 23, 1779, off the coast of Yorkshire, England, Jones encountered the 50-gun British frigate the *Serapis* and the 20-gun sloop *Countess of Scarborough*. The *Pallas* engaged the *Countess of Scarborough*, taking her after two hours. The *Serapis*, under the command of Captain Richard Pearson, and the *Bonhomme Richard* began their battle just after sunset, with an change of broadsides.

When the *Bonhomme Richard* ran bow into the *Serapis*'s stern, on hailed Jones with, "Has hip struck?" (taken down its surrender), to which Jones "I have not yet begun to nes made good his boast, with the superior ship for hours.

xplosion finally forced on to strike his colors in surrender. His officers, afraid of exposing themselves to the relentless fire, refused to do it, and the captain had to take down his own flag. Two days later, Jones had to transfer his crew to the *Serapis* as the *Bonhomme Richard*, damaged even worse than the *Serapis*, began to sink.

More than 100 men died or were wounded in the battle. Jones later wrote, "A person must have been an eye witness to form a just idea of this tremendous scene of carnage, wreck and ruin that everywhere appeared. Humanity cannot but recoil from the prospect of such finished horror, and lament that which should produce such fatal consequences."

At 32, Jones was a hero in France and America. Louis XVI awarded him the Ordre de Mérite Militaire and presented him with a gold-hilted sword. He would live another 13 years but never again have the kind of success he'd had in this one historic battle.

Put in charge of the construction of the Continental Navy's first 74-gun warship, *America*, with a promise of its command, Jones would instead see the ship given to the French at war's end. A stint with Catherine the Great's navy ended with his being charged with rape, which was never proven, and leaving for Paris, where he died at the age of 45, alone and poor. A month before his death, President George Washington had appointed him American consul in Algeria, but Jones never received notice of the appointment.

In the last months of his life, Jones wrote, "The rules of conduct, the maxims of action, and the tactical instincts that serve to gain small victories may always be expanded into the winning of great ones with suitable opportunity; because in human affairs the sources of success are ever to be found in the fountains of quick resolve and swift stroke; and it seems a law inflexible and inexorable that he who will not risk cannot win."

Jones was buried in Paris's St. Louis Cemetery. A few years later, the cemetery was sold and those buried there forgotten.

In 1905, after an extensive search headed by American ambassador General Horace Porter, the site of the former cemetery was determined and Jones's casket recovered. President Theodore Roosevelt sent a squadron of warships to transport the body home, following an elaborate send-off in Paris.

On April 24, 1905, the casket was brought to the Academy, with President Roosevelt giving the main address at a formal ceremony. After that, Jones in his coffin was stored under the main staircase in Bancroft Hall while Congress debated the appropriate funding for construction of his crypt.

Finally, funding came through and Jones's remains were laid to rest in the Academy Chapel crypt on January 26, 1913. Designed by architect Whitney Warren in the Beaux Arts style, the circular crypt and its 21-ton sarcophagus and surrounding columns of black and white Royal Pyrénées marble suggest the tombs of Napoleon and Nelson, which doubtless would have pleased Jones. Bronze dolphins and garlands of sea plants embellish the sarcophagus.

Inscribed on the marble floor in bronze are the names of the seven ships Jones commanded, and at the foot of the sarcophagus is inscribed JOHN PAUL JONES, 1747-1792, U.S. NAVY, 1775-1783. HE GAVE OUR NAVY ITS EARLIEST TRADITIONS OF HEROISM AND VICTORY. ERECTED BY THE CONGRESS, A.D. 1912.

Visitors are not allowed near the sarcophagus but are limited to a circular walkway around the crypt. Along the walkway are glass-fronted display windows in which have been placed artifacts such as Jones's gold-hilted sword and his medals.

Visitor Information
410-293-2108

www.usna.edu/Museum

Hours: The museum is open Monday through Saturday 9 a.m. until 5 p.m.; Sunday 11 a.m. through 5 p.m.; closed Thanksgiving, December 25, and January 1. John Paul Jones's crypt in the Naval Chapel is open Monday through Saturday, 9 a.m. until 4 p.m., Sundays, 1 p.m. until 4 p.m.; closed Thanksgiving, December 25, and January 1.

Admission: Free.

Accessibility: Both the museum and John Paul Jones's crypt are handicapped accessible. Those who have vehicles with a valid handicapped placard may drive onto the yard, but visitors should call ahead to make sure security arrangements have not been changed due to current security situations.

Special Events: John Paul Jones Day, held every July, features exhibits and events related to Jones's life and times, with a wreath laying, slide lectures, demonstrations, and children's activities.

Getting There: The museum is located in Preble Hall, at 118 Maryland Avenue in Annapolis, just inside the Academy's Maryland Avenue entrance (Gate 3). The chapel is across the street from the museum. Visitors must enter through Gate 3 on Maryland Avenue, and all visitors over 16 must have a valid picture ID. Visitors' cars are not permitted on the Academy yard, and parking is very limited in downtown Annapolis. Annapolis Transit runs a free shuttle bus between the Navy/Marine Corps Memorial Stadium parking lot (Rowe Boulevard just off U.S. route 50) and downtown Annapolis. (Online: www.ci.annapolis.md.us/government/depts/transport/parking.asp).

From the northeast: Take U.S. route 301 south from Delaware to U.S. route 50 west across the Chesapeake Bay Bridge and follow the signs to Annapolis.

From the south: Take I-95 to the Washington beltway and U.S. route 50 to Annapolis.

The Battle for Boston

Just days after Lexington and Concord in April 1775, colonial militia and volunteers from all over New England surrounded Boston and began a yearlong siege. After two major battles, the British evacuated the city in March 1776.

However, the battle for Boston had really begun almost 30 years earlier, when rioting Bostonians drove the governor of Massachusetts from the city during a protest against impressment of Americans into the Royal Navy. From that first major civil upheaval in 1747 to a city under siege in 1775, a seemingly inevitable journey set America on the road to independence.

Today Boston is one of America's major business and cultural centers, a city steeped in the promise of 21st-century technology, education, and science. Yet visitors can still experience the city's 18th-century history through the sites along the Freedom Trail that have been preserved by farsighted stewards of another era.

Pre-Revolution Boston

It's possible there wouldn't have been an American Revolution without Boston. As much as the other colonies were enamored of the idea of independence by the mid-1700s, it took the hardscrabble intellectuals of Boston to push the entrepreneurs of the Mid-Atlantic and the plantation gentlemen of the South into making the final break.

Boston hadn't always been trouble. Established by the Puritans of the Massachusetts Bay Colony in the 1630s, Boston was for some 130 years an orderly community whose populace prided themselves on their British heritage and on being a productive contributor to the wealth and power of the British Empire. By the 1740s, Boston was a thriving seaport of between 12,000 and 15,000 people. Its merchants sent shiploads of New England's coveted timber to Europe, along with rice from the Carolinas and wheat from Pennsylvania. Trade was also established with West Indian planters, whose profitable sugar production was made possible by African slaves. What became known as the Triangular Trade developed: sugar and molasses from the West Indies to New England, rum from New England to Africa, slaves from Africa to the West Indies.

Slavery for people of color was tolerated in Boston. Of the estimated 800 blacks who lived there in 1765, nearly all were slaves. Servitude for the town's other residents was viewed differently. In 1747 when the British navy seized 40 men from the port, thousands rioted and Governor William Shirley was forced to take refuge at a fort in the harbor. Only when the men were released was peace restored.

The Stamp Act

Things remained relatively peaceful until the 1760s, when, in an effort to pay down the enormous debt it had incurred during its war with France, Great Britain imposed new taxes and restrictive laws on its North American colonies.

Passage of the Sugar Act in 1764, followed by the Currency Act that same year and the Stamp Act a year later, confounded Bostonians in its blatant attempt to impose taxes on freeborn Englishmen without giving them representation in Parliament. Until then, the colonies had taxed themselves. Worse, passage of these laws made it clear that while Bostonians considered themselves valued members of Britain's citizenry, the Mother Country viewed them as little more than subservient colonials. Or so Boston thought. From the British point of view, these laws, particularly the Stamp Act, were fair and reasonable ways for the colonies to help defray the costs of their own defense and infrastructure.

The Stamp Act required all legal documents, licenses, commercial contracts, newspapers, pamphlets, and playing cards to carry a tax stamp similar to the one above.

Boston had also experienced economic difficulties as a result of the war. Offshore fisheries had been closed and merchant ships had been attacked and even confiscated. The Stamp Act, which imposed a tax on all documents and publications, seemed one more financial burden at a time when many were struggling. And if the moneyed classes

British soldiers *open fire on a mob of people gathered in front of the Customs Office in Boston. The first to die was a mulatto named Crispus Attucks, a native of Framingham, Massachusetts. Attucks escaped from slavery in 1750 and had become a sailor. He is considered the first martyr for American independence.*

had less to spend, so did all those who depended on their trade. The middle and poorer classes would feel the brunt of the law's impact.

On August 14, 1765, Andrew Oliver, the newly appointed stamp master, was hanged in effigy from an elm tree in the town's South End. (This elm tree would later be christened the Liberty Tree.) That evening several thousand Bostonians propped Oliver's effigy on the end of a pole, set it afire, and paraded it through the town. A small contingent attacked Oliver's house, breaking windows and tearing up his garden. Then on August 26, the home of Oliver's brother-in-law, Lieutenant Governor Thomas Hutchinson, was destroyed. Hutchinson and his family were lucky to escape with their lives. Though the mob that attacked Hutchinson was motivated more by pettiness than principle, their anger was based on the same feelings of disenfranchisement as those of the mob who opposed the Stamp Act.

An up-and-coming young lawyer of the town named John Adams understood the sentiments for self-rule that were gradually coalescing in Boston. "The people, even to the lowest ranks, have become more attentive to their liberties, more inquisitive about them, and more determined to defend them, than they were ever before known or had occasion to be." Though it would be 10 years before a formal declaration would proclaim the intent, many in Boston and elsewhere were already pulling away from Mother Britain. During this time a Boston minister nearly brought his congregation to

its feet when he quoted from Paul's letter to the Galatians, "I would they were cut off which trouble you: for, brethren, ye are called unto liberty."

The Boston Massacre

With Parliament's repeal of the Stamp Act in 1766, Bostonians and other colonials felt their concerns were being given a fair hearing in London. They were proven wrong in 1767, with the passage of the Townshend Acts mandating duties on tea, glass, paper, lead, and paint.

The Sons of Liberty was formed by Samuel Adams, John Adams's cousin, as a centralized organization to increase the effectiveness of political protests. They became the core of what would be the movement for independence. Soon after news of the Townshend Acts reached Boston, they began holding meetings to map out a protest strategy.

The Massachusetts Assembly, made up of elected representatives, wrote and circulated a letter to the other colonies, calling for coordinated action in opposition to the acts. King George III on hearing of the letter demanded that it be rescinded. When the Assembly refused, its session was halted by Francis Bernard, the Royal Governor. In retaliation, the Sons of Liberty organized a boycott of all British goods. The *Boston Gazette* supported the boycott, telling its readers, "Save your money and you save your country." This sweeping act put pressure on all levels of society and all trades and professionals to conform. Those who didn't were ostracized or even ruined. Upholding the boycott became a

Samuel Adams

Samuel Adams was the flashpoint of the Boston rebellion that grew into the Revolutionary War. His fiery orations impassioned the people to take action, while his political strategies organized their energies into an effective resistance movement.

Adams's populist manner belied his patrician background. Born into a wealthy family of brewers and landowners, he graduated from Harvard and inherited a large sum of money at a young age. Lacking an aptitude for managing money, by the time he was in his early 40s he had lost most of his fortune and was depending on friends for the support of his family.

Before and during the war he worked tirelessly for American independence, serving in the Continental Congress until 1781. Following the war, his radical ideas isolated him from the framers of the U.S. Constitution. He refused to take part in the convention because he knew that power would be given to the national government to the detriment of the individual states.

In 1794, Adams was elected governor of Massachusetts, where during his three terms in office he continued his proletarian ways by refusing to use the governor's carriage. When criticized for it, he replied, "The Almighty gave me two feet for the purpose of using them, sir! I have been walking through the streets of Boston for seven decades, and shall continue to do so until I can no longer walk!"

Though remembered most for his Yankee perseverance and passion for liberty, Samuel Adams also appreciated what the country he helped create meant to the rest of the world. "Driven from every other corner of the earth, freedom of thought and the right of private judgment in matters of conscience, direct their course to this happy country as their last asylum."

severe hardship for tradesmen with small businesses, but their economic ruin was judged an unfortunate by-product of the need to stand up to the king and Parliament.

In June 1768, four of the government's appointed customs commissioners were forced to seek refuge in a harbor fort. Governor Bernard had been urging London to send troops to control the city, and this latest action proved the need. It also gave certain elements in the British government, who had been advocating a firmer hand against the recalcitrant colonials, the excuse they needed to carry out that policy. Four regiments were dispatched to Boston to restore order. On October 1, 1768, the first two regiments, with about 700 men, arrived on 12 British warships that anchored in Boston harbor, an obvious warning. The two other regiments arrived soon after. Boston was now occupied by close to

1500 British Regulars. Half of these left the summer of 1769, but only after Boston proved itself manageable.

In the intervening year, while the British Regulars were garrisoned in Boston, many of the town's residents grew to hate them. Citizens could be challenged on the street as to who they were and where they were going. Women were openly insulted by the soldiers, and Sunday worshipers were distracted by the noise of military drills. Minor pushing and shoving matches between soldiers and citizens escalated through the end of 1768 and the beginning of 1769. Bostonians, especially those on the lower rungs of the economic ladder, had seen their wages and opportunities decrease throughout the 1760s, with no relief in sight. Now, in their eyes, they'd been insultingly reduced to the level of those in conquered

Ireland, rather than treated with the respect due British citizens. Worse, some of the soldiers were taking jobs when off duty, flooding an already tight job market.

On March 5, 1770, insults were exchanged between an angry mob of working-class men and the sentry at the Custom House, across from the State House. The mob began throwing rocks, oyster shells, and icy snowballs. Captain Thomas Preston and seven of his soldiers came to the sentry's rescue and tried to disperse the crowd. Exactly what happened next has never been clearly ascertained, but apparently the soldiers felt sufficiently threatened to fire on the crowd. Three Americans died at the scene, two a few days later.

Preston and his men were tried for murder. That the British government allowed its soldiers to be tried in an American court shows there was still an accepted common ground; nevertheless, all but two were acquitted. Those two were found guilty of manslaughter, branded on their thumbs, and released. Their lawyer did what many thought impossible. In a town hostile toward British soldiers, he convinced a jury that six of the eight had acted in self-defense toward a crowd their lawyer described as a "motley rabble of saucy boys, negroes and molattoes, Irish teagues and outlandish jack tarrs."

Playing on the prejudices of the jurors, but also presenting a reasonable argument for self-defense, the lawyer won, and in doing so garnered the respect and recognition of Boston. Thirty-three-year-old John Adams had finally begun to make his mark.

The Boston Tea Party

By 1770, England could do no right in the view of many Bostonians. Though Parliament had pulled the soldiers out of the town and repealed most of the Townshend Acts, there was a crack in the façade of the alliance. The majority of Bostonians were making the mental and emotional leap from identifying themselves as English to identifying themselves as American. In their eyes, England had disenfranchised them—in effect cutting them loose by imposing taxes without fair representation. They were now searching for a sense of who they were as a community and where their community belonged in the greater scheme of things.

The answer was found in the dealings Samuel Adams instituted with other Massachusetts towns and other colonies. Samuel Adams, an adept political strategist, understood that whatever filled the emotional vacuum left by England could have great influence. He built a network of Sons of Liberty associations throughout the colonies. He established Committees of Correspondence to share views among the towns, and he encouraged town meetings where everyone, regardless of status within the community, would have a voice in the replies. He got people talking and thinking about what they wanted from a government and how they should go about getting it. In doing so, he and his independence-minded associates planted the seed of a united coalition to deal with issues, rather than towns and colonies dealing with them individually.

In 1773, Parliament passed the Tea Act, which lowered the price of the popular beverage but dictated that only agents of the East India Company could sell it. Boston joined other Massachusetts towns and the other colonies in opposing the act as a restriction on fair trade. When three ships carrying tea docked in Boston Harbor, Sam Adams and other leaders asked the governor to send the ships and their cargoes back to England. The governor at that time was Thomas Hutchinson, the same gentleman who had had his house destroyed by the mob eight years earlier. He now adamantly refused to let the ships sail back to England and, fearing the cargoes would be destroyed once they were unloaded, refused to let the ships unload any cargo. It was a standoff.

Town meetings were organized. As Abigail Adams wrote to her husband John, "The flame is kindled, and like lightning it catches from soul to soul." When the governor's final refusal was received at a December 16 town meeting at the Old South Meeting House attended by several thousand people, Sam Adams adjourned by saying, "This meeting can do nothing more to save the country."

That was the signal for more than 100 men, reportedly dressed as Native Americans, to march to Griffin's Wharf, board the ships, and throw some 300 chests of tea overboard. Several thousand stood on the wharf watching, and thousands throughout the colonies echoed John Adams's entry in his diary:

On December 16, 1773, a band of patriots, disguised as Mohawk Indians, boarded three tea ships anchored in Boston Harbor. Once on board, the patriots went to work opening the tea chests with axes and hatchets and dumped the contents into the sea.

"There is a dignity, a majesty, a sublimity, in this last effort of the patriots that I greatly admire. This destruction of the tea is so bold, so daring, so firm, intrepid and inflexible and it must have important consequences, and so lasting that I cannot but consider it as an epocha in history."

Parliament Reacts

The consequences were quick and brutal. Parliament closed Boston Harbor. This, along with several other actions designed to squash colonial defiance, became known as the Intolerable, or Coercive, Acts. Parliament also drastically altered the government of Massachusetts, and outlawed the town meetings Samuel Adams had used so effectively. Lieutenant General Thomas Gage, commander of British forces in America, was now also appointed governor of Massachusetts, and brought with him 11 regiments to occupy Boston.

Moderates and those opposed to what they viewed as the breakdown of civil authority and the rise of mob rule now urged reconciliation with Great Britain.

On June 1, 1774, when the port was officially closed, a day of prayer and fasting was observed there and in other colonies. Boston's public buildings were draped in black, its shops closed, and church bells tolled all day. Over the course of the next few weeks, supplies poured into town from New York, Connecticut, and Pennsylvania. Still, the acts did serious damage to Boston. An already teetering economy began to fail, as trade all but ceased.

The Patriots—led by Sam Adams, physician Joseph Warren, silversmith Paul Revere, and the very wealthy merchant John Hancock—joined their counterparts in Virginia and Rhode Island in calling for a congress where representatives from all the colonies would decide on a unified response to the crisis. In September 1774, the First Continental Congress met in Philadelphia. Among its delegates were John and Samuel Adams. The Congress voted to enact a trade boycott against Great Britain. In Boston, newspapers and circulars defiantly published articles condemning Parliament and Governor Gage.

In April 1775, matters came to a head when Gage decided to confiscate powder and other military supplies being held at Concord, some 20 miles from Boston. Gage's soldiers encountered a group of militia in Lexington on the road to Concord, shots were fired, and eight Patriots lay dead on Lexington Green. The British proceeded to Concord, found little in the way of matériel, and had to fight their way back to Boston along what came to be known as the Battle Road (*see* Lexington and Concord). In response, thousands of militiamen from all over New England descended upon Boston, surrounding and laying siege to the town.

The Battle of Bunker Hill

By May of 1775, a line of Patriot militia formed a semicircle around

Boston, from Mystic River on the north, through Cambridge and Roxbury to the west, and to Dorchester in the south. The militia was something of an army by now, with Artemas Ward as its commander in chief and between 7000 and 8000 men. The majority of Boston's residents, about 12,000, had fled the city, among them all the Patriot leaders, leaving a little more than 3500 residents among some 8000 British regulars. England sent three generals to put down the rebellion: Sir William Howe, Sir Henry Clinton, and John Burgoyne.

Both the British and the Americans knew it was imperative to control the hills surrounding Boston. From these the Patriots could fire on British ships in the harbor or the British could fire on the Patriot lines. On the evening of June 16, 1775, Colonel William Prescott and 1200 men from Massachusetts and Connecticut began to build a redoubt on what they thought was the 100-foot-high Bunker Hill on the Charlestown Peninsula. It turned out to be the 75-foot-high Breed's Hill nearby, less advantageous by about 25 feet.

On the afternoon of June 17, Howe and his men came across

John Adams

From an early age, John Adams was intensely ambitious and determined to succeed. As a young man he had written in his diary, "Shall I look for a Cause to Speak to and exert all the Soul and all the Body I own, to cut a flash, strike amazement, to catch the Vulgar? . . . A bold Push, a resolute Attempt, a determined Enterprise, or a slow, silent, imperceptible creeping? Shall I creep or fly?"

The Adams family emigrated from England in the 1640s and settled in the village of Braintree, Massachusetts. In 1735, John Adams was born into a family that had become a leader in community affairs. Adams was schooled for the ministry, but his college years at Harvard turned him toward law, with an eye to some kind of public service. He was encouraged in this by his wife, Abigail Smith, whom he married in 1764. Abigail would remain his lively, intelligent, and steadfast companion for more than 50 years.

In 1765, Adams became involved in the political movement to oppose the Stamp Act. Functioning as the philosophical counterpart to his cousin Sam Adams's firebrand, Adams anonymously wrote articles for the Boston *Gazette* opposing the Act, chronicling the history of freedom in human societies and explaining the legal basis for the rights of Englishmen. From this beginning, Adams moved into the forefront of those fighting for American independence. He was a delegate to the First and Second Continental Congresses, a signer of the Declaration of Independence, and a member of the American mission in Paris that finally brought France into the war. He continued to serve after the war, first as one of the peace treaty negotiators, then as the first U.S. minister to Great Britain. He was elected Vice President in the first presidential election, and elected the second President of the United States in 1796. In 1800 he lost reelection to Thomas Jefferson, and retired with Abigail to his family home in Braintree, where he died on July 4, 1826, the 50th anniversary of the Declaration of Independence.

As one of the acknowledged Founders of the Nation, along with Washington, Jefferson, and Franklin, John Adams remains the least glamorous in the public's eye, now as then. He hadn't Washington's stature, Jefferson's reputation for intellect, or Franklin's wit and charm. He was a Yankee plebeian, hardworking, stubborn, blessed with an unshakable belief in a higher purpose and a self-deprecating sense of humor.

His philosophy of life may have been most clearly reflected in the advice he gave to his granddaughter: "Do justly. Love mercy. Walk humbly. This is enough."

Boston Harbor and landed at what is now the Charlestown Navy Yard. Ships in the harbor bombarded Charlestown, burning it to the ground, while the British advanced against the redoubt at Breed's Hill and against a Patriot line of New Hampshire militia under Colonel John Stark that stretched along a rail fence extending down the slope of the peninsula.

Atop Breed's Hill, Colonel William Prescott reportedly told his men, "Don't shoot until you see the whites of their eyes!" Though the colonial militia weren't the cowardly rubes the British purported them to be, they also weren't professional soldiers. Yet they threw back Howe's first two attacks by one of the best-trained, best-equipped armies in the world.

On the third charge the Americans were driven from the hill, but by then nearly half of Howe's 2200 men were dead or wounded. The Patriot forces lost an estimated 400 to 600 men, one of them Dr. Joseph Warren, Samuel Adams's closest friend and a founder of the Sons of Liberty.

In a letter to his mother soon after the battle, a Patriot soldier named Peter Brown described the fighting: "[A]nd after they were well formed they advanced towards us in order to swallow us up, but they found a choaky mouthful of us, tho' we could do nothing with our small arms as yet for distance, and had but two cannon and nary a gunner. And they from Boston and from the ships a-firing and throwing bombs keeping us down till they got almost round us. But God in mercy to us fought our battle for us and altho' we were but few and so were suffered to be defeated by them, we were preserved in a most wonderful manner.... I was in the fort [redoubt] till the Regulars came in and I jumped over the walls, and ran for about a half a mile where balls flew like hailstones and cannons roared with thunder."

A British officer writing about the battle lamented the terrible losses his army had suffered, admitting that "too great confidence in ourselves, which is always dangerous, occasioned this dreadful loss," and looked ahead with some discouragement. "My mind cannot help dwelling upon our cursed mistakes. Such ill conduct at the first out-set argues a gross ignorance of the most common rules of the professions, and gives us, for the future, anxious forebodings."

Dorchester Heights

Two weeks after the battle, General George Washington, who had been

After enduring two volleys that tore huge gaps in their lines, British troops are seen converging on the American fortification atop Breed's Hill. The Patriots, running out of ammunition, use their muskets as clubs against the British bayonets.

Boston Under Siege

Boston under siege quickly ran out of food and fuel and became racked with disease. As Peter Oliver, a Loyalist, wrote to his brother in England, "Our situation here, without any exaggeration, is beyond description almost." John Andrews, who stayed in town to protect his property, "as the soldiery think they have a license to plunder every one's house and store," wrote to a friend that occasionally "a carcase [is] offered for sale in the market, which formerly we would not have picked up in the street," and that their diet consisted of "pork and beans one day, and beans and pork another, and fish whenever we can catch it."

The British suffered along with the Bostonians. Supplies coming from England were often delayed, and food and fuel were often scarce for months at a time. Scurvy and smallpox soon spread among the regiments, and there were reports of officers' horses being stolen and served for dinner. As one British officer wrote home, "The soldiery, and inhabitants likewise, I am sure have done sufficient penance here for the sins of their whole lives."

To relieve the tension and boredom, theatricals were performed twice a week by the officers and some of Boston's ladies. During one of these—a farce written by General John Burgoyne called *The Blockade of Boston*—an attack commenced in Charlestown. When a sergeant ran into the theater yelling, "Turn out! Turn out! They are hard at it, hammer and tongs!" he was applauded for the enthusiasm of his delivery. Only when the bombardment grew louder did the audience realize it wasn't part of the play.

appointed commander in chief of the newly formed Continental Army by the Second Continental Congress, arrived in Cambridge to formally take charge. Not for the last time, luck was with Washington, for the British reluctance to attack gave him the time he needed to organize his fledgling forces.

In September, Governor Gage was called back to London and General Howe placed in command. King George formally declared the American colonies in rebellion and began transferring British troops from other parts of the empire to America, as well as hiring Hessian soldiers to fight alongside them. Washington wanted to take the initiative and attack, but he didn't have enough ammunition for his men and had almost no artillery. That summer, Patriots had captured Fort Ticonderoga and Crown Point (see Maine, Old Fort Western). In early November, Washington turned to a 25-year-old Boston bookseller named Henry Knox to retrieve the captured cannons from the fort and bring them back to Boston, telling him that "the want of them is so great that no Trouble or Expence must be spared to obtain them."

Knox's was a monumental undertaking and its success somewhat miraculous. It took several weeks of hard travel just to reach Fort Ticonderoga. Once there, he and his men found 44 guns, 14 mortars, and a howitzer. One gun was a 24-pounder; the rest ranged from 12 to 18 pounds. Three of the mortars were 13-inchers, weighing a ton each. Knox and his men next had to construct 43 sledges and find 80 yoke of oxen to pull them. At Lake George, the cannons, sledges, and oxen were transferred to flat-bottomed scows and floated down to the head of the lake. From there they made their way to Albany, then down icy mountain roads and up snowy valley trails. In late January, Knox and his men arrived back in Cambridge, presenting to Washington what Knox called "a noble train of artillery." They had transported the guns 300 miles, crossing the Hudson River four times along the way. Washington now had the artillery he needed to fortify Dorchester Heights in South Boston.

On March 5 the British woke to find a line of earthworks and batteries from which the Continental Army looked down upon the city of Boston. General Howe recognized that his position was untenable. In return for agreeing not to fire the town, he and his troops, plus about a thousand Loyalists, were permitted to leave without interference. On March 17 the British evacuated Boston and departed for Canada, leaving behind a plundered but free town.

Boston National Historical Park

The National Park Service's (NPS) park in Boston encompasses historical sites along the 2.5-mile Freedom Trail, plus the Dorchester Heights National Historic Site. Some of the sites are operated solely by NPS, some jointly by NPS and the Freedom Trail Foundation or private organizations.

All the sites have been preserved with an eye to maintaining each site's historical authenticity without isolating it from everyday life in today's city. Difficult and challenging choices were being made 200-plus years ago. Walking the Freedom Trail among people going about their daily routine brings home that those choices were made by ordinary people like these.

The **Freedom Trail** runs from Boston Common to the Charlestown Navy Yard and Bunker Hill. The trail follows a red line on the sidewalk, in most places made of red bricks. There are also signs along the way to direct visitors. Walking maps of the trail, brochures, audiovisual presentations, and visitor orientations are available at the NPS visitor centers (at 15 State Street, across from the Old State House; and at the Charlestown Navy Yard) and also at the Boston Common Visitor Information Center.

Boston Common

The oldest public park in America has been the site of witch hangings, militia training, a papal Mass, and Shakespeare in the Park during its 300-plus-year history. This was the homestead of Boston's first white settler, William Blackstone, who moved here in 1622. In 1766 the repeal of the Stamp Act was celebrated here, and nine years later British troops left for Lexington and Concord from the foot of the Common near Charles Street. Within the Common are a memorial to John Barry, "Father of the American Navy" (*see* Maryland, U.S. Naval Academy Museum); a bas-relief recording the entire Declaration of Independence; and a column memorializing the Boston Massacre.

The Liberty Tree

Boston's Liberty Tree, the first in the colonies, no longer exists but is honored in a freestone bas-relief set in the wall of a building on the southeast corner of Essex and Washington streets, one block east of the Boylston subway station on Boston Common. It was under that elm tree that Andrew Oliver, the official assigned to implement the Stamp Act in Boston, was forced to resign in 1765. When the Stamp Act was repealed in 1766, a large copper plate was attached to the tree's trunk, inscribed "This tree was planted in the year 1646, and pruned by order of the Sons of Liberty." The Liberty Tree was chopped down in August 1775, during the British occupation. Legend has it that one of the Loyalists chopping down a branch of the tree fell from it and died.

The Granary Burying Ground

Established in 1660, this resting place took its final name from the granary that stood at one time in a corner of the two-acre site. An estimated 5000 people are buried here, though there are only a little more than 2300 gravestones. The five victims of the Boston Massacre are buried together in one site. Also here are Samuel Adams, Paul Revere, the parents of Benjamin Franklin, and John Hancock.

Old South Meeting House

Built in 1729 as a Puritan meeting house (or church), this simple red brick building is one of the shrines of the American Revolution. As the largest building in colonial Boston, Old South was used for public meetings. It was here in December 1773 that Samuel Adams signaled the go-ahead for the Boston Tea Party. It was here, prior to the war, that commemorations were held to honor the victims of the Boston Massacre. Town meetings organized here by the Sons of Liberty in the spirit of pure democracy gave every citizen a right to be heard. Realizing the symbolic importance of Old South, the British desecrated the building during the occupation, turning it into a stable and a riding school. Today this National Historic Landmark continues its tradition as a sanctuary for free speech, with speakers taking diverse stands on issues of the day. Through interactive exhibits and displayed artifacts, "Voices of Protest" traces the 300-year history of the meeting house and those who have spoken here in the contexts of their times. The audio exhibit "If These Walls Could Speak . . ." uses actual speeches to take visitors back in time to events such as the Boston Tea Party and the British occupation.

The Old State House as seen from the circle of stones that commemorates the site of the Boston Massacre.

Old State House

From the balcony of this graceful red brick colonial building the Declaration of Independence was first read to the citizens of Boston; and from this same balcony 200 years later Queen Elizabeth II of England addressed many of their descendants. Such historical contradiction is inherent in the building that served as headquarters for the king's representatives (the Council) and those elected by the people of Massachusetts (the Assembly). John Adams wrote that here "the child Independence was born," referring to an eloquent and passionate argument presented by James Otis in 1761 opposing Writs of Assistance that infringed on citizens' rights. During the debates over the Stamp Act, in 1776, for the first time in remembered history citizens were allowed to witness legislative sessions. Owned and operated by the Bostonian Society, the museum has a fascinating permanent exhibit on Boston's history, including Revolutionary War artifacts, plus changing exhibits and programs on a continuing basis.

Boston Massacre Site

A small circle of stones beneath the balcony of the Old State House is the site of what came to be known as the Boston Massacre—an exchange of harangues and insults that escalated into rock throwing and finally to the shooting deaths of five Patriots. Strategist Samuel Adams was quick to dub the incident a "horrible and bloody massacre," and Paul Revere's famous engraving *Bloody Massacre,* though not factual, was excellent propaganda for the Patriot cause.

Faneuil Hall

Besides being historically distinctive, this is a stunningly beautiful building, with a graceful exterior topped by a golden-domed cupola and a lovely neoclassical interior accented with Ionic columns. Faneuil Hall was a gift to the city from Peter Faneuil, a wealthy merchant. That hall was built in 1742, with a market downstairs—as now—and a meeting hall upstairs. The present hall is twice as large, with additions designed by Charles Bulfinch, an architect of the U.S. Capitol, that were constructed in 1805. The idea of Committees of Correspondence was created here, and meetings were held here in protest of the Sugar Act and the Stamp Act until overflow crowds moved them to Old South Meeting House. A statue of Samuel

Faneuil Hall is where colonists first protested the Sugar Act in 1764, based on the doctrine of "no taxation without representation."

Adams stands facing the Congress Street entrance to the hall. Inside this entrance, there's an NPS information desk on the second floor. Park rangers give regularly scheduled talks about the history of the hall and the events that took place here. The hall has continued to serve as a forum for debates and public discourse from revolutionary times forward, welcoming speakers such as Frederick Douglass, Elizabeth Cady Stanton, and statesmen such as President John F. Kennedy and South Africa's Nelson Mandela. And there is a satisfying symmetry to the fact that each year new citizens take their oath of loyalty here. The grasshopper weathervane is thought to be a copy of one that topped the Royal Exchange in London, of which Faneuil was a member. A Boston landmark, the grasshopper was used to reveal spies during the War of 1812, because anyone who claimed to be a Bostonian and didn't know the form of the hall's weathervane had to be lying.

Old North Church

Even in its early days, Christ Church was known affectionately as Old North Church, the oldest church in Boston's North End neighborhood. Today it is the oldest standing church building in Boston. Constructed in 1723 based on drawings of Christopher Wren's London churches, Old North was one of Boston's Anglican churches that leaned more toward Patriots than Loyalists—although the rector was such an adamant Loyalist that the congregation stopped paying his salary. The part Old North played in Paul Revere's famous midnight ride, however, had more to do with its steeple being the highest point in the city than with its political views. A vestryman of the church, Captain John Pulling, and the church's sexton, Robert Newman, agreed to signal from the steeple's topmost window "one if by land and two if by sea" (*see* Massachusetts, Lexington and Concord). The night of April 18, 1775, the two men climbed 154 stairs up the church tower and then ascended a narrow ladder to the top of the steeple. From there they signaled Patriots in Charlestown with two candle-lit lanterns that the British were coming by sea. Christ Church remains an active Episcopal Church (part of the worldwide Anglican Communion), and visitors are welcome.

Bunker Hill Monument

This 221-foot Egyptian obelisk was dedicated in 1843 in a ceremony that featured orator Daniel Webster as the main speaker. To reach it, the Freedom Trail crosses the Charlestown Bridge from downtown Boston. The monument and its surrounding park are on what was actually Breed's Hill, the site in June 1775 of what is known as the Battle of Bunker Hill. In the observatory at the top of the obelisk, illustrated signage explains the positions of the Patriot breastworks and the rail fence. A statue of the commander of Patriot forces, Colonel William Prescott, stands at the base of the monument. The park service plans to open a new facility in 2005 across the street from the monument, which will feature exhibit space, Revolutionary War artifacts, interactive displays, and dioramas of the Battle of Bunker Hill.

Charlestown Navy Yard

It was on this site that the British came ashore to meet Patriot forces at the Battle of Bunker Hill. One of the first six navy yards established following the war, Charlestown serviced, supplied, and built ships for the U.S. Navy from 1800 until 1974. Today it is known primarily as the home of the U.S.S. *Constitution*, nicknamed *Old Ironsides* for her sturdy oak construction. She is the oldest commissioned warship afloat in the world. Located at the yard is one of the two Boston Historical Park visitor centers. A very entertaining and informative film called *The Whites of Their Eyes*, presented in the pavilion, provides a terrific overview of the Battle of Bunker Hill. The park rangers here periodically give talks on the battle.

Dorchester Heights National Historic Park

The park is located in South Boston, two miles from downtown Boston, and is not part of the Freedom Trail. The colonial-revival-style monument was dedicated in 1902. From its tower, visitors have a wonderful view of Boston Harbor, much as George Washington did in 1775. Standing here, it's not difficult to understand General Howe's decision to fold his tents and retreat to Nova Scotia. Budget cutbacks within the park service have necessitated closing the site except during the summer months, when it is open only four days a week. The park service plans to provide wayside panels at the site sometime in the next few years.

Visitor Information

617-242-5642 and 617-242-5601
www.nps.gov/bost and
www.thefreedomtrail.org
Hours: The Boston Common is open Monday through Saturday, 8:30 a.m. until 5 p.m., Sunday, 9 a.m. until 5 p.m. **The Boston Common Visitor Center** is open daily from 9 a.m. until 5 p.m. **The Granary Burying Ground** is open 8 a.m. until 5:30 p.m. daily in the spring, summer, and fall, and 8 a.m. until 3 p.m. in the winter. **The Old South Meeting House** is open daily April through October from 9:30 a.m. until 5 p.m. and November through March from 10 a.m. until 4 p.m. **The Old State House** is open daily from 9 a.m. until 5 p.m. **The Old North Church** is open daily from 9 a.m. until 6 p.m. from late June through October, and from 9 a.m. until 5 p.m. from November until late-June. **The Bunker Hill Monument** is open daily from 9 a.m. until 4:30 p.m.; exhibits daily from 9 a.m. until 5 p.m.; grounds open until dusk. **Faneuil Hall** is open daily from 9 a.m. until 5 p.m. except when the hall is being used for meetings; call ahead to be sure. **Dorchester Heights National Historic Park** is open Wednesday through Saturday, Memorial Day through Labor Day, from 9 a.m. until 5 p.m. **The Downtown Visitor Center** is open daily from 9 a.m. until 5 p.m. **The Charlestown Navy Yard Visitor Center** is open daily from 9 a.m. until 5 p.m. All sites are closed Thanksgiving Day, December 25, and January 1.
Admission: Free: Charlestown Navy Yard, Faneuil Hall, Bunker Hill Monument, Dorchester Heights National Historic Park, Boston Common, Granary Burying Ground.

There is no admission fee to Old North Church, but a behind-the-scenes tour that includes a climb up the bell tower has a significant fee. Old South Meeting House and Old State House have a moderate charge. The Charlestown Navy Yard Visitor Center multimedia presentation has a moderate fee.
Accessibility: Accessible: Boston Common and Boston Common Visitor Center, Old South Meeting House, Faneuil Hall, Charlestown Navy Yard Visitor Center, Downtown Visitor Center, Bunker Hill Monument museum, Dorchester Heights National Historic Park museum.

Partially accessible: Old State House, Old North Church. The Granary Burying Ground has one 7-inch step at the entrance. Not handicapped accessible: Bunker Hill Monument, Dorchester Heights Monument.

The Complete Guide to Boston's Freedom Trail provides a recommended wheelchair route and is available at the visitor centers or by contacting Newtowne Publishing in Cambridge, Massachusetts.
Special Events: Free 90-minute walking tours of Boston's Freedom Trail, led by NPS rangers, leave from the Downtown Visitor Center from mid-April through November. There are historical talks given at chosen sites throughout the year. Call 617-242-5642 or check the Web site for times. Freedom Trail Tours (for a fee) and audio tours are available at the Boston Common Visitor Information Center. Evacuation Day (March 17) and the Fourth of July are both celebrated with National Park Service programs and programs by the city of Boston. The privately administered sites of Old South Meeting House, Old State House, and Old North Church offer a variety of programs throughout the year. Thursday and Friday nights from June through October *Paul Revere Tonight!* is presented on the Old North Church campus (admission charged).
Getting There: The Freedom Trail begins at the east end of Boston Common in the middle of the city. The NPS Web site has detailed information on arriving by car from every direction, or call 617-242-5642.

By subway: Park Street Station, on the Red and Green lines, exits onto Boston Common. State (Blue/Orange lines) and Government Center (Green/Blue lines) stations are near Faneuil Hall.

To Dorchester Heights from downtown Boston, take an outbound Red Line train (either Quincy or Ashmont) to Broadway Station. From Broadway, take a City Point bus to G Street. Walk a short distance south from the intersection of Broadway and G Street to Thomas Park, which surrounds Dorchester Heights.

For driving directions, see www.nps.gov/bost/Dorchester_Heights_directions.htm or call 617-242-5642.

Lexington and Concord

By the rude bridge that arched the flood,
Their flag to April's breeze unfurled,
Here once the embattled farmers stood,
And fired the shot heard round the world.

Ralph Waldo Emerson's "Concord Hymn," written in 1837 for the dedication of a monument, encapsulates the imagery of brave resolution etched on our national memory. The American Revolution began in the small Massachusetts towns of Lexington and Concord. It began accidentally and brutally and needn't have happened this way. But if it hadn't happened here, it would have happened elsewhere. Both sides were itching for a fight, and instead they got a war.

A Hotbed of Rebellion

Lieutenant General the Honorable Thomas Gage, commander in chief of British forces in North America, was given the additional office of Royal Governor of Massachusetts in 1774. As overall commander of all the colonies, Gage was most challenged by Massachusetts, the hotbed of rebellion. Gage liked Americans—his wife was an American—but he disliked the concept of democracy and the chaos it threatened.

Gage was no lover of tyranny or war. He strongly felt that he could dissuade the New England population from rebellion—not with a ruthless clamping down on the Patriot movement, as some in London clamored for, but with a gradual whittling away at the power of its leaders. That whittling away included outlawing town meetings, replacing district judges with court appointees, and, in effect, closing the courts and shutting down the government, after which he decided to disarm the Patriots. This meant removing any stored arms from towns all around New England. Gage began with the gunpowder stored in the Provincial Powder House six miles northwest of Boston.

When citizens learned the powder had been removed, thousands took to the streets in protest, forcing several prominent Loyalists to run for their lives. With this, Gage realized the full extent of the Patriot fervor, that it wasn't just a few groups of agitators. He wrote to London in late 1774, asking for reinforcements. "If you think ten thousand men sufficient, send twenty; if one million is thought enough, give two; you save blood and treasure in the end."

Officials in London thought he was exaggerating. They sent 400 marines. They might have taken it more seriously had they known that at the supply depots of Concord and Worcester there were enough arms and ammunition to outfit an army of 15,000 men.

Preparing for War

Patriot leaders also reacted to the Powder House incident, determining never again to be taken by surprise. Companies called minutemen were formed after September 1774, in order to have a group of militias to "hold themselves in readiness at a minute's warning, compleat in arms and ammunition . . ."

In October 1774 the First Provincial Congress of Massachusetts created a Committee of Safety and a Committee of Supplies, modeled on committees formed during the Puritan Revolution in England a century before. That same year, Paul Revere, a Boston silversmith and influential Patriot leader, organized a secret society to monitor the movement of British troops. Revere also began establishing a communications network among the towns of New England.

General Gage was well aware of these activities but, because he believed in the letter of the law, felt there was no way he could stop them. As David Hackett Fisher writes in his excellent history *Paul Revere's Ride,* "Thomas Gage was an English gentleman who believed in decency, moderation, liberty, and the rule of law. Here again was the agony of an old English Whig: he could not crush American resistance to British government without betraying the values which he believed that government to represent."

Though the winter of 1774–75 had been unusually mild, there had been a great deal of sickness among the British stationed in New England. Addiction to rum (good for keeping warm and supposedly for keeping healthy) became a huge problem, with some soldiers even selling their muskets to pay for the libation. Desertions were growing, and to encourage the trend, a kind of Underground Railroad was established by the Patriots to provide a suit of clothes and a small sum of money to the departing soldier.

The mood in New England was somber and the atmosphere tense. Worse, the opinion of leaders began to change. Whereas before General

Gage was regarded as a man of good though misguided intentions, after months of tension in early 1775 Samuel Adams was accusing Gage of being an enemy of humanity who would willingly kill residents in defense of despotism. Reacting to the unfairness of such accusations, which appeared almost daily in the local press, Gage began to feel there was no fair way to deal with these manipulative liars.

On April 14, 1775, Gage received orders from London to arrest Patriot ringleaders and seize all munitions.

Planning the Raid

"Keep the measure secret until the moment of execution, it can hardly fail of success," the Earl of Dartmouth advised General Gage. "Any efforts of the people, unprepared to encounter with a regular force, cannot be very formidable."

For all their years of hand-wringing and shouting, debating in Parliament, considering action or nonaction, correspondence, and spying on Patriot activities, the British hadn't really been paying attention. Before Lexington and Concord, they never understood the full extent of the organization, the determination of the Patriot cause, nor the intelligence and military acumen of its leaders.

Those leaders had been warned by friends in London of the decision to take strong action. Word quickly spread to be ready but, if it came to a real fight, not to fire the first shot. A British bullet must signal the beginning of open rebellion. The revolution must be in reaction to unnecessary British force.

After several forays by his agents, Gage settled on the munitions at Concord, going by the Lexington Road. He had intelligence that John Hancock and Samuel Adams were staying in Lexington, a small farming community about five miles east of Concord, but he did not order their arrest. That aspect of his orders from London he chose to ignore, realizing how incendiary such arrests would be.

Gage's orders to the commander of the expedition, Lieutenant Colonel Francis Smith, were to proceed "with utmost expedition and secrecy to Concord, where you will seize and destroy all the Artillery, Ammunition, Provisions, Tents,

Colonel James Barrett, who owned this government-issue cutlass, was the commanding officer on the American side at the North Bridge fight.

Small Arms, and all Military stores whatever." The general was particularly clear that Smith should not go beyond those orders. "You will take care," he told the colonel, "that the soldiers do not plunder the inhabitants, or hurt private property." Gage understood that there might be resistance, but he put his faith in his conviction that "there is not a man amongst [them] capable of taking command or directing the motions of an army."

On April 8, with the information from London, Paul Revere rode to Concord to warn of an imminent raid. Though this turned out to be premature, residents began moving supplies from town to outlying communities. As a precaution, a squad of Lexington militia was guarding the house of the Reverend Jonas Clarke, where Adams and Hancock were staying, while some 30 others camped in the Buckman Tavern across town.

The Night of April 18

Dr. Joseph Warren received word early in the evening of the 18th that the British were preparing to march to Lexington to arrest Adams and Hancock and then burn the stores at Concord. Dr. Warren sent a Boston tanner of Puritan stock named William Dawes to Lexington to warn Hancock and Adams and then on to Concord to warn the militia there. Soon after, Paul Revere also left Boston with the same intention, but by a different route.

A week earlier, worried that the British might "close" Boston to keep any couriers from escaping, Revere had arranged with Patriots in Charlestown that they keep watch each night of the steeple of Christ Church, or the Old North Church, as it was called. From this tallest building in Boston, a signal would be seen across the river. There would be two lanterns lit if the British left Boston by water and one if by land.

Late at night on the 18th, Revere contacted Robert Newman the church sexton and vestryman John Pulling, instructing them to go to the church and signal with two lanterns in the steeple's northwest window.

The Charleston Patriots readied a horse for Revere and at the same time sent a courier to warn Adams and Hancock. The courier never arrived—probably detained by the British. Revere was rowed across the Charles River in a boat with muffled oars. Once across, Revere set out on horseback for Lexington, arriving around midnight at Clarke's home, where Adams and Hancock were staying. Also visiting the Clarke family were Hancock's fiancée, Dorothy Quincy, and his Aunt Lydia, one of the wealthiest women in the colonies.

About a half hour after Revere arrived, Dawes came, and all the men in the house repaired to the Buckman Tavern to consult with the militia bunking there. The priority, all agreed, now that Hancock and Adams were warned, was to alert Concord, so Revere and Dawes once again set off.

The British March

Luckily, the British had been delayed. Around two a.m. they began their nine-mile march to Lexington, with another nine miles to reach Concord. Smith's column was seen by a number of people who alerted the local militia. So all across the countryside, this supposedly covert expedition of 800 British soldiers was noted.

Around three a.m., Smith ordered Major John Pitcairn of the Royal Marines to quick-march to Concord with six light infantry companies. Remembering the British humiliation at Salem Bridge just two months earlier (*see* Massachusetts, Salem

Maritime National Historic Site), Smith was worried that too much time had been lost and local militia would secure the bridge before his army arrived.

Pitcairn had little respect for the colonials. In a letter to the Earl of Sandwich a month earlier, he prescribed an elementary solution to the problem of the New England upstarts: "I am satisfied that one active campaign, a smart action, and burning two or three of their towns, will set everything to right."

At around four a.m., the British heard alarm bells ahead. Smith sent a message to Gage in Boston that the element of surprise was lost and, as a precautionary measure, requested reinforcements. Prior to this, one of Pitcairn's advance patrols had managed to capture Paul Revere. The soldiers were in the process of taking Revere and others they had found on the road back to Pitcairn when they heard the alarm bells. When the soldiers heard musket fire (probably militia clearing their guns), they took their prisoners' horses, let the men go, and skedaddled back toward the army.

Revere's network of messengers, from Boston to Concord and beyond, had been spreading the alarm all night. It is unlikely, however, that they were shouting, "The British are coming!" because at that point these people still thought of themselves as British. More likely they were warning, "The Regulars are out!" Town militias were already on their way. These soon to be "embattled farmers," some already at their chores in

---

"The Midnight Ride of Paul Revere"

"Listen my children and you shall hear/ Of the midnight ride of Paul Revere . . ." Henry Wadsworth Longfellow's poem of "The Midnight Ride of Paul Revere" was memorized by millions of schoolchildren from the time it was published in 1863 until well into the 20th century. Though a highly romanticized and simplistic account of Revere's activities, the poem's urgent martial rhythms capture the gravity of that fateful night.

Longfellow wrote his patriotic ode when the nation had been at Civil War for two years and the pains of loss and sacrifice were beginning to take their toll. The poem's last stanza seems as much a cheering on as a looking back. "Through all our history, to the last,/ In the hour of darkness and peril and need,/ The people will waken and listen to hear/ The hurrying hoofbeats of that steed,/ And the midnight message of Paul Revere."

One of the two lanterns hung in the Old North Church is on display in the Concord Museum.

John Hancock

John Hancock was orphaned at an early age, adopted by his uncle, and left one of the largest fortunes in America while in his mid-20s. Early on, he involved himself in civic affairs, while keeping a sharp eye on business. A prosperous merchant, he was involved in smuggling—in defiance of the Stamp Act and because, as a man of business, he resented paying more than he had to—and in 1767 he was defended in court by John Adams when two of his ships were seized for trading in contraband. Hancock became one of the leaders of the Revolution, serving as president of the First and Second Continental Congresses. His oversized signature on the Declaration of Independence, he said, was to enable King George to read it without his 'specs on. It is one of the few that can still be recognized.

Though a small man, at 5 feet 4 inches, Hancock made his presence felt and had an air of authority that lent itself to public office. He was elected governor of Massachusetts in 1780, and died in 1793 while serving his ninth term. Besides his service to his country, Hancock was also remembered for his charitable nature. During the war, it was said, he supported more than 100 families in Boston.

the early morning hours when they got the word, were joined by merchants, lawyers, teachers, blacksmiths, and others, from boys of 16 to elders in their 70s. All were now heading for Concord.

Paul Revere headed to Lexington, on foot, hoping to find Hancock and Adams long gone. He found them debating—some three hours after he had left—what was best to do, while the rest of the household was packing and hiding the family silver. Adams understood they had to leave, but was only able to convince Hancock of that with the added weight of Revere's concurrence. At daybreak the three men left in Hancock's coach for the parsonage in Woburn (now Burlington), where they could hide.

The Action at Lexington

Around four thirty a.m., Major Pitcairn, still in advance of Smith's main column, stopped his men and had them load their muskets. As the British approached the edge of town, they could hear 16-year-old William Diamond beating out a call to arms on his drum, just as a British drummer had taught him.

At the head of Pitcairn's column was an Irish Marine, Lieutenant Jesse Adair, whom Pitcairn had placed in front to set the pace. The army had been told that the main road through Lexington on the way to Concord forked just before the meetinghouse. The choice would be whether to go around or through the militia now lined up on Lexington Green. Going around would leave an armed force to the left and rear of the column—not a wise choice. Going through might cause some hard feelings or even a small altercation.

Adair and the column were moving at a steady clip toward the fork when Pitcairn, realizing the column had to be turned, galloped to the front. He made the decision to take the fork to the right, through the green and the militia. The two companies behind Pitcairn, light infantry of the 4th and 10th Foot had halted across from the militia and formed a line of battle. The two lines were only a few yards apart.

What was said and what was heard formed contradictory testimony afterwards. Many of the militia said they heard a British officer shout at them, "Lay down your arms, you damned rebels!" Others heard a British officer shout to his men, "Damn them, we will have them!"

There were no minutemen at Lexington. The town militia leaders had decided to keep their unit as one and not single out any as designated minutemen. Lexington also didn't call its fighting force militia but rather labeled it with the traditional Puritan name, the training band.

Historians now believe that Captain John Parker, commander of Lexington's militia, which at that moment numbered 78 men on the green, ordered his men to disperse, though tradition long has held that he ordered them to stand their ground. The militia slowly began to leave, but they did not lay down their arms. These were not army issue; these were their personal guns, used to protect their families, some even having been handed down father to son.

A shot rang out. Later no one could say for sure where it came from, but many thought it was not fired by either group on the green. It sounded as if it came from one side or the other, from the direction of the Buckman Tavern or from behind a wall. Major Pitcairn shouted to his men, "Soldiers, don't fire, keep your ranks, and surround them!"

His soldiers had been cooped up for months, even years, in the town of Boston, many of whose citizens daily made rude remarks, threw rotten food at them, and generally treated them like an offending army of occupation. In addition, only a few months before, several of the companies had been ready to ship home but at the last minute had been ordered to Boston instead. On top of this, they had just marched all night in heavy wet uniforms. They were ripe for a fight.

Almost before Pitcairn had finished his order, his soldiers opened fire. The militia began to scatter. A few got a shot off first, but none could compete with the British soldier's lightning speed at firing and reloading. Some militia fell where they stood; others were shot as they fled.

The British officers knew they had lost control of their men, who were firing at will. Pitcairn continued to shout, and rode among the men, but there was no line. The soldiers were chasing men off the green and up to the doors of their houses.

Colonel Smith had arrived with the main column in the midst of the chaos. He had ridden into what forces were left on the green, shouting for them to cease firing. He took his senior officers aside and told them his orders were to capture the munitions at Concord and that he was determined to obey his orders. The officers pointed out that the countryside would be up in arms after what had happened and that it would be wiser to return to Boston. Smith refused.

Before ordering his men to march, he had them fire a victory salute (in order to empty their guns) and give three cheers. The soldiers then marched off the green and out of Lexington.

Eight Patriots were dead, nine wounded. An hour or so later, Captain John Parker mustered Lexington's militia once again, and this time more than 100 men answered the call.

The Shot Heard Round the World

Militia leaders in Concord had decided to withdraw across the North Bridge to Punkatasset Hill, about a mile from Concord's center. The munitions had been either removed from town or hidden, so what was the point of a fight?

The beating of William Diamond's drum called Captain Parker's company of minutemen from the Buckman Tavern to assemble on Concord common. The 18th-century fife was also played during the encounter with the British. Both are on display at the Concord Museum.

When Smith and his army entered the town, they found it empty of any man of fighting age. The British began a house-to-house search for weapons. When a house caught fire after British soldiers burned two gun carriages, soldiers and townspeople formed a bucket brigade and saved the house. The British did find three 24-pounder cannons buried in the backyard of a tavern.

Outside town at the North Bridge, several companies of British soldiers had been posted, while on the hill above the Concord militia was joined by men from Acton, Bedford, Lincoln, and other towns. The British kept an eye on them, but otherwise made no move.

Then the militia saw the smoke from the gun-carriage fire and thought the British had begun to burn the town. Just about the same time, the soldiers at the bridge were ordered to fall back. As they did, they began to pull up the planking. This, coupled with the fire, infuriated the militia, who formed a column and marched down the hill. Seeing the column advance, the British tried to form a line; but two companies hurrying back across the bridge ran into one already there, and confusion reigned.

Suddenly there was a shot. One of the British Regulars had fired. Two other shots followed immediately, and then all the British fired. Most fired high, missing their targets, but two minutemen who were in front fell dead.

The Patriot militia fired as they continued advancing, having been ordered to return fire by their commander, who shouted, "Fire, fellow soldiers, for God's sake fire!" Three British soldiers fell dead and nine wounded, four of them officers.

The column of Patriot militia split into two lines curving down the hill, as the British Regulars, with half their officers out of action and no clear commands, ran from the bridge. "The weight of their fire was such that we was obliged to give way,

then run with the greatest precipitance," wrote a British soldier. The British wounded, abandoned, crawled toward town.

Colonel Smith, supervising the search in town, had received a message for help from the bridge and was now encountering the retreating soldiers.

The militia remained at the bridge, excited at the sight of British Regulars running from their fire but waiting for what would come next. A Concord minuteman later recounted, "The [British] commanding officers ordered the hull battalion to halt and officers to the frunt march and the officers then marched to the front thair we lay behind the wall about 200 of us with our guns cocked expecting every minnit to have the word fire."

Colonel Smith halted some 200 yards from the bridge, considered the situation for about 10 minutes, then ordered his men to fall back. Four British companies that had been behind the militia came running toward the bridge and crossed it without being fired on, nor did they fire on the militia. Everyone was suddenly very thoughtful about how next to proceed.

Smith decided it was time to leave. The wounded officers were placed in commandeered carts and wagons; wounded privates who couldn't walk were left behind. The British departed Concord around noon. Ahead of them was a gauntlet of almost 18 miles before they could reach the safety of Charlestown and Boston.

The Battle Road

From Concord to Meriam's Corner, a British flanking guard separated the British soldiers from the Patriot militia by moving along a ridge that paralleled the road. At Meriam's Corner the ridge ended, and when the flankers came down off the ridge to cross the bridge, the militia fired on them. By now the militia numbered almost 1000 men.

Smith moved his troops under fire from Meriam's Corner onto a road that allowed for almost no flanking guard. The road was bordered by fields with stone fences, from behind which the militia could fire and then run ahead across the field to catch the British at the next turn. Mile after mile the weary British soldiers fought for every inch, with fresh militia appearing all the time. It was a feeding frenzy against which the British soldiers acquitted themselves with great valor.

At a hill on the approach to Lexington, Captain John Parker and his Lexington militia waited. When the British were within range, Parker's men opened fire. Many of the British officers were dead or wounded, and the soldiers began to scatter across open land on the edge of Lexington. The remaining officers were pushing the men into ranks, trying to form them while under heavy fire.

Many of the British were out of ammunition. One group of retreating British soldiers was so frightened that when they came to the farm of an old woman named Mother Batherick, they surrendered to her and begged her protection. When the story of her delivering them to a militia captain reached London, critics of the government's policy asked, "If one old Yankee woman can take six grenadiers, how many soldiers will it require to conquer America?"

Suddenly a cheer went up from the beleaguered British. The Right Honorable Hugh Earl Percy stood with his brigade in a line of battle on the heights east of Lexington Green. Percy had two 6-pounder cannons with him, which were now fired over the British soldiers and into the militia pursuers.

Meeting with his officers at Munroe Tavern, which was being used as a hospital, Percy was surprised to learn there were almost 2000 militia descending on his troops. He hadn't expected this. His men had only brought 36 rounds each, and he only had a few rounds for the cannons. Though he had almost as many men as the Patriots, those from Smith's army were exhausted and almost out of ammunition. Percy decided to form his army into a moving square, with Smith's men in the middle.

The Patriot militia halted at Lexington and also re-formed. There were about 50 regiments now from throughout New England. They

British troops march into Concord as two officers reconnoiter the surrounding area from the town cemetery. Painting within 50 years of the actual event, an anonymous artist probably based the work on eyewitness paintings and sworn depositions from the encounter. The work is on display at the Concord Museum.

chose Brigadier William Heath as their commander. Heath had never been in battle, but he was known as a scholar of military tactics, particularly those used by mobile light infantry. Seeing the British army falling into a square formation, Heath and his officers attempted to form a moving circle around that square, never challenging it in an open battle but consistently picking off soldiers from its ever-shrinking rims.

Fire was coming incessantly from all sides, including from houses along the road. Near Menotomy (present-day Arlington), where the fire became particularly heavy, the British began charging through the Patriot ring and attacking individual homes, bayoneting those they found inside. The fighting in this area was

the most lethal of the day.

As the British neared Cambridge, they saw a large group of militia waiting for them at the bridge that was the last hurdle before Charlestown. Percy decided to turn east and use an obscure road that bypassed Cambridge. Just before making the turn, he used the last of his cannonballs to scatter militia stationed on Prospect Hill, and brought his army safely into Charlestown.

The British had lost 73 dead, 174 wounded, and 26 missing; the Patriots 49 dead, 40 wounded, and five missing.

Lieutenant John Barker of the King's Own later wrote of Lexington, "Thus for a few trifling stores the Grenadiers and Light Infantry had a march of about 50 miles (going and returning) through an enemy's country, and in all human probability must every man have been cut off if the Brigade had not fortunately come to their assistance." For many of the British, this had now become "an enemy's country."

For the Patriots, there was more at stake than munitions. Years later Captain Levi Preston, age 91, was asked why he had joined the fight at Lexington. After answering in the negative to suggestions of the Stamp Act and the tea tax and the eternal principle of liberty, Preston explained, "Young man, what we meant in going for those Redcoats was this: we always had governed ourselves and we always meant to. They didn't mean we should."

Visiting Minute Man Park

Minute Man National Historical Park comprises 1000 acres along the Battle Road and in the towns of Lexington to the east and Concord to the west.

Since the park was created in 1959, the National Park Service has been restoring the area's landscape and roads to their 18th-century appearance, including re-creating the farming fields and stone walls used by the Patriots along the Battle Road Trail. Traveling the five-mile trail takes visitors to many of the park's historic sites, while crossing farming fields, wetlands, and wooded areas.

The Road to Revolution, a 25-minute multimedia presentation at the Minute Man Visitor Center, depicts the events of April 18 and 19, from Paul Revere's ride to the British retreat along Battle Road. A map of the park and the park newsletter with information about special events are available at the Visitor Center.

There is also an impressive 40-foot mural of the fighting along the Battle Road, which shows the landscape as it was in 1775. A display at the center simulates a barn space used as a hiding place for the munitions the soldiers were searching for, with barrels of gunpowder and cannonballs. Another display details information about Paul Revere's network of couriers that spread the alarm.

There are several ways to explore this area and relive the events of April 19, 1775. For those who want a complete overview of events, it is best to begin at the Minute Man Visitor Center, see the film and displays, and get a copy of the park map. Those who prefer to begin at the beginning can start in Lexington (*see* Other Lexington and Concord Sites, below), drive west to the Minute Man Visitor Center for the film, displays, and map, continue to Concord and the North Bridge Visitor Center, then head back east to Meriam's Corner, and from there begin to follow the Battle Road Trail. Those with less time or who only want to see the highlights can start at the Minute Man Visitor Center and from there stop at the Paul Revere Capture Site and Hartwell Tavern on the Battle Road. Then continue to the North Bridge in Concord.

There are excellent outdoor exhibit panels along the Battle Road Trail, giving detailed information about what happened at more than a dozen points. This was the Bay Road, a winding artery connecting Concord and Lexington that cut through wetlands and over hills until 1803, when it was straightened for use by a more mobile and growing region.

The Paul Revere Capture Site provides information about the Boston silversmith immortalized by Longfellow for his bravery, but relatively unknown for his other roles in the Revolution. He was Mercury to the Patriot cause, making dozens of trips between New York, Boston, and Philadelphia in the years leading up to Lexington and Concord, and he fought as a member of the militia during the war.

The Ephraim Hartwell Tavern is an authentically restored period home and tavern. In 1775 Ephraim and Elizabeth Hartwell had three sons—Samuel, who lived next door; John, who still lived at the tavern; and their youngest son, Isaac, who lived in nearby Lincoln. All three sons were members of the Lincoln Minute Man company.

It was to Hartwell Tavern that Dr.

Reenactors gather *in front of Hartwell Tavern, site of one of many skirmishes with the Americans as the British retreated along the Battle Road back to Boston.*

49 Patriots *fell at Lexington, but at the North Bridge in Concord it was the British who suffered the losses.*

Samuel Prescott, who had been enlisted as a messenger by Paul Revere on the night of April 18, came knocking to spread the alarm. The Hartwells sent their African American slave Violet next door to alert Samuel, and then instructed her to proceed from there to the home of William Smith, captain of the Lincoln militia. Violet was too afraid to go, so Samuel's wife, Mary, rode to Smith's house.

Soon after, the Hartwell brothers all left for Lincoln, and from there went with the militia to Concord and took part in the fight there and along the Battle Road. It's assumed that Ephraim and Elizabeth shuttered the windows and went to stay with friends. When Ephraim returned the evening of April 19, he found the bodies of five British Regulars in his front yard. With the help of a neighbor, he loaded the bodies onto an oxcart to transport them into town. Years later his daughter-in-law Mary told her grandchildren that seeing these young men dead before their time, she felt the terrible loss it must have been to their families, and so she walked behind the rude hearse mourning them as their mothers and sisters would have. Those soldiers were buried in the center of Lincoln in a mass grave. Other grave sites are marked along the Battle Road Trail, where it's believed British soldiers were laid to rest following the battle.

The North Bridge Visitor Center's 12-minute film *April Fire* is complemented by a large topographical map that shows the movements of the British and Americans at the North Bridge and depicts the town of Concord as it was in 1775. There is also a small museum whose displays emphasize the personal accoutrements of a minuteman, such as the linen haversacks used to carry food and rations and the makeshift cartridge box carried with a cloth sling over the shoulder

The North Bridge, a reconstruction of the original, is a five-minute walk from the Visitor Center. Daniel Chester French's Minute Man statue, with the first verse of Emerson's poem inscribed on its pedestal, stands on the east side of the bridge. On the west side is a marker noting the burial site for two of the British soldiers who died there.

Also included in the park is **The Wayside**. Originally the home of

Daniel Chester French's Minute Man *statue stands at the North Bridge, a symbol of "the patriot farmer, who, at the morning alarm, left his plough to grasp his gun."*

Samuel Whitney, muster master of the Concord minutemen, the house is now preserved as the home of two 19th-century writers who helped bring about the American literary Renaissance—Louisa May Alcott (this is thought to be her model for the home in *Little Women*) and Nathaniel Hawthorne. One of its final residents was Harriett Lothrop, who under the pen name Margaret Sidney wrote the children's books about the Five Little Peppers.

Visitor Information

978-369-6993 (main number)
781-674-1920 (Minute Man
   Visitor Center)
www.nps.gov/mima

Hours: Park grounds are open sunrise to sunset. The North Bridge Visitor Center is open year-round, April through October daily 9 a.m. until 5 p.m., and November through March daily 9 a.m. until 4 p.m. The Minute Man Visitor Center is generally open mid-April through the end of October from 9 a.m. until 5 p.m., with reduced hours during the winter months. Hours may be further reduced in 2005, so it's best to call first or check the Web site. The Hartwell Tavern is open weekends only, from the end of May until the middle of June noon until 4 p.m., and from the middle of June until the end of October 9:30 a.m. until 5:30 p.m., also open Patriots Day Weekend. The Wayside is open for tours from the end of May until the end of October, Saturday, Sunday, and Tuesday through Thursday. All facilities are closed Thanksgiving, December 25, December 26, and January 1.

Admission: There's a moderate charge for the Wayside House Tour.

Accessibility: Both visitor centers and the Trail are accessible.

Special Events: Information about the dozens of activities in the park throughout the year is available on the Web site and in the Minute Man Messenger newsletter available in the park. In addition, there are special events held for Patriots Day Weekend in April, and on weekends April through October, plus scheduled programs by British regiments. Regularly scheduled ranger programs include "Who Were the Minute Men?" and "Life Along the Battle Road" from May through October.

Getting There: The NPS Web site has detailed information on arriving by car from every direction, or call 978-369-6993.

From I-95, take exit 30B onto state route 2A west. The park is 1 mile west.

By bus: MBTA Commuter Rail stops at the Concord Depot. From the depot, the North Bridge Unit is a 1 1/2 mile walk. (No bus or taxi service is available.) Liberty Ride provides a guided tour of Lexington and Concord. Information on the Web site or at 508-254-7491.

Other Lexington and Concord Sites

Lexington Green

The Lexington Visitor Center, located next to the Buckman Tavern and across from Lexington Green, provides brochures and maps of Lexington, and it has an interesting diorama of the Battle of Lexington. The city of Lexington and the town of Lexington have done an admirable job of preserving many of the sites related to the battle, so that visitors today can gain some sense of what daily life was like for those living here in 1775.

On Lexington Green, also called the Common, stands the **Minuteman Statue,** representing Captain John Parker, leader of Lexington's militia. Placed on the Green in 1900, the statue honors those 78 men who fought here on April 19.

The Revolutionary Monument on the west side of the green stands on the site of Lexington's first schoolhouse. Between here and the Parker Boulder, on the east side, stood the line of Lexington's militia. The granite monument, dedicated in 1799, is thought to be the first Revolutionary War monument erected.

The Parker Boulder across the green is inscribed with the words attributed to Captain Parker to his men as they faced the British: "Stand your ground. Don't fire unless fired upon, but if they mean to have a war, let it begin here!"

The green and the Revolutionary Monument are the site each year of ceremonies on Patriots Day in April and Memorial Day in May.

Buckman Tavern, Lexington

The Buckman Tavern, located across the street from Lexington Green, looks today much as it did in 1775 when the Lexington militia used it as their headquarters. Built in 1709 by John Muzzey, it became a tavern in 1714 and remained in the family until bought and restored by the

Lexington Historical Society in 1913. Six rooms are open to the public on a guided tour that draws visitors into the world of 1775 through artifacts and information about 18th-century life in a small town.

The Tap Room is the oldest room in the house and one of the most interesting. The fireplace, about five feet tall and five feet wide, is original to the room and was discovered during the restoration. Only men were allowed in the Tap Room, and only men were allowed to spend the night in a tavern, so things could get a bit rowdy. The expression "being at loggerheads" comes from the use of metal pokers called loggerheads kept near the fireplace.

Behind the bar, a piece of Plexiglas covers some original writing found during the restoration. This is where the barkeeper would tally the pints and quarts a man was drinking during the course of an evening ("minding your p's and q's") for a tally at the end of the night. And only those men whose chin cleared the bar were allowed to drink—which was their way of keeping children out.

The table in the Kitchen next to the Tap Room was used by a Dr. Fiske as an operating table the day of the battle. He worked on 11 men that day, two of them British soldiers. The table is set with pewter original to the tavern, though the pewter wasn't used for everyday eating, mainly because of its high lead content, known even then to be unhealthy. There is also a flax wheel here. Buckman had a field of flax planted behind his tavern.

The innkeeper's family slept in the Landlord's Bedroom, added to the house in 1750. Beds were made from mattresses stuffed with straw and horsehair laid on top of a rope structure that was tightened periodically to keep the mattress from sagging—giving rise to the phrase "sleep tight." Guests slept in rooms upstairs. Those willing to sleep with someone else paid a lower fee.

The innkeeper's lantern in the window held four candles. Buckman would light all four each night as a signal that his inn offered drinks (one candle), food (two candles), overnight lodging (three), and barns and stables for horses and livestock (four).

The Ladies Parlor is also called the Nooning Room because this is where people would come from the meetinghouse on Sundays to warm themselves and have some lunch before returning for afternoon worship. An ingenious metal foot warmer is displayed here, as are copies of Paul Revere engravings of the Boston Massacre and of British ships in Boston Harbor.

The original red door (red was the color of hospitality), with a musket ball from the battle implanted in it, is displayed in the Hallway, along with two fire buckets. Every family was required to have two fire buckets with their name painted on them, and to turn out whenever they heard the alarm. Once the fire was put out, an inventory was taken of the names on the buckets and whoever was missing was fined.

The final room of the tour is part of the building that was added in 1813 to house the first post office in Lexington. Numerous artifacts are displayed, among them copies of the Doolittle paintings of the battle (*see* Hancock-Clarke House, page 72).

Munroe Tavern, Lexington

Munroe Tavern, built in the late 1690s, is about a mile east of Lexington Green. It was given to and restored by the Historical Society in 1911.

In 1775 the tavern was owned by William Munroe, a sergeant in the Lexington militia. His wife and children were hiding in a barn behind the tavern when the British under Lord Percy commandeered it as Percy's headquarters and as a hospital. A neighbor, John Raymond, had stayed behind to guard the tavern, and he was found shot dead in the hallway following the British retreat.

A guided tour takes visitors to the Entrance Hall, where the family's fire buckets hang on the wall, and from there to the Percy Room, where the British stayed while in town. The Tap Room, also on the first floor, displays the tavern's original swinging sign and a musket used in the battle. The Museum Room, originally the kitchen, has original pumpkin-wood floors and a display of more than 20 samplers whose themes are related to the war.

The upstairs Bedroom has beautiful quilts from the 1800s and a period four-poster bed. On the wall behind the bed there is a large oil-on-canvas wall hanging brought to the Munroes by a Salem sea captain in the early 1800s. The chair, table, dishes, and hat rack used by President George Washington when he was entertained here in 1789 are preserved in the Washington Room, also on the second floor. This room was used as a Masonic Lodge in the late 1700s, and displayed here is George Washington's Masonic apron.

Hancock-Clarke House, Lexington

About a quarter mile north of the Buckman Tavern stands the Hancock-Clarke House, where John Hancock and Samuel Adams were staying when the alarm was sounded the night of April 18, 1775. Two of Lexington's most beloved ministers lived in this house—John Hancock, grandfather of the Patriot, and Jonas Clarke, whose house was full of guests that fateful night.

A guided tour takes guests first to a Reception Room, where they can see William Diamond's drum, Dr. Fiske's saddlebags, and Major Pitcairn's pistols.

Of special interest are three originals and one copy of Amos Doolittle's prints of four scenes from April 19: the battle on Lexington Green, the British march to Concord, the battle at North Bridge, and the retreat on the Battle Road. These engravings were made from eyewitness accounts and are considered invaluable testimony as to what happened.

At one time this was the home of a very wealthy man, as evidenced by the wallpaper in the Family, or Keeping, Room, which was extremely rare in colonial homes. One of the room's most intriguing artifacts is a fire screen next to the fireplace. Ladies used these to shield their faces while warming themselves at a fire, a dire necessity because their makeup was made of beeswax that melted when warm.

The table in the Kitchen had to seat all twelve of the Clarke children and yet leave room for preparing meals, so it folded in the middle and was pushed aside during the day—considered very innovative in 1775.

The desk in Jonas Clarke's study is unusually high because he wrote his sermons standing up, so that he could pace as he composed. Next to the study is the Hancock-Adams Bedroom, where the gentlemen slept while visiting. Visitors may be surprised to find only one bed, but it was very common in colonial times for men to share a bed when traveling.

Upstairs are the Family Bedrooms. One of them is where all twelve children slept together, the other is where John Hancock's fiancée

Dorothy Quincy and his Aunt Lydia had a clear view of the battle from the window.

Concord Museum, Concord

Concord is a town rich in history, and this museum reflects that heritage with a collection of more than 10,000 articles encompassing the precolonial era to the 19th century. Among the Revolutionary War items displayed are the "one if by land, and two if by sea" lantern immortalized by Longfellow's poem about Paul Revere's ride. There is also a relic of the original North Bridge. Military memorabilia include powder horns, muskets, cannonballs, and fifes. Period rooms illustrate domestic life, and three centuries of decorative arts are included.

Visitor Information

For Lexington:
781-862-1450 or 781-862-5598 or 781-862-1703
www.lexingtonhistory.org
For Concord Museum:
978-369-9763
www.concordmuseum.org
Hours: In Lexington, the Buckman Tavern, Munroe Tavern, and the Hancock-Clarke House are open in the summer on Monday through Saturday from 10 a.m. until 5 p.m. and on Sunday from 1 p.m. until 5 p.m. Winter hours are 10:30 a.m. until 4:30 p.m. Friday, Saturday, and Monday, and from 1 p.m. until 5 p.m. on Sunday. Closed on national holidays, except the Fourth of July. Lexington Green, also known as the Common, is open from sunrise until sunset.

The Concord Museum is open Monday through Saturday, 9 a.m. until 5 p.m.; Sunday, noon until 5 p.m.; closed Easter, Thanksgiving Day, and December 25.
Admission: There is a moderate fee for admission to one Lexington tavern or house, with reduced fees for tickets to two or three. Children under 6 are free.

There is a significant fee for admission to the Concord Museum.
Accessibility: Lexington Green, the Buckman Tavern, and the Concord Museum are accessible.
Getting There: To Lexington, from I-95 exit onto state route 2A east then go north on state route 225.

To Concord, from I-95, take exit 30B onto state route 2A west to Concord. The museum is just past the Minute Man Park.

Salem Maritime National Historic Site

In the years immediately preceding the Revolutionary War, Salem, Massachusetts, was an influential center of trade, as well as the site of an early confrontation with the British. During the war it served as a major privateering port, contributing greatly to the disruption of British trade.

Salem Maritime National Historic Site includes twelve historic structures, plus Salem's Visitor Center. Exploring the wharves, warehouses, and other buildings along the waterfront provides a deeper understanding of why curtailment of trade was one of the main causes of rebellion in the colonies. Salem Patriots—as determined a merchant class as in any English port—were among those laying the foundations of America's commercial wealth, the fire of their patriotic fervor banked by economic opportunism. Many of Salem's richest citizens founded their fortunes during the Revolutionary War.

Intolerable Acts

Until well into the 20th century, Salem looked to the sea for its livelihood. Established in 1626 by fishermen and their families, it was then called Naumkeag—the fishing place—by local Native Americans. When the Puritans arrived a few years later, they renamed it Salem, a variation of the Hebrew word *shalom*, or peace.

By the late 1630s, shipbuilding had become the town's second industry, and in the following decades Salem would become a prosperous town, whose wealthiest citizens owned fleets of merchant ships. To its credit, Salem was not as active as other New England ports in what became known as the Triangular Trade: sugar and molasses from the West Indies to New England, rum from New England to Africa, slaves from Africa to the West Indies sugar plantations. Salem's merchants preferred to make their fortunes trading lumber, hides, masts, wool, and rum for salt, linen, hardware, and bar iron in Europe.

The Molasses Act of 1733, which placed high taxes on sugar or molasses imported from non-British islands, was the opening salvo of officious restrictions for Salem, whose shippers often traded in the French and Dutch islands. Add to this the growing dissatisfaction with British rule in general over the next decade and the influential hotbed of rebellion in Boston, only sixteen miles to the south, and it is easy to second-guess the decision of General Thomas Gage, then governor of the province, to move Massachusetts's capital to Salem in 1774 to thwart Boston's leaders.

When this didn't work—delegates elected their own representatives and based a new government in Concord—the British clamped down harder. That same year, when authorities tried to enforce the Intolerable Acts, which decreed that town meetings could be held only with official approval, Salem residents openly defied the acts, holding a town meeting and barring the doors of the town hall to British troops. The troops, under orders not to use force, could only retreat.

A Fool's Errand

An even more ignominious retreat, and one of far greater import, occurred the next year, in February 1775, when General Gage received word that a forge in Salem was converting ships' cannons into field artillery. Gage sent Lieutenant Colonel Alexander Leslie and 240 men to Salem on a Sunday morning to capture the cannons and shut down the operation. It was intended that the British would catch the townspeople, presumably in church, by surprise. The troops landed at Marblehead and began their five-mile march to Salem along what is now route 114.

Salem's John Pedrick learned of the troops' arrival, and even though he was thought to have sympathies toward the crown, he rode from Marblehead to warn the town. At this point, the campaign takes on a comic opera aspect, as one thing after another went wrong for Leslie and his men. Pedrick met them along the road, explained he was on his way to visit a sick friend, and not only was he allowed to pass but the troops moved off the road to make his way easier.

Arriving in town, Pedrick went to the nearest church and sounded the alarm. Word spread quickly throughout Salem, and worshippers from every denomination halted services to hide cannons. Others took to the Marblehead road and tore up the planking of a bridge, forcing the British to pause for repair.

Meanwhile, preparations were frantically being made to haul the cannons to nearby Danversport. By the time the British finally arrived, they found the townspeople in the streets and the North River draw-bridge—leading to the forge—was up. After being told he and his men would not be allowed to cross the bridge, Leslie made a move toward some gondolas tied nearby, but these were quickly destroyed.

This was not what Leslie had been led to expect. Only a few months earlier, Gage had written of the colonists, "They will be lyons whilst we are lambs, but if we take the res-olute part they will undoubtedly prove very meek." Leslie wasn't see-ing a lot of meekness in what was now late afternoon in Salem.

When approached by the Reverend Mr. Barnard, Leslie declared, "I will get over the bridge before I return to Boston, if I stay here till next autumn. By God, I will not be defeated!" to which Mr. Bar-nard replied, "You must acknow-ledge you have already been baffled."

Barnard offered Leslie a compro-mise. He and his troops could cross the bridge, search the forge but only the forge, and leave. Leslie, sur-rounded by bellicose townsfolk whom he did not want to fire on, chose the wiser part of valor and agreed.

As the British were retreating, an old nurse named Sarah Turrant, who lived on the outskirts of town, opened her window and taunted, "What, do you think we were born in the woods to be frightened by owls? Go home and tell your master he has sent you on a fool's errand." When one of the soldiers threatened to shoot her, she retorted, "Fire if you have the courage, but I doubt it," foreshadowing Barbara Frietschie.

This was a thoroughly demoraliz-ing episode for the British and was used to great advantage by the Patriots as evidence that the roar of the British lion was worse than its bite. The British response in Lexington and Concord just two months later is thought to have been strongly influenced by Leslie's humiliation in Salem.

The Salem Alarm, as the incident was called, also had an impact in Salem. Gradually the chasm wid-ened—between those who resented Britain's clumsy handling of its colonies but assumed something could be worked out and those who begrudged the clumsy handling and thought a change was called for. People took sides as Loyalist or Patriot. As open war drew nearer, Loyalists were subjected to beatings, tar and feathering, and financial ruin. Most would eventually leave for Nova Scotia or the West Indies.

Privateering

Once war came in earnest, trading fell off. Salem's merchants found their ships under attack and their trade routes threatened, so they turned with a vengeance to priva-teering (*see* The Continental Navy and Marines, page 80). Between 1776 and 1783, Salem's 158 priva-teering vessels took 445 prizes, or a little more than 50 percent of all the prizes taken during the war.

Many local ships were the prop-erty of the Derby family. It was to Captain John Derby, who had the fastest schooners in the colonies, that the Patriots turned when they wanted their version of what had happened at Lexington and Concord to reach England first. Derby's *Quero* landed before the British ship that had left four days earlier, enabling Benjamin Franklin to have the American account published in the London papers before the British could shape the event to their advantage.

In writing about privateering in 1776, Josiah Batchelder described it as "the most Likely Means by which we can hope to Annoy our Enemies, supply Our selves with Foreign Necessarys of life, which we have been Accustomed to, and discipline a Nursery of Seamen by which means we may soon be a formidable Nation by Sea as well as by Land."

There was a downside, of course, to Salem's privateering. Hurting British trade often meant hurting men much like themselves. In a let-ter to the Massachusetts Council in August of 1776, William Pringle, "late Commander of Ship Anna Maria," explained that he and his family faced financial ruin if his ship and its cargo were not returned to him, having bought the sugar he was transporting on credit. He also pointed out that "his extream anxi-ety of mind, which he must neces-sarily be under, arising from his being separated from his Family and Friends, and in a Country where he is an entire Stranger (tho' treated with great kindness and humanity) he apprehends will greatly injure and impair his health."

His petition was for naught, pre-sumably, because there appeared in a Boston newspaper two months

The *Friendship*

Anchored at Derby Wharf is a replica of the East Indiaman *Friendship*. (An East Indiaman was a ship that sailed to the East Indies and other exotic locales for trade.) The original *Friendship* was launched in 1797 and made 15 voyages before being captured during the War of 1812. Her fate after that is unknown. Dating from a post–Revolutionary War period, this ship nevertheless gives visitors a very realistic idea of what it must have been like to board a privateer or traverse the oceans of the world in the Age of Sail.

A model of the three-masted, square-rigged 342-ton vessel was made by her second mate, Thomas Russell, assisted by Mr. Odell, ship's carpenter, during her eighth voyage, between 1802 and 1804. From this model, currently on display in the Peabody Essex Museum, and from surviving paintings of the ship, as well as the ship's logs, the National Park Service was able to commission a replica.

The captain's cabin, *below. The master of a vessel had absolute power of command aboard ship. He was legally accountable for every aspect of the operation of the ship, the activities of her crew, and the safe delivery of all cargo.*

notice of a public auction: "At ...Wharf of Richard Derby, Esq; in ...m, The Ship *Anna Maria* and her ...go, consisting of 250 Hogsheads ...the best clayed Sugar, 50 ...ogsheads of best white ditto, and ...50 Hogsheads of brown ditto; like-wise, 30 Bales of Cotton, 280 Bags of Ginger, 160 Goards of Aloes, 2 Hogheads of Barbados Tar, 10 Hogheads of Barbados Rum, and 48 Pipes of Sterling Madiera wine. N.B. The ship is 300 tons burthen, a fine vessel, River built and well found; she will be put up precisely at 12 o'Clock." With such riches available, and a chance to contribute to the Patriot cause at the same time, it's understandable, though lamentable, that the Derbys and their fellow merchants chose not to consider the personal consequences to those they waylaid.

The end of the war brought Salem into its prominence as a trading center, with merchants like Elias Hasket Derby, Simon Forrester, William Gray, and the Crowninshield family opening America's trade to a world-wide market. In 1790, Salem was the sixth largest city in the United States and its richest per capita. In less than 200 years, it had developed from a small fishing settlement to a center of world trade.

Visiting Salem Maritime National Historic Site

Though the focus here is on the years between the Revolutionary War and the War of 1812, when Salem again would provide sea power to her fledgling nation, the setting along the wharves still evokes a sense of what the town was like during the war years.

Begin at the National Park Service Regional Visitor Center, 2 New Liberty Street, in downtown Salem. The film *Where Past Is Present* touches on Salem's role in the Revolutionary War, as does a section of the exhibit space.

From here it's a short walk to the site, which faces Salem Harbor. Salem was the only major New England port not occupied during the war, and with good reason. The one time a British sloop of war tried to invade the harbor, it got caught on a bar, was bombarded mercilessly, and barely got loose in time to save itself from sinking or capture. Most British vessels were larger than those that sailed from Salem, and the harbor couldn't accommodate them.

At the Central Wharf Warehouse

Orientation Center, 193 Derby Street, the film *To the Farthest Port of the Rich East* provides a history of Salem's trading and shipbuilding industry. There's also a three-foot-long model of the privateer *Rattlesnake*, as well as a display of equipment used for measuring and weighing at the Custom House.

The three wharves preserved on the site were among the more than 30 here during the war. The National Park Service's excellent brochure "Salem Maritime" provides a wonderful illustration of and detailed information about the activities on the wharves in their heyday. It was Salem's ships that opened such foreign ports as Calcutta, Manila, and Zanzibar to U.S. trade, returning with cargos of exotic goods, among them the first elephant ever brought to the U.S. (though the elephant was brought to New York, not Salem).

Central Wharf was once called Forrester Wharf for Simon Forrester, who came to Salem a common seaman and died a millionaire merchant. One of Salem's most successful privateers during the war, he captured four ships in just one year. The foundations of his warehouse are opposite the Orientation Center. Forrester was given command of a ship at age 28, which made him a bit long in the tooth for the job, according to the standards of the time. The average age of a crew then was around 22 years of age, including the captain and officers. When the Derby ship *Benjamin* sailed in 1792, her captain was 19 and her first mate 20. These were typical of men who went to sea at 12 or 13 and could handle a ship before they were past adolescence.

Derby Wharf today is about three times the length it was during the war, having been extended to its present length in 1806. More than a dozen warehouses lined the wharf at one time. During the Revolution, they were filled with products captured by Derby's privateers. In the heady days of trade afterward, they'd be filled with tea, spices, cotton, and goods from all over the world.

The **Derby House** is pre-Revolution built in 1762, about the same tim... as the original length of wharf, an... it's the oldest brick house in Sale... The Derbys used Hawkes House n... door, which was built in 1780... warehouse their privateering s... Elias Hasket Derby had intend...

live in Hawkes House, but he never finished building it. That was left to its next owner, Benjamin Hawkes, who had a shipyard next to Derby Wharf.

The **Narbonne House,** built around 1670, is the oldest home in Salem and one of the oldest in Massachusetts. Craftsmen and tradesmen lived here through the years. Today it is used by architectural students and the public on a daily basis to explore 17th-century house construction and visually interpret the sequence of alterations made over 300 years of occupancy. Signage explains the building techniques of the time, and there's a model used to demonstrate how the house was constructed.

Among the post–Revolutionary War structures is the **Custom House,** built in 1819. It's best known for the fact that Nathaniel Hawthorne worked here during the 1840s, but perhaps a more interesting note is that when the British left at the beginning of the Revolution, they took Salem's shipping records with them. For this reason, even though Salem's shipping history goes back to the 1600s, its records don't begin in earnest until the 1790s. The Custom House has one of the finest collections of early weighing and measuring equipment in the country, from large dock scales to Custom Service locks. Antique scales are also on display at the Scale House (1829), among them many used in he years immediately following the ar.

Though the **West India Goods** e (circa 1800) was built after the the products displayed here are similar to what a shopper find along Salem's waterfront 1770s and '80s. The some 6000 people who lived here then would have had access to a great variety of goods, what with Salem's privateering contributions and the fact that the British weren't particularly successful in their blockade attempts.

There are two other structures at the site—**St. Joseph's Hall** (1909), a religious, cultural, and social center for the town's Polish population, and the **Derby Light**—a lighthouse at the end of Derby Wharf, built in 1871.

Visitor Information
National Park Service Regional Visitor Center, 978-740-1650 Salem Maritime National Historic Site Orientation Center, 978-740-1660 www.nps.gov/sama (for both)
Hours: Both are open from 9 a.m. until 5 p.m. daily; closed Thanksgiving, December 25, and January 1. Films are shown on the half hour. Throughout the day, ranger-led tours of the historic structures begin from the Orientation Center.
Admission: Admission to the Regional Visitor Center is free. Tours of selected areas of the National Historic Site have a moderate charge; children under six are free. Check at the Orientation Center for those areas that are open without charge.
Accessibility: The Visitor Center and the Orientation Center are accessible, as is the historic wharf area. The historic houses have limited accessibility, as does the ship *Friendship.*
Special Events: Check Web site or call for information about special events, which change periodically.
Getting There: Salem is about 15 miles northeast of Boston. Once in Salem, follow signs to the Visitor Center or Waterfront.
By car: Take state route 1A north to Salem, or use I-93 north to state

...odels like ...identified ...ip were con- ...ted by seamen ...were taken ...soner during the ...th and early 19th ...centuries. Confined for many years, they sought relief of their boredom by building ship models from scraps of wood, paper, animal bones, and human hair.

route 128 north. Take exit 25A and follow Route 114 east into Salem. (Note that I-95 north and route 128 north share the same road for the loop around Boston. When the roads divide, stay on Route 128 north. At this point, the exit numbers jump from 45 to 28.)

By bus: Buses 455 and 450 from Boston's Haymarket section (on the Green and Orange lines of the subway) or Bus 459 from Logan Airport Terminal C go to Salem's rail depot.

By train: The Newburyport/ Rockport Commuter Rail Line from Boston's North Station arrives at the Salem Depot, a 5-minute walk from the Visitors Center.

Peabody Essex Museum

In 1799 the wealthy shipbuilders and merchants of Salem created the Peabody Essex Museum as a way of introducing to Salem the wonders they'd seen in their travels around the world. Today the 250,000-square-foot museum is an intriguing repository of art and architecture reflecting the town founders' fascination with ancient, foreign cultures as well as their pride in their newly established country and in their New England roots. America's oldest continuously operating museum, it contains an impressive collection of colonial and Revolutionary War–era art and historical artifacts, including ship models and navigational charts and instruments.

Visiting the Museum

The Peabody Essex Museum campus includes a renovated museum space that reopened in June 2003, 23 historic properties (four of them National Historic Landmark buildings and eight on the National Register of Historic Places), and a park and gardens.

The newest of these outdoor spaces, Armory Park, is situated between Peabody Essex Museum and the National Park Service Visitor Center in downtown Salem. The centerpiece of the park, which is designated as a commemorative space honoring the citizen soldier in America, is the Paul Revere Bell. Surrounding it are markers chronicling the role of the citizen soldier from the 1600s to the present.

With its 125-million-dollar renovation, the museum has created more space for its 2.4 million works from Asia, Africa, and the Pacific, plus Native American art, American decorative art, and photography. The majority of the exhibits are spread out over three levels. The colonial and Revolutionary War–era pieces currently on display are concentrated in two galleries of Maritime Art and History, located just off the Atrium on the first level. Unfortunately, the museum's fine collection of weapons and military uniforms is not on display, and currently there are no plans for future exhibitions.

The entrance to the first gallery is graced by an impressive six-foot-long model of the *Raleigh*, one of the 13 frigates authorized by the Continental Congress in 1777. Other ship models on display include a paper-and-wood model given to the museum in 1830 and a contemporary miniature (four-inch-long) model of the privateer *Rattlesnake*.

The painted paper model, which has a wooden hull, came with the story that the donor's father ha... built the model while he was a pr... oner of war in England. The conte... porary model is of particular in... est—first because models of p... teers are rare, as there ar... resources for researching the... of the ship's constructi...

appearance—and second because it was built by Philip Reed, thought by many to be the best model maker practicing the craft today. Reed, who takes a year or more to make each of his models, typically uses a 1-to-92 scale, which makes the detailing of miniatures such as this one even more impressive.

Privateering brought quite a few treasures into Salem. Among those displayed here is a beautiful Delft-ware bowl captured from a British vessel, engraved with a poem boasting of "heroic Britains on the main who have humbled France and Spain." There's also a commemorative silver tankard engraved with the image of the *General Pickering*, whose captain was awarded the tankard for successfully defending his ship (and its cargo) from attack. It's assumed the gift was given by either the ship's owner or the insurance company.

There are quite a few portraits of ships' captains, including one oil on canvas of Thomas Shippard of Boston, painted by Joseph Badger. Badger, one of America's earliest portraitists, began as a housepainter and glazier but took to painting portraits when he moved to Boston in the mid-1730s. Badger is now considered something of a curiosity but is admired for what he was able to accomplish without the formal European training that had become more commonplace among American artists by the 1750s.

Also displayed are two dramatic renderings of pivotal events in the war. Christian Remick's six-foot-long watercolor of the 1773 blockade of Boston Harbor presents a panorama from one end of the harbor to the other. Also known for his colored engraving of the Boston Massacre in 1770, Remick is thought to have created this painting on-site during the blockade.

French artist Joseph Roux's depiction of the battle between John Paul Jones's *Bonhomme Richard* and the H.M.S. *Serapis* is darkly compelling, showing the ships facing each other with only a cloud-covered moon lighting their way. Roux, father of a dynasty of celebrated painters, was also known as a hydrographer (making maps of water-covered areas) d a manufacturer of navigational truments.

he Peabody Essex Museum's essive collection of instruments e period includes an octant of ebony and ivory, a painted

quadrant, and a backstaff mad William Williams of the Continer Army. The backstaff, invented in t 1730s, was the successor of th cross-staff. Both were used to measure altitude, but the backstaff had the advantage of not forcing the user to look directly into the sun. (The navigator's back was to the sun, hence the instrument's name.)

Perhaps the museum's most engaging and unique collection from this era is its set of more than 300 charts of the Eastern seaboard. Commissioned by the British in the 1760s and '70s, these provided a detailed analysis of the North American coast from Labrador down to the Carolinas. The charts, made by cartographers such as Joseph Des Barres, were considered highly classified and available only to high-ranking naval officers. Because of their size, the museum can display only two or three at a time, but the selection is rotated.

Visitor Information

978-745-9500

www.pem.org/homepage/

Hours: The museum is open daily from 10 a.m. until 5 p.m., Thursdays until 9 p.m.; closed Thanksgiving, December 25, and January 1.

Admission: There is a significant entry fee for visitors over the age of 16.

Accessibility: The museum is handicapped accessible.

Special Events: Throughout the year, there are lectures, workshops, family days, and other activities.

Getting There: Salem is about 15 miles northeast of Boston. Once in Salem, follow signs to the Visitor Center or Waterfront.

By car: Take state route 1A north to Salem, or use I-93 north to state route 128 north. Take exit 25A and follow Route 114 east into Salem. (Note that I-95 north and route 128 north share the same road for the loop around Boston. When the roads divide, stay on Route 128 north. At this point, the exit numbers jump from 45 to 28.)

By bus: Buses 455 and 450 from Boston's Haymarket section (on the Green and Orange lines of the subway) or Bus 459 from Logan Airport Terminal C go to Salem's rail depot.

By train: The Newburyport/ Rockport Commuter Rail Line from Boston's North Station arrives at the Salem Depot, a 5-minute walk from the Visitor Center.

The Continental Navy and Marines

As John Adams would recall years later in his memoirs, the debate in Congress over whether to establish a Continental Navy was long and passionate. Opponents represented [the idea] as the most wild, visionary, mad project that ever had been imagined. It was an infant, taking a mad bull by his horns . . . it was said it would ruin the character, and corrupt the morals of all our seamen . . . [making them] piratical, mercenary, and bent wholly upon plunder."

Adams and his colleagues answered reasonably, presenting "the great advantage of distressing the enemy, supplying ourselves, and beginning a system of maritime and naval operations."

On October 13, 1775, a resolution establishing the Continental Navy was passed: "Resolved, that a swift sailing vessel, to carry ten carriage guns, and a proportionate number of swivels, with eighty men, be fitted, with all possible dispatch, for a cruise of three months, and that the commander be instructed to cruize eastward, for intercepting such transports as may be laden with warlike stores and other supplies for our enemies, and for such other purposes as the Congress shall direct."

In other words, the Continental Navy was established primarily for the purpose of capturing British ships and robbing them of their supplies. Even John Adams, an avid supporter of an American navy, didn't envision his new nation as a major naval power.

Organization

The Marine Committee, formed to oversee this new navy, appointed Esek Hopkins as "Commander in Chief of the Fleet of the United Colonies."(After some unfortunate command decisions, Hopkins would be dismissed by Congress with the damning pronouncement that he was "an ordinary man who had the misfortune to live in extraordinary times.") The committee also formulated rules of operation that included articles on behavior (swearing was punished by a fine of one shilling), flogging (limited to 12 lashes), religion (services twice a day, sermons on Sunday), and procedures for a court-martial at sea.

Requirements set for recruits stated they should be "able bodied and perfect in all their limbs and sight, of sound health without ruptures or other visible infirmities, above five feet four inches, and above sixteen and under fifty years of age, and if above forty they must be of robust constitution."

The term "a motley crew" certainly reflected many who put to sea under the flag of the Continental Navy. Army troublemakers were handed over to the navy to get rid of them; criminals were often offered a choice of going to prison or enlisting.

Securing a crew, the responsibility of individual captains, became such a daunting task that some captains resorted to offering bonuses, only to have volunteers accept the bonuses and then desert. In an emergency, some captains even took to impressing civilians or using captured British seamen. The brief amount of time in which the navy had to organize itself also meant, in many cases, that training was shortchanged.

Leadership was another problem, with many captains chosen because of family ties and with no more incentive than profit or prestige. A disgruntled John Paul Jones wrote, "When gain is the ruling principle of officers in an infant Navy, it is no wonder that they do not cultivate by their precepts nor enforce by their example the principles of dutiful subordination."

Though it was never officially mandated, the Continental Navy's strategy was basically *guerre de course*—hit and run actions, attacking enemy merchant vessels and smaller ships, and retreating when confronted by a stronger opponent. The alternative—*guerre d'escadre*, which entailed fleets fighting battles at sea—would have been suicidal.

The Continental Marines were also established at this time. A Congressional committee meeting at Tun Tavern in Philadelphia drafted a resolution approved by Congress on November 10, 1775, establishing the service. Robert Mullen, owner of Tun Tavern, was named a Marine captain and Samuel Nicholas, another tavern owner, was appointed Commandant of the Continental Marines.

Ships and Armaments

On October 30, 1775, authorization was given for the purchase of two ships, the 24-gun *Alfred* (previously captained by John Barry and known as the *Black Prince*) and the 20-g Columbus.

In December, Congress authorized the building of 13 frigates, w were to form the core of the

Revolutionary-Era Sailing Ships

Stephen Howarth, in his history of the U.S. Navy, *To Shining Sea*, provides an excellent guide to the ships of this era. For example, types of ships were based on their styles of rigging:

A **ship** had three masts square-rigged, the sails set across the craft.

A **barque** had two square-rigged masts and one rigged fore-and-aft.

The two-masted **schooner** had fore-and-aft sails, with an additional square topsail on the foremast.

The **brig** had two masts square-rigged.

The **brigantine** had a square-rigged foremast and an aftermast rigged fore-and-aft.

The **sloop** had a single mast and one or two fore-and-aft sails.

The main armaments on ships consisted of iron cannons on wooden carriages with wheels. Cannons were defined by the size of the solid shot they fired. Standard weights were 2, 3, 4, 6, 8, 9, 12, and 18 pounds.

Ships were rated by the number of so-called great guns (9-, 12-, and 18-pounders) they carried. **First-rate ships** had a hundred or more great guns; **second rates,** 84 to 100; **third,** 70 to 84; **fourth,** 50 to 70, **fifth,** 32 to 50, and **sixth,** up to 32.

Naval line ships (first-, second-, and third-rate ships) were those that sailed into the line of battle. Fourth-rate ships cruised independently, sometimes engaging in battle, while fifth- and sixth-rate ships (known for their speed) scouted the enemy's fleet and were called frigates.

The *Alfred*, with twelve 9-pounders, was considered a sixth-rate ship. Four- and 8-pounders were the most common in the Continental Navy.

nental Navy. Of these, only seven would ever get to sea and all of those would be sunk or captured. The remaining six would be destroyed before ever being commissioned, to prevent their capture by the British. Fortunately, shipbuilding was one of America's major industries. At the time of the Revolutionary War, colonial shipyards were so superior in efficiency to those in Europe that it cost only about half as much to build a ship here as in Britain. Consequently, about a third of Britain's merchant fleet had been launched in the colonies.

There were problems, however, one of the most serious being that there were few foundries in the colonies that had the ability to cast cannons. Trial and error resulted in damaging explosions. There was also a period of learning how to cast anchors. Additionally, the speed with which the new navy's ships had to be produced necessitated the use of green, unseasoned timber, making the ships prone to decay.

The Continental Navy was playing an impossible game of catch-up. In 1775, Great Britain had 131 ships of the line and 139 smaller vessels. The Continental Navy would never have more than 10 ships under sail in any one year.

ate Navies and Privateers

ther than depend solely on ships nmissioned for the purpose, gress turned to state navies and privateers. Eleven of the colonies (excluding New Jersey and Delaware) had been organizing their individual navies for at least a year. These state navies, which eventually totaled close to 160 vessels, consisted mainly of small ships, brigs, sloops, and schooners. For the most part, they hugged the coast, protecting their seaports as best they could.

Privateers, on the other hand, had a far greater range of operation, from Canada to the West Indies to Great Britain. These were not pirates, the distinction being that privateers had letters of marque, issued by a government, charging them to serve with its navy. Originally, these letters of marque were called letters of reprisal because their purpose was to give official sanction to ship owners to retaliate against an enemy country that had destroyed their ships. During the course of the war, some 1697 letters of marque were issued to privateers, either individuals or a consortium of ship owners.

Crews for these ships, of course, were much easier to come by, since they could count on minimal discipline and maximum profit. Competition was fierce for the best men, and advertising had to be compelling. One poster appealed to "all those jolly Fellows who love their Country, and want to make their Fortunes at One Stroke. . . . They will be received with a hearty welcome and treated with that excellent liquor call'd Grog which is allow'd by all true Seamen to be the Liquor of Life."

Once a privateer had captured a vessel, members of the privateer's crew were dispatched to the vessel to take it to the nearest designated port, where a court would decide the value of the ship's cargo. This procedure entailed a "principal Person" from the captured vessel to be examined under oath, plus present to the court "all Passes, Sea-Briefs, Charter-Parties, Bills of lading, Dockets, Letters and other Documents and Writings found on Board." Meanwhile, the privateer captain (or his representative) had to "keep and preserve" the vessel and its cargo intact while the procedure progressed (or didn't, if there was a backlog), while also ensuring the safety and maintenance of crew members.

Though angry British merchants referred to privateers as marauding pirates, it should have been obvious that true pirates never would have put up with this kind of bureaucracy.

Privateers did tremendous damage to British commerce. A report made by Lloyds of London following the war estimated that not even counting those ships that were ransomed or recaptured, American privateers took more than 600 British ships, with a loss amounting to the equivalent of $18 million in today's value. These losses meant increased insurance rates for the merchants, who berated the government for not being able to protect their ships.

John Adams was apparently right in his assessment of privateering as "a short, easy, and infallible method for humbling the English."

Engagements

The first major action ordered by the Marine Committee was that Commodore Hopkins take his small fleet and sail to Chesapeake Bay, where Lord Dunmore, former royal governor of Virginia, was patrolling with a small British fleet. There Hopkins was to determine Dunmore's strength and, if his fleet wasn't overwhelming, "immediately to enter the said bay, search out and attack, take or destroy all the naval force of our enemies."

If Hopkins managed that, he was next "to proceed immediately to the southward and make yourself master of such forces as the enemy may have in both North and South Carolina." From there he was to return to Rhode Island "and attack, take, and destroy all the Enemies Naval force."

None of this happened. Instead, Hopkins took his fleet, including the *Alfred* and *Columbus* and a contingent of Continental Marines under Commandant Nicholas, to the Bahamas, where they attacked New Providence Island, Nassau, in March 1776. Two forts were captured, yielding 88 guns and more than 16,000 shells. A fine haul for a first venture.

Not all Continental Navy ventures ended as well. The Battle of Valcour Island in October 1776 resulted in defeat and destruction of the fleet, but it did delay the British long enough to ensure victory the following year at Saratoga. There were other victories, by John Barry and the *Lexington* and *Alliance*, Lambert Wickes and the *Reprisal*, and John Paul Jones and the *Bonhomme Richard*. Also, it was the Continental Navy that introduced the concepts of mines and submarine warfare, through the inventive mind of David Bushnell (*see* Connecticut River Museum).

The Continental Marines also played an important role, their greatest contribution perhaps being the defense of settlers against Native Americans in the West.

Disbandment

Following Cornwallis's surrender at Yorktown, a surrender brought about in part by the French naval blockade that preceded it, George Washington wrote, "It follows then, as certain as night succeeds day, that without a decisive naval force we can do nothing definitive—and with it, everything honorable and glorious."

But Washington's savvy vision was disregarded by a Congress concerned with financing a new government. Both the navy and the marines were disbanded.

Though it was the French navy that would eventually ensure a naval victory against the British, the Continental Navy and its patchwork union with state navies and privateers and the Continental Marines provided needed support at pivotal moments and established a proud legacy for their successors.

Colonial Michilimackinac and Fort Mackina[c]

A British stronghold during the Revolutionary War, this area of Michigan had been under French control for more than 100 years prior to the war and would be ceded to the United States at war's end.

Today, Colonial Michilimackinac, in Mackinaw City, provides insight into the lives of those living in America's frontier during the war, as well as the lives of the British soldiers stationed here at the former Fort Michilimackinac.

Fort Mackinac is on Mackinac Island, most of which is state parkland. The Lake Huron island is near the Straits of Mackinac that join Huron with Lake Michigan at Mackinaw City. This fort, constructed by the British when Fort Michilimackinac was deemed indefensible, preserves the original fort structure while taking visitors into a later era of American military occupation.

Fur Trade and Fighting

Native American tribes such as the Ottawas and Chippewas, who settled in this area centuries before the Europeans, used Mackinac Island to plant crops and bury their dead. The name Mackinac (pronounced mack-i-naw) is derived from the Indian word for turtle. According to native lore, this island was the first land mass established by the Great Turtle, who had previously existed in a world made only of water.

French fur traders made their way to the area in the 1600s and were followed by missionaries such as the Jesuit explorer Jacques Marquette, who established a mission on the island in 1671. In 1715 the French built Fort Michilimackinac on the south side of the straits, which, along with the entire Great Lakes region, passed to the British at the end of the French and Indian War.

In 1763 area tribes rebelled against the new British occupants in what came to be known as Pontiac's Rebellion. The British garrison at Michilimackinac was massacred by a band of Chippewas, who used the clever ruse of inviting the soldiers outside the compound to observe a [b]all game in honor of King George [III]'s birthday. The British eventually [put] down the rebellion, and by the [start] of the Revolutionary War they [regard]ed Michilimackinac as one of [Britain]'s most important centers of [fur trade i]n the Northwest Territory, as [it was] called by the Americans.

[When] the newly appointed lieutenant governor of Mic[hilimack]inac, Captain Patrick Sincla[ir arrived] in 1779, he recognized th[at] Michilimackinac, though we[ll situ]ated as a trading center, being accessible by water, was vulne[rable] as a military post. He also de[ter]mined that Mackinac Island ha[d a] deepwater harbor that British wa[r] ships could use. Plans were thu[s] made to build a fort on the nearby island, and in 1781 the British established themselves at Fort Mackinac on a limestone bluff overlooking the straits. From here Sinclair launched his campaign to recapture the British outposts, including Baton Rouge, Mobile, and Natchez, that had been captured by the Spanish after Spain entered the war in 1779. Though apparently an able commander, Sinclair had a difficult time marshaling an organized effort on the part of his Native American allies and the campaign failed.

At the end of the Revolutionary War, this region was given to the United States. But the British were a long time taking their leave (in 1796), and quick to return at the first sign of trouble. An attempt by the British to regain Mackinac Island led to what is thought to be the first land action of the War of 1812. After reoccupying the region during this second war, the British again ceded it to the United States at war's end, and Mackinac once more became a major trading center.

A penniless German immigrant named John Jacob Astor—later one of America's first millionaires—began to build his fortune with a fur-trading business based in Mackinac. When fur trading moved west in the 1830s, Astor sold his business.

In 1875, Mackinac Island became the country's second national park (Yellowstone being the first); then in 1895 it was given to the state of Michigan, which created its first state park. Over time, the town of Michilimackinac shortened its name to Mackinac Island, and after the Civil War it became a major summer resort, which it remains today.

Visiting Colonial Michilimackinac

The British didn't simply abandon the fort established here when they moved across the straits to Fort Mackinac. They completely razed the structure, in part to prevent its use by the Continentals, whom they feared might try to conquer the

this reason, the com-
Colonial Michilimackinac
struction on the original
mpassing a complete work-
olutionary War–era frontier

e life of the typical British sol-
during the Revolutionary War is
l presented here, along with the
ench and Native American cul-
ures. While British soldiers provide
a military presence, with cannon,
musket, and drilling demonstrations, French fur traders arrive at the
fort's gate down by the Lake
Michigan shoreline, and Native
Americans demonstrate their crafts.
Colonial women cook over open
hearths and colonial cooking
demonstrations are given in the
Southwest Rowhouse. A French
priest conducts a wedding, with visitors welcome to join in the dancing
afterward, and Native American storytellers relate the legend of the
Great Turtle.

Archaeological crews have been
working at this site every summer

since 1959. Visitors can watch and
ask questions, as well as see artifacts
found during the reconstruction.

Visiting Fort Mackinac

Fourteen original structures remain
at Fort Mackinac, including one (the
Officers' Stone Quarters) from the
Revolutionary War period. The limestone walls, also original, have been
restored.

The fort is a National Historic
Landmark. Though its overall focus
is that of an American military post
in the 1880s, Fort Mackinac has
much to offer those interested specifically in the Revolutionary War era.

The video *The Heritage of Mackinac*,
shown in the Post Commissary,
traces the prewar history of the
island, placing the Revolutionary
War in the context of the ongoing
French-British conflict. The exhibit
"Mackinac: An Island Famous in
These Regions," located on the second floor of the Soldiers' Barracks,
displays the original deed to the
island, Native American artifacts,

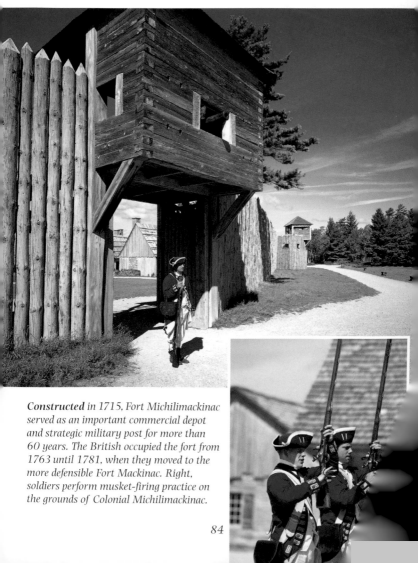

*Constructed in 1715, Fort Michilimackinac
served as an important commercial depot
and strategic military post for more than
60 years. The British occupied the fort from
1763 until 1781, when they moved to the
more defensible Fort Mackinac. Right,
soldiers perform musket-firing practice on
the grounds of Colonial Michilimackinac.*

Colonial Michilimackinac is a working 18th-century fur-trading village and British military outpost. An interpreter in colonial dress tills the vegetable garden near the Southwest Rowhouse.

and other items discovered in archaeological excavations at the fort.

"Kids' Quarters," in the Officers' Stone Quarters, affords visiting children the chance to dress up in military uniforms, fire a miniature cannon, use a telegraph, and enjoy other activities that don't have a lot to do with the Revolutionary War but provide fine entertainment.

Drum demonstrations reveal the ways in which drums were used during battle to relate movement orders. Though the specific orders may have changed in the intervening 100 years, the techniques used in this 1880s setting are very similar to those used during the Revolutionary War.

There's also a chance to compare the improvements made in arms between the 1780s and 1880s. At Fort Mackinac, visitors can see firing demonstrations by soldiers using rifles from the 1880s. At Colonial Michilimackinac, soldiers giving firing demonstrations use muskets from the 1780s. The level of difficulty between 1780 and 1880 armaments is immediately evident.

Visitor Information

906-847-3328 or 231-436-4100
www.MackinacParks.com

Hours: Colonial Michilimackinac is open daily from 9 a.m. until 5 p.m., May until mid-June; 9 a.m. until 9 p.m., mid-June until late August; and 9 a.m. until 5 p.m., late August until mid-October. Fort Mackinac is open daily from 9:30 a.m. until 4:30 p.m., May until mid-June; 9:30 a.m. until 6 p.m., mid-June until late August; and from 9:30 a.m. until 4:30 p.m., late August until mid-October.

Admission: There is a significant fee for each site; children under 5 are free. 7-day combination tickets cost only slightly more than buying tickets to both sites, and they include admission to other area attractions.

Accessibility: The majority of attractions at the two sites are accessible. At Fort Mackinac, problems may be encountered at the Guardhouse, Officers' Hill Quarters, the Schoolhouse, the Post Bathhouse, the South Sally Port, the East Blockhouse, the Gun Platforms, and the Tea Room. At Colonial Michilimackinac, accessibility is limited at the Powder Magazine, the Chevalier House, the Barnyard and Corrals, the Southwest Rowhouse, the Priest's House, the Native American Encampment, and the Cannon Firing Demonstration area. *A Guide to Access* pamphlet providing information about alternative entrances to some of these attractions is available upon request. To make special arrangements in advance, contact the museum educator at 231-436-4100.

Special Events: A community re-enactment of the 1763 Indian attack on the British is held in May, and there are festivities on the Fourth of July.

Getting There: To get to Mackinaw City, take I-75 north to Exit 339. Follow Huron Street west along the water to the Colonial Michilimackinac Visitor Center. Cars are not allowed on Mackinac Island. There are bikes for rent, as well as carriage tours available. Three ferry lines provide public access to the island from Mackinaw City and nearby St. Ignace.

Monmouth Battlefield State Park

The Battle of Monmouth, fought on June 28, 1778, was one of the largest engagements of the war, with some 36,000 troops involved. Rather than one cohesive engagement, Monmouth consisted of dueling artilleries and combat between Continental and British detachments.

The outcome, though a draw, was still a morale booster for the Patriots. Not only did it prove the Continental Army could act as a disciplined body and hold its own against a professional army, it established that the Continentals could pull themselves back together as an army in the midst of the chaos of battle, re-form, and make a fight of it.

Monmouth also proved General Charles Lee's undoing, which left George Washington free to fight the rest of the war without the distraction of Lee's coveting his command and playing politics to get it.

Washington's Opportunity

As a result of the French entering the war, Sir Henry Clinton, newly appointed commander of the British army in America, was ordered to evacuate Philadelphia and return to New York.

Britain now needed to ensure her position in the West Indies, which the French were threatening, which could mean dispatching as much as one fourth of the British troops in America to the islands. Clinton's orders were to consolidate the main army in New York. From there, fur-

ther assignments would be made.

George Washington had survived a harsh winter in Valley Forge (*see* Pennsylvania, Valley Forge National Historical Park). Now it was late spring and his men, after months of drilling and discipline under Baron von Steuben, were itching for a fight. When Washington discovered Clinton's plan to withdraw from Philadelphia, just 25 miles away, he saw an opportunity to catch the British army while it was strung out on the move. In consultation with his generals, Washington began to make plans.

General Charles Lee, second in authority only to Washington, opposed attacking Clinton. Lee, although a former British officer, was a staunch Patriot who had just returned from 15 months as a prisoner of the British—but kept in a fine house, as befit his rank. His reluctance to attack may have been based on his expressed feeling that the Continental Army couldn't defeat its British counterpart on the battlefield. He heatedly argued that the army shouldn't try to engage Clinton and should be thankful he would be bottled up in New York. Generals Lafayette and Anthony Wayne disagreed and encouraged Washington in his plan to attack.

Clinton, for his part, realized Washington might move on his troops. He considered sending the army to New York by ship, but had to scratch that idea because there weren't enough ships available in

The Battle of Monmouth included the largest land artillery engagement of the war.
At the 225th anniversary, over 20,000 spectators watched the reenactment of the bat

Philadelphia. Since the Philadelphia Loyalists could not remain in that city without British protection, he moved them out by ship, along with part of his Hessian troops. Clinton and his army would have to march to Sandy Hook, New Jersey, before embarking on ships there for New York.

On June 18, 1778, Clinton and some 20,000 men left Philadelphia. Along with them they took 1500 wagons, stretching 12 miles, and a large contingent of female camp followers. Clinton moved his baggage, containing provisions, ammunition, pontoon bridges, and other necessities, to the middle of the convoy and put his best troops to the rear, ready to engage Washington's army should it appear.

In late June, Washington held a formal council of his generals, soliciting opinions on the proposed attack. Again Lee expressed his strong opposition, and again Wayne and Lafayette—now joined by Nathanael Greene and Henry Knox—urged Washington to engage the enemy. Washington decided to send 2500 men ahead, to attack the rear of Clinton's column. Washington would follow up with the main army.

Lee, because of his rank, was to lead the attack. Washington gave him a clear and simple order: The moment the British army left Monmouth Court House (present-day Freehold) where they were now camped, Lee was to attack the rear guard.

Lafayette and Wayne were already in New Jersey with about 1000 men, s were at least 1500 militia and

Continentals, so when Lee arrived at Monmouth, he was commanding some 5000 men.

For both armies, the march to Monmouth had been hellacious. Hot, humid mornings would give way to torrential downpours, making the roads quagmires of mud; then in the afternoon the steamy heat would return. In their heavy uniforms, many of the British were dropping from sunstroke and heat exhaustion. The Americans were having similar problems but were making better time. Added to Clinton's troubles were the intermittent guerilla attacks by the New Jersey militia and the New Jersey Brigade along the way, which further slowed the British progress.

The Battle of Monmouth

The British reached Monmouth Court House midday on June 26, rested on the 27th, and prepared to leave while it was still dark on the 28th.

Lee arrived midday on the 27th and ordered reconnaissance to ensure that the British didn't slip away. Throughout that day and evening, Lee received conflicting information from militia and Continental reconnaissance parties about the deployment of Clinton's forces. Worse for Lee, the rear division he had been ordered to attack was led by one of Britain's ablest commanders in America, Lord Charles Cornwallis. Serving under him was the cream of the British army.

Lee's contradictory intelligence

In this painting by H. Charles McBarron, Washington, hurrying forward with the rest of his army to support an attack, meets General Lee amid his retreating columns and irately demands an explanation of the confusion.

translated into muddled orders to his officers. These unlucky gentlemen were not only trying to figure out what they were supposed to do, but they were also dealing with junior officers and troops with whom they were unfamiliar. Lee had shuffled all the commands the night before.

The British were moving out of their encampments, on a road between Freehold Meeting House and Monmouth Court House. This road crossed two ravines, about a mile apart, which the Continentals designated the west ravine and the middle ravine. The west ravine was the Spotswood Middle Brook, and the east ravine was the head of that brook. The middle ravine was a marshy ditch dividing two local farms.

At Monmouth Court House, the British continued north toward Sandy Hook and crossed the east ravine. About ten a.m., Cornwallis's rear guard saw Lee's forces approaching. Lee deployed 4500 men between the east ravine and the road to Sandy Hook, cutting off Cornwallis's army, which numbered a little over 1500 and included dragoons and light infantry. Lee was jubilant and convinced he was about to achieve an easy victory through sheer force of numbers.

As Lee went about the deployment, however, Clinton sent the remainder of his first division—about 8500 men—to support the rear guard. Wayne and Lafayette urged Lee to stop deploying and attack.

Lee's detachments now were under attack, and their officers had no orders how to proceed. Individual groups began to attack and retreat. When they were seen retreating, others followed suit, assuming the entire army was retreating.

Meanwhile, the field artillery of both armies had begun firing with a thunderous fury. And now Cornwallis and half the British army were returning to join the attack. Lee ordered a full retreat. The men began moving across the field back in the direction of Freehold Meeting House.

In the midst of retreat, General Washington appeared. Having been told of Lee's position and his outnumbering the British almost three to one, the general had stopped for a late breakfast, confident of Lee's success. Now he saw his army in disarray, retreating before Cornwallis's army and being pursued by Clinton.

Words were exchanged between Washington and Lee. What these were was a matter of some dispute at Lee's subsequent court-martial, though it was generally agreed that Lee was left stammering and making excuses. Preferring action to discussion, Washington offered Lee command of a line of defense to keep the British busy while Washington regrouped the army in the rear. Lee accepted the command, declaring he would be one of the last to leave the field.

Washington rode into the retreating Continentals to stop their retreat. Lafayette described the scene: "Never was General Washington greater than in this action. His presence stopped the retreat; his dispositions fixed the victory; his fine appearance on horseback, his calm courage roused to animation by the vexations of the morning, gave him the air best calculated to excite enthusiasm. . . . I thought then as now that never had I beheld so superb a man."

Washington stopped two retreating battalions in their tracks and ordered them to turn back and form a defensive line in the Point of Woods. They did, and lost many men and one of their commanders; but they bought Washington the time he needed. Then Lee, with two other battalions, slowed the British advance at a hedged fence. Washington formed the main part of his army on high ground behind the causeway that crossed Spotswood Middle Brook.

The battle resumed a little past noon and became a battle of artillery. For hours both armies' field artillery pounded each other's troops. Finally, in the late afternoon General Greene and a brigade of Virginians were able to position themselves so they could fire effectively on the British artillery, which withdrew.

Silence spread across the field, but it didn't last long. Washington attacked and more fighting ensued. Combat continued until late afternoon. When darkness fell, both armies made camp.

Sometime near midnight, Clinton's army slipped away. By June 30 he was at Sandy Hook, where his men were forced to shoot thousands of horses because there wasn't enough room for them on the ships. By July 5, the British army was back in New York.

The Americans reported 69 dead, 161 wounded, and 130 missing; the British, 65 killed, 160 wounded, and 64 missing. Washington disputed the British numbers, saying that the tally of enemy casualties found on

Molly Pitcher

The Battle of Monmouth is also known as the birthplace of the legend of Molly Pitcher, whose real name was Mary Hays. Mary followed her husband, a Pennsylvania artillery gunner, into the battle. Tradition has Molly carrying water from a nearby stream to her husband and his comrades during the action, which gave her the nickname Molly Pitcher. But historians now believe she assisted her husband's shorthanded crew by running cartridges from the bombardier at the ammunition box to the loader at the cannon muzzle.

Molly is commemorated on the Battle of Monmouth Monument, and in the traditional toast offered by artillery men: ". . . Drunk in a beverage richer and stronger than was poured that day from Molly Pitcher's pitcher."

the field for several days after, plus deserters during the battle and the wounded, numbered closer to 2000 men, or 15 percent of Clinton's army. The British also reported they had lost 59 men to "fatigue," or heat exhaustion.

Almost immediately following the battle, Lee wrote two insolent letters to Washington in which he at first insisted on a pub-

The Battle of Monmouth Monument

The monument, located in Freehold in a park at the junction of Court and Monument streets, was dedicated in 1884. The elaborate 100-foot statue, with a figure representing Liberty Triumphant at the top, graphically and beautifully depicts five scenes from the battle on bronze tablets: Lieutenant Colonel Nathaniel Ramsey, who held his position against the British Dragoons; Washington rallying the troops; Molly Pitcher with her husband fallen at her feet; Washington's council of war; and the final charge of the day by Anthony Wayne and his men.

lic hearing and then a court-martial, to clear his name. He claimed that Washington had called him "a damned poltroon" (coward) and that this aspersion on his character must be addressed. He also expected a public apology from Washington. Five days after the battle, the court-martial was convened, and Lee was found guilty of ordering an unnecessary and disorderly retreat. He was sentenced to a year's suspension from the army. When the sentence was upheld by Congress, Lee wrote a bitter letter denouncing that action and was dismissed entirely from the service.

This eccentric Englishman who had fought bravely for the cause of liberty was now undone by what some considered periods of madness and what others thought of as simply a tendency to go too far. Whichever is true, historians generally agree that Lee truly believed in the Patriot cause.

Lee died in Philadelphia, after a short illness, in 1782.

Visiting Monmouth Battlefield

The battlefield is now a lovely state park, with a little more than 1800 acres of fields, orchards, woods, and wetlands, as well as picnic areas and miles of hiking and horseback-riding trails. However, the battle is not forgotten.

The Visitor Center is located on Comb's Hill, the site from which Nathanael Greene's Virginia brigade displaced the British artillery. There is a small museum inside the center displaying artifacts from archaeological digs of the area, among these a lead musket ball with the imprint of a human tooth.

A recently restored 4-pounder cannon is also on display and is used for artillery demonstrations. In addition, several wayside exhibits

have been placed around the battlefield orienting visitors to the battle, and a mile and a half of rail fencing such as was here during the battle has been reconstructed.

The Craig House, an 18th-century farmhouse that became part of the battlefield, has been restored with period furnishings. According to tradition, John and Ann Craig hid their silverware in the well before fleeing with their three children. British soldiers, desperate for water, drained the well and found the silver at the bottom.

Visitor Information
732-462-9616
www.njparksandforests.org/parks/monbat.html
Hours: The battlefield and the park are open daily. Summer hours are 8 a.m. until 8 p.m.; fall, 8 a.m. until 6 p.m.; winter, 8 a.m. until 4:30 p.m.; spring, 8 a.m. until 6 p.m. The Visitor Center is open daily, 9 a.m. until 4 p.m.
Admission: Free.
Accessibility: The Visitor Center and recreational facilities in the park are partially accessible. Contact the park for further information, including accessibility of the battlefield.
Special Events: One of the largest Revolutionary War reenactments in the country is held here annually the last weekend in June. Various recreational activities are available in the park.
Getting There: From the New Jersey Turnpike, use exit 8 and go east approximately 12 miles on state route 33, following signs to Freehold and the park.

From the Garden State Parkway, take exit 123 to U.S. 9 south for 15 miles to business route 33 west. The park is located 1.5 miles on the right.

Morristown National Historical Park

During the winter of 1779–1780, Abigail Adams wrote to her husband John, "Posterity who are to reap the blessings, will scarcely be able to conceive the hardships and sufferings of their ancestors." Even the indomitable Mrs. Adams was humbled by what meteorologists believe may well have been the most severe winter in recorded American history.

Hundreds of miles away from the Adams farm, outside a small town in New Jersey, thousands of Patriot soldiers were huddled around fires in small log huts, waiting for spring and the chance to fight again. Visitors looking into the huts at Morristown today are likely to admit that Abigail was right—trying to imagine the misery those soldiers and camp followers endured probably falls far short of the mark.

Winters of Hardship

Parts of the Continental Army spent four winters at Morristown. The largest encampments were January through May of 1777 and the winter of 1779–1780.

The first encampment followed Washington's victories at Trenton and Princeton (see Washington Crossing State Parks and Princeton Battlefield State Parks). At that time, Morristown consisted of some 70 houses, two churches, a courthouse, a jail, and a few taverns. It was a good spot for the army to spend the next five months, as it was only 30 miles from New York City and located such that Washington could react expeditiously to British troop movements south toward Philadelphia or north toward the Hudson Valley.

A few weeks after Washington established his headquarters at Arnold's Tavern, he was joined by his wife, Martha, who began arranging modest dinners for the officers and their wives, quartered in private homes in the area.

Meanwhile, Washington was losing his army to enlistment deadlines

and the privations of the camp. The barely established supply routes were ineffectual at best, causing Washington to write a blistering letter to one of the commissaries: "The Cry of want of Provisions comes to me from every Quarter. . . . Consider, I beseech you, the consequences of this neglect and exert yourself to remedy this Evil." When provisions still did not arrive, Washington ordered that food be commandeered for his army from the surrounding area.

The supply problem was eventually, although only temporarily, solved; but an equally daunting problem was smallpox. At one time almost a third of the army was ill with it. Washington ordered that his entire force be inoculated, a daring practice at the time. Because inoculation brought on a mild form of the illness, the army was vaccinated in stages, so as not to incapacitate it entirely at any one time. This practically eliminated smallpox as a potential killer.

The problem of a dwindling army also was solved eventually, through the offer of bounties, and by the middle of May the army numbered close to 9000.

As harsh as this winter had been, it would pale in comparison in the memory of those who lived through the winter of 1779–1780. The cold extended from the northern to the southern states. In North Carolina, Patriot troops marched across the Albemarle Sound; in New York the British rolled a three-ton cannon across the Hudson River, where the ice was measured at 18 feet thick. When the Continental Army arrived in Morristown in early December, there was already a foot of snow on the ground. A January blizzard lasted four days. There were more than 20 snowstorms during that winter; the last one at the end of March left 10 inches of snow on the ground.

It was almost impossible to get supplies through to Morristown on roads blocked by six-foot drifts. Soon

Ice creepers were tied to the shoes just in front of the heel to aid in walking on ice or hard-packed snow— a necessity during the brutal winter of 1779–1780.

after the army was settled in, surgeon James Thacher wrote in his journal, "The snow on the ground is about two feet deep and the weather extremely cold; the soldiers are destitute of both tents and blankets and some of them are actually barefooted and almost naked."

The men had to construct their huts out of the surrounding forest of oak, hickory, and walnut trees, chopping away at wood hard as stone from the cold. This continued for months. The snowstorms hindered construction and left men frozen in their tents. "Some of the men were actually covered while in their tents and buried like sheep under the snow," wrote Thacher. "The sufferings of the poor wretches can scarcely be described, while on duty they are unavoidably exposed to all the inclemency of storms and severe cold; at night they now have but a bed of straw on the ground and a single blanket to each man; they are badly clad and some are destitute of shoes."

Lack of food was another major concern. Joseph Plumb Martin, a private from Connecticut, later wrote, "We were absolutely, literally starved. I do solemnly declare that I did not put a single morsel of victuals into my mouth for four days and as many nights, except a little black birch bark which I gnawed off a stick of wood, if that can be called victuals. I saw several of the men roast their old shoes and eat them."

As before, Washington authorized his officers to take what they needed from 11 districts within the state of New Jersey as soon as the roads were passable by horse, let alone wagons. The provisions taken were to be paid for at some future date.

The 10,000 half-starved men and camp followers who made it to spring received news in March that a French ship was on its way, carrying 364 cases of arms, thousands of caps, stockings, and shoes, 11,000 gunflints, and 1000 barrels of gunpowder.

Visiting Morristown

The park consists of four areas: the Washington's Headquarters unit, with the Headquarters Museum and the Ford Mansion; Fort Nonsense; Jockey Hollow, including the Wick House; and the New Jersey Brigade Encampment Area. Visitors will need a car to get from site to site.

It is best to start at the **Washington's Headquarters Museum**, where tickets can be purchased, maps and other information are available, and there is a 20-minute film depicting life in the Morristown encampments from the soldiers' point of view, taken from diaries and letters of the time.

"War Comes to Morristown" on the first floor explains the effects of the war on the people of the town. The second floor has two galleries, one devoted to changing exhibits and the other featuring weapons used during the war. Among these are a cannon captured at the Battle of Princeton, two of George Washington's swords, muskets, rifles, and fowling pieces. The most impressive item is an extremely rare Ferguson rifle (*see* South Carolina, Kings Mountain National Military Park), one of 100 experimental Fergusons made for enlisted men. This is thought to be the only one on display in the United States. This exhibit also contains a link from the chain that stretched across the Hudson River at West Point (*see* New York, West Point Museum) to deter British passage.

Leaving from the museum, visitors are taken by National Park Service rangers on a guided tour of the Ford Mansion, which was George Washington's headquarters the winter of 1779–1780. Period furnishings—including a few pieces that belonged to Mrs. Jacob Ford, Jr., a widow with four children who rented space to the general—recreate the interiors as they might have been that winter.

Nearby is the **Fort Nonsense** area. An earthwork fort was built here in the spring of 1777 as a defense position for soldiers guarding the supply depot at Morristown. Stones outline the perimeter where the fort stood. Its name is derived from the mistaken belief that Washington had the soldiers build it just to keep them busy. Interpretive signs explain the actual purpose and use of the fort.

Western Avenue takes visitors five miles south to the **Jockey Hollow Encampment**, where a short film at the Visitor Center depicts life in the huts the winter of 1779–1780. Complementing the film is a full-size hut built into the floor. Looking down into the hut's interior and aided by a spoken narrative, visitors get a better understanding of the claustrophobic space in which soldiers existed for six months.

About 100 yards from the Visitor

Center is the Wick House, which was used by General Arthur St. Clair (*see* New York, Fort Ticonderoga National Historic Landmark) that same winter. A self-guided tour takes visitors through a typical 18th-century kitchen, the sitting room St. Clair used as his headquarters, his small adjoining bedroom, and the two rooms Mr. and Mrs. Henry Wick and their daughter moved into in order to accommodate St. Clair.

A paved tour road that loops for two and a half miles around the Jockey Hollow unit features the Pennsylvania Encampment Area, where a series of replica huts designate where the soldiers stayed and how they lived. The army intended to save the original huts for the following winter, but townspeople claimed many of them, informing army personnel that soldiers had sold the huts to them before leaving. Some of the huts were used as a hospital complex after the army left.

About a half mile south of the Visitor Center is the **New Jersey Brigade Encampment Area,** now a wooded hiking area with interpretive signs explaining where and how the soldiers encamped. There are about 27 miles of hiking trails at

Jockey Hollow and the New Jersey Brigade areas.

Visitor Information
973-539-2016, ext. 210
www.nps.gov/morr
Hours: The Washington's Headquarters Museum and the Jockey Hollow Visitor Center are open daily year-round, 9 a.m. until 5 p.m. Note that at some time during the next few years the museum will be closed for renovations. The Wick House is open daily from 9:30 a.m. until 4:30 p.m., depending on staff availability. Park roads are open from 8 a.m. until sunset. The park is closed Thanksgiving, December 25, and January 1.
Admission: Moderate charge for adults, children under 16 free.
Accessibility: The Visitor Center and the first floor of the Washington's Headquarters Museum are accessible.
Special Events: There are programs throughout the year on subjects related to the Morristown encampments, the Revolutionary War, and 18th-century life. The park presents a public reading of the Declaration of Independence on the Fourth of July. A Memorial Day commemoration honors those who died here.
Getting There: Take I-287 south to exit 36 or I-287 north to exit 36A, then follow the signs to the Washington's Headquarters unit.

*A **military cocked hat** belonging to Hartshorne of Reading. Cockades of different colors were used to distinguish between regiments, particularly those without standard uniforms.*

*A **wooden canteen** carried by Isaac Whitehead during the Revolutionary War is one of many artifacts on display at Morristown National Historical Park.*

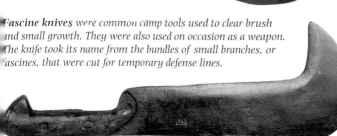

Fascine knives *were common camp tools used to clear brush and small growth. They were also used on occasion as a weapon. The knife took its name from the bundles of small branches, or fascines, that were cut for temporary defense lines.*

Old Barracks Museum

The Old Barracks Museum, in Trenton, New Jersey, provides visitors with an opportunity to better understand how British, Hessian, and Continental soldiers were quartered during the French and Indian and Revolutionary wars.

Through its historical interpretation presentations and mixture of original and reproduced furnishings, this National Historic Landmark accurately and entertainingly invites visitors to connect with the soldiers on both sides of the conflict.

History of the Museum

Built to house British troops during the French and Indian War, by December 1776 the Barracks served as a refuge for Loyalist families under the protection of Hessian troops as well as for their families. Most Hessian soldiers were quartered in houses around the town.

What the soldiers didn't steal or break, they used to keep their fireplaces going. Even Trenton's library wasn't immune. Only the 14 books that were out on loan when the soldiers came looking for fire fodder were saved, and are now among the library's treasures.

On the morning of December 26, George Washington and his army captured Trenton from the Hessians (*see* New Jersey, Washington Crossing State Park). The Barracks is thought to have been the first building shelled, but the thick fieldstone suffered no permanent damage, and the women and children escaped.

For the next six years, the Barracks served as a Continental Army hospital. In 1781 almost 600 sick and wounded soldiers from the Battle of Yorktown were brought here for treatment and recovery.

Visiting Old Barracks Museum

Guided tours are given throughout the day by costumed interpreters who enthusiastically share historical facts and interesting tales in equal measure. In 1777 this building was considered to be on the outskirts of town; even today, surrounded by the city of Trenton, visitors entering the grounds feel as if they've stepped back in time a few hundred years, isolated from the 21st-century bustle around them.

Coming off the street, visitors enter via the parade ground, where the officers drilled their men. The original parade ground is several inches below the present surface; but once it was discovered by archaeologists, the ground was filled in again in order to preserve the original.

The basement rooms of the U-shaped building are used for archaeological and architectural programs. Originally, the Barracks' four kitchens were located in this basement.

The Squad Room on the first floor represents the way Continental Army soldiers lived during the war—12 men to a 16-by-16-foot room, each room with six bunk beds, each bed shared by two men. Besides the beds, individual rooms had tables with benches or stools, a small fireplace, a window at one end, and a door at the other.

Records show that during the French and Indian War about 300 British soldiers lived in these first-floor rooms, housed in much the same way as their Continental Army successors. How the rooms were delegated when Loyalists' families were living here is unknown, but it's likely that the women organized things as best they could for the comfort and safety of their families.

The clothing displayed is reproduced but very realistic, with its patches and ample evidence of mending. Cartridge boxes, haversacks, and other personal items add to the military atmosphere.

Also on the first floor are the Surgeon's Room and the Hospital Room. Costumed interpreters give a very realistic demonstration of how Washington's army was inoculated against smallpox. There are medical instruments from the period and more detailed information about the procedures of the time than the average adult may want to hear, but kids love it. For the truly curious, the Old Barracks Web site has a full explanation of how amputations were performed.

The Gallery on the second floor has changing exhibits related to topics such as the Revolutionary War, the Battle of Trenton, and Trenton's early history.

In 1759, an Officers' House was built onto the Barracks, after British officers complained about having to share quarters with their men. This fieldstone-and-brick Georgian house was treated as a totally separate building, with no passageway between it and the Barracks. Exhibits focus on how British officers lived during the French and Indian War and provide an interesting contrast

to the soldiers' setup in the Barracks.

Whereas Continental soldiers in the Barracks ate and slept in their rooms, British officers almost 20 years earlier ate and slept in separate rooms. What is now called the Long Room, located on the first floor, was used for dining and entertaining. The table could be folded after the evening meal and set against the wall to make way for dancing. And whereas Continental soldiers were housed 12 to a room and were sharing beds, British officers slept two to a room, each with his own bed. And each likely had his own servant, or batman, quartered in the hallway or attic.

The furnishings and arrangements of the Officer of the Day's Room on the second floor demonstrate the many duties of junior officers, such as maintaining the company's accounts and handling correspondence.

Outside, in the yard behind the Barracks, is an authentic 18th-century brick-and-clay oven. Every Thursday from spring until late fall, visitors are treated to the aroma of fresh bread baking. The bread, made of unbleached flour, sea salt, and springwater, according to an 18th-century recipe, is sold in the nearby Farmers Market.

Visitors of Hessian or German descent are invited to search the records here of who fought in the battle and where they were prisoners of war after they were captured. There are plans to make this information available on the museum's Web site sometime in the near future.

Visitor Information
609-396-1776
www.barracks.org
Hours: Open daily 10 a.m. until 5 p.m.; closed Easter, Thanksgiving, December 24 and 25, and January 1.
Admission: Moderate charge; children under 6 are free.
Accessibility: Handicapped accessible.
Special Events: There are lectures, exhibits, and special events throughout the year. Reenactments include the arrival of Hessian troops in mid-December, followed by a reenactment of the fighting at Trenton. In February, there's a celebration of Washington's birthday. Summer camps are held in July and August for children ages 9 to 12 and Youth Camp-Ins are offered March through June and September and October. Check the Web site for fees and schedules.
Getting There: From routes U.S. 1, I-95, I-195, I-295, or the New Jersey Turnpike, follow the signs to state route 29, Trenton. From route 29, take the Calhoun Street exit and turn right at the traffic light onto West State Street. At the next light, turn right onto Barrack Street.

The Battle of Trenton Monument
The Battle of Trenton Monument, located nearby on North Warren Street, marks the site of an American artillery emplacement during the Battle of Trenton on December 26, 1776. Designed by John H. Duncan, who also designed Grant's Tomb in New York, the monument consists of a flat-topped triangular granite base on which rests a 135-foot Doric column topped by a 13-foot statue of George Washington. For further information, call 609-737-0623, or go to www.10crucialdays.org/html/monument.htm.

Princeton Battlefield State Park

"Though it was once the fashion of this army to treat them in the most contemptible light, they are now become a formidable enemy." This judgment of the Continental Army by British Colonel William Harcourt, as written in a letter to his father, followed the Battle of Princeton.

In a 10-day stretch from the night crossing of the Delaware on December 25, 1776, to the Battle of Princeton on January 3, 1777, George Washington changed the complexion of the conflict. What the British had viewed as the chastisement of a rebellious child had now become a battle between, if not equals, at least two determined foes each with their own way of winning.

At last Harcourt and others in the British army were realizing that "though they seem to be ignorant of the precision and order, and even of the principles, by which large bodies are moved, yet they possess some of the requisites for making good troops, such as extreme cunning, great industry in moving ground and felling of wood, activity and a spirit of enterprise upon any advantage."

The Battle of Princeton and what some historians call the Second Battle of Trenton occurred on the same day within hours of each other. Both were the result of the British, commanded by Lord Charles Cornwallis, trying to prevent Washington from raiding a supply depot at New Brunswick.

Washington Pushes On

Just two days after his triumph over the Hessians at Trenton, George Washington and his army were recrossing the Delaware. The victory at Trenton had been a morale booster for the Continental Army and for the Patriot cause. Washington wanted to take advantage of the impetus such a victory brought by pressing back through New Jersey, especially as he had just convinced the New England regiments to re-up for at least another month.

Their enlistment expired on January 1, and Washington apparently knew that only a personal appeal on his part had any chance of inducing the men to stay. As remembered by a sergeant more than 50 years later, the general said, "My brave fellows, you have done all I asked you to do, and more than could be reasonably expected; but your country is at stake, your wives, your houses and all that you hold dear. You have worn yourselves out with fatigues and hardships, but we know not how to spare you."

This, plus a reported promise of a monetary bonus, convinced many of the men to stay, and the next day they were crossing the river again and marching toward New Brunswick, where the British had a large supply depot and a cache of 70,000 pounds sterling.

Cornwallis and 7000 of his men left Princeton for Trenton on January 2, 1777, leaving one brigade under the command of Lieutenant Colonel Charles Mawhood to guard the supplies stored in Princeton.

By this time, Washington was established near Trenton with 2000 men, waiting for General John Cadwalader and his Pennsylvania Associators, who had not made it across the Delaware River for the December 26 attack on Trenton, to join them. Washington needed a delaying action against Cornwallis to establish his position and give Cadwalader time to get to Trenton.

On January 1, Washington ordered General Roche de Fermoy, a Frenchman fighting for the Patriot cause, and Colonel Edward Hand with his Pennsylvania sharpshooters to reconnoiter the British advance and do whatever they could to hinder it. For some unknown reason, de Fermoy ended up rejoining Washington in Trenton, but Hand and his Pennsylvanians proceeded to harass Cornwallis's main army (his artillery was bogged down on roads muddied by thawing ice and snow) as they retreated back toward Trenton.

About two miles north of Trenton, the Patriots made their final and strongest attack, seriously delaying the British, who took the time to form a line of battle. In a ravine of the Assunpink Creek, about a mile north of town, Hand and his men held fast, encouraged by Washington and Nathanael Greene, who had ridden from Trenton to urge the troops to hold out as long as possible. Meanwhile, the Continental Army was shoring up its defenses at Trenton's Assunpink Bridge.

The fighting on January 2 and 3 succeeded in delaying Cornwallis's army long enough so that the British didn't reach Trenton until early evening on January 2. The Hessian troops marched into town at the head of the British army, intent on revenging the defeat there the week before (*see* New Jersey, Washington Crossing State Park). As they moved through town toward Assunpink Bridge, ahead of them Hand's forces, now joined by the Rhode Island Continentals, were firing, then retreating. At the bottom of what is now Broad Street and was then Queen Street, Washington waited with his artillery. Three times the Hessians and the British assaulted the bridge and three times they were thrown back. The third time must have taken a special kind of courage, for it was observed that "the bridge looked red as blood, with [the British] killed and wounded and their red coats."

Following this attack, with night coming on, Cornwallis fell back. His men were exhausted. Besides, Washington's back was to the Delaware River, and retreating across it would take too long. The British would catch at least half of the Continentals in the act. When Sir William Erskine, an officer on Cornwallis's staff, suggested to him that "if you trust these people tonight, you will see nothing of them in the morning," Cornwallis replied, "Nonsense, my dear fellow. We've got the old fox safe now. We'll go over and bag him in the morning. The damned rebels are cornered at last."

Many of the "rebels" would have agreed with him. Washington did not. He had a plan. While nearly 400 New Jersey militiamen remained behind to bank huge campfires and make noise enough for an army, the rest of Washington's forces slipped around the British to the Quaker Bridge Road and on to Princeton. The muddy roads that had hindered the British were now refrozen, so the wagons, their wheels wrapped in cloths to muffle their clacking, had a much easier time of it. Within hours, Washington's army was gone.

The Battle of Princeton

The British commander at Princeton, Lieutenant Colonel Mawhood, had received orders to take the bulk of his three foot regiments and dragoons and march to the town of Maidenhood (now Lawrenceville), join up with other regiments from Cornwallis's forces, and push on to Trenton. Only a small force now remained in Princeton to guard the supplies.

Mawhood and his regiments had just crossed Stony Brook Bridge, about a mile and a half outside Princeton, when he caught sight of a group of militia emerging from the woods. These were General Hugh Mercer's men, some 350 of them, who were at the front of Greene's division. At first Mawhood assumed they were German troops. Upon confirming they were Patriot soldiers, Mawhood marched his men back across the bridge toward Princeton, ready to return to town to support the troops left behind.

When Mercer spotted the British, he deployed his men across the open farm fields and into the apple orchards belonging to Thomas and William Clarke, trying to shield General John Sullivan's forces a half mile to the east. Mawhood quickly divided his 1000 men, sending a third to attack Sullivan, a third to attack Mercer, and the final third to guard the high ground above Sullivan.

Mawhood and Mercer both had artillery pieces. The Americans initially drove back a British skirmish line; then the main British line, supported by artillery, forced the Americans back. Mercer's horse went down, and as the British charged with bayonets, his men— most of them lacking bayonets— began to break ranks. Mercer and his officers tried to rally them, but two of his officers were killed and Mercer was bayoneted seven times and left for dead, although he actually lived nine more days. With their officers brought down, the men ran from the field. The British grabbed the Continental cannons and turned them on the fleeing soldiers.

General Cadwalader and his Pennsylvania Associators now arrived on the field and tried to form behind the Clarke farmhouse, but the men only got off two or three rounds before they broke and ran back toward the woods. Two pieces of artillery, however, were still manned and were firing into the advancing British lines. And now more Continental forces were arriving, including regiments from Rhode Island and Massachusetts; and Colonel Hand's sharpshooters had formed and were attacking from the right.

George Washington had been with Sullivan's troops approaching Princeton, but hearing firing on his left, he and his officers charged ahead of Sullivan's troops toward Greene's position. Washington arrived in time to rally Mercer's and

James Peale probably painted The Battle of Princeton *from his brother and fellow artist Charles Willson Peale's firsthand account of his participation in the pivotal battle*

Cadwalader's panicked commands, demanding they stand their ground. He rode to the front of the retreating soldiers, some say within 30 paces of Mawhood's line, and stood his ground while the cannons fired. One of his officers said he turned away because he couldn't bear to see his commander brought down. But when the cannon smoke cleared, Washington was still on his horse, shouting for his men to attack. They charged, as more troops arrived from Sullivan's division.

Mawhood and his men were now almost completely surrounded and were outnumbered 400 to 2000. But they weren't beaten. The British commander led a bayonet charge through the Patriot lines, crossing the bridge and retreating through the woods toward Trenton. Meanwhile, Sullivan continued his advance on Princeton, where some 200 British soldiers had taken refuge in Nassau Hall at the College of New Jersey (now Princeton University). When Sullivan fired several cannon volleys at the building, the men surrendered. A cannonball scar is still visible on the south wall of the west wing of the hall.

The battles at Trenton and Princeton had regained more than two thirds of New Jersey from the British. Washington would have pushed on to New Brunswick, but his army could not tolerate more

fighting. For 10 days in the dead of winter they'd been in almost constant battle.

Still, the account of an 85-year-old Princeton resident a few months after the battle shows the incredible resilience of these men: "Immediately after the battle Genl Washingtons men came into our house. Though they were both hungry and thirsty some of them [were] laughing out right, others smileing, and not a man among them but showed joy in his countenance. It really animated my old blood with love to those men that but a few minutes before had been courageously looking death in the face in ravages of a bold and dareing enemy."

Visiting the Battlefield

This 85-acre battlefield site has a sense of timeless quietude about it. Instead of a modern building for a visitor center, the 18th-century Clarke House serves as an orientation center and museum. Instead of large monuments, a classic Ionic colonnade, designed by Thomas U. Walter, one of the U.S. Capitol architects, stands at the edge of the battlefield, and behind it a stone patio marks the grave of 21 British and 15 American soldiers.

Set into the stone in bronze lettering is a poem by the English poet Alfred Noyes: *Here freedom stood by slaughtered friend and foe,/ And ere the*

wrath paled or that sunset died,/ Looked through the ages, then, with eyes aglow,/ Laid them to wait that future, side by side.

The Clarke House was built by Thomas Clarke, a Quaker farmer, around 1772. Thomas and his brother William were farmers working the surrounding fields and orchards where the battlefield is now located. Following the battle, the Clarke home became a hospital. It was here that General Mercer died on January 12.

A wing was added to the house in the 1840s, and it is in this section of the house that two exhibit rooms now display artifacts from the period. Among these are numerous muskets, including fowlers originally intended for hunting and French Charlevilles. Guided tours are given of the 18th-century section of the house. Two of the bedrooms have period furnishings, while another room has been furnished in the style

of a 1770s storage room.

While at the Clarke House, visitors can pick up a brochure and map of the battlefield, which shows where interpretive signs are located. The map also pinpoints the former location of the Mercer Oak. It was near this oak that General Mercer was said to have lain after the attack by British soldiers. The oak itself died in 2000.

A film about the battle is scheduled to be completed in 2005 and will be shown at the Washington Crossing State Park Visitor Center (*see* New Jersey, Washington Crossing State Park), west of Princeton in Titusville.

Adjacent to the Princeton Battlefield park is a 550-acre reserve of woodlands and wetlands owned by the park's neighbor, the Institute of Advanced Study. Visitors are welcome to enjoy its hiking trails.

Visitor Information
609-921-0074
www.state.nj.us/dep/parksand
forests/princeton.html
Hours: The park is open dusk until dawn. Clarke House is open Wednesday through Saturday, 10 a.m. until noon; Sunday 1 p.m. until 4 p.m.; closed Thanksgiving Day, December 25, and January 1.
Admission: Free.
Accessibility: The park is accessible, as is the first floor of the Clarke House and the exhibit wing.
Special Events: Periodically there are celebrations on the Fourth of July and reenactments around the anniversary of the battle.
Getting There: From I-95 & I-295 at Trenton, take exit 7 to U.S. 206 north toward Lawrenceville/Princeton. After a half mile, turn right onto Quaker Road, then left onto Mercer Road (Princeton Pike) north.

From I-287, take U.S. 206 south for 18 miles. Turn left onto Lovers Lane, then right on Mercer Road (Princeton Pike).

Princeton Battle Monument
Created by designer Thomas Hastings and sculptor Frederick MacMonnies, the monument was dedicated by President Warren G. Harding in 1922. On the face of the monument, the chaos and horror of war are depicted by the fallen men and horses being trampled, while above them a calm and determined George Washington remains astride his horse facing the battle. Highly symbolic, this was not the typical straightforward war memorial of its day in that it pays homage not to war but to the men who bravely die in war. The monument is located on park property in downtown Princeton, at the corner of Stockton Road and Bayard Lane (U.S. route 206), about a mile and a half from the park.

Red Bank Battlefield Park

The successful British attacks on Forts Mifflin and Mercer in October and November of 1777 cleared the Delaware River for British warships and supply vessels, but it also delayed the pursuit of General Washington and his forces long enough for the Patriots to establish their winter headquarters at Valley Forge. By spring of 1778, the British were facing a reorganized and much more formidable Continental Army.

The Attacks on Fort Mercer

Fort Mercer, on the New Jersey side of the Delaware in what was then called Red Bank, was named for General Hugh Mercer, a casualty of the Battle of Princeton (*see* New Jersey, Princeton Battlefield State Park). By 1777 it had been restructured by the Chevalier de Mauduit du Plessis, a French engineer who recognized that there were too few men to defend so large a fort and so had an inner wall built that cut off the fort's north wing. Mercer's commander, Colonel Christopher Greene (Nathanael Greene's cousin), deployed his garrison of 400 Rhode Islanders along the interior wall, which had 14 cannons mounted on it.

On October 22, 1777, more than 1200 Hessians under the command of Colonel Carl Emil Kurt von Donop attacked Fort Mercer in what is now called the Battle of Red Bank. On the first charge, two columns of Hessians stormed the north wall, only to find themselves staring at du Plessis's new wall. Von Donop attacked simultaneously from the east; but on reaching the fort's earthenwork wall, he discovered he had neglected to bring scaling ladders.

From both sides, Greene ordered his men to open fire, aiming at the broad white belts of the Hessian uniforms. The first volley scattered the Hessians, who fell back, regrouped, and charged again, this time concentrating on the fort's south wall. This left them vulnerable to fire from Patriot gunboats on the river and they again took a powerful hit. More than 400 Hessians were killed or wounded in the first and second attacks, while the Patriots lost less than 50 men. Among the mortally wounded was von Donop, who died three days later after declaring, "This is finishing a noble career early."

Next, Howe sent five ships armed with more than 125 cannons up the river to mount attacks on both Fort Mifflin and Fort Mercer. The ships ran aground and one, the *Augusta*, blew up when her magazine was hit by fire from one of the forts. Giving up the idea of a river attack, the British now decided to concentrate on Fort Mifflin with a bombardment from batteries on the Pennsylvania side of the Delaware (*see* Pennsylvania, Fort Mifflin on the Delaware).

The Patriots were forced to abandon Fort Mifflin in November of 1777, but General Washington hoped to save his remaining Delaware River fortification at Fort Mercer. He sent Nathanael Greene and a small force in support of the fort. But Greene's forces were so greatly outnumbered by the British force ahead of them that Greene decided to turn back.

Following a heavy bombardment by the British, Mercer was abandoned on November 21, giving the British unchallenged access to the Delaware River.

Visiting Red Bank Battlefield

Visitors to the Red Bank Battlefield can tour the remains of the earthworks of Fort Mercer, where signage provides a detailed explanation of the 40-minute battle in October 1777. There is also a 75-foot monument erected by the state of New Jersey in 1905 to honor the Patriots who defended Fort Mercer from the Hessian attack.

For those interested in a more personal insight into the effects of the Revolution on families living in its war zone, the James and Ann Whitall House is a charming and informative stop. The Whitalls were a wealthy Quaker family whose 400-acre Red Bank Plantation was located on the banks of the Delaware River. In early October 1777, Colonel Christopher Greene and his army arrived, established their headquarters at the Whitall House, and began to construct a fort in the northern section of the property. Building the fort meant destroying most of the Whitall's apple orchards, which also served as the army's camp while Fort Mercer was being constructed.

On October 22 the Hessians attacked the fort, located only 600 feet from the house. The Whitalls and their nine children remained in their home, with Mrs. Whitall in her bedroom spinning. When a cannonball struck nearby, she picked up her wheel, moved to the basement, and continued spinning.

In the fall of 1777, Colonel Christopher Greene, the commander of the American forces at Red Bank, set up headquarters in the Whitall House. The Colonel decided that the family's apple orchard was the ideal location for a defensive fort, so the orchard was razed and Fort Mercer built there.

Following the battle, Hessians and Patriots alike were brought to the Whitall house, which was used as a field hospital. Mrs. Whitall helped care for the wounded, while remonstrating with her patients for trying to kill each other. The damage done to the plantation and home, plus the continued bombardment of the fort from the river, forced the Whitalls to leave Red Bank on October 25. They would not return until April of the following year.

Visitors can take a self-guided tour of the house from November through March, aided by a number of very engaging illustrated brochures with information about the battle, the house, and the Whitalls. From April through October, costumed interpretive guides lead tours of the five rooms that have been restored.

In Mrs. Whitall's Parlor and in the Colonial Kitchen, visitors learn about simple colonial family life, with information on spinning and weaving, the toys children played with, how women cared for their families, and cooking techniques. Demonstrations of many of these activities are given during Heritage Sample Days.

A Field Hospital Room has been created showing how patients were cared for during a battle. Window shades painted with scenes such as would have been seen out the windows that day add a touch of authenticity.

Mr. Whitall's Office displays a model of his grandson's ship, the East Indiaman *New Jersey*. Captain John Mickle Whitall was part of the burgeoning China–America trade that developed in the first quarter of the 19th century, making four voyages to Canton in four years.

Archaeological explorations were begun at Red Bank in 1999. One of the rooms in the Whitall House has been converted into an archaeologist's office, with displays of tools currently in use and information about the ongoing archaeological activities.

The 18th-century gardens surrounding the house are planted with herbs, trees, and flowers that would have been found here during the Battle of Red Bank.

Visitor Information
856-853-5120
www.co.gloucester.nj.us/
    parks/red.htm

Hours: The park is open from dawn until dusk daily. The Whitall House is open April through September, Wednesday through Sunday 1 p.m. until 4 p.m., and October through May on Wednesday, Thursday, and Friday, 9 a.m. until noon and 1 p.m. until 4 p.m.; closed Easter, Thanksgiving, December 25, and January 1.

Admission: Free.

Accessibility: The house is partially accessible, and the park completely accessible.

Special Events: Heritage Sampler Days on the third Sunday of each month, April through September; 18th-Century Field Day the third Sunday in October commemorates the battle; Annual Flower Show.

Getting There: The park is on the Delaware River in National Park, New Jersey, south of Camden and 7 miles west of Woodbury. (Note: It is not at the town in eastern New Jersey that is now known as Red Bank.) From I-295, take exit 22 and follow county road 644 west. After 0.4 miles, turn left on Hessian Avenue to the park.

Washington Crossing State Park

Following a series of defeats in New York, George Washington's army had been forced to retreat to Pennsylvania in December of 1776. The British general, Sir William Howe, believed the American troops were incapable of further offensive action, and that at most they would be preparing for a battle in the spring. But Howe underestimated Washington's resolve.

On Christmas Day, Washington made a daring move. While his adversaries in New Jersey celebrated the holiday and fell into unguarded sleep, he loaded 2400 men and artillery onto boats at McConkey's Ferry and prepared to cross the Delaware. (*See* Pennsylvania, Washington Crossing Historic Park.) At night, in driving sleet and snow, with many of the men in tattered clothing, they made the perilous crossing and landed in New Jersey, in position to march the nine miles to Trenton.

The British post at Trenton was garrisoned by three regiments of soldiers from the Germanic principality of Hesse-Cassel. These soldiers, numbering about 1500, had been sold into service by their prince. (Renting soldiers from other countries was a common European practice.) The prince received a certain amount per man, plus extra payment for each one killed and for each three wounded. These Hessians had only been in America, on average, for three months; but Washington and his men were well acquainted with Hessian fighters. It was primarily Hessian troops who had taken Fort Washington—one of the worst defeats of the war, with a loss of 458 killed and 2800 Americans captured.

The commander at Trenton was a German, Colonel Johann Gottlieb Rall, a veteran of European conflicts, known for his courage and for his love of gambling and wine. He and his men were not particularly comfortable at this post. They'd been quartered in the houses of Trenton's citizens, some 10 to 15 soldiers to a house, with few creature comforts, except in the case of the commander, of course, who had his own quarters. Many residents had skippered, taking just about everything with them. One Hessian wrote that he and his fellow soldiers "occupied bare walls." In addition, although this area was known to be loyal to

the Crown, every day it seemed there were people shooting at them from ambush.

The Battle of Trenton

As Rall and his disgruntled men settled into their winter quarters, Washington had set his plan in motion. Using his network of spies, he spread the rumor that those who had seen the Americans described them as unprepared and demoralized, and certainly not fit for any kind of military activity. Hearing this, Rall—convinced that the orders of his superiors to fortify the town were an overreaction—did nothing, satisfied that Trenton was safe.

Once Washington's army was across the river, they stopped for a quick meal. By now the first light of the day was coming on. As Elisha Bostwick of the 7th Connecticut regiment wrote, "[A]bout day light a halt was made, at which time his Excellency and aids came near to front on the side of the path where the soldiers stood. I heard his Excellency as he was comeing on speaking to and encourageing the

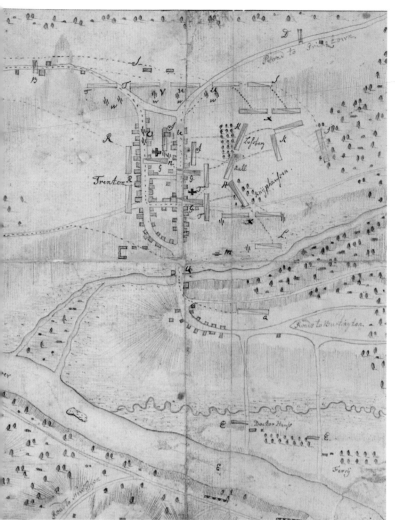

A *contemporary sketch map* of the Battle of Trenton rendered by a Lieutenant Wiederhold of one of the Hessian regiments.

soldiers. The words he spoke as he passed by where I stood and in my hearing were these: 'Soldiers, keep by your officers. For God's sake, keep by your officers!' Spoke in a deep and solemn voice."

The general now divided the force in two, sending John Sullivan to the right. Nathanael Greene would go with Washington to the left. As the troops approached Trenton, they saw a group of American soldiers in the road ahead. These turned out to be a reconnaissance party, sent without Washington's knowledge or permission, which had been ordered to check out the Hessians. They had been spotted, and ended up shooting five of the Hessian guards posted on the outskirts of town.

Washington was furious, convinced that the entire operation had been compromised. Now the Hessians would be on the alert, expecting and prepared for the attack. He needn't have worried. Colonel Rall, when advised of the incident and told that scouting parties hadn't found any signs of soldiers in the area, assumed it was

local farmers being brave. Deciding he would deal with it after the holiday, he declined the suggestion of his officers that extra guards be posted. He also canceled the daily early morning patrol along the Delaware because of the inclement weather.

The sleet and heavy snow had not stopped the Americans, even those who were leaving bloody footprints in the snow because they had only rags for shoes. Three days before, on December 23, the general had ordered his army to form ranks in order to hear Thomas Paine, a soldier now marching alongside them, read from his recently published pamphlet, *The American Crisis.* "These are the times that try men's souls. The summer soldier and the sunshine patriot will, in this crisis, shrink from the service of their country; but he that stands it now, deserves the love and thanks of man and woman. Tyranny, like hell, is not

The Americans' *early morning attack found the Hessians unprepared. Though they fought bravely, the element of surprise carried the day for the Patriot troops.*

easily conquered; yet we have this consolation with us, that the harder the conflict, the more glorious the triumph."

Approaching town, the troops were given orders to break into a trot. Both Greene's and Sullivan's forces burst upon the town almost simultaneously, the attack beginning a little before eight a.m. Caught off guard, the Hessians poured out of the houses and were met with gunfire, bayonets, and cannons. The entire battle would turn out to be one of artillery, bayonet, sword, and spontoon (a short pike), since the flintlocks of the guns on both sides were too wet to spark. The Americans had tried to keep theirs dry during the crossing and on the march, but most to no avail. Even the Hessians who fired got off only one shot off before the sleet and rain made another impossible.

Rall, rousted from sleep, took too long to organize his men in any kind of defensive position. When he finally did lead them in a charge, shouting, "All who are my grenadiers, forward!" he was hit twice and had to be carried to shelter. In a little more than an hour, all three Hessian regiments had surrendered. Colonel Rall and 22 other officers and soldiers were or would soon be dead from their wounds, and almost 1000 were Washington's prisoners. A little more than 400 had escaped.

American losses were two privates and two officers wounded. One of the wounded was James Monroe, a future President of the United States. During the 10-hour crossing, two of the soldiers waiting on the New Jersey side froze to death, the only known American casualties of the battle. The Americans had gained 40 horses, six cannons, 1000 weapons, four wagons of baggage and three of ammunition, 12 drums, and a large supply of rum.

However, half of Washington's forces had been unsuccessful in reaching New Jersey. The plan had called for Colonel John Cadwalader to take 1800 men across at Bordentown. But he had only gotten part of his command across the river before deciding the crossing was too dangerous and calling everyone back to the Pennsylvania side. Brigadier General James Ewing and another 800 men were to have crossed at Trenton Ferry, but he'd been unable to launch any of his boats.

An Extraordinary Leader

Washington's plan to continue immediately to Princeton was thus thwarted. Yet no one would say this was in any way a failure. Washington had regained the confidence of the Congress and of his army. As Bostwick wrote, "[T]hen by the pressing solicitation of his

Excellency a part of those whose time was out consented on a ten dollar bounty to stay six weeks longer, and although desirous as others to return home I engaged to stay that time and made every exertion in my power to make as many of the soldiers stay with me as I could, and quite a number did engage with me who otherwise would have went home."

General Sir William Howe was quoted as saying he found it hard to believe "three old established regiments of a people who made war a profession should lay down their arms to a ragged and undisciplined militia." Howe's confusion was to be expected. He didn't yet have a real understanding of the people his army was fighting, nor of their leader.

Paine had ended his reading that day to the soldiers with these words: "Voltaire has remarked that King William never appeared to full advantage but in difficulties and in action; the same remark may be made on General Washington, for the character fits him. There is a natural firmness in some minds which cannot be unlocked by trifles, but which, when unlocked, discovers a cabinet of fortitude; and I reckon it among those kind of public blessings, which we do not immediately see, that God hath blessed him with uninterrupted health, and given him a mind that can even flourish upon care."

Visiting the Park

Located on the Delaware River just north of I-95, this is the site where Washington's army landed after crossing from Pennsylvania. The 1399-acre park includes a Visitor Center and Museum with an impressive collection of artifacts from the period and from the war, the ferry house Washington occupied that night, and a nature interpretive center.

The Visitor Center/Museum, which opened in 1976 to commemorate the U.S. bicentennial, takes as its theme "Ten Crucial Days," which refers to the events occurring between December 25, 1776, and January 3, 1776. During that period, Washington's army crossed the Delaware and the first Battle of Trenton took place on December 26, followed by the second Battle of Trenton on January 2 and the Battle of Princeton on January 3.

The more than 500 artifacts in the museum, on loan from the Swan Historical Foundation, provide an excellent visual portal through which visitors can experience those 10 days that were crucial to independence. There are two galleries—one specifically about the period between the crossing and the Battle of Princeton, the other covering the period from the French and Indian War through the Revolutionary War. On display are firearms (Pennsylvania long rifles, Brown Bess muskets, a Ferguson rifle, a

The battle at Trenton, *fought in rain and sleet, lasted just over an hour and resulted in the surrender of almost 1000 Hessians. The Americans also captured badly needed weapons, ammunition, and supplies that would serve them well in the months to come.*

Hessian rifle), uniforms (reproductions of Hessian, American, and British uniforms), maps of the period that were used by the Continental Army during the war, a Scottish broadsword with a basketweave hilt, and household and hunting items from the colonial period. Many of the items are rare and some are particularly touching, such as a musket belonging to Second Lieutenant David Watts of the 18th Continental Infantry Regiment. On his silver ownership plate, Watts proudly had engraved "Liberty or Death 1776 DW."

From the museum, visitors can walk along the Continental Lane, a small sunken dirt road used by the army that night, when the lane was a basic farm road between two fields. Part of the army also walked along what is now route 546, meeting the other force at Bear Tavern Road, where they turned south toward the river. At the time of the crossing, this area was part of a large plantation owned by Garret Johnson, so the fields on either side of the roads would have been planted with wheat and corn, or could have been orchards.

The lane leads visitors to the Johnson Ferry House, a Dutch-American farmhouse that was used by Washington and his officers to keep warm while waiting for the entire force to cross the river. Washington apparently made a point of not spending too much time inside, periodically joining the troops outside, encouraging them as they waited in the cold for hours. This is a large house for the period, with five rooms to a floor and a central hearth to keep it warm. The Johnsons had 12 children, in addition to an African American slave and several indentured servants. At the time of the crossing, however, the house was occupied by the Slack family (with only eight children), who were running the ferry service. Costumed interpreters lead visitors through a tour of four of the rooms, two on each floor, where items related to cooking, sewing, and gardening are on display.

From the Johnson Ferry House, visitors walk across a pedestrian bridge above route 29, which cuts through the park. Near the landing site, there's a historical marker denoting the area where Slack ran the ferry service. Even though there were ferry landings four miles south and about four miles north of here,

Washington chose this landing because he hoped it was just far enough away from Trenton to escape detection. Also, this was a very wide landing, which was necessary for the number of boats being used and for the rafts bringing the horses and artillery.

The Interpretive Center, located in the northwest area of the park, displays dioramas that track the changes in the riverbank from the time of the Native Americans through the Revolutionary War era and into modern times.

The park has more than 10 miles of hiking trails. There are also picnic areas located in groves named for some of the leaders of the crossing—Washington, Sullivan, Greene, and Knox. An open-air theater features concerts and theatrical and musical performances during the spring and summer.

Visitor Information

609-737-9304 or
609-737-0623
www.state.nj.us/dep/
  parksandforests/

Hours: The Visitor Center/Museum is open Wednesday through Sunday from 9 a.m. until 4:30 p.m.; closed Monday and Tuesday, state and federal holidays (except Memorial Day, July 4, and Labor Day), and the Wednesday following a Monday or Tuesday holiday. The Johnson Ferry House and the Interpretive Center are open Wednesday through Saturday, from 10 a.m. until noon and from 1 p.m. until 4 p.m., and on Sunday from 1 p.m. until 4 p.m.

Admission: Free. A parking fee is charged Memorial Day weekend to Labor Day on weekends and holidays.

Accessibility: The Visitor Center Museum is accessible. The first floor of the Johnson Ferry House is partially accessible. Call ahead for information about access to other areas of the park.

Special Events: A major commemoration is held each year on Christmas Day. There are celebrations for Washington's Birthday and the Fourth of July. There are lantern tours during the holidays at Johnson Ferry House, plus demonstrations of colonial cooking, gardening, weaving, and lacemaking throughout the season.

Getting There: From I-95 take state route 29 north and follow the signs to the park.

Battlefield Medicine

Take Hog-Lice, half a pound, put them alive into two pound of White Port Wine, and after some Days Infusion strain and press out very hard . . . and filter for Use."

As this popular 18th-century remedy suggests, medicine in the 1700s was rudimentary at best. Yet the average colonial doctor would dazzle his listeners with the advancements being made in understanding the workings of the human body.

Among these was the notion, preached by Dr. Benjamin Rush, the country's first Surgeon General and a signer of the Declaration of Independence, that all disease was caused by nervous tension and could be cured by vigorous purging, a sparse diet, and bleeding until the patient fainted, thus relaxing the blood vessels and alleviating the tension.

In 1775, when the Continental Army's Medical Department was established by Congress, most of the 3500 physicians then practicing in the colonies had learned medicine by apprenticing themselves to practicing physicians, rather than through formal education. This meant that though advancements were being made in understanding diseases, treating those diseases continued to depend on three procedures: purging, bleeding, or blistering.

Purging consisted of cleaning out the patient's system using laxatives to cause diarrhea or emetics to induce vomiting. Bleeding involved cutting a vein in the arm with a lancet to draw as much as several quarts of blood in a two-day period. Blistering meant causing blisters on the skin through use of an irritating solution, which was thought to draw inflammation out of the body.

Not surprisingly, soldiers were as frightened of getting sick as they were of being shot. Estimates of what percentage of American soldiers' deaths during the war resulted from disease run as high as 90 percent (84 percent for the British). Diseases included typhus, malaria, dysentery, pneumonia (called pleurisy), smallpox, scurvy, and syphilis.

The most popular medicines included mercury, opium, and wine. Wine was particularly popular, with red wine used for dysentery, port for fevers, and champagne for nausea and throat ailments. All of these, however, were in short supply throughout the war because of lack of organization, and in fact the organization of an army medical system was still in process when the war ended.

In the beginning soldiers depended on their individual states to provide medical care, but after 1776 a federal system began taking shape. Congress proposed that each hospital have a director, a chief physician, surgeons and surgical assistants, an apothecary, stores keepers, and one nurse for every 10 patients. This was the ideal and was rarely met. Many hospitals were overcrowded and understaffed, incubators for disease, with the "beds" (bundles of straw on the floor) of contagious patients being used repeatedly before being changed, and clean water often unavailable. Plus, there were never enough doctors. Only about 1200 served during the war.

By 1777 large warehouse-type hospitals were being replaced by smaller log buildings with higher ceilings, allowing for greater circulation of fresh air, and with designated areas for contagious patients.

A bright spot in the army's health care plan was the mandate from George Washington that the entire army receive smallpox vaccinations. These vaccinations were considered daring at the time but Washington was a strong advocate of vaccination, especially as smallpox could decimate an army.

A vaccinated soldier had about a one-in-400 chance of dying from the pox, contrasted with a 60-in-400 chance for the unvaccinated.

Anesthetics were uncommon, so a patient usually bit down on a lead bullet during surgery. If the patient had been shot, the surgeon only removed the bullet from the wound if he could reach it with his finger. Once the doctor located the bullet, he used a forceps to remove it. If it was under the skin, then a small incision was made and the bullet removed. Once the bullet was out, the wound was covered with plaster and a bandage instead of being stitched up.

Amputation was very common. After the limb was cut off, the stump was washed with hot tar as a way of sterilizing the wound. (Infections were a major concern following amputation.) Other surgical procedures were followed by a poultice of bread and milk, bleeding, laxatives, and warm baths.

The Battles for New York

The six-month battle for the city of New York, the largest battle of the war, was fiercely fought on the islands of Manhattan and Long Island, in meadows and on hills, in the neighborhoods of Brooklyn, Greenwich, and Harlem, and downtown in the Wall Street area. In the end the Patriots were defeated, but in a real sense the battle was lost by the British, who failed several times to use their navy to its best advantage, who hesitated when they could have overrun the Continental troops, and who lost their chance to capture Washington and end the war.

Preparing for Battle

After their withdrawal from Boston, the British turned their attention to New York and Savannah, primarily because these were Loyalist strongholds and major ports. Controlling the ports meant controlling troop and supply distribution, and impeding aid shipped from the European countries to whom the rebel government had lately applied.

The British also knew that once they had New York, they had the Hudson River, so vital to trade and transportation north into Canada and west into the continent's interior.

Their plan was fairly straightforward. General William Howe would sail from Halifax, Nova Scotia, and would be joined by his brother, Lord Admiral Richard Howe. Together they would capture New York, then General Howe would move north with his army to take Albany, separating New England from the rest of the colonies. General Sir Guy Carleton, governor of Canada, would lead a force from the north, join Howe in Albany, and together they would wipe out any remaining rebellion.

Given the state of George Washington's army at the beginning of 1776, it was a good plan with a more than fair chance of success. But the British waited five months before putting it into action, and Washington used those five months to best advantage. He understood New York's importance as well as the British did.

Washington gave General Charles Lee command of the defense of New York in January of 1776. Lee's strategy was to place 5000 troops on Long Island, primarily on Brooklyn Heights overlooking southern Manhattan. Troops would also be stationed at Kings Bridge, which crossed from the northern end of Manhattan eastward to the Bronx.

Washington began sending troops to the city in early March. Manhattan homes were used as barracks, and the forest areas of wealthy Loyalists were cut down for lumber to build defenses such as a huge earthwork at Brooklyn Heights. Almost 19,000 Continental soldiers and militiamen were assembled by early June. By that time, Lee had been sent to take charge of Charleston, South Carolina, and Washington was left to handle much of the organizational minutiae himself.

On June 25, 1776, General Howe and three ships arrived at Sandy Hook in New Jersey, across from Staten Island, and a month later Admiral Richard Howe arrived with more ships and men. By the end of August, General Howe had nearly 32,000 fully equipped, professional seasoned soldiers and 300 ships with a total of 1200 guns at his disposal. Washington was facing the largest expeditionary force ever to sail from England and likely the largest to sail anywhere in the world until D-day in World War II. Remembered one Continental soldier who saw the armada, "I thought all London was afloat."

For two weeks the British encamped at overwhelmingly Loyalist Staten Island, preparing to cross the mile-wide Narrows and invade the Brooklyn end of Long Island where Fort Hamilton now stands, just off the Verrazano Bridge (*see* New York, Harbor Defense Museum).

Washington had divided his army between Manhattan and Long Island, assuming the British would attack both simultaneously or in near succession. He commanded the Manhattan position and placed General Israel Putnam in charge of Brooklyn Heights. In the farmlands below the Heights, General William Alexander commanded 1600 men in eastern Brooklyn and General John Sullivan 1500 in western Brooklyn.

General Thomas Mifflin and his brigade were at Fort Washington, which was located near the northern end of Manhattan. Other troops were stationed at Governor's Island, off the southern tip of Manhattan, and at various points throughout the city. Altogether Washington had about 20,000 poorly equipped but determined soldiers and militia defending New York.

The Battle of Long Island

On August 22 the British began a night landing on Long Island at Gravesend, eight miles south of Brooklyn Heights. Ten thousand troops under the command of generals Henry Clinton, Charles Cornwallis, and Lord Hugh Percy took up positions in the southern part of Brooklyn between Gravesend and the Flatlands. Washington immediately fortified Brooklyn Heights with more troops from Manhattan.

On the morning of August 27, General Howe sent General James Grant to attack Alexander on the east side. Meanwhile, 5000 Hessian

and 7000 Scottish Highland troops had outflanked Sullivan t the west. The 3100 Continentals and militia would have to stave off the 12,000 coming at them from all sides.

Sullivan and Alexander had placed their sharpshooters in the front lines, thinking their accuracy could stem the tide of a British line. The British took the fire and then, while the riflemen were reloading their single-shot pieces, charged with bayonets. Large sections of the American line were overrun, and Sullivan was captured. By now Washington had come over from

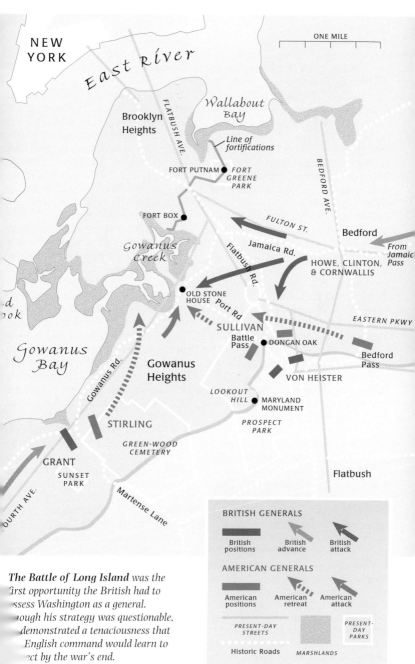

The Battle of Long Island *was the first opportunity the British had to assess Washington as a general. Although his strategy was questionable, [h]e demonstrated a tenaciousness that [the] English command would learn to [resp]ect by the war's end.*

...anhattan to Brooklyn Heights.

Alexander, meanwhile, was con-...ending with Grant. Fighting with his ...regiments were William Smallwood's Marylanders and John Haslet's Delaware regiment. The Americans numbered about 1700 and the British Grenadiers and the Scottish Black Watch together about 5000.

Realizing the futility of continuing the fight, Alexander organized a retreat down Gowanus Road toward the Freek's Mill Bridge, fighting the British all the way, doing what they could to retard the British advance. Approaching the bridge, he saw that other retreating Americans were being fired on by cannons, under the command of General Cornwallis, stationed at the Vechte House (*see* New York, Old Stone House Historic Interpretation Center). Alexander ordered the majority of his men to proceed with the retreat, while he, Smallwood's, and Haslet's regiments attacked the house.

They struck six times before finally capturing it, only to be overrun by freshly arrived Hessian troops. Many of the Americans were killed and many were captured, including Alexander; but their sacrifice allowed large numbers of Patriot forces to escape to Brooklyn Heights. Haslet and Smallwood escaped to continue the fight for New York.

A letter from an unidentified Patriot soldier, written days later, reported that General Washington, viewing the battle from Brooklyn Heights, "wrung his hands and cried out, 'Good God! What brave fellows I must this day lose!'"

In this battle, also known as the Battle of Brooklyn, the Americans estimated their losses at 1000. The bodies were strewn across the forests and fields of Brooklyn, many eventually buried where they fell.

Escape from Brooklyn Heights

Now the British hesitated. The Patriots were entrenched above them on several Brooklyn high points, some at Brooklyn Heights, others at Fort Putnam—now Fort Greene Park (*see* New York, Prison Ship Martyrs Monument). With their overwhelming numbers, the British could have rushed the Heights, but Howe had suffered huge losses attacking Breed's Hill in Boston, and he wouldn't chance making that mistake again. He dug in and waited.

Washington realized it was only a matter of time, and a change in the

direction of the wind, before British ships could begin bombarding his positions from the Hudson or bring more troops around to outflank him. He directed a unit from Marblehead, Massachusetts, to gather enough boats to ferry the Americans across the East River to Manhattan. During the nights of August 29 and 30, thousands of Continentals and militia evacuated across the river, with cover provided first by a storm and then by fog. The British didn't realize what was happening until the morning of the 31st.

A Proposal of Peace

Having won the Battle of Brooklyn, Admiral Lord Howe looked for a peace settlement with the rebellious Americans. He had approached General Washington in July before the battle, but that effort seemed doomed before a meeting even took place.

Howe now wrote a letter requesting a meeting, addressing it to "George Washington, Esq., New York." Washington's officers told the bearer of the missive that there was no person in their army with that address. After readdressing Washington as "General," Howe's representative was granted a meeting, but Washington declined to disband his army and go home.

Howe and his brother had decisively beaten the general and that he felt, warranted a second look a working out some kind of negotiate peace. Accordingly, he sent an in... tation to the Congress that rep... sentatives be sent to New York f...

The bravery of the Maryland and Delaware regiments who sacrificed themselves in a delaying action at the Old Stone House is commemorated annually.

meeting. On September 11, 1776, Lord Howe met with Benjamin Franklin, John Adams, and Edward Rutledge in a home on Staten Island owned by Loyalist Christopher Billopp (*see* New York, Conference House).

After enjoying a fine meal, the four gentlemen, with their secretaries, began the discussion on the friendliest of terms. Finally Lord Howe said, "It is desirable to put a stop to these ruinous extremities, as well for the sake of our country as yours—when an American falls, England feels it. Is there no way of treading back this step of Independency, and opening the door to a full discussion?"

The Declaration of Independence, adopted just two months prior, was the sticking point, and remained so throughout the three-hour discussion. No agreement could be reached and the party broke up, amicably.

The Fight for Manhattan

On September 3, Nathanael Greene wrote a letter to Washington, urging the general to abandon New York and burn it to the ground. He and others reasoned that this would be a tremendous hardship on the British, who expected to use it as their base and as quarters for the approaching winter, and who had to house hundreds of Loyalists who were arriving almost every day.

On September 8, Washington wrote to the President of the Congress explaining his decision to evacuate the city. He was aware that he would be subject to reproach for his decision. But to attack the British, or even to await an attack, likely meant the destruction of his army, and this Washington could not condone. His goal was to "protract the War if Possible; I cannot think it safe or wise to adopt a different System."

While Washington made plans to depart, on September 15 the British sailed up the Hudson and East rivers, flanking Manhattan. Eighty-five flatboats from dozens of warships began landing troops at Kip's Bay on the East River, at present-day 34th Street. Howe was anticipating Washington's decision to evacuate the city and was determined to trap him before that could be achieved. He issued an order that his men rely on their bayonets, as these had caused panic among the militia and soldiers in the previous battle.

The Patriot militiamen nearest the landing did indeed flee into downtown Manhattan at the first British charge, but the bombardment from the ships also encouraged their haste. Even Washington, riding south from Harlem Heights, couldn't stop the run of soldiers, and he himself just barely escaped the first wave of Hessians.

The British, instead of pressing their advantage, once again dug in, this time in what is today the Murray Hill area. Washington pulled all his troops behind fortifications at Harlem Heights.

On the morning of September 16,

Nathan Hale

"This day, one Hale, in New York, on suspicion of being a spy was taken up and dragged without ceremony to the execution post, and hung up. . . ." This newspaper account of the death of Nathan Hale is as terse as was his treatment by the British. Hale, a 21-year-old Connecticut schoolteacher, had volunteered to spy on British troop movements in New York. From September 12 until September 21, the large, red-haired Hale had moved about the town taking notes, apparently undetected until he was betrayed to a British commander—some said by his cousin Samuel. A September 22 entry in General Howe's Orderly Book tells it all: "A spy from the enemy by his own full confession, apprehended last night, was executed this day at 11 o'clock in front of the Artillery Park." Hale was hanged without benefit of trial, and also without benefit of clergy, though he made the request several hours before he died. Hale's famous last words—"I regret I have but one life to give for my country"—were not reported until some years later.

a group of Connecticut Rangers advancing down from Harlem Heights was met by the Black Watch Highland troops. A brief fight ensued, and the Rangers retreated. The Highlanders thought the Rangers were the vanguard of a full retreat. Loudly jeering as they pursued the Rangers up the heights, the Highlanders were met with a strong volley and retreated across a wheat field at what is now Barnard College at 116th Street and Broadway.

Cornwallis's arrival with reinforcements prevented Washington from pressing his advantage, but this still felt like a major victory to the Americans. It was the first time in the battle for New York that the British had retreated, and the Americans enjoyed the unusual sensation of victory.

The armies now lay within two miles of each other. Washington was still planning an evacuation, but the conditions had to be right. He wouldn't chance losing his army while trying to save it.

The New York Fire

On the night of September 20, a fire broke out on a wharf near the tip of Manhattan Island. A strong southerly breeze quickly spread the fire north and west. Fire companies were undermanned and couldn't get water to the houses quickly enough. Nearly 500 houses were destroyed, as well as Trinity Church.

The cause of the fire was never determined, but the British blamed the Americans. Ranted Howe in a letter to England, "[A] most horrid attempt was made by a number of wretches to burn the town of New York. . . . The destruction is computed to be about one-quarter of the town."

It was a blow to the British, who now had to spend manpower and resources constructing housing for their soldiers and for the displaced populace, including refugee Loyalists. Washington's reported reaction to the fire was, "Providence, or some good honest fellow, has done more for us than we were disposed to do for ourselves."

The Battle of White Plains

On October 18, Washington moved his army north to the isolated village of White Plains. Howe waited until October 22 and the arrival of a reinforcement of Hessians before confronting Washington's forces in a series of skirmishes. More than 25,000 men took part by the time of the major battle on October 28 at White Plains. Washington was entrenched on high ground in the village. When the British tried to flank Washington at Chatterton's Hill, they were pushed back by heavy artillery fire from Captain Alexander Hamilton's cannons. The hill was lost, however, when Hessians attacked from the other side. Howe captured Chatterton's Hill but waited for more reinforcements before attacking Washington head on. The delay allowed Washington to retreat north to New Castle.

Surrender of Fort Washington

Washington now expected Howe to follow him north. Instead, Howe turned south toward Fort Washington. The reason for the turnaround was discovered after the war: An American deserter, William Demont, had turned the plans of the fort over to the British.

Washington previously had considered abandoning the fort, situated on the northern end of Manhattan

Island, but had been advised by Nathanael Greene that the site was in no danger and could prove useful. Almost 3000 Patriot soldiers garrisoned the fort.

Howe sent a full force of Hessians and British Regulars against Fort Washington. The fort's commander, Robert Magaw, put up a good fight but by nightfall decided that further loss of life was useless. He surrendered, and Washington's army lost 2800 men. It was one of the largest Patriot surrenders of the war.

The surrender of Fort Washington was the final act of the battle for New York. This had been the first real test of Washington as commander of this new country's army. He had made some mistakes, but he was still able to retreat into New Jersey with part of his army still intact. He hadn't been captured, nor had the Patriot army collapsed, which had been the expectations of the British from the start.

Still, the loss of New York was a terrible blow to the Patriot cause. The city would remain in British hands until the end of the war.

Harbor Defense Museum

The Harbor Defense Museum is located on the grounds of the United States Army garrison of Fort Hamilton, on the tip of Long Island near the Verrazano Narrows Bridge, where the British first landed on August 22.

The experiences of the Revolutionary War and the War of 1812 convinced a young United States that its coastal defenses were lacking. Beginning in the 1820s, a series of fortifications was built along the American coast. Fort Hamilton was begun in 1825 and completed in 1831. It continues today as an active military base.

As part of Fort Hamilton's defenses against an assault by land, a dry moat was designed around the fort to trap attacking forces and fire on them from above. The museum is located in the fort's *caponier* (from the French for "chicken coop"), which is a battery built in the ditch of a fort from which the enemy can be fired upon. This *caponier* is thought to be the nation's oldest and among its finest examples, and is included in the National Register of Historic Places.

Visiting the Museum

The focus of this museum, the only military museum in the city, is the history and evolution of New York City's harbor defenses. A new exhibit centers on the Battle of Brooklyn (Battle of Long Island), with period muskets displayed, as well as reproductions of the uniforms of those who fought at the Battle of Brooklyn. There is also a diorama of the battle and maps contrasting what the area looked like in 1776 with how it looks today.

In addition to its Revolutionary War displays, the museum also has exhibits related to the Civil War, World War II, and the Korean War, as well as military items from European wars, such as 16th-century body armor.

Tours are given daily, or visitors can tour the museum at their own pace.

Visitor Information

718-630-4349 or 4306
www.hamilton.army.mil/ and
www.harbordefensemuseum.com/
Hours: Open from 10 a.m. until 4 p.m. Monday through Friday, and 10 a.m. until 2 p.m. on Saturday.
Admission: Free, but donations are welcome.
Accessibility: The Revolutionary War exhibit will be accessible.
Special Events: Periodic lectures and presentations throughout the year. A reference library and archives are available by appointment only.
Getting There: The main entrance to the fort is at the intersection of Fort Hamilton Parkway and 101st Street. Visitors must present a picture I.D. to enter the fort. Because of changing levels of security, it's best to check with the museum 4 hours in advance of a visit, or e-mail to visitorpass@hamilton.army.mil.

By bus: B-8 to 4th Avenue and 94th Street, B16 and B37 to 4th Avenue and 100th Street, or the B-63 to 4th Avenue and Shore Road. From 4th Avenue, walk to 101st Street and then one block east to Fort Hamilton Parkway.

By train: R Train to 95th Street, from there to 4th Avenue and proceed as above.

By car: Take the Gowanus Parkway to the last exit before the Verrazano Narrows Bridge, 92nd Street & Fort Hamilton. At the second light make a right. Proceed one light and turn right on Fort Hamilton Parkway. Go to the end, which is 101st Street, and make a left under the Verrazano Bridge into the post.

From the Belt Parkway take exit 2,

*A **tabletop model** at the Old Stone House shows British and American troop placements in and surrounding the Vechte house during the Battle of Brooklyn.*

then take 4th Avenue. After 3 lights, make a right onto 100th Street. Go one block and turn right on Fort Hamilton Parkway. At the end, make a left under the bridge.

From New Jersey take the Verrazano Narrows Bridge to Brooklyn and get off at the first exit (92nd Street). Make a left at the light. Go 2 lights and turn left on Fort Hamilton Parkway. At the end, make a left under the bridge.

Old Stone House Historic Interpretive Center

This substantial Dutch-style old stone house, recreated from the original stones, has come to symbolize the valor of the Patriots who fought in the Battle of Brooklyn in August of 1776.

The original fieldstone and brick structure was built in 1699 by the Vechte family, who farmed the surrounding rich bottomland. During the Battle of Brooklyn (also known as the Battle of Long Island), it was a stronghold for the British, who used its cover to bombard the Americans retreating across Gowanus Creek. Maryland and Delaware troops sacrificed themselves to distract the British so their fellow Patriots could escape.

During the war, the family lived under the British occupation, continuing to farm, harvest oysters in Gowanus Creek, and ferry their produce to markets in Manhattan. Following the war, the house was sold to the Cortelyou family, whose generations lived there until the 1850s.

After that it was bought by a railroad developer, and in the early 1880s was used as the club house of the Brooklyn team of the National Base Ball League, later known as the Brooklyn Dodgers. By the late 1880s it had been demolished and covered with landfill.

Recognizing the significance of the house, the city excavated it in 1930 and reconstructed it from many of the original bricks and stones, about 50 feet from where it originally stood. By the mid-1980s the reconstructed house had deteriorated but was rescued by the First Battle Revival Alliance, which was formed to renovate the house and make it a center of commemoration for the Battle of Brooklyn.

In 1997 the house was reopened as part of the Parks Department's Historic House Trust.

Visiting the House

The exhibit space is on the first floor of the house, while the second floor is used for special events.

A large tabletop model of the battle at the Vechte house is an excellent visual aid to understanding the positions of the British and Americans. Wall panels provide an explanation of the entire Battle of Brooklyn, as well as interesting details about the lives of the soldiers, such as what their uniforms were made of and what was included in a soldier's kit.

There are also a number of maps that show aspects of the battle, and the evolution of Brooklyn from the Dutch period to the present day.

Visitor Information

718-768-3195
www.oldstonehouse.org
Hours: Open Saturday and Sunday

from 11 a.m. until 4 p.m.

Admission: A small donation is suggested; children under 12 are free.

Accessibility: The house is accessible.

Special Events: The Center coordinates one of the largest annual commemorations of the American Revolution in the country. Week-long events during the month of August include memorial services, guided walking tours, and workshops. There are also lectures, concerts, and various changing exhibits throughout the year.

Getting There: Located between 3rd and 4th streets and between 4th and 5th avenues in the Park Slope/Gowanus neighborhood of Brooklyn.

By bus: B71, 75, or 77 to 5th Avenue and 9th Street. By subway: F, M, or R line to the 9th Street/4th Avenue station.

Conference House

A National and New York City Historic Landmark, this 17th-century house is the oldest manor house still surviving in New York City.

Located in Conference House Park on Staten Island, overlooking Raritan Bay, the Conference House commemorates the meeting that took place here in September 1776 between Lord Howe and representatives of the U.S. Congress.

This graceful fieldstone house was built by Captain Christopher Billopp of the Royal Navy, who was granted a title to 932 acres of land on the island in 1674. Construction of the house was begun sometime before 1680.

Legend has it that Staten Island is part of New York instead of New Jersey because of Billopp. When the British took possession of what was then New Amsterdam, in 1664, the proprietors of New York and New Jersey both claimed the island as theirs. The Duke of York decided to settle the issue by agreeing to award the island to that province whose representative could circumnavigate it in less than 24 hours. Billopp won the competition for New York.

The family fortunes took a downturn during the Revolutionary War, when Colonel Christopher Billopp, a descendant of the captain, declared himself a Loyalist. His property was confiscated by the state of New York, and he and his family were forced to emigrate to Nova Scotia.

In 1776 the British landed on Staten Island, preparatory to invading Long Island and Manhattan. Following their victory at the Battle of Brooklyn in August, Admiral Lord Richard Howe hosted a peace conference here, meeting with Benjamin Franklin, John Adams, and Edward Rutledge. The meeting was cordial but unsuccessful.

Following the war, the house was used as a private residence, a public inn, and a factory, with structural changes made as necessary.

In the early 1920s when the house was scheduled to be razed, The Conference House Association was formed to preserve the house and share its history with the public.

Visiting the House

"In approaching New York from Philadelphia by the Amboy route, few objects are more striking to the traveler's eye than a high, ancient-looking stone edifice situated near the water on the extreme west end of Staten Island. This is the old Billopp House at Bentley."

Though the surrounding area has changed somewhat since this description was written in 1846, the house itself remains an impressive and graceful structure. Furnished with 18th-century period pieces, the Billopp house has been restored to what it probably looked like on September 11, 1776.

Guided tours by costumed docents take visitors through two floors of family rooms and bedrooms, and down to the 17th-century kitchen in the basement. The surrounding waterfront park is a pleasant place for a stroll or a picnic.

Visitor Information

718-984-0415
www.theconferencehouse.org

Hours: April through mid-December, Friday through Sunday, 1 p.m. until 4 p.m.

Admission: There is a minimal charge.

Accessibility: The house is not handicapped accessible.

Special Events: Crafts workshops and family activities are held throughout the year.

Getting There: From the New Jersey Turnpike or Brooklyn, take I-278 to the Hylan Boulevard exit, just west of the Verrazano Narrows Bridge. Take Hylan Boulevard south toward the end of Staten Island. At the end of Hylan Boulevard, turn right onto Saterlee Street. The Conference House is 100 feet on the left.

Federal Hall National Memorial

This majestic Greek Revival building in New York City commemorates the extraordinary history that occurred on this site. It was built in 1842 as the U.S. Customs House.

The Original Building

The first building on this site, begun in 1699, was New York's city hall, which also served as the capitol of the Royal Province of New York. At that time, New York had only been under British rule for about forty years. Previously it was a Dutch colony named New Amsterdam. A small port town with a population of less than 5000, New York's greatest asset was its outstanding natural 11,000-acre harbor. Located at the mouth of the Hudson River, the harbor could accommodate all the navies then in existence, and had the added advantage of almost always being ice free, even in the dead of winter.

When completed in 1703, City Hall was one of only a few buildings at the tip of Manhattan. The two-story red brick capitol, with its tall chimneys and a cupola centered between the two wings on either end, had a library, government offices, meeting rooms for the Governor's Council and the New York Assembly, jail cells, and courtrooms.

The Zenger Trial

It was in one of those courtrooms in 1735 that John Peter Zenger was tried for libel when his newspaper exposed government corruption. In the 1730s, the royal governor of New York was William Cosby, a politician generally agreed to have been spiteful, corrupt, and heavy-handed in his rule. The German-born Zenger published the New York *Weekly Journal*, which from its first issue in November 1733 aimed to uncover every dubious act or outright bit of chicanery by the governor.

In 1734, Zenger was arrested on a charge of seditious libel and put in one of the jails here, where he stayed for nine months awaiting trial. When the trial finally began on August 4, his lawyer, Andrew Hamilton, admitted that Zenger had published the statements in question. But he based his defense on the premise that what Zenger had printed was the truth, and that truthful criticism of a government could not be libelous.

Chief Justice James De Lancey (*see* New York, Fraunces Tavern Museum) instructed the jury that according to English law, criticizing the governing power was dangerously libelous and could not be justified. "The jury may find that Zenger printed and published those papers, and leave to the Court to judge whether they are libelous."

Hamilton argued otherwise—that the true power was with the jury, that "they have the right beyond all dispute to determine both the law and the fact. . . . Leaving it to judgment of the court whether the words are libelous or not in effect renders juries useless (to say no worse) in many cases."

Hamilton gave a summation that defended freedom of the press as strongly as it did his client, beginning with "It is natural, . . . it is a right, which all free men claim . . . to remonstrate against the abuses of power in the strongest terms, to put their neighbors upon their guard against the craft or open violence of men in authority."

De Lancey followed Hamilton's spirited summation by, in effect, instructing the jury to disregard it. The jurors chose otherwise. Deliberating only a short time, they returned with a verdict of "not guilty." Zenger was released the next day.

Zenger's acquittal established the principle of a free press in the colonies and paved the way for the vital role the press played in the making of a revolution. Newspapers, brochures, broadsides, and pamphlets created support for the revolution and created a network of communication integral to unifying the colonies.

When the Bill of Rights was framed in 1789, in this same building, freedom of the press was guaranteed under the first amendment to the U.S. Constitution.

The Hall's Role in Revolution

In some of the colonies, the capitol building was considered the venue of the Crown, but New York's city hall was viewed as the property of the people. It often happened that while the king's business was being carried out in one part of the building, the people's business, perhaps contrary to that of the king's, was being enacted in another.

In 1765 the Stamp Act Congress, with representatives from nine of the colonies, met in session here for 19 days. It produced the Declaration of Rights and Grievances, one of the earliest formal statements of unified protest from the colonies against British policy. When New York's supply of stamps arrived, the royal governor, Henry Moore, had them stored in his military headquarters. When the city's Patriot leaders objected that the tax papers should be released to their safekeeping, the governor acquiesced and the stamps were transferred here. At the same time, irate New Yorkers were boycotting British goods and gamely imbibing a tea substitute of brewed sassafras bark and sage. New York had a "tea party," with tea being tossed into the harbor, but it didn't gain the notoriety of Boston's fete.

From April 1775 until the defeat of George Washington's forces in the fall of 1776, New York's Provincial Congress met here, while the royal governor William Tryon (*see* North Carolina, Tryon Palace Historic Sites and Gardens) and his council met on ships in the harbor.

During the British occupation of New York, from 1776 until 1783 and the war's end, City Hall served as British headquarters. In 1783, following the signing of the Treaty of Paris and the British evacuation of New York, George Washington and his troops returned to the city. Washington said farewell to his officers at Fraunces Tavern (*see* New York, Fraunces Tavern Museum) and sailed from New York Harbor, bound for home.

In January 1785 the United States in Congress Assembled—as the Continental Congress was now designated—convened its first session here and over the next few years took the first halting steps toward establishing a national government.

With the ratification of the Constitution in 1788, New York City became the capital of the United States, and a newly renovated City Hall became Federal Hall. It was here that George Washington took the oath of office as first U.S. President in 1789, here that the U.S. Congress first met, and here that the Bill of Rights was written.

New York had been chosen as the U.S. capital over Philadelphia and Boston largely because of its quality of living. It was more fun here. Philadelphia had no theater and Boston was revolutionary only in its politics. But in 1790, politics sent the federal government to

Philadelphia, and in 1812 Federal Hall was demolished.

The current building, constructed as the U.S. Customs House in 1842, continued to house various federal agencies until 1955, when it was designated the Federal Hall National Memorial.

Visiting Federal Hall
Visitors can get some sense of what this building and the 18th-century City Hall were like, first in a 10-minute film and then in an exhibit featuring models of both buildings at various times during their history.

The adjacent "Freedom of the Press" exhibit focuses on the precedent-setting Zenger trial and the right of a free press. The exhibit also highlights the tremendous influence a free press had on the spread of revolutionary spirit in America.

"George Washington's Inauguration" focuses on April 30, 1789, when the first U.S. President took the oath of office. Standing on an exterior balcony in front of a large crowd that filled the streets below, Washington repeated the oath to "preserve, protect, and defend the Constitution of the United States." Adding his own "so help me God" and kissing the Bible, he began a tradition carried on to this day.

Also exhibited are a piece of brownstone on which Washington stood while taking the oath, and a railing from the wrought-iron balcony.

Ranger-led tours of the building, which provide a wealth of colorful details, are scheduled throughout the day, or visitors may take a self-guided tour.

Visitor Information
212-825-6888
www.nps.gov/feha
Hours: Monday through Friday, 9 a.m. until 5 p.m.; closed national holidays.
Admission: Free.
Accessibility: Handicapped accessible.
Special Events: Occasionally scheduled. Check the Web site or call 212-825-6888.
Getting There: Subway: #4 and #5 subway trains stop at Wall Street and Broadway, one block west of Federal Hall.

Bus: By route M-15 on Water Street, 3 blocks to the east. Driving is not recommended due to limited and expensive parking.

Fraunces Tavern Museum

Although Fraunces Tavern is known primarily as the site of George Washington's farewell to his officers in 1783, this building, the oldest in Manhattan, has a rich history dating to New York City's colonial period.

The tavern on the first floor continues to function as a popular Financial District restaurant. The Fraunces Tavern Museum on the floor above and in four adjacent 19th-century buildings provides a fascinating glimpse into the city's colonial and Revolutionary War period.

History of the Tavern

This was originally a fashionable townhouse, built in 1719 by Stephen (Etienne) De Lancey, a Frenchman who came to New York in his 20s and became one of the city's wealthiest merchants.

The De Lancey family figured prominently in the city's political and judicial life during the colonial period. De Lancey's son James served on the provincial supreme court and was the presiding judge at John Peter Zenger's trial (*see* New York, Federal Hall National Memorial). De Lancey's grandson, also James, was a leading Loyalist and one of the few compensated for loss of property after the war. In 1734, Stephen De Lancey moved to Broadway, and for a time this building was used for offices and as a warehouse.

When Stephen died in 1741, the property passed to his son James, who sold it to Samuel Fraunces in 1762. Fraunces, thought to be a Haitian of French descent, had arrived in New York seven years earlier and by 1762 had established himself as one of the city's leading innkeepers. He also operated a wax museum in a large mansion across town that contained 70 historical and biblical miniature wax figures.

By 1770, Fraunces Tavern was a popular gathering place, attracting prominent members of the independence movement, of which Fraunces was openly supportive. The Sons of Liberty met here regularly, and once the war began and the Continental Army was headquartered in New York City, General Washington became a regular patron.

When the British occupied New York, Fraunces supposedly moved his family to Elizabeth, New Jersey, and joined the Continental Army. In 1778 he was brought back to New York by the British and served as chef for a British general. It's said that Fraunces took advantage of this position to give what aid he could to Patriot prisoners held in city jails and that he spied on the British for Washington. It is known that Fraunces was later awarded 200 pounds by the Congress for his services during the war.

In November 1783, the last of the British army evacuated the city. George Washington and 600 troops paraded from upper Manhattan to this downtown tavern, where Washington and city, state, and national officials enjoyed a celebratory dinner on what became known as Evacuation Day.

Following the war, Fraunces became the first steward of the first President of the United States. The tavern, which Fraunces sold in 1785, was used for offices by the Congress for a time, and later housed the U.S. Department of Foreign Affairs (State Department), the Treasury Department, and the War Department.

When President Washington and the federal government moved to Philadelphia in 1790, Fraunces went with them, continuing to serve as the President's steward until 1794, when he opened a restaurant. A year later he died.

In acknowledging Fraunces's efforts for the cause, George Washington once wrote to him, "You have invariably through the most trying times maintained a constant friendship and attention to the cause of our country and its independence and freedom." Fraunces is buried in an unmarked grave in St. Peter's Episcopal Church Cemetery in Philadelphia.

By the turn of the 20th century, Fraunces Tavern had suffered numerous fires and was slated for demolition. It was rescued by the Sons of the Revolution, an organization founded in 1876 by descendants of those who fought in the war or otherwise placed themselves at risk for the Patriot cause. The members hired architect Leonard Mersereau to design and oversee the restoration of the building, making this one of the earliest historic restoration projects in the country.

The restored Fraunces Tavern opened in 1907, with much the same arrangement as today—a restaurant on the first floor and a museum upstairs. Later, four of the adjacent buildings were bought and

Fraunces Tavern has stood at the corner of Pearl and Broad streets since 1719, when it was the home of Stephen De Lancey, one of New York's wealthiest merchants.

consolidated into the museum complex that now serves as the Fraunces Tavern Museum.

Visiting the Museum

Through its lecture series, changing exhibits, and family events, this museum showcases the city's Revolutionary War history in ways that appeal to both the casual visitor and the avid historian.

A 15-minute video shown in the Orientation Center on the second floor acquaints visitors with a history of the tavern. Also on the second floor is what is now called the Long Room, where George Washington said farewell to his senior officers "with a heart full of love and grati-

tude" on December 4, 1783. This room, which is decorated and furnished with period pieces suitable to an upscale 1700s public dining room, was the scene of many private dinners hosted by General Washington.

Adjacent to the Long Room is the Elizabeth and Stanley DeForest Scott Washington Portrait Gallery, which displays a delightful collection of portraits of the Father of His Country. Some are fanciful, others respectful, all present an interesting perspective on how the great man was viewed in his own and the following century worldwide.

Beside the Portrait Gallery is the Clinton Room, named for George Clinton, the first American governor of New York. Clinton's sword hangs over the fireplace. It was Clinton who hosted the first Evacuation Day celebration here at the Tavern in 1783. Many of the guests were probably served in this room. The room has been decorated in the style of a 19th-century private dining room. Its

Sons of the Revolution

The Sons of the Revolution was founded in 1876 by descendants of those who fought in the war or otherwise placed themselves at risk for the Patriot cause. Among its major projects in New York City have been the restoration of Fraunces Tavern, erection of a statue honoring Nathan Hale in City Hall Park, and the placement of commemorative plaques and memorials relevant to the war in sites around the city.

George Washington was a regular patron of Fraunces Tavern when his troops were quartered in New York. At the end of the war he chose the Long Room to host a farewell dinner for his senior officers.

mural wallpaper, which is original to the Mersereau restoration, depicts scenes from the Revolutionary War. A replica of this wallpaper was chosen by First Lady Jacqueline Kennedy for one of the public rooms in the White House in the early 1960s.

The Warren Jennings McEntee Gallery on the third floor is devoted to a history of the Sons of the Revolution and to the organization's collection of Revolutionary War and period artifacts and documents. A British army canteen, an engraved powder horn, a bugle, and a pistol owned by Lafayette are among the objects displayed.

The Loeb Gallery features an exhibit on the heroes of the war. The Mesick Gallery has changing exhibits dealing with numerous aspects of the colonial period as well as the war, such as medicine and the healing arts in colonial America, the role of women, and New York City under British occupation.

The Davis Gallery displays the organization's impressive collection of flags and is known informally as the Flag Gallery. Among the fifty flags exhibited here are a rare late-18th-century Stars and Stripes.

Visitor Information

212-425-1778

www.frauncestavernmuseum.org

Hours: Open Tuesday, Wednesday, and Friday, 10 a.m. until 5 p.m.; Thursday, 10 a.m. until 7 p.m.; Saturday, 11 a.m. until 5 p.m.; closed Sunday and Monday, Thanksgiving Day, December 25, and January 1.

Admission: There is a moderate charge for adults, minimal for students to age 18 and for seniors; children 6 and under are free.

Accessibility: Visitors with special needs should call ahead. The interior of the museum and its galleries is accessible.

Special Events: There are lunchtime and evening lecture series and Family Saturdays, in addition to Open House on George Washington's birthday, Flag Day (June 14), and the Fourth of July.

Getting There: The museum is at the corner of Pearl and Broad Streets in the city's Financial District.

By car: Take Franklin D. Roosevelt Drive to the Battery Park/South Ferry exit.

By bus: M6 or M15 to South Ferry.

By subway: routes 4 or 5 to Bowling Green, routes 1 or 2 to Wall Street, routes N or R to Whitehall Street.

Prison Ship Martyrs Monument

This is the largest Revolutionary War burial site in the country. Located in the center of Fort Greene Park in Brooklyn, the Prison Ship Martyrs Monument honors American prisoners of war who perished on the British prison ships moored in the East River off Long Island from 1776 until 1782.

History of the Prison Ships

There are no reliable statistics on the number of prisoners taken by both sides during the war. Neither side was adequately prepared to deal with them, and the first problem they faced was one of definition.

The British were reluctant at first to recognize Patriot soldiers as prisoners of war (POWs) because the British government did not recognize the United States as a legitimate nation. The Patriots were reluctant to give captured Loyalists POW status because Loyalists were considered traitors, not soldiers of another nation. Even sorting out these issues didn't mean the problem of prisoners was sufficiently addressed.

Prisoners held by both sides during the war died from disease and harsh living conditions. Some suffered horribly. Among these were British soldiers imprisoned in abandoned mines in New England and Americans captured on privateering vessels and thrown into British prisons.

There were exceptions. Some prisoners were exchanged and some were paroled (released after taking an oath not to fight again in the war); some escaped, with little effort at pursuit by their captors; and some ended up in local jails or barracks in fairly comfortable situations.

It is generally agreed, however, that the decommissioned British ships in New York waters used as prisons were unequaled in the rankness of their conditions and the misery of their prisoners.

Excerpts from the December 1776 journal of William Slade, a young Connecticut boy, cryptically relate the lack of humanity shown American prisoners by their British captors: "No fire. Suffer with cold and hunger. We are treated worse than cattle and hogs. . . . One dies almost every day . . . People gone bad with the pox [smallpox]. . . . Bisd. [biscuits] At noon rice and cornmeal. About 30 sick . . . Last night was spent in dying grones and cries. . . . now gro poorly."

Slade, who survived, perhaps fared a bit better for not having been on the *Jersey*, the most notorious of the prison ships. She was nicknamed Hell Afloat by her inmates, which often numbered near a thousand.

According to Ebenezer Fox, who also survived, "The Jersey, from her size and lying near the shore, was embedded in the mud and I do not recollect seeing her afloat during the whole time I was a prisoner. All the filth which accumulated among . . . a thousand men [was] thrown overboard [and] would remain there until carried away by the tide. The impurity of the water may be easily conceived and in this water our meat was boiled." These conditions were endured not only by men but also by women and children.

Over a period of six years, some 11,500 prisoners died aboard the *Jersey* and other British ships. Thousands of these prisoners were only a few miles from their families on land. Their bodies were buried in shallow mass graves along nearby shorelines. Eventually, with the tides washing up on the shores, the skeletons of the dead were exposed and broken.

Building the Monument

Following the war, concerned citizens who had collected the bones wanted to rebury them beneath a monument honoring these Patriot martyrs. A strapped Congress refused to fund the project, and it was not until the early 1800s that enough money had been raised to erect the first Prison Ship Martyrs Monument. In 1806 the bone fragments, in coffins, were enclosed in a vault located on Hudson Street in Brooklyn, near what is now called Vinegar Hill. On the cornerstone was inscribed, "In the name of the spirits of the departed free, Sacred to the memory of that portion of . . . seamen, soldiers and citizens who perished in the cause of liberty and their country on board the prison ships of the British."

The entombment was attended by a number of dignitaries, including DeWitt Clinton, mayor of New York and nephew of George Clinton, who had fought with Washington and was a member of the Continental Congress. Unfortunately, the vault was made of wood, and it decayed with age.

In the 1840s, the poet Walt Whitman, as editor of the Brooklyn

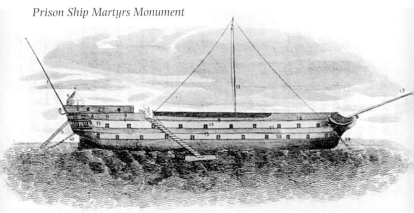

HMS Jersey *was used as a prison ship for captured Continental Army soldiers. Thousands of prisoners were crammed belowdecks where there was virtually no natural light or fresh air and few provisions for the sick. As many as eight corpses a day were buried from the* Jersey *alone before the British surrendered at Yorktown.*

Daily Eagle, called for the creation of a public park in Brooklyn on the site of what had been the military post Fort Putnam. During the War of 1812, the fort was named Fort Greene, in honor of Nathanael Greene who supervised its construction in 1776. In 1847, Washington Park was established on the site. It was renamed Fort Greene Park in 1897.

In 1855 the Martyrs Monument Association was formed, to erect a suitable monument to those who had died in the prison ships. In 1873 a large stone crypt was built in the park. The bone fragments were taken from the old wooden vault and reinterred in the crypt.

In 1898 the Prison Ship Monument Association hired the prestigious architectural firm of McKim, Meade and White to design a monument to be erected near the crypt. Because of the park's significance in the Battle of Brooklyn (Long Island), the park had been the site of patriotic demonstrations over the years, specifically in the park's center in an area called "The Saluting Ground." An adjacent hillside was chosen for the monument, which was designed by Stanford White in 1905 and unveiled in 1908.

Visiting the Monument

The 147-foot-tall Doric column unveiled in 1908 was the tallest such column in the world. It still seems tall, visible from the Manhattan and Brooklyn sides of the East River.

Located in the center of a large plaza, with a wide granite stairway fronting it, the monument is an impressive and moving sight. Originally the bronze lantern at its crown was electrically illuminated, and the column was lit by electric lights set into four granite shafts, each graced by a bronze eagle. An elevator took visitors up to the observation deck near the top of the column.

The illumination is now saved for special occasions, and the eagles have been removed for restoration. The observation deck has been closed because of safety concerns.

In the nearby crypt, twenty slate coffins contain the bone fragments of the approximately 11,500 prisoners who died on the prison ships. The harsh reality of the sacrifice they made doesn't change.

The Committee for the Restoration of Fort Greene Park is currently raising funds to restore the monument in time for a 2008 centennial rededication. Further information regarding the project is available at 718-596-0899.

Visitor Information

800-201-PARK or 718-596-0899
www.nycparks.org and
www.fortgreenepark.org
Hours: Dawn until dusk.
Admission: None.
Accessibility: The park is accessible.
Special Events: There is an annual wreath laying at the monument in August. There are hundreds of activities at the park throughout the year. Check the Web site.
Getting There: Fort Greene Park is located east of Flatbush Avenue between DeKalb and Myrtle avenues, less than a mile from the exits of the Brooklyn and Manhattan bridges.

By bus, take B25, B26, B38, B41, B52, B54, or B69. By subway, take the A or C lines (Lafayette Avenue stop), the G line (Fulton Street stop), the B, M, Q, or R lines (DeKalb Avenue stop), or the 2, 3, 4, or 5 lines (Atlantic Avenue or Nevins Street stop).

Historic Richmond Town

This living-history village and museum complex invites visitors to step back in time and walk the streets of a community whose buildings span the 17th to the 20th centuries.

More than a dozen structures are open for tours. Most are original structures transported to this location in order to preserve them and to create a physical timeline of Staten Island history.

History of Richmond Town

Richmond Town was the county seat of Richmond County in the 1700s. The British changed the Dutch name, Staten Island, to Richmond when they took control of this island in 1664. In the early 1700s, Richmond was a thriving farming and trade community.

During the British occupation of New York in the Revolutionary War, British troops were bivouacked in residents' homes and farmers' barns. Following the war and into the mid-1800s, Staten Island was a popular retreat for Manhattanites. When the island became a borough of New York City in 1898, Richmond Town lost its function as the county seat.

In the 1930s the Staten Island Historical Society spearheaded a movement to preserve the town's older structures as a village. In 1958 it contracted with the City of New York to maintain and develop Historic Richmond Town as a museum village.

The society's missions of collection, restoration, and research continue today. Its collections comprise more than 70,000 artifacts, as well as maps, books, and photographs.

Visiting Richmond Town

In the summer months, costumed interpreters demonstrate the crafts and everyday skills of their particular era. During the off-season, costumed tour guides provide insights into the interactions that made Richmond Town a close-knit community.

At the Visitor Center, located in an 1837 courthouse, a map of the town with brief descriptions of all the buildings is available, and there is a 15-minute film covering the 300-year history of Staten Island. Nearby is the Historical Museum, housed in an 1848 building that served as the County Clerk's & Surrogate's Office. Changing exhibits focus on Richmond's history.

Currently there are four Revolutionary-era buildings: the Voorlezer's House, circa 1695; the Christopher House, circa 1720; the Guyon-Lake-Tysen House, circa 1740; and the Boehm House, circa 1750. Each building is furnished with reproductions representing the social standing and professions of those who lived there.

Voorlezer is the Dutch name for a lay minister of the Reformed Dutch Church and a teacher. The Voorlezer House, thought to be the oldest existing elementary school building in the nation, served as a church, school, and residence for the Voorlezers when Staten Island was a Dutch community.

Next door is the Boehm House. An exhibit on traditional colonial-era building techniques includes reproductions of tools, as well as displays explaining how houses were built.

Next to that is the Christopher House, the reputed meeting place of the town's Committee of Safety before and during the Revolution.

The Guyon-Lake-Tysen House across town is considered remarkable because of the large amount of interior paneling and woodwork that survives.

Visitor Information

718-351-1611

www.historicrichmondtown.org

Hours: September through May, open Wednesday through Sunday, 1 p.m. until 5 p.m., June through August, open Wednesday through Saturday, 10 a.m. until 5 p.m. and Sunday, 1 p.m. until 5 p.m. Closed Easter, Thanksgiving, December 25, and January 1.

Admission: Moderate charge; Staten Island Historical Society Members and children under 5 free.

Accessibility: Wheelchair access is available on a limited basis. Contact the Visitor Center for assistance.

Special Events: Numerous programs and activities are held throughout the year related to Revolutionary War history. Check the Web site for further information or call the Visitor Center. In even years, there are Revolutionary War encampments.

Getting There: Located in the heart of Staten Island, Historic Richmond Town is a 15-minute drive from all the bridges and a 30-minute ride from the Staten Island Ferry via the S74 bus. Detailed directions from various locations in New York City are available on the Web site or by calling the Visitor Center.

Bennington Battlefield State Historic Site

The Yankee hardheadedness of John Stark, a New Hampshire Patriot, proved the undoing of General John Burgoyne's grand scheme to conquer New England. Because he refused to take orders from a Continental Army general, Stark and his New Hampshire Militia were perfectly situated to intercept a detachment from Burgoyne's army on its way to raid a supply depot. The ensuing battle and Patriot victory cost Burgoyne more than 900 men and denied him those supplies, irrevocably hampering his campaign.

Bennington Battlefield, named for the Vermont town the British were trying to reach, is located just across the border in New York and is now part of a 208-acre state park.

Burgoyne's Plan to Raid Bennington

In 1777, Burgoyne's army was experiencing delays, mainly because of lack of horses and supplies. Lack of horses was especially a problem for Baron Friedrich Adolph von Riedesel and his Brunswick Dragoons, who were outfitted for riding, not marching. (Their 12-pound jackboots kept tripping over the long broadswords hanging from their waists.) Lack of food was a problem for the entire army, including Burgoyne's restless Iroquois allies.

As Burgoyne would write later in explanation of his actions, "It was well known that the enemy's source of supplies in live cattle from a large tract of country, passed by the route of Manchester, Arlington and other parts of the Hampshire Grants [Vermont], to Bennington, in order to be occasionally conveyed to the main army. . . . A large depot of corn and of wheeled carriages was also formed at the same place, and the usual guard of militia, though it varied in numbers from day to day." The image of meagerly guarded supplies at Bennington must have been too tempting to pass up. The decision was made to raid this Continental Army supply center.

Burgoyne gave command of the expedition to Hessian lieutenant colonel Friedrich Baum. Baum's detachment was made up of the Brunswickers without horses, some Canadians, Loyalists, British sharpshooters, Iroquois, and a German musical band—some 500 in all.

Burgoyne's orders to Baum were "to try the affections of the people, to disconcert the councils of the enemy . . . and to obtain large supplies of cattle, horses and carriages." Baum was to impose taxes on several of the districts he was raiding. In addition he was to take as prisoners "all persons acting in committees, or any officers acting under the directions of Congress, whether civil or military." Hopes of encouraging the local Loyalists to join Burgoyne's campaign were faint, given these heavy-handed tactics.

Several weeks prior to Baum's taking command of his detachment, the General Court of New Hampshire, hearing of Burgoyne's advance, had enlisted John Stark to raise a militia and "check the progress of Burgoyne." Meanwhile, the Continental Army's general Philip Schuyler was gathering forces at Stillwater, just to the west of Bennington in New York. Schuyler sent General Benjamin Lincoln to meet Stark in Manchester, New Hampshire, and order him and his militia to join the Continental Army at Stillwater.

Stark refused, saying that he only took orders from the authorities in New Hampshire. When threats and cajoling didn't dislodge Stark from his position, General Lincoln sent a message to Schuyler suggesting they quit arguing with Stark and instead use his determination to engage Burgoyne's army to their advantage. Schuyler agreed.

Sending a message to Colonel Seth Warner and the Green Mountain Boys to join him in Bennington, Stark turned his army south. Baum and his army set out on their 40-mile march on August 11. A scouting party sent ahead by Stark attacked the detachment on August 14. Alerted, Baum sent his scouts ahead and learned there was a large force of Patriot militiamen in the area. He then dug in on a hill overlooking the Walloomac River five miles from Bennington and sent for reinforcements.

The Battle of Bennington

It rained all day on the 15th, giving Stark time to take up position two miles from Baum. Stark had about 1500 men, Baum about 800. "The morning of the 16th," a Hessian officer named Glich wrote, "rose beautifully serene; and it is not to the operation of the elements alone that my expression applies. All was perfectly quiet at the outposts, not an enemy having been seen nor an alarming sound heard for several hours previous to sunrise." This serene state may have caused Baum to drop his guard. When a group of Stark's men were seen approaching carrying their muskets butt end up over their shoulders in the Loyalist fashion, Baum assumed these were some of the eager locals come to fight for Burgoyne, and gave the signal the sentries were not to stop their approach.

Glich and many of the other men had misgivings about allowing these men to approach unchecked. Stark had waited until all his forces were in position, then signaled the attack with the shout, "See there, men! There they are! We'll beat them or Molly Stark will be a widow tonight!"

Baum's army was surrounded. "Columns were advancing everywhere against us," wrote Glich, "and those whom we had hitherto trusted as friends had only waited till the arrival of their support might justify them in advancing."

The Iroquois fled, but the Brunswick dragoons and the British marksmen would not give up. Stark later described the fighting as "the hottest I ever saw in my life. It represented one continued clap of thunder." When part of the British ammunition, stored in a wagon, blew up, the Americans rushed Baum's positions. "For a few seconds," remembered Glich, "the scene which ensued defies all power of language to describe. The bayonet, the butt of the rifle, the saber, the pike, were in full play, and men fell, as they rarely fall in modern war. Col. Baum, shot through the body by a rifle ball, fell mortally wounded, and all order and discipline being lost, flight or submission was alone thought of."

Stark assumed the fighting was over, but was soon informed there was "a large reinforcement on their march within two miles of us." Lieutenant Colonel Breymann, with more than 600 men, had arrived from Burgoyne's camp in support of Baum. At almost the same time, Seth Warner and his troops arrived to support Stark. The fighting began anew.

"The battle continued obstinate on both sides till sunset," wrote Stark. "The enemy was obliged to retreat."

Breymann's retreat began in an orderly fashion but soon became a rout. His drums beat a call to parlay for surrender, but the Patriot militia were not familiar with the intricate messages and kept firing. In spite of being shot in the leg, Breymann held his remaining men together and escaped with them into the darkness.

"We pursued them till dark," reported Stark. "But had daylight lasted one hour longer, we should have taken the whole body of them. We recovered four pieces of brass cannon, some hundred stands of arms, eight brass barrells, drums, several Hessian swords, about seven hundred prisoners [and] 207 dead on the spot. The number of wounded is yet unknown. . . . Our loss was inconsiderable, about 40 wounded and thirty killed. I lost my horse, bridle and saddle in the action."

Burgoyne lost almost a third of his army. After the defeat, he proceeded doggedly toward Albany and his supposed rendezvous with St. Leger and Howe.

Congress, at last recognizing Stark's value as a strategist and commander, appointed him a brigadier general in the Continental Army.

Visiting the Battlefield

As with so many battlefields, years after the horrific sounds and smells of battle have faded, Bennington today is a lovely spot, with verdant stretches of park area bordered by trees.

Once through the entry gate, visitors drive up a roadway to a small shelter, where public restrooms are located. There is a topographical bronze panorama of the battlefield, showing the movements of those who fought in the battle, and printed information and a map of the battlefield are available.

Four monuments dot the battlefield, each commemorating the participation of Patriots from one of four states: Vermont, Massachusetts, New Hampshire, and New York.

Visitor Information

518-279-1155
www.nysparks.state.ny.us/parks/
(click on Grafton Lakes State Park in list at left, then scroll down and click on Bennington Battlefield State Historic Site)
Hours: Open May 1 through Labor Day, 10 a.m. until 7 pm., Labor Day through Columbus Day, weekends only from 10 a.m. until 7 p.m.
Admission: Free.
Accessibility: Handicapped accessible.
Special Events: None.
Getting There: The historic site is about 35 miles northeast of Troy, New York, just a few miles from Hoosick Falls. Take NY route 7 east or Vermont route 9 west to New York 22 north. Go north 6 miles to New York route 67 east to the battlefield.

Crown Point State Historic Site

The ease with which Seth Warner and his troops captured the British fort at Crown Point in May of 1775 would have seemed incongruous to those who had spent the previous century vying for this hotly contested property.

Before and during the French and Indian War, the French and British recognized the strategic importance of this peninsula at the head of Lake Champlain. It remained strategically important to the Patriots during the Revolutionary War until the British retook it in 1776. Remnants of what was once the largest British fort in America can still be seen today, as can partial remains of the French fort that existed before it.

History of Crown Point

The French were the first to claim this area, which they called *Pointe à la Chevelure* (Crown Point). In 1731 they constructed a small fort for a garrison of 30 men, and three years later began construction of the more formidable Fort St. Frédéric. A substantial community was eventually established in the vicinity of Frédéric that discouraged British incursions into the valley for more than 20 years.

With the outbreak of the French and Indian War in 1755, the British determined to take the fort, but it took over four years to capture it. Soon after, the British began construction of His Majesty's Fort of Crown Point, creating a complex covering almost five square miles. Besides the fort, there were three redoubts, seven blockhouses, and a stump fence closing off the peninsula. Included were more than 120 cannons. The new fort was about 300 yards from the remains of Fort St. Frédéric, which the French had razed before vacating.

With the Treaty of Paris in 1763, the British gained sovereignty over Canada, and Crown Point became the center of communication between the colony of New York and its fellow colony to the north. Crown Point also served as the police authority for the settlers and Native Americans in an area that included Fort George and Fort Ticonderoga. With a wide swath of the North American continent under mostly uncontested British rule, the troops focused on keeping the peace rather than fighting battles.

On April 21, 1773, a fire burned down the wooden fort. Rather than undertake another massive building project, the British moved the area's central administration south to Fort Ticonderoga, leaving nine men to garrison what was left of the fort.

Two years later, in May 1775, the undermanned fort surrendered to Seth Warner and his men during the Patriot army's sweep of the Champlain Valley (*see* New York, Fort Ticonderoga National Historic Landmark). Benedict Arnold and his troops removed more than 100 pieces and thousands of cannonballs from Crown Point, transporting them to Fort Ticonderoga. Some of this matériel was sent to New York City; the rest was at Ticonderoga later that year when Henry Knox returned for it (*see* Massachusetts, Boston National Historical Park).

In June of 1776, survivors of the failed Canada campaign (*see* Maine, Old Fort Western) arrived at Crown Point, some 3000 of them seriously ill. A soldier named Charles Cushing wrote to his brother from Crown Point on June 13 that "a great part of the army were sick, many with the small-pox, and many of those who had had it were sick with the flux. Here we were obliged to wait for boats eight days, where we could get nothing but pork and flour . . . and such a number of men on so small a spot, and many of them sick—the place stunk enough to breed an infection."

Once the sick were removed, the majority of the army left for Fort Ticonderoga, leaving a Pennsylvania regiment as a rear guard. In August the Pennsylvanians built a new wooden fort just south of where the lighthouse is today, but were forced to burn it when Arnold lost the Battle of Valcour Island (*see* Vermont, Lake Champlain Maritime Museum) and the Americans retreated out of the valley.

Crown Point fell back into British hands in 1776 and would remain in their hands until the end of the war.

Visiting Crown Point

One of the earliest tourists to visit Crown Point was George Washington, who stopped by in July of 1783, traveling from his headquarters in Newburgh where he was waiting for the conclusion of the peace talks in Paris. Visitors today will find a museum where they will be given an informative map of the grounds of the French and British forts.

Maps from the 1700s are dis-

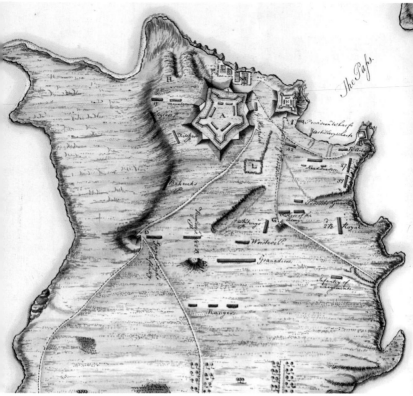

*A **contemporary map** in the collection of the Library of Congress is labeled "Plan of the newly constructed fort and fortress at Crown Point with the disposition of the British army under the command of General Amherst in 1759."*

played in the museum, showing the area at the time of the Revolution, and scale models of the two forts provide a clearer idea of their size and structure. Also on exhibit in the museum are a rare French Pierrier small breech-loading swivel gun (one of only four known to still exist), a bronze British cannon taken from a French ship, and a captured French cannon.

The self-guided walking tour takes visitors to the site of Fort St. Frédéric. Stonework, cut in a style typical to the French, is visible in the surviving end walls of the guardhouse. Just below these walls are the remains of four beehive ovens built by the British to bake bread—on average, 900 loaves in a single day. One of the most interesting items described on the map is the Bastion du Moulin, or stone windmill, built by the French across the bay where the Champlain Memorial now stands. Though it was used for grinding grain for flour, it also served as a defensive outpost and was fortified with cannons.

The shells of two barracks survive in the British fort. The impressive stone walls are what remain of the officers' barracks, with a large chunk blown out during the fire of 1773. Visitors can also see remnants of the stone foundation that was located at the corner of the bastion where the

fort's well was dug. Beyond the outlines of the fort is the visible ruin of the Light Infantry Redoubt. The view from the top of the fort, looking ten miles down the wooded shoreline of Canada, is breathtaking.

Crossing the field south of the fort brings visitors to Gage's Redoubt, and next to it a 19th-century lime kiln.

Visitor Information
518-597-3666
nysparks.state.ny.us/hist/
(click on Crown Point on the left)
Hours: The museum is open May through October, Wednesday through Monday, from 10 a.m. until 5 p.m. The grounds are open until Columbus Day to sunset.
Admission: There is a moderate charge for admission to the museum, and a moderate vehicle charge on weekends and holidays.
Accessibility: The museum is accessible. The self-guided tour trails and hiking trails are partially accessible.
Special Events: An annual French and Indian War Encampment, the second weekend in August.
Getting There: From state routes 9N and 22 about 15 miles north of Ticonderoga, take route 903 east toward the Lake Champlain Bridge. The historic site is just before this bridge to Vermont.

Fort Stanwix National Monument

In New York, as in many of the other colonies, the British found themselves entangled in local conflicts that could be used to their advantage but could also hinder their cause. This was certainly true in the Mohawk Valley, where the struggle for control was as much between settlers and Native Americans and between feudal-type landowners and middle-class farmers and merchants as it was between Britain and her subjects seeking independence. Each of these conflicts figured in the siege of Fort Stanwix.

Today's fort, reproduced on the site of the original in what is now Rome, New York, focuses on the impact of the siege; but even more so, it pays tribute to those who withstood the 19-day ordeal.

Burgoyne's Plan

The Mohawk Valley was part of what traditionally has been referred to as General John Burgoyne's three-pronged approach to cutting off New England from the rest of the states. British military leaders were certain that doing so would shatter the Patriot cause.

Under Burgoyne's plan, one army would come down from Canada via Lake Champlain and the upper Hudson River, another would come up from the lower Hudson, and a third, smaller army would come through the Mohawk Valley from Fort Oswego on Lake Ontario.

Colonel Barry St. Leger led the army dispatched from Fort Oswego to rendezvous with Burgoyne at Albany. St. Leger's second in command was Sir John Johnson, a Loyalist who had been chased off his large New York estate by his Patriot neighbors. Their army consisted of about 500 British and Hessian troops, some French-Canadian militia, and about 1000 Native Americans from the various Indian nations, including the Iroquois.

Fort Stanwix had been built by the British in 1756 and named for the officer in charge of construction. The Patriots called it Fort Schuyler in honor of the American general Philip Schuyler. It was commanded by 28-year-old Colonel Peter Gansevoort, scion of a patroon family that had both Patriots and Loyalists among its members. (Patroons were Dutch landowners granted large estates in what is now New York by the Dutch West India Company in the early 1600s.) The fort was in disrepair when Gansevoort and his troops arrived in the spring of 1777. Aware of the threat of British insurgency, Gansevoort immediately set his men to work on repairing the fort's walls, barracks, and palisades.

The Siege

St. Leger and his army arrived at Fort Stanwix on August 3, 1777. William Colbraith, a soldier stationed at the fort, recorded the event in his journal: "About 3 o'clock this afternoon the enemy showed themselves to the garrison on all sides, carried off some hay from a field near the garrison, at which a flag brought by Captain Tice came into the fort with a proffer of protection i[f]

The Iroquois Confederation

The Iroquois people did not form one group. They formed a confederation of nations that consisted of the Mohawks, Oneidas, Onondagas, Cayugas, Senecas, and Tuscaroras. The alliance of their confederation, or nation, with Britain was more than 100 years old and was sustained by Britain's assistance to the Iroquois in their conflicts with the Algonquins and the French. Only the Oneidas and Tuscaroras would side with the Patriots during the war.

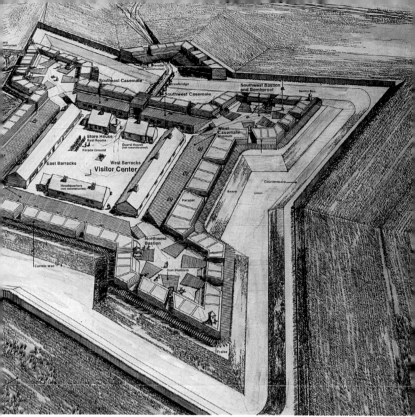

This painting *gives a good idea of how Fort Stanwix looked during the Revolutionary War. Except for certain buildings and outworks, the current fort is a faithful reconstruction of the original.*

Image labels: Southeast Casemate, Drawbridge, Southwest Casemate, Southwest Bastion and Bombproof, Sentry Box, Store House (Rest Rooms), West Casemate Museum, Guard House (not reconstructed), Parade Ground, Headquarters (not reconstructed), East Barracks, West Barracks, Visitor Center, Counterscarp, Glacis, Parapet, Curtain wall, Northwest Bastion, Gun Platform, Fraise

the garrison would surrender, which was rejected with disdain."

Seeking to reinforce Fort Stanwix, on August 4 General Nicholas Herkimer set out from Fort Dayton, about 50 miles to the east, with 800 men. They were ambushed and suffered heavy damage at Oriskany. General Herkimer was mortally wounded and died ten days later. (*See* New York, Oriskany Battlefield State Historic Site.) Not knowing about Oriskany but in keeping with Herkimer's request for a diversion, Gansevoort sent his second in command, Lieutenant Colonel Marinus Willett, with a detachment to create a diversion and draw St. Leger's forces away. Willett was able to raid some of the Indian camps, and from his prisoners learned about the bloody standoff at Oriskany.

On August 8, Colbraith reported a more formal demand for surrender: "About 5 o'clock this evening Colonel Butler, with a British captain and a doctor from the enemy, came to the garrison with a flag, whose message from Gen. St. Leger was that the Indians, having lost some of their chiefs in a skirmish with our party . . . were determined to go down the Mohawk River and destroy the women and children; also that they would kill every man in the garrison when they got in; that Gen. St. Leger had held a council with them for two days in order to prevent them, but all to no purpose, unless we would surrender. The general

therefore, as an act of humanity, and to prevent the effusion of blood, begged we would deliver up the fort, and promised if we did, not a hair of our heads should be hurt."

The next day Gansevoort replied in writing, "I have only to say that it is my determined resolution, with the forces under my command, to defend this fort, at every hazard, to the last extremity, in behalf of the United American States, who have placed me here to defend it against all their enemies." With that, the British bombarded the fort with artillery while Indian snipers picked off soldiers trying to repair the cannons' damage. But Gansevoort and his men held out.

Even before hearing of Oriskany, Major General Benedict Arnold and 1000 New York and New England Continental troops had begun a march from near Albany to reinforce Fort Stanwix. Even with these 1000 reinforcements, the Americans would still be outnumbered. But then something happened that put balance to the scales.

A Ruse Saves the Day

An advance party for Arnold's regiment, led by Lieutenant Colonel John Brooks of Massachusetts, captured two Loyalists—Ensign Walter

Butler and Jan Yost Schuyler, a distant cousin of General Schuyler. This bit of serendipity led to a scheme being hatched, for as James Thacher, a doctor attached to Arnold's regiment, wrote in his journal, "An object which cannot be accomplished by force is often obtained by means of stratagem."

Brooks offered Schuyler clemency in return for his acting "as a deceptive messenger to spread the alarm and induce the enemy to retreat," wrote Thacher. "General Arnold soon after arrived and approved the scheme . . . [Schuyler] would return to the enemy and make such exaggerated report of General Arnold's force as to alarm and put them to flight. Someone suggested that [Schuyler]'s coat should be shot through in two or three places to add credibility to his story." Schuyler returned to the Indian camp, "where he was well known, and informed their warriors that Major Butler was taken, and that he himself narrowly escaped, several shots having passed through his coat, and that General Arnold with a vast force was advancing rapidly towards them."

The Indians took the bait and decided to leave. "The consequence was that St. Leger, finding himself deserted by his Indians, to the number of seven or eight hundred, deemed his situation so hazardous that he decamped in the greatest hurry and confusion, leaving his tents with most of his artillery and stores in the field." It wasn't a dignified retreat, and reports afterward said that some of the Loyalists were scalped and killed by the Indians in retaliation for their losses.

In this way the siege of Fort Stanwix was broken on August 22— the British defeated by the courage of the people defending the fort, the sacrifice of those who fought at Oriskany, and the Yankee guile of Colonel Brooks.

The fort was garrisoned until 1781, though there was no further fighting. In 1784, representatives of the Iroquois nation met here with representatives of the U.S. government to negotiate the Treaty of Fort Stanwix. The members of the

Iroquois nation such as the Mohawk, who had fought with the British were forced to cede large tracts of land to the U.S. Those such as the Oneidas who had chosen the winning side were allowed to keep their land, though, as it turned out, not for much longer.

After that the fort fell into disuse and was leveled in 1830.

Visiting the Fort

Fort Stanwix provides a fascinating living-history experience for visitors, with furnished rooms accented with period artifacts and reproductions that elicit a strong sense of what it must have been like more than two centuries ago for the soldiers and their officers. Visitors receive not only the usual excellent National Park Service illustrated brochure, with its detailed information about the fort, the battle, and the leaders involved, but also a terrific self-guided walking-tour booklet with material about each of the 23 sites within the fort that are open to the public.

A new Visitor and Education Center, which will include a museum, is currently being built and is scheduled to open in 2005. In the meantime, visitors can see the monument's compelling 23-minute orientation film that provides a first-hand experience of the siege through the words of a journal kept by one of the soldiers.

Touring the North Casemate, visitors see the barracks where the officers and commandant lived, as well as the staff dining room. The Officers' Quarters displays a traveling camp bed, which could be disassembled for transport. Soldiers, for the most part, carried their possessions on

The Stars and Stripes

There is a long-standing tradition that the Stars and Stripes were first hoisted above a military installation at Fort Stanwix, though no incontrovertible documentation exists to prove it. William Colbraith recorded in his journal, "Aug. 3d, Early this morning a Continental flag, made by the officers of Colonel Gansevoort's regiment, was hoisted." Historians now believe this flag was actually what was known as a Grand Union flag—the British Union flag with thirteen red and white stripes added. Also included in the tradition is that the flag was made from pieces of a white shirt on which were sewn strips of red cloth from a petticoat and a piece of blue cloth. The only documented fact is that the blue cloth was from a captured British officer's cloak.

A wooden bridge leads to the sally port that allowed the garrison of the fort to attack besiegers. When not in use, the sally port was closed by a massive timber gate.

their backs. Officers had baggage wagons and so could have transportable beds. The Staff Room/Dining Room was used as Gansevoort's office during the day and in the evening converted to a dining room for the officers. The creature comforts of Gansevoort's Commandant Quarters bespeak his wealth and education, while the Artillery Officer's Quarters are filled with that officer's mathematical and scientific tools.

The Soldiers' Quarters, located in the East Barracks, usually housed 28 to 36 men, who cooked, ate, and slept in the one room. Ranks were mixed, so that a private and a sergeant, as well as drummers and fifers, might share accommodations. The Suttler's Quarters provide a glimpse of consumerism at the fort. Suttlers were civilian merchants who followed the army and set up shop at army installations. In this small store, soldiers and their families could buy the extras that made life a little more comfortable. Suttlers made it a point to maintain good trade relationships with the local Indians.

In the Soldiers' Barracks in the Southeast Casemate, visitors see long beds called cribs that slept 10 to 12 men side by side. Though probably not very comfortable, this arrangement was certainly warm in the winter.

Bastions at each corner of the compound (a bastion is a diamond-shape corner of a fort) provided soldiers a view of the surrounding army, as well as a point from which to bombard them with cannon fire. A tall red brick building that can be seen from the Northeast Bastion marks the spot from which British cannons were firing, about 600 yards away. Just beyond that building was the site of the main British camp. A makeshift hospital was located in the Southwest Bastion, where visitors can see some of the rather scary medical implements of the period.

The fort's drawbridge, as reproduced here, is similar in design to those of the time. It used the counterweight principle, with 1200-pound weights on a track on either side. Pushed by the men, the weights would roll down the track to raise the bridge. To lower it again, the men probably used long poles that pushed the bridge down until its weight brought the weights on either side back up to the top of the track.

Visitor Information

315-336-2090
www.nps.gov/fost

Hours: Open daily April through December, 9 a.m. until 5 p.m.; closed Thanksgiving Day and December 25. When the Visitor Center is ready in 2005, it will be open daily year-round, 9 a.m. until 5 p.m., except for Thanksgiving Day and December 25.

Admission: Free.

Accessibility: The Visitor Center is accessible, and the museum opening in 2005 will be accessible. Natural light is used in the living-history areas of the site, resulting in dimly lit rooms that may present a problem for some. Programs can be adapted to take into consideration those with special needs.

Special Events: The annual Revolutionary War Fall Troop Muster in late fall brings together reenactment groups (Patriot and Loyalist) from all over the Northeast for military drills, open-hearth cooking, and other aspects of military life in the fort at the time of the siege. Daily living-history programs are scheduled throughout the season.

Getting There: By car: All major state routes through Rome—26, 46, 49, 69, and 365—pass within sight of the fort. To get to Rome from I-90 (the New York Thruway), take exit 32 at Westmoreland to state route 233 north to route 365 west, following the signs to downtown Rome.

Fort Ticonderoga National Historic Landmark

During the French and Indian War, this massive stone fortification on Lake Champlain was the sight of British defeat at the Battle of Carillon, the bloodiest battle on American soil prior to the Civil War. Seventeen years later, in 1775, the Americans captured it from the British almost without a shot being fired, and two years later gave it back to the British in a hurried retreat.

Throughout these events, the fort and its environs were home to successive generations of Native American, French, and British pioneers. Today the restored fort's rich history of conquest and settlement is integrated in a diverse and entertaining living-history experience that includes impressive museum collections, daily demonstrations, and special events.

A Quick and Easy Victory

Ten days after Lexington and Concord (*see* Massachusetts, Minute Man Park) Benedict Arnold was addressing the Massachusetts Committee of Safety, proposing he be given sufficient arms and men to capture Fort Ticonderoga in northeastern New York. Arnold felt strongly that in these opening days of armed conflict, the Patriots had to take the initiative, even though Congress had authorized only defensive actions.

Fort Ticonderoga was a strategically important location. The British fort sat on a promontory 100 feet above where Lake George empties into Lake Champlain, which is why the Iroquois called it ticonderoga— "between two waters." At this point the passage between the headlands on the east and west sides of Lake Champlain is less than a quarter of a mile wide. Positioned on the main course between Canada and the Hudson Valley, Fort Ticonderoga controlled that narrow passageway, the gateway to Canada.

Making the fort equally attractive to Arnold was its artillery, which he knew would be sorely needed in the coming engagements.

Arnold wasn't alone in his reasoning. Members of the Connecticut Committee of Safety had directed Ethan Allen and his Green Mountain Boys to capture the fort.

Since Arnold had considerably fewer men than Ethan Allen, when their two forces came together in early May 1775, Arnold graciously agreed to share command. With 83 men, the two leaders arrived at Fort Ticonderoga at daybreak on the 10th of May. They were confronted by a sentry whose gun misfired, after which he fled into the fort.

The fort's commander, Captain William Delaplace, likely more confused than threatened by this motley

The Green Mountain Boys

The Green Mountain Boys, with Ethan Allen, pictured below, as their leader, were a group of Vermont men who came together in 1770 to protect the land claims of themselves and their neighbors. At that time, Vermont was called the New Hampshire Grants because those who lived there had been granted their land by New Hampshire. At the same time, New York claimed the area west of the Green Mountains, which runs through the center of Vermont. When New York sent sheriffs to evict those with New Hampshire grants from what it considered New York land, the Green Mountain Boys fought back. They evicted the "Yorkers,"

burned their houses and barns, and took their cattle. Once the war started, Vermonters appealed to the Congress to have their territory recognized as a separate state. New York repeatedly blocked this move, and in 1777 Vermont declared itself an independent country. For the next 14 years it printed its own money and maintained its own militia, even as its men, including the Green Mountain Boys, were fighting for the Patriot cause. In 1791, Congress admitted Vermont into the union.

The capture *of Fort Ticonderoga itself wasn't especially important, but the fort's artillery was. The captured cannons from Ticonderoga were later transported to Boston, where a grand display of them from the fortified American position of Dorchester Heights caused the British to pack up and leave the occupied city.*

band, asked by what authority they were there. "In the name of the Great Jehovah and the Continental Congress!" shouted Allen. Or so he wrote years later in his autobiography. Historians now believe he said something much less dramatic. Whatever he said, Delaplace got the idea.

Delaplace had requested reinforcements only the week before, suspecting there might be an attack on the fort. But they had not yet arrived, so with his entire garrison consisting of two officers, two artillerymen, several sergeants, and 44 privates, plus a small group of women and children, he had no choice but to surrender. Ticonderoga was taken.

Two days later the British fort at Crown Point was also captured (*see* New York, Crown Point State Historic Site). Between them, these forts netted 78 artillery pieces, six mortars, three howitzers, and a large supply of cannonballs and muskets to the Patriot cause. The matériel could not be immediately claimed, however, because of lack of transport. In December 1775, Washington sent Henry Knox to Ticonderoga to collect the artillery for use in the Battle for Boston (*see* Massachusetts, Boston National Historical Park).

Also late in 1775, Ticonderoga was one of the staging areas for the invasion of Quebec, and a year later 3000 of those forces retreated back to the fort, riddled with smallpox and

dysentery and near starvation. Benedict Arnold also retreated to Ticonderoga after the Battle of Valcour Island (*see* Vermont, Lake Champlain Maritime Museum).

Divide and Conquer

In the spring of 1777, Major General John Burgoyne arrived from England with a plan to capture New York and thereby separate New England from the southern states. Called Gentleman Johnny by his officers and troops, Burgoyne was viewed by his supporters as the most laudatory of a particular type of 18th-century British officer—daring, innovative, intelligent, literate (he was a playwright), educated, and an able and inspiring commander.

Burgoyne had already seen service during the war in Boston and Canada, and felt that what was needed was a coordinated squeeze of Patriot forces. His plan involved his coming down from the north through the upper Hudson Valley, while another force came west to east through New York's Mohawk Valley (*see* New York, Fort Stanwix National Monument). These two forces would then triumphantly join with General Sir William Howe at Albany, leaving behind them defeat and submission as they moved into New Jersey and Pennsylvania.

General Howe, though, had decided now was the opportune time to take Philadelphia, and he apparently

This 1777 map of the fort and its environs shows its strategic importance to the defense of Lake Champlain. Defensive lines and redoubts are indicated in red. The lines were "covered by an amazing abbattis [sic] of fell'd trees with their boughs to the enemy." The map also shows a clearing, northwest of the fort, hewn from the nearby woods that protected it from surprise attack and offered a clear field of fire.

A MAP of
TICONDEROGA
with the Old and New Lines and Batteries.
taken from
an Actual Survey & other Authentick
INFORMATIONS.
1777.

Fathoms

had no intention of joining Burgoyne in New York. Burgoyne learned of Howe's intention before leaving England; but against all reason, he assumed Howe would have the time and wherewithal to capture Philadelphia and return north for their rendezvous.

Burgoyne Attacks

On June 17, 1777, Burgoyne's army began its march south from Canada to Lake Champlain. The force consisted of some 7000 British and German infantrymen and artillerymen, a small number of Canadians and American Loyalists, and about 400 Native Americans, mainly Iroquois.

On June 23, Burgoyne issued a proclamation from his camp. He listed the wrongs done by the Congress and state governments in their disloyalty to the Crown, "unprecedented in the Inquisitions of the Romish Church." He called upon "All Persons, in all Places where the Progress of this Army may point, and by the Blessing of God I will extend it FAR, to maintain such a Conduct as may justify me in protecting their Lands, Habitations, and Families." Finally, he concluded with a threat: "The Messengers of Justice and of Wrath await them [the Patriots] in the Field, and Devastation, Famine, and every concomitant Horror that a reluctant but indispensable Prosecution of Military Duty must occasion, will bar the Way to their Return."

The next day at the same camp, Burgoyne spoke to his Native American forces through an interpreter, telling them, "The Great King, our common father and the patron of all who seek and deserve his protection, has considered with satisfaction the general conduct of the Indian tribes from the beginning of the troubles in America." He explained that the Europeans and Canadians fighting alongside them would guide them as to the proper conduct in this conflict, and proceeded to lay down the rules, name-

ly that there should be neither bloodshed nor taking of scalps outside of battle. But he promised "you shall be allowed to take the scalps of the dead when killed by your fire and in fair opposition; but on no account, or pretence, or subtilty, or prevarication, are they to be taken from the wounded or even dying."

An Iroquois chief answered that the Indians loved the king and "with one common assent we promise a constant obedience to all you have ordered."

Having called for the enlistment of Loyalists in the cause, warned the Patriots of their coming chastisement, and set the boundaries for his Native American allies, all in gentlemanly fashion, Burgoyne was ready to proceed.

In early July, Burgoyne divided his force. The Germans under Baron Friedrich von Riedesel would capture Mount Independence on the east side of Lake Champlain, while the British would move down the west side to Fort Ticonderoga.

By now, much of Fort Ticon-

deroga had been refortified. Block-houses had been repaired and small redoubts built. But it was garrisoned by a skeleton force of only about 2500 men, described as "mere boys [and] one third unfit for duty." The commander, Major General Arthur St. Clair, had arrived at the fort just a few days before Burgoyne began his march south from Canada. A Scotsman who had fought in the French and Indian War and then settled in Pennsylvania, St. Clair is generally considered a competent man who was given a very difficult task. Not only had he few men, he had little in the way of arms, equipment, ammunition, and supplies.

The Americans knew Burgoyne was coming. On June 20, General Philip Schuyler arrived with orders that St. Clair was to hold Fort Ticonderoga as long as possible and then retreat across the lake to Mount Independence (*see* Vermont, Mount Independence State Historic Site). There the combined armies were expected to hold the British at bay for at least several months, depleting

Burgoyne's forces and supplies and putting the skids on his grand design.

Americans Abandon the Fort

About two miles northwest of Ticonderoga is a hill rising 750 feet above the water. It was then called Sugar Loaf; the British would rename it Mount Defiance. Declaring it inaccessible, the Americans hadn't bothered to fortify it.

Burgoyne dispatched his chief engineer, Lieutenant Twiss, to see if the Americans were wrong. Twiss reported that the hill commanded Fort Ticonderoga at 1400 yards and Mount Independence at 1500 yards and that a road could be opened and guns hauled to the top in 24 hours. As Major General William Phillips, Burgoyne's chief artillery officer, said, "Where a goat can go a man can go, and where a man can go he can drag a gun."

Fort Ticonderoga had by now been reinforced with 900 fresh troops. But by July 5, with British guns looking down from Sugar

This howitzer gun is typical of those captured by the Americans and later transported overland by Henry Knox to drive the British from Boston.

Loaf, St. Clair ordered a retreat to Mount Independence and from there to Skenesborough at the southern end of Lake Champlain (*see* New York, Skenesborough Museum).

Fort Ticonderoga was once again in British hands, where it would remain until the end of the war. It was a crushing loss, and St. Clair was court-martialed but acquitted. He later served as governor of the Northwest Territory in the late 1790s.

Still, Patriot leaders consoled themselves that this first easy victory would be Burgoyne's undoing. "I am in hope," wrote Alexander Hamilton, "that Burgoyne's success will precipitate him into measures that will prove his ruin. The enterprising spirit he has credit for, I suspect, may easily be fanned by his vanity into rashness."

Visiting the Fort

With its equal emphasis on the French and Indian War, the living-history experience of this restored fort provides an excellent opportunity to discover the many connections between that war and the Revolutionary War.

Thirty-minute guided tours of the fort are especially informative, or visitors can choose self-guided tours using the map that is provided. There are musket demonstrations throughout the day, daily artillery demonstrations and fife and drum corps performances in July and August, plus interactive programs for families every Monday and Thursday during the summer.

Defensive works have been preserved on the Ticonderoga peninsula, also called the Garrison Grounds. These include French earthworks on the west side of the fort and a French glacis, or slope, on the north side. Hollow trenches, deep enough to hide a standing soldier, extend from east of the fort to the Lotbinière Battery.

Fort Ticonderoga has the largest collection of 18th-century artillery in North America. Nearly 200 French, British, and American pieces are displayed on the ramparts of the fort, part of the Fort Ticonderoga Museum that covers four floors within two 1756 barracks buildings.

This museum holds many treasures from both wars. Its collection of more than 170 powder horns provides a particularly fascinating window into the personalities of the men who fought here. It was the militiaman, generally, who carried a powder horn—made from the horn of a bull—not the professional soldier. Decorations were one way of making these utilitarian pieces individual. Some have crude maps, others depict the surrounding landscape or patriotic insignias. A couple of dozen are on display here at any one time.

Personal items are also displayed, such as Ethan Allen's blunderbuss, sword, and canteen, and items belonging to Henry Knox.

The fort's sword collection includes the fighting weapons of American, British, French, and

German officers, as well as presentation swords given to an officer to commemorate a particular battle. Also in the edged-weapons collection are bayonets and polearms.

The collection of nearly 1000 muskets is among the largest in the country and covers the French and Indian War, the Revolution, and the War of 1812. Included are British, French, and German pieces, as well as early examples of muskets developed by Eli Whitney in Springfield, Massachusetts. Among the museum's most prized treasures is a French Infantry Musket, Model 1746, one of only four known to exist.

Artifacts such as tools, personal effects, and musical instruments interpret the French presence in the Champlain Valley and explain the history of the French conflict with the British that came to include the American fight for independence.

For a taste of Fort Ticonderoga's later history, visitors are encouraged to stop by the King's Garden, created in 1920 for Stephen and Sarah Pell, who bought and restored the fort with an eye to both tourism and historic preservation. The garden design is based on ones depicted on 18th-century French and English maps of the fort. With its pathways and ornamental sculpture, it's a lovely stop after a day of muskets and drill.

From Fort Ticonderoga, visitors can drive to the top of Mount Defiance, located to the southwest of the fort. From here the overlook provides an awesome view of parts of the Champlain Valley and the Vermont lakeshore. There is a picnic facility at the top of the summit.

Visitor Information

518-585-2821
www.fort-ticonderoga.org
Hours: Fort Ticonderoga and Mount

Fort Ticonderoga is in the process of redesigning and redistributing its collections. Items currently displayed in the museum may be displayed elsewhere in the fort after May 2005.

Defiance are open daily from early May to mid-October, 9 a.m. until 5 p.m. The King's Garden is open June to October, 10 a.m. until 4 p.m.

Admission: There is a significant charge for adults, a reduced fee for youngsters, and children 7 and under are free.

Accessibility: Much of the fort is accessible, with hard-packed dirt walkways and ramps, though assistance may be required in some areas. The second and third floors of the museum, located in a historic building, are not accessible. Please call ahead for further information and assistance.

Special Events: The annual Grand Encampment of the French & Indian War, held the last weekend in June, involves more than 700 enactors, including French and British Regulars, American and Canadian provincial troops, and northeastern Native American groups. Some years, naval forces also participate. Music, dancing, food, demonstrations, and children's games are included. In July there is an annual commemoration of the Battle of Carillon. Check the Web site for additional upcoming Revolutionary War–related events.

Getting There: From I-87 (the Northway), take exit 28 to state route 74 east and follow that for 18 miles. In Ticonderoga, follow the signs for a continuation of route 74 east (a sharp left-hand turn at the blinking light) to the entrance of the fort.

The Battle of Carillon

Visitors approaching Fort Ticonderoga drive across the battlefield where the Battle of Carillon took place in 1758, during the French and Indian War. Though outnumbered five to one, the French withstood eight hours of attacks by the British, resulting in great loss of life for both sides. This was the greatest and the last victory for the French in that earlier war. Wayside panels and historical markers dot the tranquil landscape, which was an open field at the time of the battle. Two monuments have been placed here. One was erected soon after the battle by the Marquis de Montcalm, commander of France's North American forces during the war, in thanksgiving for the victory. The other is a cairn erected in 1997 by the Black Watch Regiment. This Scottish regiment, which lost more than half its men in the battle, sent stones from every clan whose ancestors fought in the battle.

New Windsor Cantonment State Historic Site

Our God and soldier we alike adore,/ Just at the brink of danger and not before. So wrote Ensign Benjamin Gilbert of the 5th Massachusetts Regiment in 1780. As he and others discovered, there wasn't much adoration for the Revolutionary War soldier after the danger had passed, either.

The Continental Army spent the winter of 1782 in New Windsor, near Newburgh, New York. It might be said that this was the site of George Washington's last "battle" of the Revolution and, arguably, the first battle of his political career. It was here that a cabal of officers began to agitate over the issue of pensions. And it was here that Washington yet again brought to bear his character and reputation among his men to turn the tide and prevent disaster.

The Camp at New Windsor

In October 1782, Washington and his army of around 7500 soldiers, plus some 500 wives and children, came into the Hudson Highlands and established their winter quarters a few miles from the village of New Windsor.

Just 60 miles south were 12,000 British soldiers camped in and around New York City. Savannah and Charleston were also still under British control. The French, for the most part, had left North America to shore up their West Indies holdings as the war with Britain wound down. Washington had every expectation that the war was over, but he still had to remain at the ready for whatever might ensue.

New Windsor was a familiar area to Washington and his army. In the fall and winter of 1780–1781, a major part of the artillery from all over the Northeast was collected here. New carriages were made, and the gunners were trained in ricochet firing. All this was in preparation for an attack on New York City, which was supplanted by the march to Virginia and the attack on Yorktown.

With the victory in Yorktown a satisfying memory, the general decided his army would winter here. There was a reliable water supply, camping on the side of the hills west of town meant good drainage, and the area was surrounded by forests, which were essential to building the huts in which the soldiers (and families) would live.

When the army first arrived, they set up from 1500 to 1800 tents across the meadows and immediately began felling trees. Though the tents had small fireplaces, there was still a push to get into warm log cabins as soon as possible.

Army blacksmiths produced nails and hardware and repaired axes and saws while the soldiers were hewing timbers, splitting shingles, and finally building the huts. The huts contained two rooms, with bunks for beds and fireplaces used for cooking.

When by mid-December the majority of the huts had been constructed, the Reverend Israel Evans, a New Hampshire chaplain, asked that Washington authorize the building of a chapel for Sunday services. This Temple of Virtue was decorated in the style of a meetinghouse, and was also used for courts-martial and officers' functions, among other activities.

It was in this building that Washington met with his officers to quell what could have been a mutiny with far-reaching consequences for the new nation.

A Question of Money

The trouble began when Congress promised officers a pension system that paid an officer half his salary for life following retirement. Some officers had gone a significant time without being paid the most rudimentary salary, and these pensions were a way of making up that sum as well as expressing a nation's gratitude.

However, state governments had failed to ratify an impost tax act passed by Congress in 1781, which was to fund the pensions. This meant many officers found themselves with large debts and little hope of getting any money out of the country's legislative body, which was itself broke and couldn't squeeze any funds out of the states' governments, which were fairly broke themselves.

Concurrently, a group calling themselves the Nationalists, consisting of men like Alexander Hamilton and Robert Morris, were pushing for the right of the national government, through Congress, to impose taxes. In their view, the officers were convenient tools to frighten taciturn lawmakers into taking action. The Nationalists hoped that the officers would successfully bully Congress into passing another impost tax law.

In the winter of 1782, a delegation led by General Alexander

The Purple Heart

The New Windsor Cantonment State Historic Site is the future location of the National Purple Heart Hall of Honor. Since World War I, more than 800,000 Purple Heart medals have been awarded to those who were killed or wounded while in the service of their country.

The precursor of the Purple Heart is the Badge of Military Merit created by George Washington to honor Revolutionary War heroes. In his general order, Washington directed that "whenever any singularly meritorious action is performed, the author of it shall be permitted to wear  on his facings, over his left breast . . . the figure of a heart in purple cloth . . ." The heart was embroidered with laurels and the word Merit.

Three were awarded at the end of the war. One to Sergeant Daniel Brown of Stamford, Connecticut, for leading the first party to charge Redoubt No. 10 at Yorktown; another to Sergeant Daniel Bissell of Windsor, Connecticut, for his actions as Washington's spy during the war; and a third to Sergeant Elijah Churchill of Enfield, Connecticut, for his part in several engagements on Long Island. Churchill's Badge of Merit is on display at Washington's Headquarters in Newburgh.

In the years following the Revolutionary War, the Badge of Merit fell into disuse but was revived in 1932 by President Herbert Hoover as the Purple Heart. The Purple Heart is a gold-framed heart with a purple background and the silhouette of George Washington in the heart's center.

Criteria for the award have been extended to include civilian nationals who work for U.S. Armed Forces, those who are wounded or killed due to an international terrorist attack, and military personnel on peacekeeping missions.

McDougall made a personal appeal to Congress to make provisions for payment. In spite of recognition that the officers were justified in their demands, Congress again voted against the tax.

Army leaders now plotted another strategy. They realized that once the peace had been settled they'd have little leverage. In March 1783 Major John Armstrong, aide to Major General Horatio Gates, penned what came to be known as the Newburgh Addresses. Newburgh was where General and Mrs. Washington were wintering. (*See* New York, Washington's Headquarters State Historic Site.)

Seeking to incite his fellow officers to do whatever it took to get their monetary due, Armstrong pulled no punches, writing that the Continental Army had "conducted the United States of America through a doubtful and bloody war! It has placed her in the chair of independency, and peace again returns to bless-whom? A country willing to redress your wrongs, cherish your worth, and reward your services . . . Is this the case? Or is it rather, a country that tramples upon your rights, disdains your cries, and insults your distresses?"

A meeting was called for March 11, but Washington forbade it. Instead, he scheduled a meeting a few days later in the Temple Building. In the meantime he met individually with officers, cajoling them to be patient. By the time the meeting was held, Washington had good reason to believe he'd be given a respectful, if not a warm, reception.

Rising to read his reply to the Addresses, Washington's powerful words expressed his loyalty to the army. "As I have been the constant companion and witness of your distresses, and not among the last to feel, and acknowledge your merits . . . As my Heart has ever expanded with joy, when I have heard its praises— and my indignation has arisen, when the mouth of detraction has been opened against it . . ."

He promised to pursue the matter and asked for their patience. In this way he acknowledged the power the army had to disrupt the "last stage of perfection" in finally forming the nation he and they had fought seven long years to attain. At the same time, Washington firmly established a principle he had supported throughout the war—the primacy of civil authority.

The officers acquiesced to the general's wishes and wrote a conciliatory letter to Congress. Some years later some meager pensions were awarded.

In April 1783 official proclamation of the peace was announced and the army disbanded. Officials auctioned off the buildings here, all of which eventually were torn down.

Visiting New Windsor Cantonment

An audiovisual presentation at the Visitor Center provides an overview of the winter spent here by both soldiers and their families. A brochure with a map of the site is provided, and there's an interesting exhibit on the Purple Heart.

Several galleries in the Exhibit Building are currently under renovation, including the artillery gallery, where visitors will see 13 cannons used in the war, ranging in size from 3-pounders to a massive 32-pounder, whose barrel alone weighs 6000 pounds. There will also be a detailed history of 18th-century artillery and the role it played at Yorktown.

In the upstairs gallery (also being renovated), visitors will see a drawing of a large section of the cantonment, as rendered by a Massachusetts private, and a model of one of the huts.

The reconstructed Temple of Virtue, with its spare furnishings, evokes the same sense of quietude its original likely provided for the men who worshipped here. Behind it is the Temple Hill Monument, erected in 1891 in honor of the Masons who served here, including George Washington.

Visitor Information

845-561-1765
nysparks.state.ny.us/hist

Hours: New Windsor is open Mid-April through October, Wednesday through Saturday, 10 a.m. until 5 p.m., Sunday, 1 p.m. until 5 p.m. Also open Memorial Day, Independence Day, and Labor Day.

Admission: Moderate charge: children under 5 admitted free.

Accessibility: The site is accessible.

Special Events: From June through August there are daily demonstrations of musket drills, blacksmithing, military medicine, camp life, and building the log huts.

Getting There: Take I-87 (N.Y. Thruway) to exit 17 and turn right on 17K, then left on state route 300 and go south 3 miles to the site.

New York State Military Museum and Veterans Research Center

This impressive collection of more than 10,000 artifacts related to New York State's military forces and veterans is housed in the massive Saratoga Springs Armory. Designated as a National Historic Landmark, the armory with its castle towers evokes another era of warfare but one not all that removed from the bayonets and swords of Revolutionary War combat.

This collection, whose pieces date from the Revolution through the early 1990s, is among the largest of its kind in the country, and includes uniforms, weapons, battle flags, photographs, artwork, and other priceless memorabilia. In the summer of 2004 the museum opened its new exhibit, "Battleground for Freedom—New York during the Revolutionary War," which includes an absorbing selection of Revolutionary War artillery pieces and weapons.

History of the Museum

In 1865 the New York State Legislature formally established the state's collection of military memorabilia as a way of honoring its veterans and preserving its history. It also approved the creation of a museum to house the collection.

The Division of Military and Naval Affairs was responsible for the collection for the next 100-plus years, storing the artifacts in various locations throughout the state. In the late 1980s, these items were brought together at the Washington Avenue Armory in Albany, and 10 years later at the Watervliet Arsenal Museum. In 2002, the decision was made to house the collection permanently in the 1889 Saratoga Springs Armory.

The on-site displays and the museum's Web site—which provides access to newspaper clippings, photographs, and oral histories—actualize the history of New York's military contributions to the nation's defense.

Visiting the Museum

The newly renovated Revolutionary War exhibit focuses on the major battles that took place in New York. Illustrations and signage examine in detail the strategies that evolved on both sides as the war progressed and the ways in which New York's battles affected the fighting in other states.

In addition to the maps and reproduced uniforms, there are original pieces such as swords and knives; Continental Army, Brown Bess and Charleville muskets; a British artillery piece captured at Yorktown; and one of the cannons captured by Benedict Arnold in Quebec.

In addition, the holdings in the Veterans Research Center include a 2000-volume library of military and New York State history, military files, and soldiers' diaries. Many are useful in genealogical research. Visitors are welcome to use the center for in-depth research or curiosity-inspired browsing.

Visitor Information

(518) 583-0184
www.dmna.state.ny.us/historic/
  mil-hist.htm.

Hours: The museum is open Tuesday through Saturday, 10 a.m. until 4 p.m.; closed on federal holidays. The Veterans Research Center is open Tuesday through Friday, 10 a.m. until 4 p.m., and Saturday by appointment.

Special Events: Check the Web site for upcoming Revolutionary War–related events.

Admission: Free.

Accessibility: The museum and the Research Center are accessible.

Getting There: From the south: Take I-87 north to exit 13N; proceed north on U.S. 9 and turn right on state route 29 (Lake Avenue).

From the north: Take I-87 south to exit 15; take south state route 50 south and turn left on U.S. 9; proceed to state route 29 (Lake Avenue). The museum is 3 blocks ahead on Lake Avenue, in the armory building.

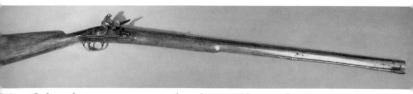

The rifled musket *was more accurate than the smoothbore musket. However, riflemen were at a disadvantage in close quarters fighting against disciplined infantry armed with muskets and bayonets, because the rifle was slower to load.*

Old Fort Niagara

Fort Niagara was the strategic center of British operations in the Great Lakes area during the Revolutionary War, as well as the northern headquarters of Loyalist activities and the center of vitally important British–Native American relations.

It was from Fort Niagara that Loyalists and Native Americans staged devastating raids against frontier settlements, and it was at Fort Niagara that supporters of Britain sought refuge throughout the war. With more than a dozen 18th- and 19th-century buildings preserved on this site, Old Fort Niagara provides a unique and fascinating living-history experience of the lives of British Regulars, Loyalists, and Native Americans during the war.

Early History of the Fort

It was the French who first understood the necessity of having a station at the mouth of the Niagara River, controlling access to the Great Lakes as well as travel in all directions. The French built two posts here. The first was established in 1679, by the French explorer René-Robert Cavelier de La Salle, and another in 1687–1688, before construction of a more permanent fort in 1726.

This last fort, captured in 1759 during the French and Indian War, formed the foundations for the British Fort Niagara. Over the next decade, the British connected a network of British posts, with Fort Niagara as its hub. These included Fort Detroit, Fort Michilimackinac (*see* Michigan, Colonial Michilimackinac and Fort Mackinac), a supply depot at Fort Erie on the west shore of Lake Ontario, and a small wooden stockade on the site of modern-day Ogdensburg, New York.

Duty here was arduous—bitter cold in the winter and isolated—but absolutely necessary to British operations. By the time the 8th Regiment Afoot, one of the most celebrated in the British army, left Fort Niagara in 1785, it was described as being made up of "invalids [rather than] soldiers . . . the worst looking soldiers, and drunkenest men that ever carried a musket." It would be five years before this once proud unit, also known as the King's Regiment, was considered restored to its full strength.

Britain's Allies

With the coming of the Revolutionary War, the fort's commandant, Lieutenant Colonel John Caldwell, was faced with three vital tasks. One was protecting and maintaining the supply routes between Canada and the Mid-Atlantic colonies (or states). Another was providing a haven to what would become a large community of Loyalists, supplying not only shelter, but food and clothing as well, to thousands of men, women and children.

The third was the trickiest and the most potentially volatile: maintaining good relations with the Six Nations of the Iroquois. The Six Nations (Mohawk, Oneida, Onondaga, Cayuga, Seneca, and Tuscarora

Old Fort Niagara

Fort Niagara's *mix of architectural styles includes the French castle fronting Lake Ontario and the North and South Redoubts with their unusual pagoda-style roofs.*

were a powerful force in this region. Add to that the fact that access to Fort Niagara and its supply routes was through Iroquois territory and the absolute necessity of favorable dealings with this very complex cultural and political entity becomes evident.

During the buildup to war, this involved preserving the neutrality of the Nations. As the war escalated, however, and as the Patriots did their best to draw the Nations to the Patriot side, the British had to work hard to retain their longtime alliances with the Iroquois. Once they had brought four of the six Nations in on their side, they had to work equally hard to keep their allies supplied and under control (*see* Native Americans in the Revolution, page 34).

Critical to British endeavors was an Irishman, Sir William Johnson. Though he died in 1774, before the war began, his powerful influence among Native Americans in the region established a foundation for goodwill and trust between them and the British government. Johnson had come to America in 1738 to manage his uncle's New York properties and soon became known to the locals as a major land speculator. After fighting in the French and Indian War, Johnson was appointed British Indian Superintendent for the Northern Department, in which capacity he dealt with tribes from New England to the Mid-Atlantic and west into Ohio country.

Adding to his stature among the Iroquois was his Iroquois marriage to Mary (Molly) Brant, with whom he had several children. Molly was sister to the leading war chief of the Six Nations, Joseph Brant, and was powerful in her own right. The Iroquois were matriarchal in that their leaders were chosen by the women of the Nation, which gave Molly a great deal of authority.

Between 1775 and 1777 the fort was employed mainly in its role as a supply center, and Caldwell and his successor, Lieutenant Colonel Mason Bolton, who took command following Caldwell's death in 1776, spent much of their time courting and supplying the Six Nations.

In the late autumn of 1777, Molly Brant arrived and, probably influenced by her brother Joseph, began pressuring the Nations to engage in military operations on the side of the British. The Iroquois were not allowed inside the fort, except for short stays and only if they had a written pass, so Brant built a cabin outside the walls and held court there until the summer of 1779. Also arriving at the fort beginning in 1777 were Loyalists who had been driven from their homes in the Hudson and Mohawk valleys. Among these were father and son John and Walter Butler. John Butler had worked as an Indian agent for Johnson and by the time of the war was one of the wealthiest men in the region. His son Walter had studied law and opened a practice in Albany. Known as Loyalists, the Butlers were forced to escape to Canada, leaving behind all their property and most of their possessions. In 1777 they came to Fort Niagara to offer their services to the British. Walter was commissioned an ensign in the 8th Regiment Afoot, but soon after left the British army to form the most famous of the Loyalist regiments, Butler's Rangers, with his father.

With the coming of winter in 1777, Commandant Bolton was faced with a huge problem. Inside the fort, in addition to his British Regulars (some 600 men), he had hundreds of Loyalists to feed and shelter. Though many of the women and children had gone to Montreal, some insisted on staying with their husbands and fathers. Outside the fort, by January of 1778, he had more than 2700 Iroquois, who had built a native community stretching eight miles from the fort and who also needed to be fed. And the Niagara River had frozen, making it almost impossible to bring in fresh supplies. The rations of the Regulars were cut to feed as many people as possible, but there were still terrible deprivations and suffering that winter.

Raids and Retaliation

In the spring and summer of 1778, Fort Niagara became a staging area for raids by the Iroquois and Butler's Rangers and other Loyalist ranger companies. The two most famous, or infamous, of these raids were those carried out in the Wyoming Valley of Pennsylvania and the Cherry Valley of New York.

These raids had a dual purpose: to disrupt Patriot supplies, and to intimidate the settlers and drive them off the frontier, away from Indian lands. The raiders burned homes and crops and killed families, annihilating entire communities.

By 1779 the rangers were reaching south into New Jersey, providing intelligence to the British along with destruction to the Patriots. That summer the Continental Army retaliated.

Led by Major General John Sullivan

Loyalists

In 1774 the Continental Congress called for "a committee in every county, city and town . . . to observe the conduct of all persons touching this association . . . to the end that all foes to the rights of British America may be publicly known and universally contemned as enemies of American liberty." This was one of the earliest official prohibitions against Loyalists—those who remained loyal to Great Britain.

Also known as Tories, after the conservative British political party, Loyalists were active in every state, with some 30,000 taking up arms in defense of the Crown. While it's difficult to determine exactly how many remained loyal to the Crown, an estimated 75,000 Americans left the United States during and after the war, most settling in parts of Canada.

---

and Brigadier General James Clinton, the Continentals clashed with Brant and about 800 warriors, plus some 250 Loyalists and a few British Regulars at Newtown, New York. Sullivan and Clinton, with more than 4000 men, defeated Brant and his forces. They then proceeded to raid Indian villages and towns in retaliation for the earlier raids, burning homes and destroying crops. Once again the British were in the position of having to care for their Indian allies, and once again that put a strain on their supply system.

Sullivan and Clinton kept up their raids for several months, but stopped short of attacking Fort Niagara. Brant and Butler's Rangers resumed their raids in 1780 and 1781, though not as many as before. While retreating from militia following one such raid, Walter Butler was killed.

The Postwar Fort

By 1782, with the surrender at Yorktown the previous year and peace negotiations ongoing in Paris, the British at Fort Niagara knew they would soon be departing. However, because of the dispute over compensation to Loyalists, a small garrison remained at the fort until 1796, 13 years after the war was officially over.

The British would again capture the fort during the War of 1812 and again give it back in 1814. The fort was used as a training facility during the Civil War, the Spanish-American War, and World War I, and as a German POW camp in World War II. The last U.S. Army units departed in 1963, making Fort Niagara possibly the longest continuously utilized military installation in North America.

Today this National Historic Landmark is operated by the Old Fort Niagara Association in cooperation with the New York State Office of Parks, Recreation, and Historic Preservation.

Visiting the Fort

Twelve original, historic buildings (six predating the Revolution), plus a spectacular view across Lake Ontario to Toronto, are complemented by entertaining and informative activities year-round.

From June through Labor Day there are dozens of hands-on activities for families, and daily living-history demonstrations and programs. It is hard not to become engrossed in the 300-year history and culture of the three nations that have garrisoned this fort.

The new Visitor Center, scheduled to open in the spring of 2005, will feature a surround-sound orientation film, an exhibition gallery featuring period artifacts, as well as a reproduction of a guardroom depicting the daily life of a British Regular.

A tour of the fort begins at the 1762 Provisions Storehouse, which could hold up to 7000 barrels of food. Behind it stands Dauphin Battery and the original entrance to the fort, which the French called the Gate of the Five Nations.

The 1757 Powder Magazine includes exhibits on the history of the fort and a mystery about a prisoner who disappeared while imprisoned here. The North and South Redoubts, built between 1770 and 1771, are curiosities because of their Chinese-style pagoda roofs, indicative of the influence of a growing Asian trade route for Great Britain.

The 1762 Bakehouse was constructed by the British on the foundations of an earlier French bakery destroyed by fire. Baking demonstrations are given during the summer.

The remaining 18th-century building is the grandest—the French Castle. The oldest building in the North American Great Lakes region, this multichimneyed building was the only one on this site in 1727. When the British expanded the fort's facilities, the Castle was used to house officers and their families. The interiors provide a fascinating insight into how the French quartered their soldiers and defended their position.

The Trade Room on the ground floor reflects the prosperous fur trade that was a staple of French settlements in the late 17th and early 18th centuries. A 25-foot-deep well

located in the castle vestibule was used from the early 1700s until the early 1800s. It is said to be haunted by a murdered French officer who lost his head and rises from the depths of the well to search for it when the moon is full.

The self-guided tour has many other offerings. There is the 18-pounder Battery, with earthwork walls and a casement gallery, and the brick Land Defenses. The Millet Cross honors French soldiers who died of disease and starvation during the winter of 1687–1688, and the Rush-Bagot Memorial commemorates a British–U.S. treaty limiting naval forces on the Great Lakes. The River Defenses were erected to counteract the 1814 British construction of Fort Mississauga on the opposite Canadian shore. The Log Cabin, erected in 1932, typifies one originally built by the French in 1757 and is used as a museum shop.

In honor of the three nations that have held Fort Niagara, three historic flags are flown in the center of the compound: a white French flag flown here from 1726 until 1759, a British Union flag used here from 1759 until 1796, and a Stars and Stripes flown from 1796 until 1818.

Visitor Information

716-745-7611

www.oldfortniagara.org

Hours: The fort opens daily at 9 a.m. Closing hours are 4:30 p.m. from November through March; 5:30 p.m. in April, May, and September; 6:30 p.m. in June; 7:30 p.m. in July and August. On weekends in May, June, and September it stays open an extra hour.

Admission: Significant fee for adults and children to age 12; children under 6 free.

Accessibility: The ground floors of the historic buildings are accessible.

Special Events: The American Long Rifle Association stages a reenactment of colonial and Revolutionary War life once a year.

Getting There: From Niagara Falls on the American side, follow the Robert Moses Parkway north from I-190.

From Niagara Falls on the Canadian side, cross the Rainbow or Queenston Bridge and follow the Robert Moses Parkway north.

From the New York State Thruway, take exit 50, and follow I-290 west to I-190. Take I-190 north to exit 25B and follow the Robert Moses Parkway north.

Oriskany Battlefield State Historic Site

"We will unite and join with the different Districts of this County in giving whatever relief is in our power to the poor distressed inhabitants of Boston, and will join and unite with our brethren of the rest of this colony in anything tending to support our rights and liberties."

This resolution—passed at the first meeting of the Palatine District Committee in Tryon County, New York, on August 27, 1774—would come to a bloody fruition three years later at the Battle of Oriskany.

Background to the Battle

This area, near Utica, New York, was known as German Flatts, named for the Palatine Germans who had come here in the early 1700s after being forced from their land during Germany's Palatine War and its chaotic aftermath. The land they settled on was the domain of the Mohawks, members of the Iroquois Confederation. The Mohawks and their leader Joseph Brant (*see* New York, Old Fort Niagara) had allied themselves with the British, in the hopes that some if not all of their land would be returned to them as reward.

Relations between the settlers and the Mohawks fluctuated—at various times friendly, guarded, or violent. The Herkimer family, one of the area's most prominent, built a compound near here, called Fort Herkimer, which served as a refuge for settlers when there were troubles with the Mohawk.

When Nicholas Herkimer—a brigadier general, leader of the Tryon County militia, and one of the wealthiest men in New York—began to view the Mohawks as a growing threat, he petitioned George Washington for military and matériel assistance. Washington replied he had little to spare, and Herkimer and his people would have to fend for themselves.

Preparing for a Long Siege

Word reached Herkimer that the British were marching down from Canada through the Mohawk Valley on their way to rendezvous with General Burgoyne (*see* New York, Fort Stanwix National Monument). Herkimer called out the Tryon County militia. Not long after, they learned that Fort Stanwix was under siege, and, some 800 strong, they set out to relieve the fort. Molly Brant, Joseph Brant's sister, hearing of this large force marching toward Fort Stanwix, sent a warning to the British commander, General Barry St. Leger. St. Leger dispatched a company of about 800 men, made up of Canadian and American Loyalists and a few British Regulars, but principally of Mohawks and Senecas.

Herkimer and his Tryon County militia were making good time, cov-

ering 40 miles in four days. The militia's four regiments were bringing 15 oxen laden with supplies, in preparation for a long siege at the fort. When Herkimer was about 10 miles from Stanwix, he sent messengers to the fort's commander, Colonel Peter Gansevoort, asking that Gansevoort fire three cannons as a signal that he was commencing a diversionary attack on St. Leger's forces. Herkimer and his militia could then come up from behind, attack St. Leger while he was busy with Gansevoort, and then slip into the fort.

Serious Miscalculation

Herkimer miscalculated the amount of time it would take his messengers to get to the fort. Assuming the messengers should have arrived and the signal given, his men grew impatient waiting for the sound of cannons and began pressing Herkimer to proceed to the fort. Herkimer was a veteran of war and knew the game had to be played carefully. Most of his men, on the other hand, had taken part in drills rather than battles and were eager to prove themselves. When they questioned his commitment, since Herkimer's brother was a Loyalist, as well as his courage, the old warrior bristled and, against his better judgment, resumed the march toward the fort on August 6.

The Loyalist plan, which historians credit to the Native Americans, focused on a ravine some six miles

from the fort, near an Oneida village called Oriska. The Oneidas were also part of the Iroquois Confederation, but had sided with the Patriots in the war. This battle would be the first time in many generations that the Iroquois Nations had fought each other. The road leading to Fort Stanwix crossed this wide ravine, about 50 feet deep and bordered by large trees on both sides. Behind these trees, the Indians and their British, Canadian, and Loyalist allies waited.

The first three Patriot regiments were leading the column. After them came the oxen and behind them the fourth regiment. The first and second regiments had gone down into the ravine and were starting up the other side, followed by the third regiment.

As the beginning of the third regiment got to the bottom of the ravine, the trap was sprung. Herkimer, having insisted on being in front of the first regiment to prove his courage, was among the first to be hit. His horse was shot dead under him and his leg shattered by a bullet. Most of the men in the front with him were killed. The first two militia regiments charged their attackers, trying to get to high ground. The third regiment was trapped from going forward by the regiments ahead and prevented from retreating by the milling oxen behind. The ravine became a blood pool. The fourth regiment, hearing the war whoops and firing, took to their heels and ran.

Herkimer was carried to beneath a tree, where tradition has it he calmly lit a pipe and directed his men. The militia had formed a defensive circle, but there weren't enough of them to fight shoulder-to-shoulder, and into the spaces between them scrambled the Indians and Loyalists. A vicious battle began. The Indians, depending more on tomahawks than guns, would wait for a militiaman to fire his rifle, then strike him down while he was reloading. Seeing this, Herkimer had his men pair off, so that while one was reloading, the other would be firing.

The battle lasted at least four hours, possibly as much as six. In the end, it was almost all hand-to-

*A **wounded** Nicholas Herkimer directs his ambushed militia from beneath a tree. He died ten days later from an unskilled amputation of his wounded leg.*

hand—tomahawk and knife, fighting not for the defense or capture of a fort miles away but fighting savagely for their families' futures, the pride of their people, the right to return to their homes. In the end, it was personal.

The Indians and Loyalists left the field first. The Mohawks hadn't counted on losing so many of their men, especially their chiefs, nor on such a protracted fight. Their anger would resonate through the valley in the coming years, as they and their Loyalist allies led raiding parties, massacring and burning and pushing the frontier back almost to Albany (*see* New York, Old Fort Niagara).

Herkimer had lost two thirds of his men. He would die 10 days later, following the amputation of his leg. The families of German Flatts would face a hard winter because most of the men weren't there for the harvest. Every family in the area lost at least one man to the battle, and most lost more than one. The horror of the loss bound families here together for generations and into the present day.

Each year a solemn commemoration ceremony is held, and descendants of those who fought and died come together. At the 225th anniversary ceremony in 2002, an elderly woman approached a clan mother of the Oneidas and thanked her on behalf of her family. Her ancestor, left dying on the field after the battle, had been rescued by an Oneida from the nearby village and nursed back to health. Whether he was Patriot or Loyalist didn't matter anymore. They were all now members of a community bound by common memories of loss and of regeneration.

Visiting the Battlefield

In the late 1790s, the battlefield was cleared for farming; but as the pain of the battle gave way to pride and a sense of the importance of what happened here, a movement began to establish it as a memorial. In 1884, the Oriskany Monument was dedicated, and three years later 65,000 people attended the three-day centennial commemoration. In 1927 the first five acres were designated as a state historic site, and in 1963 the battlefield was designated a National Historic Landmark.

The Visitor Center has a small

Oriskany Descendants

Oriskany Battlefield personnel have developed a helpful tool for those interested in researching the possibility that an ancestor fought at the Battle of Oriskany. The Descendants Registry database in the Visitor Center contains the names of more than 2500 participants in the battle, including Patriots, Loyalists, and a few Native Americans. They can be searched with the assistance of on-site staff. There's also a Descendants Registry dinner held annually.

---

museum with displays detailing the battle and putting it in the context of the Revolutionary War and the conflicts in the Mohawk Valley.

The tour of the battlefield is self-guided, using a map available at the Visitor Center. There's also interpretive signage at strategic points on the battlefield. Bronze plaques on the granite 85-foot Oriskany Monument list the names of many of the members of the Tryon County Militia who fought here. There is a 1912 stone marker on the spot thought to be where Brigadier General Herkimer sat during the battle. There is also a marker, placed by the Daughters of the American Revolution in 1928, that honors the Unknown Soldier, as well as all those who were buried in a mass grave.

Visitor Information

315-768-7225
nysparks.state.ny.us/hist/ (scroll to Oriskany Battlefield in the list on the left and click on it); and
www.oriskanybattlefield.com

Hours: Mid-May through mid-October; Wednesday through Saturday, 9 a.m. until 5 p.m.; Sunday, 1 p.m. until 5 p.m.; and Monday holidays, 9 a.m. until 5 p.m.; closed Thanksgiving, December 25, and January 1.

Admission: Free.

Accessibility: The Visitor Center, museum, and battlefield are all partially accessible.

Special Events: A commemoration ceremony is held every August, featuring speakers and luminaries for each fallen member of the militia. The annual Descendants Registry dinner is held the first Saturday of August. All who would like to attend are welcome. Contact in advance for details, including the cost of the dinner.

Getting There: From I-90 (NY Thruway), take exit 31 and go south on route 8 toward Utica. Take state route 5a west for 2.5 miles, then state route 69. The battlefield is 2 miles west of Oriskany.

The Continental Army

The Continental Army was an amorphous concept during the first three years of the war, evolving from a nucleus of New York and New England militias in 1775 to a professionally trained army following the 1777–1778 winter encampment at Valley Forge. Creating an army and the bureaucracy to run it was a formidable undertaking and one that continued to progress until the end of the war.

On June 10, 1775, the Second Continental Congress designated the New England militia as the foundation of the Army of the United Colonies. Ten days later it appointed George Washington commander in chief of "all the continental forces."

Each of the 13 colonies was directed to provide a designated number of companies to the army.

Creating an Army

In October 1775, a Congressional Committee met with Washington and issued a report calling for the establishment of a Continental Army consisting of at least 20,000 men organized into 26 standard infantry regiments and separate units of riflemen and artillery.

In November, Congress approved the committee's recommendations. Congress also established a War Office and a Board of War. To this board fell the task of keeping the army supplied, promoting officers, recruiting men for duty, and overseeing the army's overall conduct.

This group spent the majority of the war working out how to accomplish all these tasks, never getting it right but somehow getting it right enough to maintain a modicum of military organization. Keeping the army supplied was not fully mastered until the appointment of Nathanael Greene as quartermaster general in early 1778.

Washington intended to begin implementing the army's new organization in January 1776, but because many enlistments didn't come to an end until July, he had to wait.

Following his loss at the Battle of Long Island, Washington wrote to Congress, "I am persuaded . . . that our Liberties must of necessity be greatly hazarded, if not entirely lost, if their defence is left to any but a permanent standing Army."

Congress agreed. In September 1776, Congress passed legislation authorizing the establishment of the Continental Army and enlistments for three years or the duration of the war. An enlistment bounty of 100 acres of land was also authorized.

The Continental Army consisted of 88 regiments, made up of eight companies, each company divided into four squads. For each regiment there was one captain, two lieutenants, one ensign, four sergeants, four corporals, and 76 privates, plus two drummers and two who played the fife.

The quotas for each state in terms of men and matériel were based on population.

Training

The year 1777 saw the surrender of the British army at Saratoga, brought about in large measure with the assistance of militia forces.

This success of the militia and failure of the army weren't lost on those who were still concerned about having a strong standing army. Washington and his backers in Congress argued that there was much about the army that was working and that its successes could be built on.

The question was how to do that. The answer came in February 1778, when Baron Friedrich Wilhelm von Steuben, a veteran of the Prussian army, arrived at Valley Forge. Washington assigned von Steuben the task of establishing a system of "discipline, maneuveres, evolutions, [and] regulations" for the army.

Steuben drew on training principles from British, French, and Prussian systems. He decided on a system that improved the speed with which columns deployed on the battlefield. He increased the marching pace and began intensive training in the use of the bayonet. He also made it much easier for the army to travel and arrive ready for a fight.

Disbanding an Army

The army that emerged from Valley Forge was no longer a nascent fighting force. From the spring of 1778 until the victory at Yorktown, the Continental Army, supported by local militias, was not only effective at defending its country but also at successfully taking the offensive against the British army.

Once General Charles Cornwallis and his army surrendered at Yorktown in September 1781 and peace talks began in earnest, the bulk of the Continental Army returned to New York State.

The Continental Army was officially disbanded November 2, 1783.

Saratoga National Historical Park

The Second Battle of Saratoga was a pivotal event in the Revolutionary War. The victory brought France into the war on the side of the Americans, and without that alliance it is unlikely there would have been a victory at Yorktown four years later.

The First Battle of Saratoga

Following the Battle of Bennington in August 1777 and the loss of 900 of his men, General John Burgoyne had a choice: retreat to Canada or continue to Albany (*see* New York, Bennington Battlefield State Historic Site). Whether it was arrogance or duty that led him to continue with the plan to rendezvous with General William Howe is a matter long debated by historians.

On September 13 the British army, consisting of 4200 British Regulars, 4000 German troops, and some 1000 Loyalists, Native Americans, and Canadians, crossed from the east to the west bank of the Hudson River at what is now called Schuylerville. Moving south four miles, the army came to the town of Stillwater, where 9000 of General Horatio Gates's Patriot troops and militia awaited them. The Polish engineer Colonel Thaddeus Kosciuszko had designed the American positions on Bemis Heights, a plateau above the Hudson. The entrenchment consisted of a three-sided breastwork two and a half miles long, with artillery placed at each corner.

On September 19, Burgoyne advanced his army in three columns: two, commanded by General Simon Fraser and General Burgoyne, through the wooded area west and east of Freeman Farm; and one, commanded by Baron Adolf von Riedesel along the banks of the Hudson River. In an open field farmed by Loyalist John Freeman, Colonel Daniel Morgan's regiments encountered Burgoyne and the center column, about a mile north of the American position at Bemis Heights.

While that battle raged, the British western column under Fraser ran up against troops led by Benedict Arnold, who had convinced General Gates to let him attempt to take the British right flank. Forced to fall back in the face of Fraser's heavy artillery, Arnold joined Morgan at Freeman Farm. The battle went back and forth for three hours and was finally decided by the arrival of von Riedesel's regiments from their river route. The Patriot forces, low on ammunition, withdrew to Bemis Heights.

In holding the field, the British had won the battle; but with darkness setting in and uncertain of the American position, they had to remain in their position at Freeman Farm.

Burgoyne considered his next move. The Americans were well positioned on the Heights, and the three-to-one axiom—that the army attacking an entrenched defensive position needed three times as many men as its opponent—seemed to be the case here. With troops about equal in number to the Americans', Burgoyne was at a disadvantage. Having given up on Howe, Burgoyne appealed to Sir Henry Clinton in New York and settled in to wait.

Clinton hesitated to send too much of his army to aid Burgoyne, fearing that Washington would take advantage of the situation and attack New York. Actually, Washington was engaged elsewhere, desperately trying to prevent Howe from taking Philadelphia.

Clinton delayed until October 3, when he finally sent 3000 men up the Hudson River. Forts Montgomery, Clinton, and Constitution fell to the British, and Burgoyne's relief seemed imminent. Clinton sent a letter by messenger to Burgoyne saying, "*Nous voici* [we are here]." But the messenger was intercepted. Caught swallowing a bullet with the message enclosed, the unfortunate man was given a large dose of emetic tartar, which brought forth the evidence.

Adding to Burgoyne's woes was that around this time Howe sent word to Clinton ordering additional troops sent to Philadelphia. Clinton abandoned the forts he had taken and abandoned Burgoyne, and sent the expeditionary force south to Howe. It was now the beginning of October. Burgoyne's situation had grown desperate in the three weeks he had been waiting, with lack of supplies and an army growing weaker by the day. He decided to attack.

The Second Battle of Saratoga

On October 7 a force of about 1500 British and German soldiers moved southwest and deployed in the area of Barber Farm. The Patriot forces met them in three columns, com-

The Neilson Farm, the only original structure remaining on the battlefield, was farmed by John Neilson, who fought in both battles here.

manded by Morgan, General Ebenezer Learned, and General Enoch Poor. Arnold had been relieved of command when he quarreled with Gates about what Arnold considered a lack of recognition of his part in the first battle, but he joined Learned's brigade.

The Americans pushed the troops back toward Freeman Farm and the Balcarres Redoubt, the most fortified section of the British line, and the Breymann Redoubt on its west flank. Arnold joined Learned's brigade in pushing the Germans, who formed the British center, back to Freeman Farm. In less than an hour, Burgoyne had lost eight cannons and more than 400 men and officers, including Brigadier General Simon Fraser.

Arnold joined in the assault on the Breymann Redoubt, and the troops finally overwhelmed the Germans defending it. Arnold was wounded in the leg and was carried from the field.

Darkness brought an end to the fighting. Burgoyne realized his situation would only get more desperate with each battle, and he decided to retreat north with an army that now numbered about 8000.

Steady rain and mud on dirt roads forced the army to take refuge on the heights of Saratoga. Here the American army, now numbering about 17,000, caught up with them. Burgoyne would not sacrifice his men in a hopeless effort at escape. On October 17 he asked for terms,

but did not surrender.

Gates would later be dragged over the coals for the agreement he made with Burgoyne, but apparently he was concerned that British reinforcements might arrive at any moment. For whatever reason, in effect he allowed Burgoyne to dictate the terms of surrender, contained in the Saratoga Convention. Among the conditions agreed upon were that the army be allowed to march out of their camp and be allowed to return to Great Britain in exchange for taking an oath not to serve again in the war.

In January of 1778, while Burgoyne and his army waited in Boston for transport to England, Congress, in effect, discarded the Saratoga Convention, threw the army into prisoner of war facilities, and dispatched Burgoyne to England.

Visiting Saratoga

Saratoga National Historical Park is made up of three separate units—the battlefield at the north edge of the town of Stillwater, the Philip Schuyler House about eight miles north of the battlefield, and the Saratoga Monument, which is three quarters of a mile west of the Schuyler House.

The battlefield encompasses almost 3000 acres, through which

wind a 9.5-mile Tour Road for bikes and autos, the 4.2-mile Wilkinson National Recreation Trail for hiking, and several secondary hiking trails. The Wilkinson Trail is named for British Lieutenant William Wilkinson, whose 1777 maps of the area later helped locate many of the roads used during the battle. It takes visitors to a little less than half the major sites on the battlefield, but evokes a true sense of what it was like for the British and German troops finding their way through this beautifully wooded area. The Tour Road gives visitors the bigger picture, stopping at 10 sites on the battlefield.

The battlefield today is about 80 percent accurate in terms of the 1777 setting of wooded areas and open fields.

There is an engaging orientation film at the Visitor Center called *Something More at Stake,* taken from a quote by one of the soldiers who fought here, who said, "We who fought for six pence a day had something more at stake." The film was shot in 2003 at a reenactment of the Battles of Saratoga.

The center's museum has five original artillery pieces, including several cannons that were surrendered by the British here, and several muskets. Also on display are personal items used by the soldiers, such as a powder horn, a small prayer book, some tools, and a fascine knife for cutting woody brush to make fascines—bundles of sticks used to strengthen fortifications.

Two dioramas provide views of the battles. One is an aerial view of what the area looked like just before the battles—farmhouses, wheat fields, and woods. The other is a detailed view of the British Breymann Redoubt.

The **Freeman Farm Overlook** is where the first Battle of Saratoga converged on September 19. Freeman's farm was confiscated by local Patriot authorities following the battle.

The **Neilson Farm** was at Bemis Heights. Though today the entire plateau is called Bemis Heights, in 1777 the Heights was simply a ridge on that plateau. It was named for Jotham Bemis, whose tavern was located at the foot of the Heights. The Neilson farmhouse is open seasonally, with a ranger on duty to answer questions. Off-season, visitors can see inside the house through the windows.

The **Chatfield Farm** and **Barber Wheatfield** were open areas in 1777. The farm was used as a listening post by the Americans. The wheat field acted as a distraction. On October 7, Burgoyne sent about 1400 men south to find high ground for the army to occupy. Their journey took them through the wheat field of a farmer named Barber. The wheat was ripe and ready for harvesting, and the soldiers were hungry. As they began picking the heads of the stalks of wheat and stuffing

Benedict Arnold was wounded in the assault on Breymann Redoubt, where Hessian forces were overwhelmed.

Balcarres Redoubt held during the battle on October 7, but the Breymann Redoubt had little chance, with fewer than 200 German troops defending it against more than 1000 American troops.

The **"Boot Monument,"** near the Berryman Redoubt, was erected in 1887 by a New York Civil War general, John Watts DePeyster, who felt that tribute should be paid to Benedict Arnold's valor in the battles here. Its name comes from its design, a boot with a general's epaulet on it; it stands near where Arnold was shot in the left leg. The text says it was erected in memory of the "most brilliant soldier of the Continental Army, who was desperately wounded on this spot." But like the memorial to Arnold at West Point, it pays tribute to his deeds without naming the man who later betrayed his country.

them in their pockets, two of the officers sent word back to Burgoyne to send a foraging party forward for the wheat. It was then that the Americans attacked.

At the **Balcarres Redoubt,** located just south of the Freeman farmhouse, the British cannons are pointing in the direction they were aiming after the September 19 battle, when Burgoyne had a fortified line constructed between the river and the Breymann Redoubt. The

The site of **Burgoyne's headquarters,** which in 1777 consisted of large tents, is just west of the Great Redoubt. Burgoyne's system of fortifications, built to guard the British hospital, artillery park, Indian camp, and supply station, was served by an improvised bridge. The British had constructed the bridge by chaining bateaux together across the river, anchoring the chains on both sides of the river, and nailing down boards

News of Burgoyne's surrender was heard around the world, and brought France into the war on the side of the Americans.

on the top of the bateaux so soldiers could carry supplies across. From this redoubt, visitors have a fine view of the park, looking down on the Old Champlain Canal and the Hudson River. The British probably didn't have this view in 1777, since the area was mostly forest.

General Simon Fraser's burial site is reached by a one-mile loop trail. Tradition has it that during the funeral, the British were fired on by the Americans, with cannonballs hitting the surrounding earthworks and sprays of dirt falling on Burgoyne and his officers during the burial.

There are several other monuments on the battlefield, including those honoring Kosciuszko, Morgan, and Fraser.

The Philip Schuyler House

This was the home of Philip Schuyler, one of the first four major generals appointed by Congress in June 1775 to serve under Washington.

The heir of one of New York's most prominent Dutch families, Schuyler was a delegate to the Second Continental Congress and a leader in political circles in his home state. With the outbreak of the war, he was given command of the Northern Department of the army, organized the invasion of Canada, was blamed for the capture of Fort Ticonderoga by Burgoyne in 1777, and was relieved of command just six weeks before Saratoga. Following Burgoyne's defeat on October 7, the Saratoga Convention was negotiated on the southern end of Schuyler's property.

This is the third house on this property. The first was burned down in a French–Indian raid in 1745, and the second was burned by the retreating British in 1777. The house now here is a restoration of the one Schuyler built after 1777, and it is furnished to look much as it did when Schuyler and his family lived here.

The home is open seasonally, and is shown on a 30-minute guided tour.

The Saratoga Monument

This granite obelisk, 155-and-a-half-feet tall, is located on the grounds of Burgoyne's last camp on October 8, on a high bluff in a village named Victory. Life-size sculptures of General Philip Schuyler, Colonel Daniel Morgan, and General Horatio Gates stand in three of the niches of its broad base. The empty fourth niche represents General Benedict Arnold—once again a case of the deeds, not the man, being honored.

Stairs to the top of the monument lead to viewing platforms at five levels and past a number of bronze plaques portraying various scenes from Burgoyne's campaign of 1777. The monument is open seasonally, and an interpreter is on-site to answer questions.

Visitor Information

518-664-9821
www.nps.gov/sara

Hours: The Visitor Center in Stillwater is open daily from 9 a.m. until 5 p.m.; closed Thanksgiving, December 25, and January 1. The Tour Road is usually open from April 1 until mid-November, depending on weather conditions. The Schuyler House and the Saratoga Monument are open for guided tours Memorial Day through Labor Day, Wednesday through Sunday, from 9 a.m. until 4:30 p.m. On October 9 and 10 and on October 16 and 17, the Battlefield and Visitor Center at Stillwater, the Schuyler House, and the Saratoga Monument are open to commemorate the battles of Saratoga.

Admission: For the battlefield and Visitor Center at Stillwater, there is a moderate fee per car, slightly less for hikers or bikers age 16 and older; an annual pass is available. Admission to the Schuyler House and the Saratoga Monument is free.

Accessibility: The Visitor Center is accessible and the orientation film is formatted with captions. The stops on the Tour Road have paved walkways but may be steep in certain sections. The interiors of the Schuyler House and the Saratoga Monument are not accessible at this time. More detailed information about the accessibility of particular sections of the park is available on the Web site or by calling 518-664-9821.

Special Events: Annual commemorations of the Battles of Saratoga with a wreath laying, a winter festival in January, natural history walks on Saturdays in May and June, evening strolls on Saturdays in July, 18th-Century Day in August, an Oneida Indians and Stillwater Heritage Day in October.

Getting There: The park is 40 miles north of Albany and 15 miles southeast of Saratoga Springs. From exit 12 of I-87 (the Northway), signs direct drivers to the park. The NPS Web site has detailed information on arriving by car from every direction, or call the Visitor Center.

Skenesborough Museum

This small museum inventively tells the story of the creation of the Continental Navy in 1776, as well as the history of this region on the southernmost tip of Lake Champlain. It was here that Benedict Arnold and hundreds of New England craftsmen accomplished the nearly impossible construction of an American fleet capable of challenging the British navy in what came to be known as the Battle of Valcour Island (*see* Vermont, Lake Champlain Maritime Museum).

The museum's displays detail the construction of the fleet over a period of three months in the town's shipyard, originally built by Philip Skene. In appreciation for his service in the French and Indian War, in 1759 Skene was granted 34,000 acres on Lake Champlain and appointed governor of Crown Point and Ticonderoga. He founded the town of Skenesboro (now Whitehall) and prospered by building sawmills and a shipyard.

Skene was taken prisoner when the Patriots captured Crown Point and Ticonderoga in May 1775. After being exchanged for Patriot prisoners and briefly settling in Canada, Skene volunteered as an advisor to General John Burgoyne's campaign in 1777. Skene had a lot at stake in the war. For some time he had been negotiating with the British government to create a separate province, with himself as governor, that would encompass the Lake Champlain region, including parts of present-day New York and Vermont.

Fortunately for the Patriots, Skene proved a disaster as an advisor. First he advised Burgoyne to take the land route from Skenesboro south rather than the water route, even though going by water would have provided Burgoyne easier and quicker transport of horses and artillery.

Skene's second miscue was in convincing the German commander Friedrich Baum that the area around Bennington, Vermont, was a Loyalist stronghold, setting him up for the Patriot trickery that helped John Stark and his army defeat the Hessians (*see* Vermont, Bennington Battlefield State Historic Site).

His final bit of advice reveals his opinion of those whom he would have been governing. When Burgoyne sought an alternative to surrender at Saratoga, Skene is said to have replied, "Scatter your baggage, stores and everything that can be spared at proper distances, and the militiamen will be so busy plundering them that you and the troops will get clean off."

Following Saratoga, when the British whom Burgoyne had left behind at Fort Ticonderoga retreated into Canada, they burned Skenesboro to the ground, fearing it would be of use to the Patriots. Skene lost everything, and after being exchanged once again, he settled in London.

At war's end, he applied to return to New York, where he still had a great deal of property, and become an American citizen, but the state refused to lift its charge of treason against him and confiscated all his property. In 1785, Skene was granted a pension by the British government and a bonus that allowed him to buy an estate in northern England, where he died in 1810.

The Skenesborough Museum contains a number of artifacts from the Revolutionary War, such as a 12-inch mortar bomb, as well as some beautiful models of ships from Arnold's fleet and maps of the area. There are also some fascinating Native American artifacts from colonial times, and items used by 18th-century farmers and artisans.

A 16-foot diorama, part of a light-and-sound program, depicts the town as it was when established and shows various ships under construction.

The museum shares the depot site with the Whitehall Urban Cultural Park Visitor Center. The park itself, where the museum is located, is a lovely waterfront promenade of Victorian buildings from Whitehall's heyday.

Visitor Information

518-499-0716
www.whitehallchamber.com/
WhitehallNewYork.htm
Hours: Mid-June through Labor Day, Monday through Saturday, 10 a.m. until 4 p.m.; Sunday, noon until 4 p.m. From Labor Day through mid-October, Saturday, 10 a.m. until 3 p.m., Sunday, noon until 3 p.m. Closed major holidays.
Admission: Free.
Accessibility: Handicapped accessible.
Special Events: Whitehall has a winter festival on the second Saturday of February, which features special activities at the museum.
Getting There: Take I-87 (the Northway) to exit 20, then left to state route 149. After 12 miles, at Fort Ann turn left on U.S. 4 to Whitehall and go 11 miles to Skenesborough Drive.

Stony Point Battlefield State Historic Site

"Give the order, Sir, and I will lay siege to hell!" When "Mad Anthony" Wayne spoke these words to George Washington in the summer of 1779, he wasn't boasting. Given Wayne's reputation for daring and bravery, he likely would have marched into hell if Washington had ordered it. Luckily for Wayne, the General is said to have replied, "Take Stony Point first."

Actually, the task of taking the earthen fort at Stony Point might be considered somewhat hellacious from an attacker's point of view. The fort was located on the tip of an 87-acre peninsula rising 150 feet above the Hudson River. Surrounded on three sides by water, it could only be reached by a narrow causeway across a swamp.

The fact that Wayne and his troops succeeded in capturing the fort was a milestone for the Continental Army. It proved that these rebel farmers and clerks, as the British liked to portray them, were in fact a disciplined army capable of mounting a stealthy and complex attack.

Though nothing of the actual fort remains today, walking the battlefield gives visitors a clear sense of the difficulties Wayne and his men faced attacking a fort on a spit of land jutting 150 feet above the Hudson River in the dark of night.

History of the Battle

Stony Point had been a small Continental Army post, still under construction, until May of 1779, when the British captured it without a fight. The Continentals knew a large British force was approaching, one they couldn't possibly match, so they burned one of the completed blockhouses and left. The British proceeded to finish building the fort.

Both armies recognized the strategic importance of Stony Point, a promontory that thrust half a mile out into the Hudson River opposite

Verplanck's Point. Fort Lafayette on Verplanck's Point also was now under British control.

Together these two points controlled Hudson River traffic going north toward the American positions at West Point and Fort Putnam. More important, they controlled King's Ferry, which crossed the river below and was a major link between New England and states south.

But Stony Point wouldn't be easily recaptured. It was virtually an island, with only that causeway providing access by land.

Not depending solely on natural impediments, the British had placed a curved line of abatis—a barrier made of trees, set at an angle, whose limbs have been sharpened to points—to the west and east of the fort and had felled all the nearby forests to ensure a clear view of anyone (or army) approaching. Inside the fort was a garrison of some 600 men, including Loyalists, commanded by Lieutenant Colonel Henry Johnson.

Washington knew he didn't have the wherewithal in troops or matériel to occupy Stony Point, but

he also knew he had to dislodge the British. Accordingly he spent weeks sending agents into the area to reconnoiter the situation, at one point deploying Allen McLane of the Delaware Regiment to visit the fort under the guise of accompanying a Loyalist mother visiting her sons.

McLane was able to gauge the defenses and their possible vulnerabilities on this and one other visit. He returned four days later, according to his journal, with "the widow Calhoon and another widow going to the enemy with chickens and greens."

To Brigadier General Anthony Wayne went the assignment of figuring out how best to take the fort. Historians have debated whether the brutal loss of Wayne's men at Paoli, Pennsylvania impacted his strategy at Stony Point. At Paoli, Wayne's men suffered a surprise attack by the British, who used only bayonets and clubs. When the surviving Americans surrendered, they were put to death, without a shot being fired. The experience must have taught Wayne the value of silent killing in a surprise attack.

Four regiments were assigned to Wayne. The men, numbering a little more than 1300, were the cream of the Continental crop, hardy veterans, many of whom had either been drilled in bayonet fighting by Baron von Steuben or had drilled using his infantry manual.

On the morning of July 15, 1779, the brigade assembled at Sandy Point, five miles below West Point, and from there set out around noon on a 13-mile march. Once they were within about a mile of Stony Point, Wayne halted the march, and only then did the men learn what their mission was. And they learned they were to take Stony Point silently, using fixed bayonets. No firing of muskets, except by a small diversionary force firing from the causeway.

The brigade was formed into three columns, one of which was the diversionary force. In advance of each of the other two columns were to be a detachment of men with axes who would cut through the abatis. And with each of these "ax detachments" was a squad of one officer and 20 men who would be the first to push through the axed openings

"Mad Anthony" Wayne, inset, accomplished a seemingly impossible feat when he captured this peninsular fort 150 feet above the Hudson River (North River).

Around two a.m. the morning of the battle, Wayne sent a message to General Washington: "The fort and garrison with Colonel Johnson are ours. Our officers and men behaved like men who are determined to be free."

and engage in hand-to-hand combat. These were called the forlorn hope. Today we'd call them the suicide squad.

Each man in the brigade was to wear a piece of white paper in his hat, which was the way Continental forces identified each other during night attacks. Once they had entered the fort, they were to begin shouting, "The fort's our own!" and continue shouting it, to confuse the British.

Prior to setting out a little before midnight, the men were told one last thing—the first five to enter the fort would be given a cash reward.

Wayne's attack plan worked, even though one of the columns was detected as it waded through waist-high water and was fired upon from above. Wayne was wounded and had

to fall back, but his men pushed ahead of him. In less than an hour, the fort was taken, with only 15 American lives lost. More than 500 British officers and soldiers were captured, along with 15 pieces of artillery and large amounts of supplies.

Once the fort at Stony Point was taken, Washington, not having the resources to maintain it, ordered it destroyed.

The attack had served a larger purpose. Nathanael Greene, writing that same month, recognized the propaganda value of the victory. "The attack was . . . conducted with great spirit and enterprise, the troops marching up in the face of an exceeding heavy fire with cannon and musketry, without discharging a gun. This is thought to be the perfection of discipline and will for ever immortalize Gen. Wayne, as it would do honor to the first general in Europe."

The British, indeed, found a new

Immovable Women

Along with the British soldiers captured at Stony Point, there was a large contingent of women and children—the families of those garrisoning the fort. Soon after the battle, the men, women, and children began a march from Stony Point to a prison camp in Pennsylvania. A few days into the hike, the women decided neither they nor their children could survive so strenuous an exercise and, sitting down in protest, refused to move until wagons were brought. When neither threats nor cajoling could move the women, the soldiers guarding the group found wagons, loaded the women and children, and recommenced the march. The prisoners were kept in the Pennsylvania prison camp through the winter.

respect for the Continental Army. British Commodore George Collier wrote in his journal of "the surprisal in the night of the strong post at Stony Point . . . which was carried by the rebels with very little loss and the garrison all made prisoners or killed . . . The rebels had made the attack with a bravery they never before exhibited."

Visiting the Site

In time for its 225th anniversary in 2004, Stony Point opened its newly renovated museum. Previous exhibits have been reconfigured and additional space has been created to display items from Stony Point's archaeological collection.

An audiovisual presentation about the battle complements the museum's two galleries, where visitors see displays about Anthony Wayne and his Light Infantry, the strategic importance of Stony Point, and British units stationed here.

Among these was the 71st Highlanders, the first Scottish regiment raised for service in the Revolutionary War. Among the artifacts from the 71st are a Scottish pin and regimental buttons.

The buttons were recovered in 1953, when visitors noticed a bone protruding through the battlefield soil. The bone was part of the body of one of two soldiers who had been buried together in an unmarked grave. Though little of the soldiers was intact, the buttons on their shirts had survived.

Among the arms displayed is a French-made Charleville musket. (Note the manufacturer's mark, a fleur-de-lis.) There's also a dramatic grouping of five bayonets similar to ones used in the attack.

A very informative brochure includes quotes from those who participated in the battle, both British and American. The walking trail laid out in the brochure takes visitors around the battlefield, stopping at points where specific events in the battle took place.

The trail includes Stony Point Lighthouse, which was built in 1826 and is the oldest lighthouse on the Hudson River. Near the lighthouse are viewing sheds, where visitors can enjoy a breathtaking view up the Hudson River into the mountains.

April through October, a British encampment is reproduced on the lawn just outside the museum, with costumed interpreters answering questions about the lives of those who were garrisoned here and giving firing, cooking, and woodworking demonstrations. This realistic re-creation testifies to the difficult lives not only of the soldiers but also of the families who shared this spartan outpost.

Visitor Information

845-786-2521
nysparks.state.ny.us/hist
(In the list at left, scroll to Stony Point and click on it.)

Hours: The museum and battlefield are open 10 a.m. until 4:30 p.m., Wednesday through Saturday, Sunday, 1 p.m. until 4:30 p.m., mid-April until October 31, including holidays. The grounds are open 10 a.m. until 4 p.m., every day, weather permitting, March 1 through November 30. (There's a brochure box in the parking lot.) Tours of the lighthouse are given mid-April through October 31, weekend afternoons. Please call ahead for exact hours.

Admission: There is a minimal fee on weekdays and a parking fee on weekends to be determined.

Accessibility: The lighthouse is not accessible. The viewing sheds are partially accessible.

Getting There: Take Palisades Interstate Parkway to exit 15, and follow the signs to Route 106/210 (east) to Route 9W (north). Travel 1 mile north on 9W and turn right on Park Road.

West Point Museum

Before West Point was a military academy, it was a strategic point of fortification for the Patriots during the Revolutionary War. As such, it became the target of British intrigue, and the site of Benedict Arnold's infamous treason. West Point Museum, though founded more than 70 years after the war, had its genesis in items captured following Burgoyne's surrender at Saratoga.

Together the academy and the museum give visitors a clearer understanding of the integral part the New York and Hudson River campaigns played in the war and, as a plus, afford a breathtaking view of the Hudson River.

A Strategic Site

The importance of maintaining colonial control of the Hudson River was well recognized from the outset of the war. Not only was the Hudson on the main British invasion route from Canada, but following the loss of New York City, the Hudson Highlands was also the junction of a vital transportation network between the New England, Mid-Atlantic, and Southern states.

This plateau overlooking the Hudson was perfectly situated for defense. Tidal changes twice a day—at one point moving upstream, at another down—coupled with strong winds meant ships had to slow down as they approached the bend in the river and then came around it past the point. This presented ample opportunity to target any unfriendly vessels. Though earlier fortifications in the area had concentrated on Constitution Island to the east of West Point, after the British advance through here in 1777, the Continental Army began a more concerted effort to fortify the point. The task was given to General Israel Putnam. His engineer was Colonel Thaddeus Kosciuszko, who had been and would continue to be invaluable in several key battles.

Over a 28-month period, Kosciuszko turned the plateau into a formidable stronghold. Fort Arnold, named for Benedict Arnold, sat at the eastern edge. Fort Putnam, named for Colonel Rufus Putnam, who supervised the Massachusetts regiment that built it and was Israel's cousin, stood on a rise above Fort Arnold. There were three redoubts covering the southern approaches to the point, and four more in the hills behind Fort Putnam. Along the shoreline were several gun batteries.

It's easy to understand why the British coveted West Point. Less understandable, or less knowable, are the reasons behind Benedict Arnold's betrayal. Some historians attribute it to thwarted ambition, others to resentment of the advancement of less qualified men, still others to the need for money to support

*A **memorial** at Trophy Point displays thirteen links of the chain that blocked the ships of the British fleet on the Hudson River.*

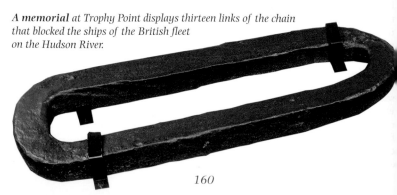

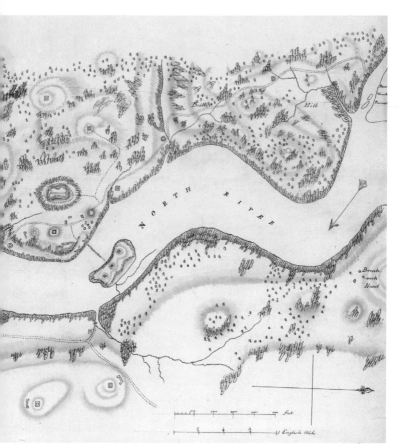

West Point's strategic placement on a plateau above the Hudson River (labeled North River on the map) prevented the British fleet from sailing up the river. Note the chain stretched across to Constitution Island.

his lavish lifestyle. It should be noted that in addition to Arnold's extravagances, it was nonpayment of monies owed him by Congress, for expenditures in several campaigns, that put him in debt. Of course, being owed money by Congress wasn't exclusive to Arnold. Most officers went into debt supporting their armies.

Though lauded as the hero of Valcour Island (*see* Vermont, Lake Champlain Maritime Museum) and promoted to major general, Arnold still smarted from the unjustified slights he'd suffered from Congress. In 1778, when he was appointed military commander of Philadelphia, he was full of resentment.

Marrying above his income, to the daughter of a wealthy Philadelphian with Loyalist tendencies, Arnold began to adopt an affluent lifestyle. In 1779, Arnold asked for a courtmartial to clear himself of charges made by his enemies that he was misusing Continental funds.

Concurrently, Sir Henry Clinton's aide, Major John André, received an anonymous letter intimating that a senior Continental Army officer was willing to render "his services to the commander-in-chief of the British forces in any way that would most effectually restore the former government . . . whether by immediate-

ly joining the British army or cooperating on some concealed plan."

André (acting for Clinton) and Arnold began a correspondence focused on Arnold's compensation for whatever was required of him. Correspondence stopped when Arnold balked at Clinton's measly recompense (two guineas per captured soldier) and mundane plan that had Arnold leading an army into a trap. In the meantime, though, Arnold had been passing along information on troop movements, strategies, and plans.

Arnold resumed contact in May 1780, still in the midst of his courtmartial. He wanted 10,000 pounds as down payment for delivery of West Point. He could cajole command of the area from Washington, he promised Clinton, after which he would so weaken the defenses that the British could easily capture the fort. And when they did, he wanted an additional 20,000 pounds.

Clinton knew the value of what Arnold was offering, and agreed. Arnold began to set the plan in motion by turning down a command

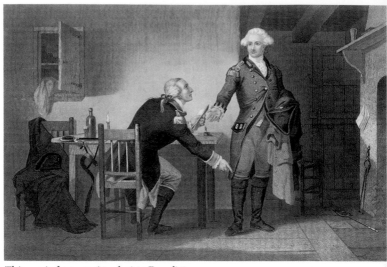

This period engraving depicts Benedict Arnold suggesting that Major John André hide the secret documents in his boot.

in the upcoming Southern Campaign. Convincing Washington that his leg wound (now several years old) still made him unfit for frontline duty, Arnold requested command of West Point instead, and got it, assuming command in August of 1780.

Betrayal

Arnold now set about weakening West Point's defenses. He sent hundreds of men away from the forts on woodcutting detachments for long periods. Knowing the chain across the river was in need of repair, he delayed repairing it. In incremental ways, he prepared West Point for surrender.

On September 21, 1780, John André arrived aboard the British sloop *Vulture* to discuss with Arnold the surrender of West Point. Using the alias John Anderson, André met with Arnold in the woods near the point and worked out a plan, after which André intended to return to the ship and sail back to New York. The *Vulture*, meanwhile, had come under attack and sailed away without him. This left André no choice but to go by land. Using a pass signed by Arnold, he made his way as far as Tarrytown, where he was picked up as a questionable character and interrogated by Major Benjamin Tallmadge, Washington's chief of intelligence. Tallmadge just happened to be in the area, doing reconnaissance for a meeting between Washington and the French general Rochambeau (could André have had worse luck?). He was suspicious of this obviously educated and erudite individual traveling by night so near West Point.

It was soon found that André had

the detailed plans of West Point's defenses, as well as confidential orders issued by General Washington, in one of his boots. Arnold, hearing that André had been captured, said a hurried good-bye to his wife and made his way via his barge to the *Vulture*, which was now sitting near Stony Point. Arnold and the *Vulture* were long gone by the time his treachery was discovered. Because André had been captured out of uniform, the unlucky major was tried as a spy and hanged.

West Point was saved from the British, but just barely. If things had not gone so decidedly wrong for André, it's likely the plan would have worked and West Point would have fallen into British hands.

The near miss did have consequences. Morale was low enough following the terrible defeat at Camden and the collapse of resistance in the South. The defection of one of the army's great heroes and most talented generals made recruitment even more difficult.

The Marquis de Lafayette, who was with Washington at West Point immediately after the incident, wrote a fellow Frenchman that he was personally humiliated by Benedict Arnold's treachery ("[W]hat will the officers of the French army say when they see a general abandon and basely sell his country after having defended it so well!") and that he fully expected Arnold to kill himself once he realized his dishonor. "My knowledge of his personal courage led me to expect that he would decide to blow his brains out (this was my first hope); at all events, it is probable that he will do so when he reaches New York."

Arnold did not blow his brains out. He joined the British army, in which he served enthusiastically (*see*

Connecticut, Forts Griswold and Trumbull) before moving to London in 1781, where he was viewed as a somewhat distasteful figure, and died in straitened circumstances 20 years later at the age of 60. One of his sons made a career in the British army, as did his grandson, who was a major general in World War I.

On August 15, 1821, John André's body was removed from its burial plot in Tappan Landing (some 25 miles from West Point) and returned to England, where it was reburied in Westminster Abbey. Atop his tomb is an elaborate monument, personally paid for by King George III, on the front of which is a relief showing George Washington receiving André's petition not to be hanged and André being led to the gallows. Long memories.

A National Military Academy

Following the war, President Washington repeatedly proposed establishing a military academy. In 1802 this site was chosen and the United States Military Academy formally established. Early curriculum focused on civil engineering. U.S.M.A. officers were instrumental in the construction of the new nation's infrastructure, supervising the building of bridges, harbors, roads, and later of railway lines.

Major John André

Much has been made of Washington's hanging André, instead of granting the British officer's request to die as a gentleman in front of a firing squad. On the eve of his execution, André appealed to Washington in a letter: "Buoyed above the terror of death by the consciousness of a life devoted to honourable pursuits, and stained with no action that can give me remorse, I trust that the request I make to your Excellency at this serious period, and which is to soften my last moments, will not be rejected.

"Sympathy towards a soldier will surely induce your Excellency and a military tribunal to adopt a mode of my death to the feelings of a man of honour.

"Let me hope, Sir, that if aught in my character impresses you with esteem towards me, if aught in my misfortunes marks me as the victim of policy and not of resentment, I shall experience the operation of these feelings in my breast, by being informed that I am not to die on a gibbet."

Alexander Hamilton, who witnessed the hanging and was sympathetic to André ("Never, perhaps, did a man suffer death with more justice, or deserve it less"), wrote that the only time André seemed to lose his composure was when he saw the gallows and asked, "Must I then die in this manner?" Clinton himself corresponded with Washington about the possibility of a trade, though whether the suggested trade was Arnold for André historians can't agree. Nor can they agree whether it was Clinton or Washington who wouldn't consent to the trade.

Major John André being read his death warrant.

George Washington was an early and determined proponent of an American military academy. In this painting by George Peale Polk, part of the museum's fine art collection, Washington i portrayed at Princeton.

Honor, Country. It remains the oldest continuously occupied military post in the United States.

Visiting the Museum

Though it wasn't officially established until 1854, the West Point Museum actually came into existence following the Battle of Saratoga (*see* New York, Saratoga National Historical Park), when Henry Knox brought back a number of items captured in the battle. It was then that Fort Arnold (on the site that later became West Point) was designated the repository of captured war trophies.

Providing military leadership in the Mexican and Indian wars, and especially in the Civil War (450 generals and hundreds of officers were trained at the Point) brought national recognition to the Academy. In the years following the wars, the Academy adopted an expanded curriculum more reflective of the army's needs.

Leadership was again provided in the two World Wars and in America's military conflicts in the second half of the 20th century. The academy also led the way in producing an army skilled in science and technology and capable of understanding and dealing with the cultures of other countries.

In celebrating its bicentennial in 2002, the academy renewed its commitment to its pledge of Duty,

In 200-plus years, the collection has grown impressively, becoming the largest as well as the oldest military museum in the U.S. Items from 3000 B.C. to the present are displayed here, in six galleries on four floors. Revolutionary War–related items are found in each of the galleries, but primarily in the "West Point" and "History of U.S. Army" galleries.

Starting in the "West Point" gallery, visitors learn about the garrisoning of West Point during the war, its strategic importance, and its place in the context of the Hudson River Valley campaigns. Among the items displayed are a portrait of George Washington by Gilbert Stuart and Thaddeus Kosciuszko's sword.

The "History of the U.S. Army" gallery features dioramas of battle plans, such as the Battle of Saratoga (now used as a teaching tool here at the Academy), two portraits of Washington—one of which, by Charles Willson Peale, depicts the young Washington as a

---

Visiting the Academy

The museum is located in Olmsted Hall in the Pershing Center, behind the Visitor Center. Both of these facilities are open to the public without an appointment or having to show a picture I.D. In order to see other points of interest at the academy, however, visitors are encouraged to take one of the tours that leave throughout the day from the Visitor Center. Entry to the academy grounds requires a picture I.D., and those who are not part of a tour may not be allowed access to areas of the grounds. Security levels are subject to change, so it's best to call the Visitor Center before coming to West Point. The Visitor Center has informational videos about the Academy and free pamphlets.

colonel in the Virginia militia fighting for King George—and a sword believed to have belonged to Burgoyne. The most prized (and rare) items here are a pair of Washington's flintlock pistols, which he used during the war.

There are also flintlocks in the "Small Weapons" gallery. And in the "Large Weapons" gallery is a Coehorn mortar (a light artillery piece used by the British and the French) that was captured from the British. The "American Wars" gallery exhibits a very early uniform from the war and has period officers' trunks on display.

The Old Cadet Chapel, a neoclassical structure built in 1830, sits on a promontory overlooking the Hudson River. (It originally stood elsewhere on the grounds, and was dismantled and reconstructed stone by stone on the present site in 1910.) This was the first place of worship built at the Academy, and is one of the oldest buildings still in use here. Plaques have been placed on the east wall honoring the generals of the American Revolution, with name, dates, and rank. No plaque names Benedict Arnold; but one gives just his birth year, 1741, and his rank of major general.

At Trophy Point, located at the western edge of West Point, there's a statue of Thaddeus Kosciuszko, dedicated July 4, 1828. This was one of the first memorials raised at West Point. One of the cadets designed it, and the cadets themselves collected the money to have it sculpted. Thirteen links of the original chain that spanned the Hudson River are displayed here, one for each of the original 13 states. Even looking at this small sample of the chain gives visitors an idea of how massive it was. Each of its iron links was some 12 inches wide, 18 inches long, and 2 inches thick. Each winter the

chain was hauled back to the river's west bank, using a windlass; otherwise, it might have been broken by the huge cakes of ice that floated along the river in winter.

Visitor Information
845-938-2203 or 3590
(for the museum);
845-938-2638 (Visitor Center);
845-446-4724 (guided bus tours)
www.usma.edu; and
www.usma.edu/Museum
Hours: The Visitor Center is open daily from 9 a.m. until 4:45 p.m. The museum is open daily from 10:30 a.m. until 4:15 p.m. Both are closed Thanksgiving Day, December 25, and January 1.
Admission: Free.
Accessibility: Visitor Center and museum are wheelchair accessible.
Special Events: May 1 is Kosciuszko Day, with a ceremony at the Kosciuszko statue and access to Kosciuszko's Garden.
Getting There: Take I-84 to exit 10, U.S. route 9W south. From 9W, take the "West Point, Highland Falls" exit, which goes into Highland Falls.

From I-87 (NY Thruway) take exit 13 north onto the Palisades Interstate Parkway. Take the PIP north to its end at the Bear Mountain traffic circle, and get on U.S. route 9W north (3d exit off traffic circle).

Follow the signs to the West Point Visitor Center and the museum (located in the Pershing Center behind the Visitor Center).

John Ward Dunsmore's The Drummer Boy. *Dunsmore was a painter of Revolutionary War subjects, including the famous rendition of Betsy Ross sewing the first American flag, part of the Fraunces Tavern Museum collection.*

Washington's Headquarters State Historic Site

Following his Yorktown victory in late 1781, George Washington and about 7500 of his troops returned to New York State in stages to await word from Paris that a formal treaty had been signed and the war was ended. While the army camped at New Windsor (*see* New York, New Windsor Cantonment State Historic Site), the general and Mrs. Washington made their home at Newburgh a few miles away.

Four major events are associated with Newburgh: Washington rejected a proposal that he become king; he dealt with a possible mutiny among his officers; he created the Badge of Military Merit, predecessor to the Purple Heart; and he wrote his "Circular to the States," which listed the objectives he considered essential to the United States's becoming a strong and unified nation.

A Home for the Washingtons

The task of finding a residence for the general and his lady was under the purview of Colonel Timothy Pickering, the army's quartermaster general, who assigned it to his second in command, Lieutenant Colonel Hugh Hughes.

Hughes was in a delicate position. He had to find not just a residence suitable for the Washingtons but one where the general and his aides could set up headquarters for an indeterminate amount of time. And once he found such a place, he had to convince the current residents to turn over their home to the army and find another place to live.

Hughes finally settled on the home of the Hasbrouck family, where he and Colonel Pickering happened to be staying, along with the colonel's wife and children. Bivouacking officers in private homes was common practice during the war—Washington had stayed in more than 100 homes in the previous seven years.

The Widow Hasbrouck and her two daughters had graciously accommodated a number of Continental Army officers since the death of her husband. She may have been reluctant about being displaced once again, because it's said she met Colonel Hughes's request with "sullen silence." It's likely there was even more silence when Hughes explained that certain changes would be made to the house, though she may have welcomed the improvements at government expense. A fireplace would be added in the bedroom, a kitchen would be enlarged, and the function of some of the rooms would be altered.

Mrs. Hasbrouck and her daughters eventually left, as did Hughes and the Pickerings. Mrs. Pickering said she didn't mind moving, but she insisted Colonel Hughes find a home that had room for a cow, as she needed milk for her babies.

From late summer to early fall of 1782 Washington was at Verplanck's Point on the eastern end of the Kings Ferry river crossing, where the army was practicing amphibious landings in case they had to invade Manhattan. And once the French returned from Virginia, they maneuvered with the Continental Army in full view of the British. Nothing was absolutely certain.

While Washington was busy with military affairs and affairs of state, Mrs. Washington was supervising the household. Her hands were always busy, whether it was with needlework, writing letters, or sharing in the letter copying that was the work of the military secretaries.

George Washington kept a copy of just about everything he wrote. Though Mrs. Washington wouldn't have been privy to military or state correspondence, she did copy his accounts. Washington didn't receive a salary for his service during the war, but he was reimbursed for his expenses, and for that it was necessary to keep very detailed records, which Mrs. Washington copied. In December 1783, when Washington left the army, he submitted an accounting of all his expenses since 1775. These included the cost of supplies, travel expenses for himself and Mrs. Washington, payments to spies, and entertainment expenses incurred when playing host to visitors. The total was 1972 pounds, nine shillings, and four pence. Auditors reviewing the accounts found they were off by less than one dollar.

The Washingtons had a beautiful sleigh at their disposal, and when the ice was off the river they could travel by barge on the Hudson. Mrs. Washington also had friends in the Hudson Valley whom she visited and who came to Newburgh to visit her. She spent the summer of 1782 away at Mount Vernon.

Visiting the Headquarters

Washington's Headquarters is considered something of a mecca by preservationists, as it was the first publicly operated historic site in the United States. In 1850 the governor of New York, Hamilton Fish, whose father Nicholas Fish had fought under Washington at Yorktown, orchestrated the acquisition of the house from Jonathan Hasbrouck's grandson for the sum of 2400 dollars. In presenting the idea to the New York State Legislature, Fish stated that part of the purpose in buying the house was its preservation. This was one of the first times preservation of a historic site was represented as a public responsibility.

Hasbrouck House today is a fascinating representation of the headquarters when the Washingtons lived here, with furnishings that are both reproductions and period originals.

A tour of the house, which lasts about 30 minutes, takes visitors into all eight of the rooms. Written tours of the house are available in English, Braille, French, German, Chinese, and Spanish. The house is the oldest building in the city of Newburgh, and was built sometime between 1725 and 1750, with later additions made around 1770.

The Dining Room is a true curiosity—a room with eight doors and one window. This was the result of Colonel Hasbrouck's adding extensions to the house, each necessitating a door to the main room. Architecture as a profession hadn't yet caught on in America. The room is unusual also because of its Dutch-style fireplace that is jambless, or without sides. A huge flue above the fireplace took up the smoke and sparks. Not having the fire contained by walls made the room warmer, but could be a hazard when the window was open on a windy day.

Several other rooms surround the Dining Room. The Parlor was used for after-dinner socializing. The Washingtons' Bedroom is where they ate breakfast together—probably one of their few private moments. The Aides' Room is thought to have been the busiest in the house, with three to five aides working and guests presenting themselves. There are also a Dressing Room and the Aides' Bedroom.

The Hallway served as a reception area for civilian guests, while those on military business entered on the other side of the house. Washington's Office, originally the Hasbrouck kitchen, was where he washed and

was shaved by his servant. The desk was used by Washington when he was at New Windsor in 1781.

Visitors are welcome to wander through the museum located nearby, where among the treasured artifacts are a Barwise pocket watch that belonged to Mrs. Washington, a lock of George Washington's hair, and portraits of the Washingtons.

Also on the grounds is the Tower of Victory, a commemorative peace monument, which has lost its roof in the years since its 1880s centennial construction. It remains, however, true to its original mandate that it should be "a structure of rude but imposing nature [to] typify the rugged simplicity of the times and personages" it was commemorating. The 53-foot-tall Romanesque-styled limestone tower looks something like a square blockhouse. Inside its arches stands a life-size bronze statue of General Washington, raised on a pedestal of red granite.

Visitor Information
845-562-1195
nysparks.state.ny.us/hist/ (click on Washington's Headquarters in list at left.)

Hours: Open mid-April through October, Sunday, 1 p.m. until 5 p.m.; Wednesday through Saturday, 10 a.m. until 5 p.m.; closed all major holidays except President's Day, Memorial Day, Fourth of July, Labor Day, and Columbus Day.

Admission: Moderate charge, minimal for children 5 through 12.

Accessibility: All facilities are handicapped accessible.

Special Events: During President's Day weekend, there are military demonstrations, musical performances, family entertainment, craft demonstrations, and lectures. Special celebrations include "George Washington's Birthday Celebration" in February; "The General's Lady," a celebration of Martha Washington and the women of her time in June; and "Kites Over the Hudson" in August.

Getting There: From I-87 (New York Thruway) take exit 17, or from I-84 take exit 10 or 10S for Newburgh, proceed to state route 17K (Broadway) and follow it east for 2.75 miles to Liberty Street. Turn right onto Liberty Street and then take the third left and turn east onto Lafayette Street. Drive two blocks on Lafayette Street and go straight into the on-site parking lot inside the fence.

Guilford Courthouse National Military Park

"We feel at the moment the sad and fatal effects of our loss on that Day, nearly one half of our best Officers and Soldiers were either killed or wounded, and what remains are so completely worn out by the excessive Fatigues of the campaign, in a march of above a thousand miles, most of them barefoot, naked and for days together living upon Carrion which they had often not time to dress, and three or four ounces of ground Indian corn has totally destroyed this Army. . . ."

So often in the previous six years, sentiments of this sort had been expressed about the Continental Army—weary, barefoot, starving—that it is a shock even now to read them in regard to the British army. But such was the decimation of that army following its Pyrrhic victory at Guilford Courthouse in March of 1781.

The importance of this battle is attested to by the fact that in 1917 Guilford Courthouse became the first national park established to commemorate a Revolutionary War battle.

Looking for a Fight

Britain's Southern Campaign was in trouble. Though by early 1781 Georgia and South Carolina were under British control, Patrick Ferguson and his forces had been defeated at Kings Mountain (*see* South Carolina, Kings Mountain National Military Park) and Ferguson killed, Banastre Tarleton had lost at Cowpens (*see* South Carolina, Cowpens National Battlefield), and Lord Charles Cornwallis was being led a not very merry chase by Nathanael Greene, commander of the Patriot forces in the South.

Equally discouraging was the lack of support from southern Loyalists, who would turn out in great numbers when the British army came to town but few of whom would take up arms.

Greene was tired of playing cat and mouse with Cornwallis. In February 1781 he began pestering the British in earnest, through a series of quick, hard-hitting raids. One of these came to be known as Pyle's Massacre, named for the Loyalist colonel John Pyle whose 400 North Carolina Loyalists were savagely cut down in an attack by a company from Light Horse Harry Lee's legion. This brutality went a long way toward discouraging

British supporters to join the fight.

These same "supporters" were reluctant to share provisions with the British troops. For the first time in the war, the British army was in danger of starving.

The Patriot army, however, was well-enough provisioned to continue harassing an opponent contending with growing desertions and becoming more desperate to engage the Patriots in a definitive battle.

Cornwallis got his wish on March 15, when Greene chose a wooded area west of Guilford Courthouse in North Carolina to stand and fight.

Little Horsepen Creek was south of the woods. On either side of the creek were cornfields framed by a rail fence, and beyond those were more woods. Greene placed his North Carolina militia and a company of Delaware regulars behind the fence with their backs to the woods. To their rear was the second Patriot line, made up of Virginia militia, positioned on a slight rise within the woods. The third American line was 500 feet behind the Virginians, on a hill in front of the courthouse. Here Greene placed his best troops, Continental soldiers from Virginia and Maryland.

The intelligence Cornwallis re-

ceived from his Loyalists failed him on two counts: One, he was told Greene had about 10,000 troops (Greene had some 4400); and two, he had little idea of the terrain. Still, Cornwallis wanted this fight. He needed to defeat Greene before Greene reached Virginia and reinforced the southern Patriot army, and he needed to do it before any more of his dwindling army of about 2000 deserted.

The Winner Loses
The battle began with a 30-minute exchange of artillery fire, after which the British advanced across the cornfields toward the rail fence. When they were 150 yards from the fence, the North Carolinians opened fire. Hundreds of British fell, wounded or dead. Those who remained re-formed and came on, stepping over their comrades.

British sergeant Roger Lamb later described what happened when the British came within 40 yards of the line: "It was perceived that their whole line [the Patriots] had their arms presented, and resting on a rail fence. . . . They were taking aim with the nicest precision. At this awful moment, a general pause took place; both parties surveyed each other with a most anxious suspence. [Then the British colonel] Webster rode forward in front of the 23rd Regiment and said, with more than his usual commanding voice . . . 'Come on, my brave Fuzileers.' . . . They rushed forward amidst the enemy's fire; dreadful was the havoc on both sides."

The Carolinian militia had been told they could retreat after firing two rounds, which they now did, dropping ammunition boxes, canteens, and even weapons—anything that might slow them down.

During the next 90 minutes, the British fought their way through the second Patriot line in the heavily wooded area, then advanced across open fields to the third line by the courthouse, where the remains of the first two lines had regrouped behind the Virginia and Maryland Continentals.

Cornwallis's 2nd Guards Battalion charged, and part of the Maryland line broke, leaving the 1st Maryland to face the Guards. It was

***North Carolina** militia fire their rounds as British regulars launch their attack. The militia then fled. A second line offered stiffer resistance but also withdrew.*

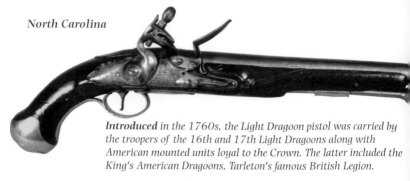

Introduced *in the 1760s, the Light Dragoon pistol was carried by the troopers of the 16th and 17th Light Dragoons along with American mounted units loyal to the Crown. The latter included the King's American Dragoons, Tarleton's famous British Legion.*

at this point that a bugle signaled the charge of William Washington and his dragoons to the rear of the Guards. Taken by surprise, the Guards were cut down in great numbers, but then were regrouped by their valiant commander, Lieutenant James Stuart, who was killed in the ensuing fight.

As the Guards faltered after Stuart fell, Cornwallis saw his troops being attacked from the front and sides by Washington's cavalry and Continental infantry. In danger of losing the battle, he ordered his artillery to fire grapeshot into the midst of the fighting, knowing he was firing on his own men as well as the Patriot forces.

When the firing scattered the Patriots and Greene saw that his artillery had been captured, he ordered a retreat. The British had neither the men nor the will at the end of the battle to charge the retreating Americans.

Technically Cornwallis had won the battle, since he held the field; but in terms of the damage done to the armies, Greene was the clear winner. More than a quarter of Cornwallis's army was either dead or wounded, including half of the Guards.

Seven months later, without reinforcements from New York, Cornwallis was forced to surrender at Yorktown.

Visiting Guilford Courthouse

This military park preserves 228 acres of the estimated 1000 acres covered during the battle. The best way to experience the battle is by starting with the film and exhibits at the Visitor Center, then either driving or biking the two-and-a-half-mile trail that stops at eight sites on the battlefield.

An excellent two-hour CD or cassette tour can be purchased that explains what happened at each site and provides information on the 28 monuments honoring those who fought here. Wayside panels along the route also provide information, as does the free brochure available at the Visitor Center.

The film at the Visitor Center, *Another Such Victory,* takes its title from a taunt made by Opposition Leader Charles James Fox when the Tories tried to present Guilford Courthouse as a victory to the House of Commons. "Another such victory," shouted Fox, "would ruin the British Army." The 30-minute film uses testimony taken from the letters and reports of those who fought here to engender a sense of what it must have been like the day of the battle. Complementing the film is a 10-minute program with a computer-animated battle map that shows the movements of the British and Patriot troops.

The center's museum features artifacts such as drums and powder

A snare drum *on display at the park was reportedly carried into battle by Luther W. Clark. Drums kept troops in step during marches and signaled when soldiers should load their weapons, fire, cease firing, and retreat.*

The Greensboro Historical Museum

The Greensboro Historical Museum, located nearby in the city of Greensboro (named for Nathanael Greene in 1808), has several displays and numerous artifacts related to the Revolutionary War and the Guilford Courthouse battle.

Among these are a 1770s map of the battle and a period map of North and South Carolina. There are also cavalry swords used in the battle, a bronze bell from the original Guilford Courthouse, a chair used by Cornwallis during his retreat, a Scottish dirk (dagger) that a wounded British soldier gave to a local family in gratitude for their nursing him back to health, a silver cup that belonged to Nathanael Greene, and a pair of silver spurs that George Washington left here after his visit in 1791.

The "Citizen Soldier" exhibit in the Military History section includes interesting information about those who fought in the battle (and in other battles up to and including World War II) and the impact of war on the home front.

Also featured in the museum is an interesting exhibit on native daughter Dolley Madison, wife of the fourth president and perhaps best known for saving the Gilbert Stuart portrait of George Washington when the British torched the White House during the War of 1812.

The museum is housed in a turn-of-the-last-century church listed on the National Register of Historic Places, and there are two restored log houses in the museum's park whose re-created interiors reflect the changing history of Greensboro. The museum is open Tuesday through Sunday, and admission is free. Call 919-373-2043 for further information or visit their Web site at www.greensborohistory.org.

---

horns. There are also interactive video and audio exhibits with illustrated wall panels and displays to explain the Southern Campaign and the conflict at Guilford Courthouse.

The auto tour stops take visitors to the Americans' first, second, and third lines, the graves of two of North Carolina's signers of the Declaration of Independence—William Hooper and John Penn—the site of the former courthouse, and the monuments, including one dedicated to British lieutenant James Stuart.

The Cavalry Monument honors those who "charged and ran through and over the 2nd Queen's Guards in the valley below."

Among the inscriptions on the base of the equestrian statue monument to Nathanael Greene are a congratulatory message received from George Washington and, in its way, an even more laudatory quote from Cornwallis—"Greene is as dangerous as Washington. I never feel secure when encamped in his neighborhood."

Visitor Information
336-288-1776
www.nps.gov/guco
Hours: Open daily from 8:30 a.m. until 5 p.m.; closed Thanksgiving, December 25, and January 1.
Admission: Free.
Accessibility: The Visitor Center and park trails are accessible, although the historic road can be challenging in spots. The Visitor Center film, battle-map program and museum audiovisual programs are offered with captioning upon request.
Special Events: Commemorative events on the anniversary of the battle each year and living-history programs at other times (check the Web site or call).
Getting There: The park is in northwest Greensboro. Take U.S. route 220 (Battleground Road) to the entrance at New Garden Road. The NPS Web site has detailed information on arriving by car from every direction, or call 336-288-1776.

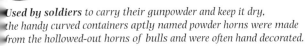

Used by soldiers to carry their gunpowder and keep it dry, the handy curved containers aptly named powder horns were made from the hollowed-out horns of bulls and were often hand decorated.

North Carolina

Historic Halifax State Historic Site

The first formal declaration for freedom by an American colony was
made here. "Resolved, that the
Delegates of this Colony in the
Continental Congress be impowered
to Concur with the Delegates of the
other Colonies in declaring Independency and forming foreign alliances—reserving to this Colony the
Sole and Exclusive right of forming a
Constitution and Laws for this
Colony, and of appointing Delegates
from time to time (under the direction of a General representation
thereof) to meet the Delegates of the
other Colonies, for such purposes as
shall be hereafter pointed out."

The Halifax Resolves, adopted on
April 12, 1776, and signed by 83 delegates to North Carolina's Fourth
Provincial Congress, provided needed impetus for the Continental
Congress meeting in Philadelphia to
move away from reconciliation and
toward declaring independence.

Visiting Historic Halifax

Visitors to Historic Halifax will find
the buildings and other sites much
as they were at the time the Resolves
were adopted. Surrounded on two
sides by modern-day Halifax, a town
of about 400, and on two sides by
the Roanoke River, this preserved
enclave conveys an authentic sense
of the typical small 18th-century
town whose citizens were making
momentous decisions in the most
commonplace of settings.

Sixteen sites make up the tour.
Visitors may take a self-guided tour
or be accompanied by a tour guide.
At the Visitor Center, across from
the parking area, visitors see a 13-
minute audiovisual presentation on
the history of Halifax and the events
that led up to the Halifax Resolves.
An accompanying exhibit provides
an overview of the history of the
Roanoke River Valley and has quite
a few interesting artifacts from the
precolonial, colonial, and Revolutionary eras.

General Charles Cornwallis briefly
occupied Halifax during his march
north to Yorktown. British soldiers
and Loyalists stayed here while on
parole during the war, occasionally
deciding to switch sides. The Owens
House, circa 1760, belonged to George
Owens, a merchant of the town, and
is furnished with a striking collection of 18th- and early 19th-centu-
ry furnishings that were locally
made.

Inside the Eagle Tavern, there is

an interesting exhibit on the history
of 18th- and 19th-century taverns
in America. The exhibit includes
information on food, gambling, and
sleeping arrangements (usually
three to a bed).

While the majority of furnishings
in these buildings are authentic to
the period, the Tap Room, located
across from Eagle Tavern, has been
furnished with reproductions so
that visitors can experience what it
was actually like to be in an 18th-
century tavern.

Post–Revolutionary War buildings include an archaeology building with displays of artifacts found
on the site, a church site and cemetery, a law office from the early
1800s furnished as an attorney's
place of business, an African
American cemetery from the late
1800s, and the Federal-style Sally-
Billy Plantation House, circa 1808.

The site of the Market Square is
noted, as this was an important
focus of the town, serving as park,
pasture, and marketplace. The
Magazine Springs—natural water
springs first used by Native
Americans and later by local settlers—was named for a nearby factory that operated during the war,
producing clothes and ammunition.

The River Overlook, about three
and a half blocks from Historic
Halifax, provides a beautiful view of
the river and the Roanoke Valley.
There are plans to construct a
canoe-and-kayak landing here as
part of the Roanoke River Trail.

Visitor Information

252-583-7191
www.ah.dcr.state.nc.us/sections/
   hs/halifax/halifax.htm
Hours: Tuesday through Saturday,
10 a.m. until 4 p.m.; closed Sunday,
Monday, and most state holidays.
Admission: Free.
Accessibility: Handicapped accessible.
Special Events: Halifax Day on April
12 includes living-history activities,
tours, and commemorative obser-
vances; *First for Freedom* is an outdoor drama presented on the Fourth
of July weekend in the town of
Halifax.
Getting There: Halifax is in northeastern North Carolina.

Take I-95 to exit 168, go south on
state route 903 about 8 miles, and
follow the signs to Historic Halifax.

Moores Creek National Battlefield

The clash between North Carolina Patriots and Scottish Loyalists at Moores Creek in February of 1776 could be characterized as a 17-day campaign that ended in a three-minute battle. And with that speedy defeat came the end of a royal presence in North Carolina, the first colony to rid itself of its royal governor.

Moores Creek was very much a battle between the Old World and the New, with a heavy sense of irony in the fact that Scottish Highlanders were fighting against a repressed people seeking independence from England. With the rallying cry, "King George and the broadswords," the Scottish charged a bridge, and in that moment many lost their chance to be part of defeating a king and birthing a democracy.

Rebellion

At the end of the French and Indian War in 1763, many in the king's Highland Regiments were rewarded with land grants in the colonies. A large number settled in the Cape Fear River region of North Carolina.

Thousands from Scotland joined them in the following decade, bringing with them their loyalties to kin and clan and their broadswords and dirks (a straight-bladed dagger). Among the latecomers were Allan MacDonald and his wife, Flora, who arrived in 1774. Flora was a Jacobite heroine, having helped Bonnie Prince Charlie to escape after the Battle of Culloden.

The Highlanders charged to the sound of bagpipes at Moores Creek.

North Carolina had been a fractious colony under the previous royal governor, William Tryon, who had put down a rebellion by back-country small farmers, the so-called Regulators, in 1776. Defeating them at the Battle of Almanac Creek, with a 1000-man militia mostly made up of coastal plantation owners, Tryon hanged their leaders and forced the rest to take an oath of allegiance to the king.

Tryon's successor, Josiah Martin, would be the fifth and last royal governor of the colony. In 1774, Martin refused to allow the Assembly to meet to choose representatives to the First Continental Congress. The Assembly met anyway. In the spring of 1775, Martin called the North Carolina Assembly into session; but the Assembly chose instead to convene in its own right the day before the date Martin had set.

Martin wrote to the government in London, decrying the situation and giving witness to "the Sacred Majesty of my Royal Master insulted, the Rights of His Crown denied and violated, His Government set at naught, and trampled upon, his servants of highest dignity reviled, traduced, abused . . ."

Thinking to bring North Carolina to heel for his royal master, Martin formulated a plan. He would defeat the Patriot cause by bringing together a large force of British troops with recently immigrated Scottish Highlanders at Wilmington. Once combined, this army would turn from the coast and restore order in the colony, one region at a time. Joining with them, Martin assured British officials, would be backcountry farmers who had been defeated by the coastal plantation owners who now led the Patriot cause. With these included, Martin said he could raise an army of 10,000.

By now, Martin had found it necessary to take up residence on a British sloop of war off the coast near Wilmington. From there he solicited the aid of Allan MacDonald and others to raise a force to join the anticipated British troops at Wilmington.

The Battle

In early February a force of about 1600, mostly Scottish Highlanders, began their march toward Wilmington. Brigadier General Donald McDonald and Lieutenant Colonel Donald McLeod were in command.

*A **diorama** on display at the park portrays the Scots bravely continuing across the bridge, even as the cannon Old Mother Covington decimates their ranks.*

Allan MacDonald marched with them.

News of this expedition reached the North Carolina militia. Colonel James Moore of the 1st North Carolina Continentals, Colonel Richard Caswell of the militia (Caswell would later be governor of North Carolina), and a force of about 1100 men rode from present-day Fayetteville to stop them.

At that time, there were only two roads in southeastern North Carolina: the King's Highway, a well-maintained roadway used for travel and for shipping goods into the region, and Negro Point Head Road, a bumpy side road used to transport slaves. Obviously the Loyalists would want to use King's Highway, so the Patriots blocked it sufficiently to force the Loyalists to funnel their army of 1600 and their supply wagons onto the Negro Point Head Road. The two armies now began a game of cat and mouse, the Patriots destroying bridges the Loyalists needed to cross creeks and streams, then retreating in the face of the Loyalists' superior numbers.

On February 25 a Patriot advance column under Colonel Alexander Lillington arrived at Moores Creek Bridge and began digging earthworks on the east side of the bridge. When the rest of the army arrived the following day, Moore and Caswell realized that digging in on the east side meant they had their backs to the creek—not a good position militarily.

Caswell set up camp with his men on the river's west bank, but not before a Loyalist had reported to the Highlanders that the Patriots were camped on the east bank. Meanwhile, the Patriots removed the bridge's planks. leaving only the sides, or stringers, and these they greased.

On the morning of February 27, the Loyalists arrived at the bridge thinking to surprise the Patriots, who were out of sight behind cover on the west bank. When they saw the fires left burning, as Moore had commanded, the Loyalists assumed the Patriots were either on the run or had gone into the woods. Either way, the Scots thought they had the element of surprise on their side.

The Scottish Highlanders, to the sound of bagpipes and drums, made a charge across the stringers, with the cry "King George and the broadswords!" Those who made it across, without falling off the greased sides and either drowning or being shot as they struggled in the water, were hit by swan shot from the Patriots' two cannons. Swan shot was a canvas bag filled with twenty or so lead pellets that, when shot from a cannon, spread over a wide area. The cannons, called Old Mother Covington and her daughter, were a two-and-a-half-pounder on a carriage and a half-pound swivel gun. Together they devastated the charging forces.

In a matter of minutes the battle was over. Between 30 and 40 Loyalists were dead or wounded; one

Patriot, John Grady, had died and two others had been wounded. In writing his report of the battle, James Moore wrote that Captain McLeod "received upwards of twenty balls through his body." More than 800 Loyalists were captured after the battle.

The British would not return to North Carolina in force until 1780.

Visiting the Battlefield

Parts of the Visitor Center are under renovation and will be reopening in June 2005 with a new orientation film and exhibits featuring period artifacts, including a Highland broadsword. Prior to completion of the renovated area, visitors can watch a 12-minute audiovisual presentation on the battle and on colonial North Carolina. There are two trails in the park. Both are interesting and one, through the Cypress Swamp, is dramatically beautiful.

The one-mile History Trail takes visitors around the battlefield to the reconstructed Moores Creek Bridge, named for an early settler in the area. There are cannons of the period and the original earthworks. Wayside exhibits give details of the battle and the positions taken by the two armies.

There are six monuments along the History Trail. The Stage Road Monument marks Negro Head Point Road, along which part of the History Trail runs. Used by the Loyalists to get to the bridge, Negro Head Point Road ran from the slave market in Wilmington (Mount Misery) to North Carolina's interior. The Battle of Moores Creek Bridge Monument commemorates the battle. The Patriot Monument honors the Patriots who fought here, particularly John Grady, who died in the battle. And the Loyalist Monument honors those on the other side "who did their duty as they saw it." The Moore Monument honors the first president of the Moores Creek Battleground Association, an early organization instrumental in the preservation of the battlefield.

The Heroic Women's Monument honors the women of the lower Cape Fear region who hazarded all with their husbands to support the Patriot cause, providing for their families while their husbands were off fighting, making clothes for the men in the field, and sometimes even facing the hostility of invading forces.

Buried at the base of the Heroic Women's Monument are Mary Slocumb and her husband Ezekiel. Every North Carolina schoolchild knows the legend of Mary Slocumb and her ride to Moores Creek Bridge the day of the battle. Two nights before, Mary had a nightmare in which she saw her husband dead at the bridge. She rode 70 miles on horseback and reached the bridge after the battle was over. Ezekiel was unhurt, but Mary stayed there, helping nurse the wounded and dying. It's a lovely story, but completely untrue. Unfortunately, in the 1930s, when Mary and Ezekiel were uprooted from their family cemetery and brought here to be honored, the story was still considered fact rather than legend.

The Tarheel Trail is a third-of-a-mile loop trail whose boardwalk takes visitors through a portion of the Cypress Swamp. The trail is currently under development, with new wayside exhibits scheduled to be in place in 2004. Through the waysides, visitors will learn about one of colonial North Carolina's leading exports, naval stores—that is, tar, pitch, and turpentine made from the long-leaf pine tree. This colony was the leading producer of naval stores in the world. Four kilns used in the process of making pine tar are located along this trail. Called tarkels by the locals, these are small mounds surrounded by ditches and are original to the site.

Visitor Information

910-283-5591; www.nps.gov/mocr
Hours: The park is open daily from 9 a.m. until 5 p.m.; closed December 25.
Admission: Free.
Accessibility: The Visitor Center, the battlefield, and the trails are all accessible.
Special Events: Commemoration Day is held the last weekend of February. Colonial Day, held every April, features colonial crafts and demonstrations of colonial life and work. Scots Heritage Day in June highlights Scottish culture.
Getting There: The park is about 20 miles northwest of Wilmington, North Carolina, located on state route 210 about three miles west of U.S. 421.

By car: From I-40 take exit 408 and go west on state highway 210 about 15 miles to the park. From Wilmington, take U.S. 421 north 16 miles to state route 210 west.

By plane: Cars can be rented at the Wilmington airport.

Tryon Palace Historic Sites and Gardens

Tryon Palace was constructed between 1767 and 1770 by North Carolina's royal governor, William Tryon. The palace was the first permanent colonial capitol and, later, the first state capitol of North Carolina. This lavish residence was intended not only to provide a suitable home for Tryon, his wife, and their daughter, but also to represent to the colonials the grandeur of England's vision and her eminence among the nations of the world.

Today's palace recreates a point in time when North Carolina was at the juncture of colonialism and democracy. Walking through the reconstructed palace's rooms and its beautiful surrounding gardens, visitors can connect with 18th-century colonials in admiring the splendor of this palatial building.

History of Tryon Palace

Governor Tryon brought English architect John Hawks with him when he came to North Carolina in 1765, and he gave Hawks the task of designing a residence that would serve both as a home for Tryon's family and as the center of North Carolina society. Hawks succeeded in building an impressively graceful and majestic Georgian mansion that became one of the most noted public buildings in all the colonies.

As pleased as Tryon was with the results, he and his family only lived in the palace for one year before Tryon accepted an appointment as royal governor of New York. Once up north, Tryon would prove an efficient commander, spending the better part of the war leading Loyalist raiding parties and destroying such towns as New Haven, Connecticut.

Tryon's stint as governor of North Carolina had not made him particularly popular in the colony (*see* North Carolina, Moores Creek National Battlefield), leaving a legacy of mistrust to be dealt with by his successor, Josiah Martin. This was unfortunate for Martin, as things were beginning to heat up throughout the colonies and some residual goodwill might have gone a long way in smoothing the transition North Carolina faced. After a series of power struggles with the colony's legislative body, Martin fled the palace in May 1775 at the outbreak of the war. His furnishings and just about everything else left behind were auctioned by the new state government.

Following the war, the palace was the residence of four state governors while New Bern was the state capital. The building's most famous visitor was President George Washington, who dined and danced here on his southern tour in April 1791.

In 1794 the state capital was moved to Raleigh, and the palace became a rental property used for a variety of purposes, including a private school and a boardinghouse. Four years later it burned down. The cause of the fire was never determined. What little was left standing of the palace was demolished in the early 1800s, and businesses and houses were built on the property.

In 1944 a Greensboro resident and native of New Bern, Mrs. James Edwin Latham, established a trust fund for the reconstruction and furnishing of the palace. In the process more than 50 buildings had to be moved or torn down. The palace's original foundations were discovered during excavations. Coupled with John Hawks's original architectural plans, the palace that opened to the public in April 1959 was as near a duplicate of the original as possible.

Visiting Tryon Palace Sites

Touring the palace, visitors are reminded that this was not only a residence but also the seat of North Carolina's early state government, when it served as the first state capitol building from 1777 until 1794.

The constitution that brought that state into existence in 1776 called for a General Assembly consisting of two houses, a Senate and a House of Commons. A landholder with at least 300 acres could be a state senator; one with at least 100 acres could be a member of the house. The General Assembly elected the governor, who had to have property worth at least 1000 pounds sterling. Only Protestants could hold office. And only free men, black or white, who owned at least 50 acres could vote for a senator; all public taxpayers could vote for a house member.

In November of 1789, North Carolina agreed to ratify the U.S. Constitution here and became the 12th state in the Union. For all the hardscrabble history that took place within these palace walls, it remains an elegant expression of 18th-century luxury, its primarily English furnishings accented with antiques and decorative arts.

A short film at the Visitor Center orients visitors to the site.

There are seven primary historic buildings and 14 acres of gardens at Tryon. Among the buildings is the Hay House, where visitors can see how middle-class craftsmen lived and worked in the early 1800s. The newest of the historic houses to open here, this is a "please touch" museum that welcomes hands-on exploration.

Another of the historic buildings, the Stanly House, had been standing empty for a number of years when George Washington came to New Bern in 1791. The locals opened it, cleaned it, and filled it with their own furnishings so the general could spend two nights there. This building is original to the Revolutionary War era, constructed around 1780.

Guided tours are given of the Stanly and Hay houses, along with the Palace and the Dixon House. Tours of the Kitchen Office, where there are craft demonstrations throughout the day, the New Bern Academy Museum, and the Gardens are self-guided.

Tryon Palace has two collections that are particularly relevant to the Revolution. Though these are not on display, they can be accessed on the Palace's Web site. The map collection includes original maps of America and of the Carolinas during the colonial period and the Revolutionary War.

The North Carolina Paper Currency Collection includes examples of several denominations of 12 different issues of paper currency authorized by the North Carolina provincial government between 1748 and 1780.

Portraits of King George III and Queen Carlotta overlook the Council Room, seat of royal government in the colony and where, after 1776, the North Carolina General Assembly met to elect four state governors.

Visitor Information

800-767-1560

www.tryonpalace.org

Hours: The palace, gardens, and other historic sites are open Monday through Saturday, 9 a.m. until 5 p.m.; Sunday 1 p.m. until 5 p.m. From Memorial Day weekend through Labor Day weekend, the gardens are open until 7 p.m. Closed Thanksgiving Day, December 24, 25, and 26, and January 1.

Admission: There is a significant fee for entry to the Gardens, Kitchen Office, Blacksmith Shop, and Stables, or a higher fee provides admission to all buildings and gardens. Student rates are moderate. Admission is valid for two days.

Accessibility: The Visitor Center and the first floor rooms of the Palace are accessible to visitors using wheelchairs. The gardens are accessible to all visitors, but 18th-century-type walking surfaces may be uneven in spots. Those with special needs are invited to call in advance to discuss any assistance they will need during their visit.

Special Events: Demonstrations of crafts and colonial-era skills are scheduled throughout the day. Holiday celebration tours are held in December.

Getting There: New Bern is 125 miles southeast of Raleigh and 83 miles northeast of Wilmington, at the intersection of U.S. highways 17 and 70. Signs on each of the highways direct visitors to New Bern.

The Battle for Philadelphia

Brandywine Battlefield Park

At the time of the Revolutionary War, Philadelphia was the largest city in the country, and one of the largest cities in the British Empire. It was also the economic and cultural center, as well as the capital, of the United States.

Contradictorily, it was a Loyalist stronghold. While the Congress went about its business at Independence Hall, the city's Loyalists waited eagerly for the British to deliver them from what they viewed as an unnecessary breach with the Mother Country that would lead to sure economic ruin. The city's Quaker population was also unhappy with the war. Their pacifist principles dictated that differences between Great Britain and her colonies could be solved without bloodshed.

Add to this the fact that southeastern Pennsylvania, where Philadelphia is located, was a vital supply center for the Continental Army. Food, cloth for uniforms, iron, wagons for transportation, paper for currency, and gunpowder from three powder mills were produced here.

Howe Covets Philadelphia

All these factors made Philadelphia a prime target for British general Sir William Howe.

The British were daily receiving reports on the deterioration of the Continental Army and its commander's resolve. There were problems with inflation; the army was grousing, as armies are wont to do; and the populace was impatient with the pace of the war. General Howe hoped to capitalize on this situation by taking Philadelphia and, he hoped, breaking the spirit of the rebellion.

Howe began planning the Philadelphia campaign in April, but his troops didn't embark from New York until July 23, 1777. He believed Washington had posted troops along the Delaware River, the most direct route to Philadelphia, to impede the British army's advance. So Howe chose to take his 264 ships the longer route around Cape Charles, Virginia, and then up the Chesapeake to disembark at Head of Elk in Maryland, about 60 miles from Philadelphia.

Washington on the Offensive

This delay gave Washington time to prepare. His army of 11,000 marched southwest from Philadelphia with the aim of defeating the British in open battle. "Our army are in amazing high spirits," wrote one Continental officer, "and very healthy."

Following some minor skirmishes, Washington determined to stop

Reenactors representing the 5000 Hessians who fought at Brandywine take part in an annual reenactment of the battle in September.

The Marquis de Lafayette

One of the paticipants in the Battle of Brandywine was the Marquis de Lafayette, eager to fight in his first battle for freedom. The 20-year-old Marie-Joseph-Paul-Yves-Roch-Gilbert du Motier, Marquis de Lafayette, had come to America in July of 1777 on a ship he had bought and supplied himself for use by the revolutionaries. The wealthy French nobleman was in love with the idea of liberty and pledged his life and a good deal of his fortune to the Patriot cause. During the war, Washington was plagued with opportunistic European aristocrats who presented themselves as seasoned and able commanders and fell far short of the mark in battle. Lafayette presented himself as a sincere Patriot and won Washington's love through his bravery in battle and his complete loyalty to the cause and its leader. It is said that Washington thought of Lafayette as the son he never had, and they remained close until the general's death in 1799.

After joining his own revolution at home in 1789 and then becoming disenchanted with its bloody excesses, Lafayette lived in exile in Austria until the reign of Napoleon Bonaparte. In 1824 the old patriot visited the United States and was greeted with wild adulation. Medals were struck, monuments dedicated, and parks and probably babies named for him. Almost 100 years later, he was still remembered by a grateful nation. When the American Expeditionary Forces arrived in Paris in 1917 to join their French allies in World War I, General John J. Pershing is reputed to have declared, "Lafayette, we are here!"

Howe and his second in command, Lord Major General Charles Cornwallis, at Brandywine, 25 miles south of Philadelphia.

On September 9, Washington established his line along Brandywine Creek. The creek was located in a largely wooded and hilly area dotted with farms and populated mainly by Quakers. Recent rains had swollen the creek, making it difficult to cross. Washington thought he had all the possible fords covered. The main army, under Anthony Wayne, Nathanael Greene, and John Armstrong, would be at Chadds Ford, behind an artillery redoubt on a hill near the house of John Chadd. To the northwest, above Brinton's Ford, were John Sullivan, Adam Stephen, and William Alexander. Farther northwest, above Painter's Ford, was Theodorick Bland. Moses Hazen and his troops were at Wistar's Ford, the northernmost crossing that needed to be covered, according to the reconnaissance Washington had received of the area.

Howe, who had more reliable intelligence, probably supplied by local Loyalists, learned of another ford north of Wistar's that could be crossed. Accordingly, he sent 5000 Hessians under Baron General Wilhelm Knyphausen to attack Washington at Chadds Ford, while the main British army of 7500 men under Howe and Cornwallis would cross six miles north and come around to attack the Patriot forces from behind. Washington's dilemma would be determining which of these was the main British offensive—the advance on Chadds Ford or Cornwallis's flanking movement.

Contradictory Intelligence

The day of September 11 broke foggy but soon turned clear and very hot. There were minor skirmishes throughout the morning, with both sides trying to gauge the other's strengths, during which time Washington received contradictory intelligence about British troop movements. Bland reported he had seen troops going toward Trimble's Ford, but Sullivan's reports dismissed that possibility.

Howe was indeed headed in that direction. Taking the Great Valley

Road (now U.S. route 1), he was halfway to Trimble's Ford by noon and from there would proceed to Jeffries's Ford, where his army would cross Brandywine Creek and begin moving southeast to come up behind Chadd's Ford. At the Quaker Kennett Meetinghouse, the British encountered some militia, and a skirmish broke out around the house while the Quakers continued to hold their midweek meeting inside. The retreating militia sent word to Washington, but this was among several messages he received, none of them sufficiently conclusive in his judgment.

As the British continued toward Jeffries's Ford, the Hessians had taken their position on a hilly area facing Washington's main force across Brandywine Creek at Chadd's Ford. Around one p.m., a local farmer named Thomas Cheyney arrived at Washington's headquarters with the news that he'd been fired upon by the British moving southeast on Washington's side of the creek. Soon after, a message arrived from Bland that the British were advancing on the area of Birmingham Friends' Meetinghouse, flanking Washington from behind.

The Battle of Brandywine

Washington immediately sent orders for Alexander's, Stephen's, and Sullivan's divisions, under Sullivan's command, to move out to meet the British and cut them off before they could completely flank Chadd's Ford. Wayne's brigade, the light infantry, and a detachment of artillery were to remain at the ford, as were Greene's two brigades, whom Washington was holding in reserve.

Sullivan positioned his forces on the slope of a hill southeast of the meetinghouse, with four artillery pieces and three outposts in front of the lines, a wooded area behind them. Cornwallis, atop a hill facing them, remarked, "The damn rebels form well."

Unfortunately this well-formed line didn't hold long. The first blast from both sides' artillery could be heard in Philadelphia. It was followed by a bayonet charge by the British and Hessians. They met short resistance from three regiments, who retreated into the woods, leaving the right flank exposed.

Sullivan had left his men to direct the artillery. Without him, they formed a ragged line to fill the hole on the right, but were quickly overrun. The center with the artillery remained intact, but now the left flank dissolved.

Washington sent Greene to support Sullivan. Washington himself desired to observe the battle. Coming upon the scene, he saw some 3000 Continentals holding off close to 7000 British and Hessians in a fierce and bloody battle. For almost two hours they had been fighting, it was

later reported, "almost muzzle to muzzle, in such a manner that General [Thomas] Conway who has seen much service says he never saw so close and so severe a fire."

The Continentals were driven back five times, and each time they returned to push back the British. Finally, though, the Americans were too weak to go on, and the order was given to withdraw. In doing so, they ran into Greene's column arriving. Greene sent them to the rear and met the pursuing British and Hessians about a mile from the meetinghouse at a place called Sandy Hollow.

The fighting again became fierce, and a little after sunset, their forces depleted, the Americans began to withdraw. The exhausted British and Hessians did not pursue them.

There had also been heavy fighting at Chadd's Ford. Once Knyphausen heard Howe and Cornwallis attacking, he launched a full-scale attack on the ford, bombarding Wayne's position with six 12-pounders, four howitzers, and his light artillery. The Americans had nothing comparable with which to counterattack, and soon after the Hessians charged across the ford, the Americans gave way and retreated. The battle was lost.

Estimates at the time set the Patriot losses at around 1300 killed, wounded, or captured, and the British at around 1500.

Washington, in reporting to Congress, blamed the defeat on faulty intelligence, and assured them that "[N]otwithstanding the misfortune of the day, I am happy to find the troops in good spirits; and I hope another time we shall compensate for the losses now sustained."

While the Patriot army headed for Chester, 15 miles southwest of Philadelphia, Howe and his forces camped at Brandywine, stripping the area of whatever the Patriot army hadn't already commandeered.

Final Defense of Philadelphia

Washington's sole aim now was to keep his army between Howe and Philadelphia. On September 16, with the British army once again in pursuit, a skirmish broke out at Malvern Hill, west of the city, and both armies began to form lines for battle. The fighting had barely started when a torrential storm erupted. The Continental Army did manage a cavalry charge before the storm, when Polish general Casimir Pulaski attacked an advance of Hessian troops. Both sides were immediately drenched, and the area between them became a gully of rushing water and sucking mud. Muskets could not be fired, and the muddy gulch between the lines prevented a bayonet charge by the British. Both sides wisely withdrew. This later became known as the Battle of the Clouds.

Unfortunately, as Henry Knox wrote to his wife, "nearly all the musket cartridges of the army that had been delivered to the men were damaged, consisting of about 400,000. This was a most terrible stroke for us, and owing entirely to the badness of the cartouch-boxes which had been provided for the army."

Now Washington was forced to replace those cartridges, necessitating a march to the Warwick Furnace at Reading, almost 30 miles away. The army marched the rest of the day in the rain, camped that night without tents on the cold, wet ground, were up at three a.m., marched the rest of the day to Reading, then a day later turned around and marched back to within 12 miles of Philadelphia.

On September 20, Washington sent General Anthony Wayne and

An 18th-century German engraving depicts American, British, and Hessian soldiers at the Battle of Brandywine.

his division of 1500 men and four cannons to Paoli to attack the British rear guard and baggage train. Alerted by local Loyalists, Howe dispatched Major General Charles Grey to catch Wayne by surprise. Grey ordered his men to remove the flints from the locks of their muskets, so they wouldn't be tempted to fire and could use only their bayonets.

Wayne and his men were taken completely by surprise at their camp that night. Though most escaped, including Wayne, the 150 Patriot corpses found after the battle were so mangled with bayonet slices that the attack became known as the Paoli Massacre.

Washington's army had marched a total of almost 150 miles in little more than a week, on half rations and many without shoes, and it had experienced the disheartening butchery of some of its soldiers. And yet the army and its commander still thought they could prevent the British from taking the city. Howe proved them wrong. He outmaneuvered Washington, and on September 23 the British marched into the City of Brotherly Love.

Philadelphia Occupied
From the journal of Mrs. Henry Drinker: "Well! Here are the English in earnest! About 2 or 300 came in through Second Street without opposition. Cornwallis came with the troops. Gen. Howe has not arrived. . . . Some officers are going about this day numbering the houses with chalk on the doors. A number of the citizens taken up and imprisoned."

Congress had left town a few days earlier, "chased like a covey of partridges," as John Adams wrote. They went first to Lancaster and then to York, where they would be until the British evacuated Philadelphia nine months later.

Since the city had a large contingent of Loyalists, when General Howe made his triumphal entrance on September 26, crowds lined the streets to cheer him as a liberator. In a few months' time, when many faced near starvation because so few supplies could make it through the surrounding Patriot lines or up the frozen Delaware River, both Howe and his supporters would remember that day.

Some thousands of miles away in Paris, Benjamin Franklin clearly assessed the situation. When it was said to him, "The British have cap-tured Philadelphia," Franklin smiled wisely and replied, "You have it wrong. It is Philadelphia that has captured the British."

The Battle of Germantown
While the British established themselves in the city, Washington's army was receiving reinforcements. Thousands of soldiers and militia were arriving from Virginia, New Jersey, New York, and Massachusetts. With his army renewed and numbering about 10,000, Washington decided to strike the approximately equal number of Howe's army that was quartered at Germantown.

Washington's battle plan entailed four columns marching miles apart to arrive at the same place at the same time and attack an established defensive position. This four-pronged attack at dawn on October 4 would follow a night march through unknown and rough terrain. This would have been difficult even with an army of professional soldiers trained in joint maneuvers, but with the Continental Army, it was asking the impossible.

Washington placed his two strongest forces, Continentals led by Sullivan and Greene, in the center. His two weaker forces, militias led by William Smallwood and John Armstrong, he placed on the left and right sides. The final stage of the plan had the four columns arriving at their individual staging areas at two o'clock in the morning, resting a few hours, then attacking precisely at five a.m. with a bayonet charge.

Washington was unsuccessful in part because the residents of the village of Germantown had chosen to enclose each of their homes with a rail fence. The general apparently didn't realize that it couldn't be a clean, straightforward bayonet charge with all those rail fences. He was also ignoring the standard three-to-one ratio—the military principle that dictated an army attacking a well-established defensive position should have three times as many men as the opposing army.

Part of the charge did work, that of Anthony Wayne's men, who came at the British yelling, "Remember the Paoli massacre!" After withstanding two charges by the Continentals, the British began to surrender and the Americans shamefully slaughtered many before being restrained by their officers.

It was the British 40th Ligh

Henry Knox's insistence that American troops capture rather than bypass the Chew house resulted in a Patriot defeat at the Battle of Germantown.

Infantry under Colonel Thomas Musgrave that was the Americans' downfall. Taking refuge in the stone house of Supreme Court Justice Benjamin Chew, the British stationed themselves at the second-story windows and began firing on the advancing Continentals.

Now came a conference of Washington and his generals. Should they simply move around the house with its 120 or so soldiers barricaded inside, leaving a small force behind to keep Musgrave and his men pinned down, or take the time to flush out the house's defenders? Most didn't see any purpose in halting here when they had the British on the run, but Henry Knox, chief of artillery, prevailed in convincing Washington that it would be dangerous to leave a force behind them that could attack from the rear.

For an hour Knox's artillery bombarded the fine Georgian house, only making dents in its thick stone walls. A proposal for surrender would have been made, but the soldier approaching the house bearing the white flag was shot. Washington next tried to storm the house, but his men were beaten back.

While Washington and his men labored at this small stone house, the battle raged in other sectors, for a time in the Americans' favor. Then in the fog that had come up, the brigades commanded by generals Anthony Wayne and Adam Stephen began firing on each other, killing and wounding many of each other's

men before realizing their mistake. Worse, the Americans were running out of ammunition. Sullivan was surrounded at one point, and only Greene's intervention and orderly fighting withdrawal saved Sullivan's men and his own.

Washington, finally having left the Chew house, came under fire while trying to rally his retreating troops, who raised their empty cartridge boxes as they moved past. Some of the men were so thoroughly exhausted they actually fell asleep when the troops paused to turn and fire at the British.

At this point the British were being reinforced by three fresh battalions from Philadelphia under the command of General Charles Cornwallis, thus outnumbering the Americans.

Washington drove his men until the British gave up their pursuit eight miles from Germantown. He stopped for neither sleep nor refreshment—though of that there was little, for as one captain wrote, "We eat nothing and drank nothing but water on the tour."

Though the battle was lost, and with it the possibility of taking Philadelphia from the British, the men were buoyed by their victories in the battle. T. Will Heath, a Continental officer, wrote soon after, "Tho we gave away a complete victory, we have learned this valuable truth: [that we are able] to beat them by vigorous exertion, and that we are far superior [in] point of swiftness. We are in high spirits. Every action [gives] our troops fresh vigor and a greater opinion of their own strength. Another bout or two must make their [the British] situation very disagreeable."

Visiting Brandywine Battlefield

Most of the 10 square miles that encompassed the battle at Brandywine Creek have been developed into housing or businesses. Fortunately, this 52-acre park preserves sections of the battlefield, the house where Lafayette stayed, and Washington's Headquarters.

An 18-minute audiovisual presentation at the Visitor Center presents an overview of the battle, while putting it in the context of the Philadelphia campaign. There's also an electronic map with a chronological detailing of the campaign and a narrative of the Battle of Brandywine.

Two items of particular interest in the center's Museum are a Ferguson rifle—a kind first used in this battle (*see* South Carolina, Kings Mountain National Military Park)—and a Lafayette Memorial Ribbon, created in 1824 to commemorate his tour of the eastern United States. There are also powder horns, a fife, Brown Bess muskets, and two cannons. Mannequins on display are dressed in the uniforms of a British and a Continental soldier. Reproduced 1777 maps and several dioramas give visitors an idea of what the surrounding area looked like at the time of the battle. Changing exhibits focus on varying aspects of the Revolution such as the role of women and agriculture during the war.

Guided tours of Washington's Headquarters and Lafayette's Quarters are given throughout the day.

The Benjamin Ring House is a reconstruction of the home of the Quaker farmer and businessman as it was when Washington used it for his headquarters at Brandywine. It's assumed Benjamin, his wife Rachel (four months pregnant at the time), and their seven children stayed on the top floor during the Continental Army's occupation.

The battle was a terrible hardship for all the farmers in the area. The Continental Army and militia commandeered much of their livestock and crops before the battle, even taking the seed for spring planting, and the British finished the pickings after the battle. In addition, both armies raided the area during that winter of 1777–1778, when families were already coping with epidemic sickness brought by the armies and with a lack of food and clothing. It took almost five years for the area to recover following the battle.

The interior of the Ring House has mostly period furnishings, with a few reproductions. The family dining room, where Washington held a dinner the night before the battle, the kitchen, the upstairs bedroom, and Ring's office reflect the quiet, orderly life the family led before the battle. The transformation of their parlor into Washington's War Room demonstrates the upheaval of those few days in September when everything changed.

Following the battle, area residents applied for reimbursement from Congress for what had been stolen or destroyed. Ring did not apply, even though his next tax listing indicated his only property was one cow. However, the following spring, Ring did receive a reimbursement from General Washington for the food used during the dinner the general held before battle.

The Marquis de Lafayette spent the night before the battle in the home of another Quaker farmer, Gideon Gilpin. Gilpin, his wife, and six children lived in a small two-rooms-up/two-rooms-down stone house, which later was enlarged with a side addition. Visitors to the house learn something about 18th-century architecture, as well as about farming in the area. Gilpin did file a claim for recompense and stated among his losses 10 milch cows, one yoke of oxen, 48 sheep, 28 swine, and one history book.

The museum sells an excellent and very detailed map of the entire battle that guides visitors to 28 sites in the 10-square-mile area, including the Birmingham Friends' Meetinghouse (still active), the John Chadd House, and the Lafayette Cemetery, which has three monuments commemorating those who fought in the battle.

Visitor Information

610-459-3342

www.ushistory.org/brandywine

Hours: Tuesday through Saturday, 9 a.m. until 5 p.m.; Sunday, noon until 5 p.m.; closed Monday, Tuesday and Wednesday from December through February; also closed Easter, Thanksgiving Day, December 25, and January 1.

Admission: There's a moderate charge, children under 6 free.

Accessibility: Every effort will be made to accommodate those with special needs. Please call in advance of visit.

Special Events: Celebrations on Washington's birthday and the Fourth of July, an annual reenactment of the battle in September, plus lectures, educational programs, special tours, and family events throughout the year

Getting There: The park is in Chadds Ford, Pennsylvania, 20 miles west of Philadelphia and 8 miles north of Wilmington, Delaware. It is located on U.S. route 1 between U.S. 202 and state route 100.

Independence National Historical Park

Boston lit the fuse, Lexington and Concord fired the shot, but Philadelphia was the epicenter of the earthquake that was American independence—the place where revolution was formally declared and a new government was established.

On the eve of the Revolutionary War, Philadelphia was a bustling port, with wharves that stretched more than two miles. Its streets were daily filled with residents—rich, poor, and middle-class, titled and tradesmen—and visitors from all over the continent and the world. There were some 30 bookshops, and twice as many taverns.

The war, of course, changed much about the city, especially after Philadelphia was occupied by the British in September 1777. On the one hand, the British brought a gaiety and European flair the city hadn't experienced before, but the occupation also brought near famine during the winter of 1777–1778, when the city experienced massive supply problems.

Fortunately, Philadelphia was never the site of battle, and many of its lovely colonial- and Federal-style buildings survived into the 20th century, when Independence National Historical Park was designated a National Historic Landmark and put under the administration of the National Park Service (NPS).

At the beginning of the 21st century, a 314 million dollar makeover of the park was initiated, which includes creation of the Independence Visitor Center and the Liberty Bell Center, plus the National Constitution Center. The park covers 45 acres and has about 20 buildings open to the public.

Visiting Independence Park

There is much to see here, and this park is a treat for anyone and everyone. The avid historian will find as much detail as desired, while the casual viewer will enjoy the 18th-century ambiance, Ben Franklin's intriguing inventions, an award-winning film, beautiful costumes, and exemplary NPS guides. In addition, there is excellent shopping.

Visitors will need at least a half day to see the highlights, but should really take one or two days to immerse themselves in this microcosm of Philadelphia in the 1700s, accented with modern reflections of a still-thriving metropolis.

Independence Visitor Center

This 50,000-square-foot facility is a panoply of colorful displays, costumed interpreters, restaurants, shops, information services, and just about anything else a visitor to the park or the city of Philadelphia could require in the way of orientation.

The 28-minute film *Independence* provides an overview of the park's historic buildings and events, as does the excellent 60-minute tour leaving daily from the Center at 11 a.m. Maps are available in 12 languages, and there are special services available for children, non-English-speaking visitors, and those with disabilities.

Liberty Bell Center

Directly across Market Street is the new home of the Liberty Bell, one of the world's most recognizable icons of freedom. Inside this gleaming marble-and-granite showcase, the bell hangs in perfect symmetry with Independence Hall, which can be seen through the glass window behind the bell.

The colony of Pennsylvania commissioned the bell in 1751 from the Whitechapel Foundry in London for the tower of Pennsylvania's new state house, now known as Independence Hall. When the bell arrived, however, its tone was off and the clapper cracked the first time the bell was rung, so Pennsylvania demanded the foundry recast the bell and replace the clapper. Whitechapel might have agreed to make repairs, but it wouldn't pay the shipping charges involved in sending the bell back to England, so two local metalworkers, John Pass and John Stow, were hired to do the job. The bell was broken up and recast twice before satisfying the State Assembly, which hung it in the tower in 1753, where it became familiarly known as the State House Bell.

Not until the 1820s did people start viewing it through the aura of the Revolutionary War. Lafayette's return in 1824 made all things Revolutionary *au courant*, and it began to be referred to as the Independence Bell or the Bell of the Revolution.

It was the Abolitionists, in 1835, who picked up on the biblical verse on the bell: "Proclaim Liberty throughout all the Land unto all the Inhabitants thereof." Though there's no documentation as to why this verse was chosen, historians believe it is related to the fact that the original order for the bell was placed in 1751, the 50th anniversary of William Penn's Charter of Privileges for the Citizens of Pennsylvania, which guaranteed religious freedom. The verse itself, from Leviticus, refers to the practice in ancient Israel of pardoning prisoners and forgiving debts every 50 years.

The bell's famous crack wasn't discovered until 1845; a year later, when the bell was being spruced up for a celebration of Washington's Birthday, efforts were made to repair it. The stop-drilling method, a common technique then and now for repairing cracked bells, apparently fixed it; but when the bell was rung, the crack reappeared even larger. It was never rung again.

In early times, bells were thought to have the power to thwart demons and lift spells. Hung in a small, shrinelike room where visitors are encouraged to view the bell in silence, the Liberty Bell's solid presence elicits a sense of that power. It is only a piece of metal, really; but it's been invested with the hopes and expectations of generations, and therein lies its magic.

The Center has a nicely laid out indoor panel exhibit focusing on the bell's early history as the State House Bell, its transformation into the Liberty Bell, and its importance as a world symbol.

Independence Hall
Across Chestnut Street stands the Liberty Bell's former home, Indepen-

---

Liberty Bell Facts
- The bell weighs 2080 pounds, and its yoke 100 pounds.
- The bell measures 3 feet from lip to crown. The crown's circumference measures 6 feet 11 inches. The circumference around the lip is 12 feet.
- The bell is composed of approximately 70 percent copper and 25 percent tin, with traces of lead, zinc, arsenic, gold, and silver. The yoke is made of American elm.
- The cost of the original bell was 150 pounds, or about $225.50.
- The spelling "Pensylvania" on the bell is not a mistake. This was an acceptable spelling of the state's name at the time.
- The strike note of the bell is E flat.
- Cast on the bell are the names of its makers (Pass and Stow), where it was made (Philadelphia), a biblical verse, the year it was completed (1753, in Roman numerals), and why it was made ("by order of the Assembly of the Province of Pennsylvania for the State House in Philadelphia").
- The bell was not rung in celebration of the passage of the Declaration of Independence. The tower atop Independence Hall had begun to crack, and there was some concern that if the bell were rung, the tower would topple.
- During the British occupation of Philadelphia, the Liberty Bell was hidden in the basement of the Zion Reformed Church in Allentown, Pennsylvania. Most of the other bells in the city were also removed, but not for safety's sake. The Patriots were afraid the British would melt them down to make cannonballs.

dence Hall. It was built to house the State Assembly but was loaned to the Second Continental Congress in 1776. It was here the Congress passed the Declaration of Independence and the Articles of Confederation and here that a postwar assembly pounded out the Constitution of the United States.

Congress met in the Assembly Room on the first floor. A large room (40 feet by 40 feet), it was appointed with fine paneling, marble-framed fireplaces, a crystal chandelier, and ample sunlight from its high windows. Tables arranged in a semicircle, with Windsor chairs on loan from the Pennsylvania government, faced the chair of the president of the Assembly or Congress.

When Congress was in session here throughout the war—except for a brief hiatus in York—the Pennsylvania legislature met on the second floor. During the British occupation, the first-floor rooms were used by the army administrators and the second floor became a prison and military hospital for Continental Army officers.

The tour includes the Assembly Room and the Chamber of the Supreme Court of Pennsylvania across the hall. Most of the furnishings are period pieces, and the rooms are arranged as they would have been when in use in the mid-1770s.

The hall's West Wing contains the "Great Essentials" exhibit, which displays original copies of the Declaration of Independence, the Articles of Confederation and Perpetual Union, and the U.S. Constitution.

Tomb of the Unknown Soldier of the American Revolution

Kitty-corner from Independence Square is Washington Square and the Tomb of the Unknown Soldier, burial site for some 2000 prisoners who died during the nine-month British occupation.

Most of the soldiers buried here (some are British) died of disease and starvation, but not under the same horrific conditions as on the prison ships in New York Harbor (*see* New York, Prison Ship Martyrs Monument). The British in Philadelphia suffered along with their captives from a lack of food and medical supplies.

This square was a graveyard almost from the establishment of the city, serving first as a potter's field or those who couldn't afford burial

elsewhere, then as a cemetery for Roman Catholics and African Americans.

A statue of Washington graces the square, and an eternal flame commemorates those who died and were buried here in the cause of liberty.

Carpenters' Hall

Two blocks east on Samson Street stands Carpenters' Hall, built in 1770 by the Carpenters' Company of the city and county of Philadelphia, the oldest guild in America. Though most famous as the meeting place of the First Continental Congress in September 1774, Carpenters' Hall has been the site of numerous historically important events.

In June 1774 the Committee of Correspondence of the city and county of Philadelphia met here to initiate measures for calling a General Congress of the Colonies. From 1773 until 1791, it housed the Library Company founded by Benjamin Franklin, which evolved into the first Library of Congress.

In November 1774 the 1st Troop Philadelphia City Cavalry was formed here, making it the oldest mounted military unit in continuous service in the U.S. armed forces. The Committee of Safety met here, and following the British evacuation it was used by commissary general Henry Knox.

The Hall is still owned by the Carpenters' Company, whose volunteer docents answer visitors' questions about the hall and its place in Revolutionary War history. The first floor of the Hall is furnished as it would have been in 1775.

New Hall Military Museum

The original of this reconstructed building on Chestnut Street was built by the Carpenters' Company in 1791 and served as the offices of the first Secretary of War, Henry Knox. The museum chronicles the history of the armed forces from the Revolutionary War through the 1790s.

The first floor covers the U.S. Marine Corps, which was founded by a congressional committee meeting at Tun Tavern. A diorama depicts the tavern as the marines' first recruiting station, and pictures new recruits marching down the street near the tavern.

The second floor exhibits on the history of the army and navy include original weapons, such as Charleville and Brown Bess muskets and a hand grenade.

An entertaining 20-minute presentation is given daily on "A Soldier's Life," detailing what must have been the extraordinarily miserable and equally exhilarating existence of the Continental soldier.

Declaration House

When Thomas Jefferson lived here at Market and Chestnut streets, it was considered country. Jefferson moved in soon after arriving in Philadelphia for the Second Continental Congress because he was tired of the bustle of the city and wanted a more pastoral

setting. The original house (this is a reconstruction) was surrounded by fields, with a stable across the street. Jefferson complained about the horseflies the stable attracted, but he appreciated the peace and quiet the location afforded, especially as he was writing the Declaration of Independence during a hot June in 1776.

Two rooms Jefferson rented can be seen by visitors today. They are furnished with period pieces arranged as they might have been when Thomas Jefferson was in residence.

A short film on the writing of the Declaration is shown on the first

Benjamin Franklin

Of all the inventors that this country has produced, perhaps America should be proudest of Benjamin Franklin. In addition, he was an author, scientist, politician, diplomat, businessman, abolitionist, and a Founding Father at the age of 70. Though some might call him a Renaissance man, Franklin was entirely American—a pragmatist with the soul of a poet and the mind of a hardheaded Yankee trader.

Born in Boston in 1706, the tenth of 17 children, Franklin had one year of schooling before being apprenticed to his brother as a printer. When he arrived in Philadelphia in 1723, he had very little money and lots of ambition. Franklin eventually became a successful printer and author, and by 1737 was involved in the city's politics. This led to leadership in state, colonial, national, and finally international affairs. In the 1760s he was living in London as the agent to the British government for four of the colonies, including Pennsylvania.

In 1775 he returned to Philadelphia and served as a Pennsylvania delegate to the Second Continental Congress. He quickly became one of the leaders of the Congress, and in 1776 he was a member of the committee delegated to write the Declaration of Independence.

Franklin was America's ambassador to France during the war, where his charm and bargaining powers helped bring France, Spain, and the Netherlands into the war as allies of Franklin's new nation. After the war, during the treaty process, America's more experienced allies might have taken advantage of her but for Franklin's skills as a diplomat and businessman. He knew how to finagle and he knew how to close a deal.

Franklin was dedicated to the idea that the United States would thrive through the energies of "the middling people." He celebrated America's middle class, inventing items such as the clean-burning stove and bifocals. He developed the lending library and the fire brigade. And he gave us pithy sayings such as "a penny saved is a penny earned" in his *Poor Richard's Almanack.*

When Benjamin Franklin died in 1790 at the age of 84, his funeral in Philadelphia was as much pageant as farewell, with thousands crowding the streets. He is buried in Christ Church burial ground, across the street from Independence Visitor Center.

The National Constitution Center

Using multimedia exhibits and multicultural references, the National Constitution Center, a privately owned nonprofit facility, presents the Constitution as a living document integral to the life of every citizen.

Visitors are invited to experience rather than observe, so they can sit at a senator's desk, decide a Supreme Court case, take the presidential oath of office, and walk among life-size statues of the delegates at the Constitutional Convention.

The production *Freedom Rising* employs film, a live actor, and video projection on a 360-degree surround-screen theater. It leads visitors into the center's permanent exhibit, "The American Experience," where more than 100 interactive and multimedia exhibits explain and examine the Constitution in the context of its time and present-day America.

floor, where there is also an interesting exhibit on Jefferson as a writer. A daily 20-minute presentation on Jefferson in Philadelphia profiles Jefferson as he went about his daily life and provides insights into his tastes and character.

Franklin Court and the Underground Museum

Located between 3rd and 4th streets off Market, Franklin Court is easy to find. What was once the home of Benjamin Franklin is represented by a whimsical "ghost" house—a white steel frame complete with squares for chimneys—sitting above the Underground Museum.

Though Franklin's own home was torn down in 1812, three of those he built as rentals have survived and face the court on Market Street. One of these now operates as a printing shop. Inside, visitors can see demonstrations of the 18th-century-style printing process and buy copies of pamphlets, books, and papers being printed in the shop.

The Underground Museum, entered off Franklin Square, covers all aspects of this extraordinary American's life, including reproductions of many of his inventions. One of the most intriguing is a musical instrument called a glass armonica. Its name taken from the Italian word for harmony, the armonica is based on the traditional practice of making music with water-filled glasses.

Visitor Information

215-597-8974 or 215-965-2305
www.nps.gov/inde
215-409-6600
www.constitutioncenter.org
Hours: The Liberty Bell Center, Independence Hall and its "Great Essentials" exhibit in the West Wing, the Tomb of the Unknown Soldier, and Franklin Court are open 9 a.m. until 5 p.m. daily. Timed tickets are required for Independence Hall from March until December. Independence Visitor Center is open from 8:30 a.m. until 5 p.m. daily. Carpenters' Hall is open from 10 a.m. until 4 p.m., Tuesday through Sunday. New Hall Military Museum is open from 2 p.m. until 5 p.m. daily. Declaration House is open from 9 a.m. until noon daily. Closing hours vary at other NPS sites, but all open at 9 a.m. except the Second Bank Portrait Exhibit, which opens at 2 p.m. The National Constitution Center is open from 9:30 a.m. until 5 p.m., Monday through Friday, and from 9:30 a.m. until 6 p.m. on Saturday and Sunday.
Admission: All NPS sites are free. The National Constitution Center has a moderate charge; children 4 and under are free.
Accessibility: The National Constitution Center is accessible. All NPS sites are accessible at least on the first floor, except Carpenters' Hall, for which an accessible entrance is in the planning stages.
Special Events: Special events, family programs, lectures, and educational events are held throughout the year. For dates and detailed information, please check the Web site. There are four daily programs: "Jefferson in Philadelphia" at the Declaration House, "Franklin's Glass Music" at the Franklin Underground Museum, "Paths of the Founders" at the Visitor Center, and "A Soldier's Life" at the New Hall Military Museum. Check at the Visitor Center for times.
Getting There: Independence Park is in the center of Philadelphia, and the Visitor Center is at 6th and Market streets. The NPS Web site has detailed information on arriving by car from every direction, or call (215) 597-8974. Underground parking is offered adjacent to the Visitor Center. The National Constitution Center is at 6th Street

David Library of the American Revolution

Located only a few miles from Washington Crossing Historic Park in Pennsylvania, this library holds an extraordinary collection of books, manuscripts, and microfilm on the history of America, circa 1750 to 1800.

The museum's founder, Sol Feinstone, a businessman, philanthropist, and collector of Americana, amassed the library's core collection over five decades. In 1974, he opened it as a noncirculating library, housed in a renovated barn on his estate.

The collection has grown to include 40,000 printed materials in bound volumes and microcards, as well as 10,000 reels of microfilm containing original American, British, Loyalist, French, and German records. There is also a wealth of material on women, African Americans, and Native Americans during this period of history. The catalog is accessible on the library's Web site.

Among the library's British collection are American Loyalist claims, Colonial Office correspondence, and papers of Lord Cornwallis and Sir Guy Carleton. Personal and official papers of Americans such as George Washington, Nathanael Greene, Henry Knox, the Lee family of Virginia, Baron von Steuben, and Benjamin Franklin are also represented.

The military service records collection is extensive and includes the entire Revolutionary War Pension Application and Bounty Land Warrant files, as well as compiled service records and naval records.

The library has more than 140 newspapers from Revolutionary War–era states spanning most of the 18th and early 19th centuries. Among these are the Connecticut *Courant* (1764–1800), the Boston *Gazette* (1719–1798), and the South Carolina *Weekly Gazette* (1783–1786).

In addition, in recent years the library has been enhancing its collection of materials related to the French and Indian War and the colonial period.

Those interested in visiting the library are encouraged to call ahead for a reservation. The library's four reader-printers are allotted on a first-reserved, first-served basis, and some days may be busier than others. This library is a wonderful resource and one that welcomes anyone who has any interest in the American Revolution.

Visitor Information

215-493-6776

www.dlar.org

Hours: Open Tuesday through Saturday from 10 a.m. until 5 p.m.; closed Sunday, Monday, federal holidays, December 25, January 1, and the Saturday before federal holidays.

Admission: Free.

Accessibility: Those with special needs should contact the library beforehand.

Special Events: There are fall and spring lecture series (information available online) and periodic exhibitions in the Feinstone Conference Center adjacent to the library.

Getting There: From the north, take the New Jersey Turnpike to exit 7A, follow signs to I-195 west; take I-195 west to I-295 north, which eventually becomes I-95 south; follow I-95 south to exit 51, the first exit in Pennsylvania; proceed 4 miles north on Taylorsville Road to state route 532 and turn right; proceed 1 mile and turn left onto state route 32 (River Road); the library is 1.3 miles on the left.

From the south, take I-95 north to exit 51; make a left at the end of the ramp, onto Taylorsville Road north, and proceed as above.

The Boston Gazette *for November 13, 1775, contains King George's "Proclamation for Suppressing Rebellion and Sedition."*

Fort Mifflin on the Delaware

Once General William Howe had occupied Philadelphia in September 1777 (see Pennsylvania, Independence National Historical Park), he looked for the most direct delivery route to ensure the city would be well supplied during the coming winter. More than 200 British ships lay anchored south of the city, loaded with necessary food and materials, but their course was threatened by two Patriot garrisons on the Delaware River—Fort Mercer on the New Jersey side and Fort Mifflin on Mud Island a few miles downriver near the Pennsylvania side. Mifflin was at that time called Fort Mud.

Though neither fort had a large number of cannons, their strategic placement still made it costly for any ship to try to run the gauntlet. In addition, the Patriots had sunk iron-spiked barricades called chevaux de fries at various points along the river. Anchored just below the water's surface, these barricades could rip large holes in a ship's bottom.

The Battle for Fort Mifflin

On November 10, 1777, after the British had been unsuccessful in capturing Fort Mercer (see New Jersey, Red Bank Battlefield Park), they turned their full attention on Fort Mifflin, the less fortified of the two forts. For five days they bombarded the fort from batteries built on the Pennsylvania shore. Two 32-pounders, six 24-pounders, one 18-pounder, two 8-inch howitzers, and one 13-inch mortar reduced the fort to, as one British officer put it, "a picture of desolation. The whole area was ploughed like a field. The buildings [were] hanging in broken fragments, the guns all dismounted."

That Fort Mifflin's defenders held out against this bombardment is considered among the most heroic acts of the war.

One of the Patriot soldiers, Joseph Martin, wrote of the ordeal, "The British batteries in the course of the day would nearly level our works, and we were, like the beaver, obliged to repair our dams in the night. As the American defenders made repairs, a soldier would stand guard, and when he saw the muzzle flash of a British artillery piece, he would call out—'A shot!'—upon which everyone endeavored to take care of himself, yet they would ever and anon, in spite of all our precautions, put up some of us."

By now there was almost no food left in the fort. Most of the men had no shoes and few had breeches or coats. When a late season hurricane hit, it rained for three days, with temperatures near freezing. The story is told that with only one of the fort's cannons remaining—a 32-pounder—Mifflin's commander, Major Simeon Thayer, offered one gill of rum to every man who retrieved one of the British 32-pounder cannonballs that landed in the mud. These were then shot back at the British.

Some believe that Loyalists sabotaged the underwater barricades, because by November 15 the British were able to move six of their now 35 ships within range. Coupled with the shore batteries, the ships began a devastating barrage of an estimated 1000 shots per hour at one point. By that night there was almost nothing left of Fort Mifflin. Thayer, realizing further defense was impossible, ordered the fort abandoned. Under cover of darkness, he and his men escaped upriver to Fort Mercer. Because Thayer never struck the fort's colors (lowered its flag), officially the fort never surrendered.

During the defense of Fort Mifflin, the Patriots had lost close to 250 men, killed or wounded; the British, less than 20.

Visiting Fort Mifflin

The British had only begun to rebuild the fort in 1778 when the decision was made to abandon Philadelphia and the troops were ordered north. The theater of war was moving away from this area, so neither side saw any need to rebuild here during the war. It was in the early 1800s that the fort was reconstructed and named Fort Mifflin. During the War of 1812, some 300 soldiers were stationed here.

The Fort Mifflin that visitors see today is restored to its 1834 appearance, though several of the surviving structures were built later. Mifflin was used as a prison for Confederate soldiers following the Civil War battle at Gettysburg, and for artillery training in World War I. It remained an active military base until 1952.

The flag flying above the fort is a reproduction of the one still flying when the British entered it in 1777. There is some evidence that the original was sewn by Betsy Ross, famous flag maker of the Revolutionary period. The distinctive red, white,

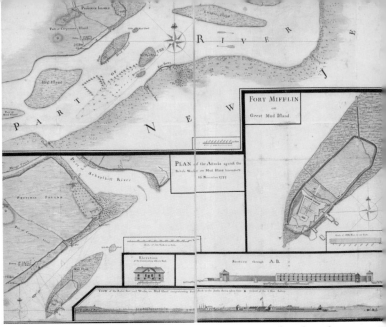

Fort Mifflin's location on Mud Island and its proximity to Red Bank can be seen on this 18th-century map rendered by British general Howe's chief engineer. Elevations and plans of the fort show it to be a formidable structure.

and blue striped Pennsylvania Navy flag is about 45 feet by 32 feet and has been dubbed the Valiant Defender, in honor of those who served here.

The Main Entrance to the fort, made of massive stones and with wooden doors from the Civil War era, has a headstone dedicated to President John Adams. It was Adams who pushed for the construction of a line of forts along the East Coast in the early 1800s, when peace with Great Britain was still tenuous.

Tickets and maps for self-guided tours are available in the Hospital, which was built prior to 1802. Guided tours by costumed interpreters are offered on weekends. There is some information here on the building's original purpose, but more detailed information about Revolutionary War medicine is provided in the Soldiers' Barracks.

The tin-roofed barracks, built between 1794 and 1795, housed 75 soldiers. Their living conditions are re-created in a barracks room circa 1840. A representative room circa 1812 is exhibited in the Officers' Quarters, which was built sometime around 1814.

The only remaining building from the British rebuilding effort in 1778 is the Blacksmith's Shop, where blacksmithing demonstrations are given during special events.

The 1837 Artillery Shed, the oldest of its kind in the country, displays several cannons, as does the 1816 Arsenal, which also displays reproductions of U.S. flags spanning the years the fort was an active military base. The 12 restored buildings also include a Powder Magazine with vaulted brick interiors and a Torpedo Magazine. The Army tested torpedoes here as early as 1875.

The Commandant's House, which burned down in 1983, is currently being rebuilt. When completed, its exhibits will include a room representing how the fort's commander lived in the mid-1800s.

Visitor Information

215-685-4167

www.fortmifflin.org

Hours: Open April 1 until November 30, Wednesday through Sunday, 10 a.m. until 4 p.m.; closed Easter.

Admission: There is a moderate charge; children under 6 free.

Accessibility: Partially accessible; call ahead for special needs.

Special Events: Celebrations on Flag Day and the Fourth of July; commemoration ceremony and events in November; Colonial Days the third Saturday in April, with reenactments, drilling, cannon and musket demonstrations, and other activities.

Getting There: Fort Mifflin is adjacent to Philadelphia International Airport. From southbound I-95 take exit 15, Island Avenue/Enterprise Avenue, onto Enterprise Avenue. Turn left onto Fort Mifflin Road; follow the road through the short tunnel, turn left, follow signs to the fort. From northbound I-95 take exit 13 Valley Forge/west 291. Bear right and follow sign for Island Avenue then turn left onto Island Avenue then left onto Enterprise Avenue and right onto Fort Mifflin Road. Proceed as above.

Fort Roberdeau Historical Site and Natural Area

Fort Roberdeau was originally built to protect the men working in the local lead mines, but it became just as important as a refuge for settlers on what was then the western frontier.

From the beginning of the Revolution, lack of ammunition was a major problem. By 1777 the dearth of bullets was becoming crucial to the success of the war. Only a few lead mines were in operation at the beginning of the war, and these couldn't keep up with the demand.

In March 1777 the Supreme Executive Council of Pennsylvania learned of large lead deposits here in Sinking Spring Valley. General Daniel Roberdeau, a member of the Continental Congress and a generous benefactor to the war effort, was sent to the area to determine if the deposits justified the time and expense of setting up a mining operation.

Visiting the Fort

Roberdeau decided in favor of the enterprise and, with his own money, began construction of what would become Fort Roberdeau, or the Lead Mine Fort as it was known locally. Some sort of fortification was necessary because of the frequent raids by Loyalists or their Native American allies. Even with this protection, Roberdeau had a hard time attracting miners to the operation. By the fall of 1778, supplies were coming from America's new ally France, and the situation took on less urgency.

Though the mines continued in operation until 1780, the fort's function as a home for miners became secondary to its service as a refuge for settlers under attack. For this purpose, the fort was garrisoned by companies of rangers raised from among the surrounding male population who signed up for nine months—from the spring thaw until early winter—for a bounty of a suit of clothes or a straight monetary payment.

Fort Roberdeau today, part of a 230-acre park, is a reconstruction of the original, built as part of the nation's bicentennial celebrations in 1976. Based on period drawings and archaeological findings, this fort is a near replica of the original.

An eight-minute film in the Visitor Center, the Barn, provides a broad overview of the area, beginning with the ancient peoples who settled here 4000 years ago and continuing through the Revolutionary War.

The focus of the exhibit area is divided between the mining operation and the lives of the people who settled Sinking Spring Valley. One of the displays, designed with children in mind, is just as informative for adults. "Could You Survive on the Frontier?" features period artifacts and reproductions to explain the hardships endured by Pennsylvania's 18th-century pioneers. Mining exhibits show how the mines were lit and how the men extracted the ore.

Costumed guides take visitors through Fort Roberdeau, where eight sites recreate the lives of the men who worked and lived here. Examining the buildings, visitors may wonder not at their small size but that they were built at all, given the difficulty of anchoring anything in the moist earth.

Visitors can view the Officers' Quarters, a small Storehouse, two Barracks, a stone Furnace, and the Blacksmith's. There are also a cabin that was reserved for those with knowledge of smelting, whose quarters were better than the barracks but not as "luxurious" as those of the officers, and a Powder Magazine because the fort was used as a supply depot for munitions. All these are furnished with reproductions for hands-on explorations.

From the fort, visitors are welcome to walk along several nature trails, where signage explains the difficulties encountered by the miners in getting through the strata of rock to the ore.

Visitor Information

814-946-0048

www.fortroberdeau.org/

Hours: May 1 through October 31, Tuesday through Saturday, 11 a.m. until 5 p.m.; Sunday and Monday, 1 p.m. until 5 p.m.; closed major holidays.

Admission: There is a minimal to moderate charge; children under 3 are free.

Accessibility: The site is handicapped accessible.

Special Events: Arts & Heritage Festival every May; theater presentations and concerts in the summer.

Getting There: The site is 8 miles northeast of Altoona. From the Pennsylvania Turnpike, take exit 11 and go north on U.S. 220/I-99. Take the Bellwood exit and follow signs to the fort.

From the north on I-80, take U.S. 220/I-99 south to the Bellwood exit and follow signs to the fort.

Valley Forge National Historical Park

One of the most abiding images of the war is that of George Washington and his men enduring the winter of 1777–1778 at Valley Forge.

A favorite of 19th-century painters, the image of the general wrapped in his cloak, snow up to his knees, his huddled men gathered around him, has come down to us as a paradigm of steadfastness, courage, and sacrifice.

So strong is this image that some visitors to the park today find it hard to believe that in fact, for all the suffering by the Patriot army over a long winter, morale was generally high and pride and comradeship strong. In spite of the army's beleaguered state by the time it reached Valley Forge, this was a tough fighting force, and it needed only cohesion and organization to make it a formidable one.

The Winter Encampment

The number of troops and other personnel who died at Valley Forge lies between 1500 and 3000, the highest death total of the eight winter encampments of the war. The deaths were mostly attributed to starvation and disease.

There was food to be had, but the delivery system was so slipshod that supplies rotted in warehouses or in abandoned wagons. Blankets and clothes didn't arrive, because of a lack of horses and wagons.

Following the loss at Germantown (*see* Pennsylvania, Brandywine Battlefield Park), Washington pushed his men to Whitemarsh to escape the pursuing British army. After a series of small skirmishes and with winter coming on, Washington and his officers opted for a period of restoration for their weary men. The decision was made to forgo a winter campaign and establish a cantonment at Valley Forge.

Valley Forge, located at the junction of the Schuylkill River and Valley Creek, 20 miles from Philadelphia, was less a valley than a two-mile long thickly wooded slope. The army arrived here on December 19, 1777.

The men were divided into groups of 12 to build their huts. Each hut was 16 feet long by 14 feet wide by six and a half feet high. Bunk beds were built into the four corners, oiled paper served as a window, and there was a fireplace. Since the only wood available for burning was newly cut green wood, the huts were almost constantly filled with smoke. Some 1000 were built over the winter.

There were also hundreds of women at Valley Forge that winter, wives of enlisted men, who were paid to work as laundresses, or in the artificer corps repairing equipment, or as nurses. Some received pensions after the war for their service.

Even as the army was building its camp in the dead of the cold winter, some members of Congress were pushing for an attack on the British in Philadelphia. Washington upbraided them—which was unusual for the general—in a sharply worded letter. "The gentlemen reprobate the going into winter quarters as much as if they thought the soldiers were made of sticks or stones. I can assure these gentlemen that it is a much easier and less dis-

Replicated huts mark the site where General Muhlenberg's Brigade anchored the oute line of defense. Here interpreters in period costume demonstrate conditions of soldier li

In December 1777, Lafayette, left, went with Washington and the army into winter quarters at Valley Forge. Several officers were interested in persuading Congress to relieve Washington of his command and tried to secure the cooperation of Lafayette, but failed.

tressing thing to draw remonstrances in a comfortable room, than to occupy a cold bleak hill, and sleep under frost and snow without clothes and blankets. However, although they seem to have little feeling for the naked and distressed soldiers, I feel superabundantly for them, and from my soul I pity their miseries which it is neither in my power to relieve or prevent."

The winter proved one of the harshest. The description by surgeon Albigence Waldo of Connecticut draws a vivid picture: "Poor food—bad lodging—cold weather—fatigue—nasty clothes—nasty cookery—vomit half the time—smoked out of my senses—Here all is confusion—smoke and cold—hunger and filthiness—a bowl of beef soup, full of burnt leaves and dirt . . ." Yet he also states that "they [the army] still show a spirit of alacrity and contentment not to be expected from so young troops."

That spirit is evident in a narrative attributed to a soldier named James Sullivan Martin, who recounts a "Continental thanksgiving ordered by Congress. . . . We had nothing to eat for two or three days previous, except what the trees of the fields and forests afforded us. But we must now have . . . a sumptuous thanksgiving to close the year . . . Well—to add something extraordinary to our present stock of provisions—our country, ever mindful of its suffering army, opened her sympathizing heart so wide, upon this occasion, as to give us something to make the world stare. . . . it gave each and every man half a gill of rice and a table spoon full of vinegar! After we had made sure of this extraordinary superabundant donation, we were ordered out to attend a meeting and hear a sermon delivered upon the occasion."

As the winter wore on, men and horses began to starve, with "meat wagons" collecting the dead from huts every day and details assigned to bury horses twice a week. Washington used these conditions as an opportunity to force Congress's hand. That august body had established departments but had left key positions vacant, and jobs weren't getting done.

In January 1778, Congress's Board of War came to Valley Forge. They saw the deprivations and the disease, but they also saw that in spite of these the army was going about its business—drilling, maintaining weapons, and storing and making repairs to what matériel it had. This display of resolve won the board's support. With it, Washington finally was able to convince Congress of the necessity of developing a bureaucracy that could sustain this army so it could win the war.

One result was the appointment of Nathanael Greene as quartermaster general. He quickly organized a system of supply that provided food and clothing for the army. Another result was the arrival of Friedrich Wilhelm von Steuben, a veteran of the Prussian army.

The 47-year-old Steuben had been introduced to Benjamin Franklin in Paris, and in 1777 he came to America with a letter from Franklin that recommended the baron for a position with the American army. Although Steuben's title was questionable, his military skills were not.

Arriving at Valley Forge in February 1778, Steuben impressed Washington with his suggestions for improving the fortifications there. By the end of March, Steuben had been given the job of supervising the

Friedrich Wilhelm von Steuben

Friedrich Wilhelm von Steuben was born into a military family and became a soldier at the age of 16. During the Seven Years War, he advanced in the Prussian army, even serving for a time on the general staff of Frederick II. Once in America, he became enamored of its people, and after the Revolutionary War he settled in New York City. Congress awarded him a substantial amount of money and 16,000 acres in New York State for his service during the war, where he had been a volunteer; but by the late 1780s he had fallen deeply into debt. In 1790, Congress voted he be given a life pension of 2500 dollars, on which he lived until his death in 1794.

The Steuben Memorial State Historic Site in Remsen, New York, features a replica of Steuben's frontier home and period furnishings. The memorial is currently undergoing a renovation that will more fully engage visitors in the baron's life. The cabin will look as it did immediately after Steuben's death, with his possessions packed and ready to be sent to his designatees. Visitors will be greeted as those paying their last respects and taken on a tour of the home by costumed interpreters. Information about the memorial and the renovation is available at www.steubenmemorial.com.

---

reform of the army's discipline. Soldiers were taught how to march, how to use a bayonet, how to dig a trench, how to arrive at and leave a battlefield as a compact group that was ready to deploy into a line and back into a column efficiently—all the basics they had been too busy fighting to learn.

The manual Steuben wrote that spring, *Regulations for the Order and Discipline of the Troops of the United States*, served as the U.S. Army's training manual until after the War of 1812.

With the coming of substantial food and supplies in March, thanks to quartermaster general Greene, and with the daily instruction of Baron von Steuben, the men at Valley Forge began to coalesce into a coherent unit. Among those who survived the winter were future Chief Justice of the United States John Marshall and future President James Monroe.

The bond formed here would carry the army through four more years of heavy fighting.

Visiting Valley Forge

At the Welcome Center, visitors can view the 18-minute film *Valley Forge: A Winter Encampment* and visit the museum, which has been imaginatively laid out in the fashion of miniature versions of the huts in which the men lived. Each hut covers a theme related to life at Valley Forge, including the role of African Americans and women, military justice, and engineering.

There are 18 miles of trails at Valley Forge, including a 10-mile stretch of road with interpretive signage for visitors taking the self-guided automobile or bicycle tour. Cassette tapes and CDs for the tour are sold in the Museum Shop.

At Washington's Headquarters, visitors learn how Mrs. Washington maintained a household while the general maintained a headquarters at which he conducted army business and received local officials and foreign dignitaries.

Replicated huts at the outer line of defense where General Peter Muhlenberg's brigade lived are the backdrop for summer-weekend demonstrations of a soldier's life, and at the Dewees's House park rangers explain how military justice was maintained at Valley Forge. The Grand Parade, where Baron von Steuben trained the troops, fronts Varnum's Quarters, the home of General James Varnum during the encampment. On weekends May through October, park rangers talk about what it was like to be a civilian living in the area that winter.

Brigadier General Henry Knox was also instrumental in transforming the army. Dozens of cannons at Artillery Park, ready for defense of

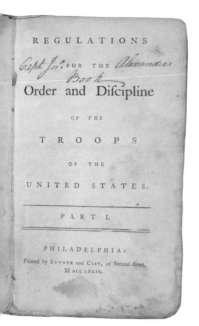

the encampment, were used by Knox to train and drill his artillery corps. A long line of cannons sits at rest in the park. A number of redoubts have also been preserved, plus more than 40 markers, statues, and memorials, including those honoring individual states and brigades and the well over 1000 African Americans who passed through Valley Forge that winter.

A 19th-century marker erected by the Daughters of the American Revolution is particularly poignant: "Here lie the remains of a Revolutionary Soldier shot on a neighboring farm during the winter of 1777–1778." Tradition has it that the soldier was milking a cow when he was shot by the farmer. The D.A.R. also erected a granite memorial in 1911 to the Unknown Soldiers who are buried at Valley Forge.

Visitor Information
610-783-1099 or 783-1077
www.nps.gov/vafo
Hours: Welcome Center and Washington's Headquarters open daily, 9 a.m. until 5 p.m. Muhlenberg Brigade open 10 a.m. until 4 p.m. daily in the summer, open Saturday and Sunday, September until mid-June. Varnum's Quarters open daily, 10 noon until 4 p.m., May through October. Dewees's House open intermittently all year. Check at the Welcome Center for availability. Closed December 25.

Admission: There is a moderate fee for a 7-day admission ticket for Washington's Headquarters from April 1 until November 30. All other park facilities are free.

Accessibility: The Welcome Center, Washington's Headquarters, and the Muhlenberg Brigade huts are accessible. The *Valley Forge: A Winter Encampment* film is shown captioned on request, and assistance for the hearing impaired is also available. The Multi-Use Trail is paved and accessible.

Special Events: At the Muhlenberg Brigade, park rangers present "Life of a Regular Soldier" daily. "Living with an Army" is presented at Varnum's Quarters.

Getting There: Valley Forge is about 20 miles northwest of Philadelphia. From the PA Turnpike (I-76/276) use the Valley Forge exit. The NPS Web site has detailed information on arriving by car from every direction, or call 610-783-1077.

By bus: SEPTA bus route 125 stops at the Valley Forge Visitor Center, the nearby Sheraton Hotel, and King of Prussia Mall.

Artifacts on display at Valley Forge include a cartridge box, left, worn around the waist.

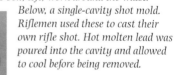

Below, a single-cavity shot mold. Riflemen used these to cast their own rifle shot. Hot molten lead was poured into the cavity and allowed to cool before being removed.

To fashion a musket cartridge, below, the soldier would create a cylinder by wrapping a wooden dowel with paper. Then he would tie off one end, insert the lead ball and pour gunpowder over it. Finally, he folded or twisted the open cartridge end. It would now be ready to fire.

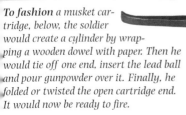

Washington Crossing Historic Park

Perhaps the most famous image of the Revolutionary War is Emanuel Leutze's painting *Washington Crossing the Delaware.* As dramatic and powerful a representation as it is, Leutze's portrayal seems impossibly romantic, with little connection to the actual event. The crossing from Pennsylvania to New Jersey was in the middle of the night, with almost no visibility because of the pelting sleet and snow, so there wouldn't have been that bright light on the horizon. Unlike the men in the painting, many of the soldiers didn't have warm coats and scarves. Incredibly, some only had lightweight summer clothing for cover. The frightened expressions on the men's faces are certainly realistic. Few of them could swim, and they were terrified of drowning in the choppy, freezing waters. And those large chunks of ice floating in the river are realistically portrayed. They threatened every moment to capsize boats as they bumped past.

Most important, Leutze's George Washington is true. While Washington wasn't posing in the bow of the boat, he was standing, simply because the boats they crossed in had no seats. The steely spine, the set of the jaw, the inspiring face forward that bespeaks determination—all are true to the man. This was the leader his men would have followed into hell, even the icy hell of the Delaware River.

What Leutze captured in his painting was the emotional core of the moment, a pivotal moment in American history when the character of a leader and the needs of a country were perfectly met, on that Christmas Day in 1776.

Howe's Mistake

The summer and fall of 1776 had been difficult for George Washington and the Continental Army. The loss of Long Island was followed by the loss of New York City, then the defeats at White Plains and Fort Washington, and finally the evacuation from Fort Lee, followed by the retreat across the river into Pennsylvania.

With each retreat, soldiers were deserting in droves. Hundreds at a time simply slipped away. The enthusiasm for becoming a separate nation had diminished in the harsh reality of battle. Worse, everywhere confidence in the commander in chief was fading.

By autumn of 1776, that confidence had deteriorated to the point where there was talk among some in Congress and in the highest ranks of the army that Washington should be replaced. In late November, Adju-

tant General Joseph Reed wrote a very flattering letter to General Charles Lee in which Reed opined that Lee wouldn't have made the mistakes Washington was making and that "an indecisive mind is one of the great misfortunes that can befall an army." Lee, for his part, was not amiss to accepting Reed's, and others', praise, and his response ended that he would "fly" to rejoin Washington "for to confess a truth I really think our Chief will do better with me than without me." And in a letter to General Horatio Gates, Lee baldly stated his opinion that "a certain great man is damnably deficient." Lee was captured by the British soon after, and temporarily posed no more threat to the great man.

What did pose a threat at that point were British forces in pursuit, though they were becoming increasingly frustrated. One British officer complained, "'Tis almost impossible to catch them. They will neither fight, nor totally run away, but they keep at such a distance that we are always a day's march from them. We seem to be playing at bo peep."

Finally, on December 7 and 8, Washington and his troops crossed the Delaware into Pennsylvania and the British stopped on the river's New Jersey side, halting their pursuit. British general Sir William

Howe knew of the desertions, knew that as of December 31, the enlistments of thousands of Continental Army soldiers would be up and it was unlikely they'd reenlist, knew that Washington's army wasn't receiving sufficient supplies from the Congress nor from the states. Why waste his men and supplies in pursuit? Why not just let human nature take its course? Besides, most armies didn't fight in the winter in those days. It was to be expected that Washington, known to be a cautious man, would take this opportunity to hole up somewhere and rethink his strategy for a spring offensive. So Howe strung out a chain of posts on the New Jersey side of the Delaware River, one of which was at Trenton, and looked forward to a merry holiday.

What Howe had not considered was that though Washington was admittedly cautious, when his back was to the wall, he had the courage to be daring. He demonstrated that courage now with a plan to take the post at Trenton.

Washington's Daring Move

The British garrison at Trenton was staffed by Hessians under the command of German colonel Johann Gottlieb Rall. Washington's agents had convinced Rall that the American troops were demoralized and unprepared for action during the cold winter. Surprise would be Washington's strongest offensive weapon. He planned now a daring nighttime crossing of the Delaware River, which he hoped would allow him to capture Trenton and march onward to Princeton.

Washington divided his army into three forces. Earlier he had written to Joseph Reed, "[O]ur numbers, sorry I am to say, being less than I had any conception of: but necessity, dire necessity, will—nay, must—justify any attempt." Washington and Nathanael Greene would take 2400 men to McConkey's Ferry, about nine miles upstream from Trenton on the Pennsylvania side, and cross to New Jersey. Colonel John Cadwalader, who had recently been released from captivity by the British, would cross at Bordentown with 1800 men. Brigadier General James Ewing and another 800 men would cross at Trenton Ferry.

Washington and Greene would

Emanuel Leutze's famous painting Washington Crossing the Delaware.

Reenactors prepare to recreate the Patriot crossing of the Delaware River. The event is staged each year on December 25 with hundreds of participants and replica Durham boats.

lead the main attacking force, while the others would come around the town on either side to prevent escapes. Once the town was taken, the three armies would come together as one and move on to Princeton.

The password, or countersign, for the operation was "victory or death."

Washington's forces began crossing late Christmas Day. He had calculated the crossing at McConkey's Ferry would take a few hours. It took almost 10. The men were transported in Durham boats. Named for the inventor, John Durham, these long, narrow (40 to 60 feet long, 8 feet wide), almost flat (2 feet deep) boats were suited to the Delaware River because they had a very shallow draft.

While the majority of men were crossing the choppy waters in Durhams, others were crossing on large ferryboats transporting the artillery (eighteen 3- and 6-pounders) on carriages and the horses to pull them. These men had the hardest job—keeping the horses calm in the driving sleet, keeping the cannons and their carriages from sliding off as the ice coated the rafts.

That march would lead the Americans to Trenton. The Hessians there never expected a winter attack, certainly not at night and at Christmastime. Caught sleeping, they were defeated in about an hour. (*See* New Jersey, Washington Crossing State Park.)

Visiting the Park

This 500-acre park is on the Delaware River, east of Doylestown, Pennsylvania. It's in two sections, divided by the Delaware Canal State

Park. The first section, which contains the Visitor Center, is the "McConkey's Ferry" section to the west of the state park, and the second section is the "Thompson's Mill" section to the east of the state park. The distance between the two sections is about six miles. The Thompson's Mill section is itself divided into two sections, which include a mill, a house, and the wildflower preserve in one part and Bowman's Hill Tower in another part.

Visitors use their cars to travel between sections.

The park's Visitor Center is currently under renovation, scheduled for completion sometime in the next few years. A 17-minute orientation video, *Of Dire Necessity*, continues to be shown during the renovation. This video provides not only a fine overview of the crossing but also a deeper understanding of what was at stake and the horrific conditions suffered by the soldiers that night.

Plans are for the renovated Visitor Center to include displays of artifacts from the period. Also on display once again in the center's auditorium will be a digitally mastered photomural of Leutze's *Washington Crossing the Delaware*, the original of which hangs in the Metropolitan Museum of Art in New York. Leutze created his painting in 1849 as a commemoration of the event, but also as an inspiration for the democratic movement in his home of Wurttemberg, part of the German-

Prussian provinces. The painting brought him great fame in the U.S., where he died in Washington, D.C., in 1868.

The guided tour of the first section of the historic park leaves from the Visitor Center and includes six structures, one of which—McConkey's Ferry Inn—was here during the crossing. The inn was owned by Samuel McConkey in 1776 when, according to tradition, George Washington and his officers ate here on Christmas Day before beginning the crossing. The interior of the inn has been decorated with period pieces as well as reproductions, creating a sense of what taverns were like at the time.

The Durham Boat House is a modern structure housing replicas of the Durham boat. John Durham began making his boats in the 1750s, and they soon became the staple vessel for transporting iron ore down the Delaware River.

The Mahlon K. Taylor House, the Hibbs House, and the Taylorsville Store are all early-19th-century buildings where visitors can learn about crafts such as spinning, weaving, and carpentry, see cooking demonstrations, and learn how people lived in the decades following the war.

A six-mile drive along the river on state route 32 brings visitors to the upper section of the park, to the Thompson-Neely House. This early-18th-century home served as the headquarters for the Continental Army during that December, and as a hospital following the battle. Part of the tour includes a look at hospital implements and information about Revolutionary War field medicine. The central portion of the house began as a cabin built in the mid-1770s. Both Thompson and Neely were millers.

The area's original gristmill, built by a wealthy Quaker around 1740, was located approximately 100 yards downstream from the Thompson-Neely Grist Mill. There are plans to make this a working mill. In the meantime, information provided by the guide on the importance of this mill to the surrounding farm area is complemented by an excellent brochure explaining the process of milling in detail.

A path from the Thompson-Neely House takes visitors to the Soldiers' Gravesite, where it's believed Revolutionary War soldiers are buried. (The path is part of the Delaware Canal Park.) The graves are marked, though the names in most cases are unknown.

Two miles above the house and mill is Bowman's Hill Tower, built in the early 1900s on what was thought to be a lookout point for Washington's troops. The tower, 125 feet tall, was constructed using more than 2400 tons of material. From its top, visitors have a lovely view of Bucks County, Pennsylvania, and of the Delaware River looking across into New Jersey. Near the tower is the entrance to the Bowman's Hill Wildflower Preserve, where native plants, flowers, and birds provide a soothing ambiance after a day of touring.

Visitor Information
215-493-4076
www.phmc.state.pa.us/bhsm/toh/
   washington/washington
     crossing.asp
or www.bucksnet.com/washxing
Hours: Open Tuesday through Saturday, 9 a.m. until 5 p.m.; Sunday, noon until 5 p.m.; closed Monday and federal holidays except Memorial Day, July 4, Labor Day, Thanksgiving Day, and January 1. Bowman's Hill Tower is open from April through early November.
Admission: There is a moderate charge; children under 6 enter free. The ticket price includes one tour of the McConkey's Ferry section, the Thompson-Neely section, and the Bowman's Hill Tower, and is valid for one year from date of issue. A park ticket doesn't include admission to the Bowman's Wildflower Preserve.
Accessibility: The Visitor Center, Durham Boat House, Thompson-Neely House, Bowman's Hill Wildflower Preserve, and Soldiers' Graves are accessible. Those needing special assistance should call ahead to discuss their particular needs.
Special Events: A major commemoration is held each year on December 25 at 1 p.m., when hundreds of reenactors in Continental military dress cross the Delaware in replica Durham boats. There are celebrations for Washington's Birthday and the Fourth of July, sheepshearing and Hessian weekends in the spring, and Harvest Day in the fall.
Getting There: From the Pennsylvania Turnpike, take exit 351 to U.S. 1 north to I-95 exit 51; from I-95 south, take exit 31B and go north on state route 32.

Historic Camden Revolutionary War Site

From May 1780 until April 1781, the town of Camden, South Carolina, was occupied by British troops, who used it as a major supply center for their forces in the South.

The Battle of Camden in August 1780 was an unsuccessful attempt to dislodge General Charles Cornwallis, then in residence, and to disrupt the British supply line. The Battle of Hobkirk's Hill the following April, though also a defeat, was one in a series of events that forced the British to evacuate Camden. Today the Hobkirk Hill battlefield is a residential development. The Camden Battlefield is designated as a National Historic Landmark, identified only by a roadside marker.

The part of Camden town occupied by the British, however, has been restored and preserved as Historic Camden and provides a revealing window into what it was like for Patriots under British occupation.

The Battle of Camden

In April 1780, George Washington sent Major General Johann Baron de Kalb south with an army to aid Continental forces defending Charleston, South Carolina.

De Kalb, a Bavarian mercenary turned wealthy landowner through marriage, had arrived in America with the Marquis de Lafayette in 1777. Unlike Lafayette, de Kalb's claims to nobility were phony. Yet this son of peasant stock was an able soldier, a good strategist, and a brave commander.

On his way south that spring of 1780, de Kalb learned that Charleston had surrendered, so he camped about 30 miles south of what is now Greensboro, North Carolina, while deciding his next move. He was hoping to encounter some local Patriot militia to augment his forces; but few turned up, so he set off again on June 21, intending to distract the British whenever he encountered them.

This was a tough march, made even more exhausting by the summer heat, the insects, and the lack of wagons, which meant the men had to carry all their baggage. De Kalb also was running short of supplies, but repeated requests to the North Carolina government were ignored. Wrote one soldier, "We marched from Hillsborough about the first of July, without an ounce of provision being laid up at any one point, often fasting for several days together, and subsiding frequently upon green apples and peaches; sometimes by detaching parties, we thought ourselves feasted, when by violence we seized a little fresh beef and cut and threshed out a little wheat; yet, under all these difficulties, we had to go forward."

While de Kalb struggled in North Carolina, the Continental Congress appointed Horatio Gates commander of the southern forces. De Kalb was by far the better officer, but he was a foreigner and had no political connections. Gates joined de Kalb on July 25, with orders to prevent further British incursions into the Carolinas. The first step was taking Cornwallis's supply center, currently being established at Camden.

De Kalb favored a circuitous route southward toward Camden that would provide better cover for the exhausted army. Plus, the areas he wanted to traverse were known for their Patriot sympathies and would likely be more forthcoming with supplies. Gates rejected this plan, even after all the officers sided with de Kalb. Instead, Gates marched his forces in something of a straight line through areas almost barren of farms, having numerous swampy patches and swollen streams, and

***Major General** Johann Baron de Kalb endured 11 wounds before being captured. He died three days later.*

known to be among the most strongly Loyalist in the region. The men were marching 18 miles a day, living on whatever they could find along the road. Food was so scarce, the officers tried thickening the soup with their hair powder.

Along the way, Gates picked up some Carolina militia, so that by the time he neared Clermont, north of Camden, he had nearly 4100 men. Somehow Gates convinced himself he had nearer 7000, and nothing could convince him otherwise. However many there were, only about 900 were disciplined soldiers who had fought before. (These were the Maryland and Delaware regiments.) And almost all were half starved and exhausted.

It got worse. Gates decided to do a night march toward Camden. Night marches were difficult at the best of times, but with undisciplined troops, unsure of the terrain, it was even trickier. In addition, on the day of the march, August 15, Gates had ordered rations of molasses from the hospital store be given the men in place of the rum supply, which had run out. The men were fed half-cooked meat, half-baked bread, and corn meal mixed with molasses. The result was an outbreak of diarrhea so severe that it was later reported troops were breaking ranks along

the march all night and "much debilitated before the action commenced."

Action commenced in the early morning hours, when Gates and his forces suddenly found themselves almost face-to-face with Cornwallis and his men, marching from Camden intent on a surprise attack. A brief spurt of gunfire was followed by both armies falling back. Neither wanted to fight in the blackness of night, in a thick forest framed by swamps.

Before daybreak, both sides formed their lines. Gates stationed de Kalb with the Maryland and Delaware regiments on the right flank, the North Carolina militia in the center, and the Virginia militia on the left flank. Gates positioned himself 600 yards behind the line.

As if prescient, the British initial attack the morning of the 16th was on the left flank. The majority of these men from North Carolina and Virginia had never engaged in formal battle. Some had never fired a gun. Exhausted, starved, sickly, terrified, and faced with a charging line of British regulars, they ran without firing a shot. Almost as a unit, 2500 men fled the field. One group of

North Carolinians stayed. Under the command of Lieutenant Colonel Henry Dixon and posted next to the disciplined, battle-hardened Maryland and Delaware regiments, they held.

With the American left flank gone, Cornwallis threw everything at de Kalb and the right flank. Colonel Otho Williams took charge of the Maryland regiment, which rallied several times before finally being routed. Now only de Kalb and Brigadier General Mordecai Gist, whose mettle had been proven in the Battle of Long Island, remained on the field with their troops. With the smoke of battle and the confusion of the field, it's unlikely they knew they were alone. They fought as if they were winning—roughly 600 against some 2000.

The fighting was fierce, with repeated bayonet charges by both regiments. When the American line was finally broken, very few escaped the British onslaught. (Only about 700 survived the battle.) Gist managed to get away in the confusion, but de Kalb took 11 wounds before being captured. He was propped up against a wagon—bleeding to death and being stripped of his coat and boots—when Cornwallis came to his rescue and put him in the care of British field surgeons. De Kalb died three days later.

And what of the commander of the southern forces, General Horatio Gates? When Gates saw the left flank break, he took to his horse. The 52-year-old general made the 180-mile trek to Hillsboro in three days, wearing out several horses along the way.

Gates's hasty retreat caused a scandal. As Alexander Hamilton wrote to a friend, "What think you of the conduct of this great man? . . . [W]as there ever an instance of a general running away, as Gates has done, from his whole army? And was there ever so precipitate a flight? One hundred and eighty miles in three days . . . It does admirable credit to the activity of a man at his time of life. But it disgraces the general and the soldier."

A Congressional inquiry in 1782 found Gates innocent of wrongdoing—none officially using the charge of cowardice—but the stigma was permanent. Gates was relieved of command following Camden, and though he remained in the army, he never again had a battlefield command.

The Battle of Hobkirk Hill—also north of Camden and not far from the 1780 battlefield—eight months later in April 1781, again resulted in an American defeat. This time the Patriots were led by Nathanael Greene and stood their ground, but eventually gave way to the superior tactics of Lord Francis Rawden, who had distinguished himself at the Battle of Camden. The losses suffered by the British, however, were among the factors leading to their withdrawal from Camden soon after.

Visiting Historic Camden

This 107-acre outdoor museum complex, a charming and informative echo of colonial and Revolutionary times, sits on the fringes of modern Camden, about 25 miles northeast of Columbia, South Carolina.

A self-guided tour brochure is available, but the guided tour provides a great many more interesting tidbits about life here during the British occupation. Note that the map reproduced in the brochure is a copy of an original map of the town drawn by the Polish Patriot general Thaddeus Kosciuszko.

Visitors begin at the Cunningham House, which serves as tour headquarters. The house was built in 1835 and moved here from across town. Its name comes from the tradition that it was a wedding present for Mrs. Joseph Cunningham. At the Dog Trot (a roofed open-air passage connecting two buildings), visitors can see a 12-minute slide presentation on the history of Camden, including its Revolutionary War occupation.

Other houses in the complex include the Craven House, one of only two 18th-century buildings left in Camden, which displays portraits of Patriot heroes such as Nathanael Greene and Baron de Kalb; the McCaa House, built around 1800 and currently appointed as an 18th-century tavern; and the Kershaw House, which the British used as their headquarters and which also served as a residence for Cornwallis.

Joseph Kershaw, considered the founder of the town, was a staunch Patriot. When Cornwallis descended on Camden, he banished Kershaw to Bermuda. While in Bermuda, Kershaw mortgaged much of his property to purchase a ship to carry supplies to the colonies. The British captured the ship and its provisions, leaving Kershaw to spend the rest of his life trying to pay the debts he had incurred. South Carolina refused to

The Kershaw-Cornwallis House *was built for Joseph Kershaw, a native of Yorkshire, England, who arrived in 1758 and established a store for a Charleston mercantile firm. He prospered and by 1768 the town was the top inland trade center in the colony. The house served as British general Cornwallis's headquarters during the Battle of Camden.*

reimburse him, with the excuse that his actions were not authorized by the state.

The Kershaw-Cornwallis House is a reconstruction. The original was used by the Confederates as a storehouse during the Civil War and subsequently burned by Union forces when they occupied the town. Decorated with period furniture, the house displays a number of items known to have belonged to Joseph Kershaw.

An extensive exhibit on Camden's colonial and Revolutionary history is displayed in the Bradley and Drakeford log cabins, early 19th-century structures dismantled and transported here by truck. Artifacts in the Bradley House touch on the Native Americans who first settled the area and the early settlers who came after. The Drakeford House continues the exhibit through the Revolutionary War years. Items include a model of the Kershaw House as it's thought to have looked during the occupation, with bayonets, and a dummy nicknamed Charles who's dressed in the uniform of the British 54th Regiment Afoot.

There are also a blacksmith shed, where demonstrations are given periodically during the year, a reconstructed palisade wall much like the

one constructed by the British, a replicated 1777 powder magazine with 48-inch walls, and northeast and southeast redoubts. A nature trail completes the complex.

Visitor Information
803-432-9841
www.Historic-camden.net
www.camden-sc.org/Historic.asp
www.historic-camden.org
Hours: The museum complex is open Monday through Saturday, 10 a.m. until 5 p.m. and Sunday, 1 p.m. until 5 p.m.; closed major holidays.
Admission: The log cabins with exhibits, the museum complex grounds, and the nature trail are free. Self-guided tours of the entire complex are free. Guided tours of the entire complex have a moderate charge for adults, a minimal charge for ages 6 to 18, and are free for children under 6. A tour of the Kershaw-Cornwallis House has a minimal charge for adults and children over 6.
Accessibility: Only the Kershaw-Cornwallis House and the Dog Trot (where a slide presentation is given) are handicapped accessible.
Special Events: Scheduled periodically. Please check the Web sites.
Getting There: By car: From I-20 east or west, take exit 98 (east of Columbia) onto U.S. 521 north.

Cowpens National Battlefield

The surrender of Charleston, South Carolina, to the British in May 1780, followed by defeat at Camden in August of that year led many in Congress to believe that the South was lost to the Patriot cause.

Even the victory at Kings Mountain in October couldn't stop the rumors that if a peace were made, the South would remain under British control. "It is agreed on all hands," wrote a Rhode Island delegate, "the whole state of So. Carolina hath submitted to the British Government as well as Georgia. I shall not be surprised to hear N. Carolina hath followed their example."

But then came a clash on South Carolina's northern border that dispelled that gloomy outlook and gave new life to the cause in the South. Daniel Morgan's defeat of Banastre Tarleton at Cowpens in January 1781 has been called brilliant by military historians. Even those who can't appreciate the fine points of a classic double envelopment (the maneuver used by Morgan) can appreciate that what had been an army in disarray only the month before had pulled itself together to decisively defeat one of the British army's most accomplished commanders.

Shaping an Army

When Nathanael Greene formally took command of the Grand Army of the Southern Department of the United States of America, in December 1780, that "grand army" was in pretty sad shape. It had only moderate amounts of supplies and matériel, minimal artillery, and a total force of only about 2500 men, most of whom were existing on starvation rations. Understandably, morale was low and discipline almost nonexistent.

Before arriving in Charlotte, North Carolina, Greene had made the rounds in Congress and elsewhere trying to scare up everything needed to transform his men into a viable army again. He had been given mainly promises and some 100 wagons for transport, plus almost 200,000 dollars in Continental currency. Unfortunately, most vendors would not accept Continental money as payment.

Greene, a Rhode Island Quaker with a gift for inventiveness and a strong streak of stubbornness, didn't give in to pessimism. Instead he began at the beginning, his first concern being to whip his army back into shape. Soldiers had fallen into the habit of leaving without permission and returning when it suited them. Greene had a soldier returning from an unauthorized leave hanged. The message was clear.

Greene instructed Colonel Thaddeus Kosciuszko, the Polish patriot who seemed to turn up nearly everywhere at some point in this war, to find a new encampment for the army—or, rather, half an army. Greene was dividing his army in two. Traditionally, dividing an army in half was a recipe for disaster, and must have seemed particularly so in this case. This army barely deserved the name. By dividing it, Greene was dissipating what strength it had left. Or so it seemed to General Charles Cornwallis, who at first couldn't believe his luck.

But on second consideration, he realized the Patriot commander had made a savvy decision. As Greene himself explained it, "It makes the most of my inferior force for it compels my adversary to divide his, and holds him in doubt as to his own line of conduct."

Greene's choice to lead the other half of this army was Daniel Morgan. A man of little formal education, described as rowdy and given to drink, Morgan had made a success of farming and of fighting, and had been an integral part of the victory at Saratoga (*see* New York, Saratoga National Historical Park). Unhappy at not being recognized through promotion for his contributions, Morgan had returned to his Virginia farm. The events of 1780, however, had brought him back into the fight. He knew once the Carolinas were completely cowed, Cornwallis would turn his attention to Virginia.

Greene could not have found a better man to lead his army. Over six feet tall, Morgan was an imposing figure and rough in his manner. He was a plain man leading others much like himself. The men respected him and had faith in his leadership.

Morgan and his army camped along the Pacolet River. Greene and his men were at Cheraw Hill, the "camp of repose" Kosciuszko had found for them.

After contemplating his position, Cornwallis did Greene one better. He divided his army into thirds. One would hold at Camden, while another, commanded by Banastre

Tarleton, would move swiftly to crush Morgan. The third, led by Cornwallis, would move back up into North Carolina and perform mop-up duty for those who escaped Tarleton's expected defeat of Morgan.

Greene sent a message to Morgan, "Colonel Tarleton is said to be on his way to pay you a visit. I doubt not that he will have a decent reception and proper dismission."

A Despised Enemy

Proper dismission with a vengeance was every Patriot's hope for Banastre Tarleton. By this point in the war, Tarleton had gained a nickname—Bloody Tarleton—reflecting his reputation as a ruthless opponent and an even more ruthless victor. Born into a wealthy merchant family in Liverpool, Tarleton ran through a large inheritance from his father in less than a year. He'd already tried studies at Oxford and two years studying law when he turned to the military, buying a commission in the King's Cavalry.

In 1776 he volunteered for the war in America, and once here he quickly endeared himself to his superiors with his fearlessness and determination. His temperament was not for the subtle strategies and patient campaign. His technique was dash and slash, as it came to be known, and he used it to greatest effect.

His capture of General Charles Lee in New Jersey in 1776 brought promotion, and he was given command of the newly formed British Legions, a company of Loyalist cavalry and light infantry. The Legion took part in the surrender of

Charleston, after which Tarleton was given the job of mopping up Patriot resistance in the Carolina countryside. He mopped up with relish, burning and looting homes and farms, attacking citizens and soldiers alike. His dogged pursuit of Abraham Buford—during which Tarleton and his men rode their horses to death, and then stole replacements, in the summer heat of 1780—resulted in Buford's men being slaughtered after they'd surrendered. "Tarleton's quarter" became synonymous with no quarter at all, and he became one of the most hated and feared men in the South.

When Tarleton received word from Cornwallis that Morgan was marching on the Loyalist post at Ninety Six, he mustered his cavalry and set off, far ahead of the rest of his army. Cornwallis's intelligence turned out to be mistaken. Morgan wasn't heading for Ninety Six. He was, in fact, north of there, near the Broad River. Cornwallis agreed that Tarleton should push Morgan to the river, where a waiting Cornwallis would combine with Tarleton to destroy the Patriot army.

Heavy rains caused Cornwallis to

Banastre Tarleton's portrait was painted by Joshua Reynolds shortly after Tarleton returned to England in 1782. The artist chose this rather unconventional pose to hide the two missing fingers Tarleton lost at the Battle of Cowpens. His uniform is generally considered to be an accurate representation of the British Legion uniform—although the breeches should be doeskin or nankeen—but the background elements are pure fantasy.

wait out the weather Tarleton, however, began bearing down on Morgan with great speed.

Morgan's Dilemma

Morgan was not moving at as fast a pace as Tarleton. He had personnel issues. Greene had vetoed Morgan's plan to move into Georgia for better forage, and now Morgan was trying to keep his underfed army together. Making matters worse, his militia had brought their horses with them, as was the custom in the South, so Morgan had to feed not only the men but also their horses, which consumed 25 pounds of oats and hay a day. At any given time, large numbers of men would be out foraging, forcing Morgan to call the roll every two hours just to be sure how many fighting men were on hand.

When Morgan had circulated messages urging men to join with him in the fight, he had asked them to subject themselves "to order and discipline" and promised that "I will ask you to encounter no dangers or difficulties, but what I shall participate in." Now he was finding it hard even to keep them in camp.

Even after rendezvousing with William Washington, who was a distant cousin of George's and an able veteran, and his 80 cavalrymen, Morgan was reconsidering his command. On January 15 he wrote to Greene, "My force is inadequate. Upon a full and mature deliberation I am confirmed in the opinion that nothing can be effected by my detachment in this country, which will balance the risks I will be subjected to by remaining here."

While writing this letter, Morgan got more bad news, which he shared with Greene: "We have just learned that Tarleton's force is from eleven to twelve hundred British." Use of the word British signaled these were regulars—trained, well-fed, disciplined experienced troops.

Morgan consulted with the leaders of his militia, suggesting that they cross Broad River and make a stand on the other side. The leaders explained that if he crossed the river, Morgan would lose at least half his men. Rivers were considered borderlines in the backcountry. Their men would consider the other side of the river someone else's concern and head home.

An Ingenious Plan

On the morning of January 16, scouts arrived with the news that Tarleton was only six miles from camp. Morgan's army immediately moved out in the direction of Cowpens, which had been suggested by the militia leaders as a good meeting place. It turned out to be a good place to make a stand. That night Morgan outlined his plan to his officers; then, even though he was almost crippled with the pain of a sciatic hip, he moved through the camp, explaining it personally to the men.

As with most ingenious plans, it was relatively simple. Morgan's forces consisted of militia from Georgia and the Carolinas under the command of Andrew Pickens; Maryland and Delaware Continentals, among the best in the Continental Army, under the command of John Howard; and cavalry under the command of William Washington. Morgan knew his militia were crack shots with their rifles, but they had no bayonets and, after a few shots, would be defenseless against Tarleton's dragoons with their sabers. (Dragoons were mounted infantrymen who rode to battle, then dismounted and fought as infantry.) He also knew some of these men hadn't seen battle before and likely wouldn't be able to stand long against the terror of a bayonet charge. With the river to their back, retreat would be difficult. They'd have no choice but to stand and fight.

He instructed the militia to fire two or three shots and "pick off the epaulets" (officers), then retire behind the Continentals, re-form, and attack the British flanks. "Just hold up your heads, boys, give them three fires, and you will be free," is how it was recalled years later by a then 16-year-old cavalry volunteer. "Then when you return to your homes, how the old folks will bless you, and the girls will kiss you."

Behind the Continentals, Morgan planned to place his cavalry. He also placed a line of skirmishers in front of the militia, to pick off as many as they could before Tarleton charged.

The next morning, Morgan greeted his men with, "Boys, get up, Benny's coming!" Tarleton was coming—as usual, eager for the charge and the fight. He sent his dragoons in first, against the skirmishers Morgan had placed in front of his militia to draw Tarleton out. Within minutes, 15 of the 50 dragoons were dead and the skirmishers had fallen back into the line of militia.

Preceding the crucial moment *depicted in this painting, Lieutenant Colonel Howard had ordered his company to turn to face the British. The order was misunderstood, and the company began to march toward the rear, causing the entire American line to withdraw. The British saw the backs of the Americans and, sensing a victory, broke ranks to come on "like a mob." Morgan selected a spot, and when Howard's men reached it, he ordered them to face about and fire. The soldiers turned as if on parade and sent a volley crashing into the faces of the oncoming British.*

Tarleton now formed his line of battle: infantry in the middle, 50 dragoons on each flank (there was also a group of dragoons in the rear, in reserve), a battalion of Highlanders and 200 cavalry in reserve, plus 18 artillerymen and two light cannons. Tarleton issued the order to take no prisoners, and he moved forward so rapidly that his second in command hadn't even finished placing his officers.

The militia fired their two or three shots, killing or wounding two thirds of Tarleton's officers before moving back behind the Continentals. Tarleton took their movement as the first signs of a rout, positive he had them on the run. But if he had paid closer attention, he would have noted they didn't run. They moved in formation behind the other line, about 150 yards back.

Tarleton sent his dragoons on the right in pursuit, but these were driven back by Washington's charging cavalry. Now the British infantry charged the Continentals, and vicious fighting began. Tarleton, seeing his advance hesitate, called up the Highlanders. This posed a threat to Morgan's right flank. Howard ordered his Continentals to fall back

to regroup, but in the confusion of battle some thought a retreat had been ordered and they began to march to the rear, reloading as they moved. Seeing this, Morgan rode to Howard's position and, as Howard wrote in his report, "expressed apprehensions." Likely Morgan's expressions were somewhat heated, even as Howard was assuring him that the men weren't retreating.

Tarleton sent word to his cavalry, 400 yards away, to charge the Continentals, but they refused and fled the field. His infantrymen, without most of their officers, charged up the slight slope in front of the Patriot infantry in almost complete disorder, yelling for blood.

Morgan, meanwhile, had re-formed the Continentals, who now surprised the British infantry with a volley of gunfire. He ordered the militia to swing out and attack the British left flank, while the cavalry swung around to the rear and attacked the right. This double envelopment, a classic military maneuver, completely unhinged the British infantry, who turned and ran.

Tarleton's artillery continued to fire, while he tried to turn back his infantry, who would have none of it.

He sent word to the dragoons in the rear to come to the aid of the 71st Highlanders, who were now alone on the field. The dragoons didn't budge.

Charging across the battlefield to personally issue the order, Tarleton got his horse shot out from under him. The dragoons, as one Highlander put it, "fled through the woods with the utmost precipitation, bearing down such officers as opposed their flight."

Tarleton's Defeat
Now took place the last major confrontation of the battle. Forty horsemen had not fled. Tarleton rallied them and 14 officers in an attempt to save the artillery. Seeing this, Washington ordered a charge and was so eager to capture Tarleton, who had humiliated him in two previous battles, that he advanced well beyond his men and found himself in the middle of a fray with Tarleton and several of his officers.

One of the officers was about to run Washington through when Washington's young black servant rode up and fired at the officer, wounding him in the shoulder. Another officer slashed at Washington with his sword, but Washington was saved by a junior officer who arrived in time to parry the move with his sword. Tarleton fired at Washington but missed, then galloped after his retreating officers. The hour-long battle was over.

It was a devastating defeat for Tarleton, who lost 85 percent of his army. Some 100 were killed, including 10 officers, 200 wounded, and almost 600 taken prisoner. In writing his memoirs years later, Tarleton blamed the defeat on the "total misbehavior" of the troops.

Visiting the Battlefield
The Cowpens battlefield, just north of Spartanburg, South Carolina, was established as a commemorative park in 1929, on an acre of ground that marked what was thought to be the heaviest fighting of the battle. In 1978, in honor of the battle's bicentennial, the park was expanded to more than 800 acres. The Visitor Center offers informative resources on the battle. There's a wonderfully evocative 22-minute film about

the battle, called *Daybreak at the Cowpens*, which tells the story from the perspective of a grandfather relating his experiences to his grandson.

A 13-minute lighted-map program explains the battle in particular and the Southern Campaign in general. In the exhibit space, which is currently undergoing renovation, visitors can see authentic weapons from the period, such as a Brown Bess and a Charleville musket, a dragoon officer's pistol, and several

A reproduction of the sword awarded by the Continental Congress to Colonel Andrew Pickens for his "spirited conduct" at Cowpens. During Tarleton's attack his men held their ground, retired as ordered, then re-formed and struck the British left flank to break their resistance and complete the double envelopment.

The painting captures the moment when William Washington's young black servant rode up and fired at a British officer, wounding him in the shoulder. Another officer slashes at Washington with his sword, but Washington was later saved by a junior officer who arrived in time to parry the move with his sword.

sabers and spontoons (a spearlike edged weapon). A painting by military artist Charles McBarron, commissioned for the Center, depicts Morgan rallying his infantry following the misunderstood order.

The granite obelisk monument in the courtyard outside the center, dedicated in 1932, was originally placed in the center of where Morgan's Continentals formed.

There are two trails related to the battle. A one-quarter-mile walking trail, or interpretive trail, takes visitors through the heart of the battlefield (a map is available at the Visitor Center), with wayside exhibits at pertinent stops. An auto-tour road, a little under four miles long, travels the perimeter of the battlefield and also includes wayside exhibits and overlooks.

Visitor Information

864-461-2828
www.nps.gov/cowp
Hours: Open daily, 9 a.m. until 5 p.m.; closed Thanksgiving, December 25, and January 1. Tour road and picnic area close at 4:30 p.m.

Admission: Free. There is a minimal charge for the film, with proceeds coming back to the park in the form of a donation.

Accessibility: All the major sites in the park are wheelchair accessible. The audiovisual program is closed-captioned.

Special Events: The Battle of Cowpens Celebration is held annually on the weekend closest to the anniversary of the battle.

Getting There: From I-85: If northbound, take exit 78 and turn left toward Chesnee on U.S. 221. At the intersection of 221 with state route 11 in Chesnee, turn right. The park is about 3 miles on the right. From I-85 southbound: take exit 92 near Gaffney, and go west toward Chesnee on state highway 11. The park is about 10 miles on the left.

From I-26: If eastbound, take exit 5, east toward Chesnee on state highway 11. The park is about 20 miles on the right (3 miles past Chesnee).

From I-26 westbound: Take I-85 north, and proceed as above.

Kings Mountain National Military Park

British General Henry Clinton acknowledged the significance of the Battle of Kings Mountain when he wrote that it "unhappily proved the first link in a chain of evils that followed each other in regular succession until they at last ended in the total loss of America."

The decisive victory here of the Patriots over the Loyalists just one month after the terrible defeat at Camden gave new hope to the American cause in the South and forced the British to regroup and pull back.

Standing today amid the quiet solitude of Kings Mountain National Military Park, visitors may have a hard time imagining the primitive hatreds that set neighbor against neighbor in this 18th-century civil war. Yet walking the trail can't help but evoke admiration for both those who charged the plateau atop Kings Mountain and those who defended it.

Patriots Harass the British

Following Camden, the Continental Congress again took up the question of who should lead the Southern Campaign. After the disaster suffered by Gates's army at Camden, George Washington once again recommended Nathanael Greene, and this time he was given the command.

Greene himself may not have been thrilled with the opportunity. He realized that what army was left in the Carolinas was in shambles and that engaging the British in any formal battle was out of the question. The only practical tactic that autumn of 1780 would be hit and run or, as he called it, a "fugitive war."

In September 1780, Cornwallis held Charlotte, North Carolina, and Camden, South Carolina, but his supply lines between those two and other British posts were frequently attacked by Patriot raiding parties. Cornwallis wanted to rid the Caro-

---

Ferguson and the Breech-loader

Prior to the invention of the breech-loader, loading a rifle was a cumbersome operation that involved using a ramrod to push the powder cartridge down the barrel. This necessitated standing next to the rifle, which was a problem in the field when a soldier might find himself running or lying on his stomach. The breech-loading rifle allowed a soldier to load it through the breech, or rear end, of the barrel. Turning a screw let the breech drop down, leaving a space into which the powder cartridge could be dropped.

The breech-loader first appeared in Germany in the 16th century. In 1721 a French Huguenot gunmaker named Isaac de la Chaumette further refined the design and efficiency of the breech-loader. Chaumette's rifle was an improvement, but it fouled (got clogged) easily. According to historian John Buchanan in his book *The Road to Guilford Courthouse*, Patrick Ferguson's main contribution to breech-loading design was in modifying it in such a way as to prevent fouling and thereby ensure a smoother, faster operation. He also fitted it to accommodate a bayonet.

Ferguson demonstrated his rifle before King George in 1776. Even though there were heavy rains and wind, Ferguson was able to fire the rifle successfully while walking and prone, hitting targets 200 feet away. The king was so impressed, he ordered 100 rifles made.

The rifle was being tested at the Battle of Brandywine in 1777 when Ferguson was severely wounded. By the time he'd recovered from his wounds, the war had moved on and he had more pressing responsibilities. It's also known that further work on the design was necessary to correct some technical deficiencies that made it impractical for infantry battalions.

Considered by some to be a turning point in America's war for independence, the defeat of Loyalist troops at Kings Mountain destroyed the left wing of Lord Cornwallis's army and temporarily ended the British advance into North Carolina. Commanding British general Henry Clinton is reported to have called the defeat "the first link in a chain of evils" that led to the collapse of the British plans to quash the Patriot rebellion.

linas of Patriot militia, recruit large numbers of Loyalists into the regular army, and move on Virginia. Once Virginia was under British control, it was a simple matter of moving up into Pennsylvania, which he felt "would fall without much resistance and be retained without much difficulty."

With this in mind, Cornwallis sent Major Patrick Ferguson into the foothills between North and South Carolina to protect Cornwallis's left flank, to pick off any Patriot raiding parties, and to recruit and train Loyalists. The Scotsman Ferguson was a daring commander, admired by his men for his determination and his cleverness. (*See page 212.*) Ferguson, though, could be foolhardy, as he proved in the cat-and-mouse game he now played with a group of commanders he had been pursuing for months.

These men had been forced to retreat before Ferguson's relentless advance across the Appalachian Mountains, and they now hungered for an opportune moment to return and fight again. Ferguson provided it when he sent word to the "overmountain" men that "if they did not desist from their opposition to British arms, he would march his army over the mountains, hang their leaders, and lay their country waste with fire and sword." In other words, swear allegiance to the Crown or die.

The enraged Americans, many of Scots-Irish descent and most from the Carolinas, came together at Sycamore Shoals in what is now Tennessee to begin their march south. More local militia joined them along the route, swelling their numbers.

The Battle of Kings Mountain

Ferguson, realizing he was now outnumbered, turned in the direction of Charlotte, North Carolina, to join Cornwallis. But on October 6, when he reached Kings Mountain, a mile and a half south of the North Carolina border, he thought better of it and decided this was an excellent position from which to take a stand.

It seemed a wise choice. Kings Mountain rises 150 feet above the surrounding forested slopes. Its flat summit was almost barren of trees, with the plateau measuring 600 yards long by 60 yards wide at the southeast end and twice that at the northeast end. From this lofty position, Ferguson and his army of 1000 Loyalists waited.

The approaching Patriots had two primary advantages. One, they would have cover among the trees, whereas Ferguson's troops were in the open. Two, they weren't regular army, which meant that instead of having to use army-issued muskets with a range of 80 yards, they could use their own weapons—long rifles with a range of 200 yards. Kings Mountain was the only battle in the war in which Patriot forces used long rifles as their main weapon.

The Patriot commanders sent 900 of their best marksmen ahead, not knowing Ferguson had settled atop Kings Mountain and fearful he might get away. Reaching the mountain in the rain on October 7, they were able to take the Loyalists by surprise, the rain having muffled the sounds of their approach. Surrounding Ferguson's position, they began the attack, effectively using the forests on the slopes as cover.

While Ferguson had spent months training his Loyalist troops, and his

Loyalist troops fought fiercely, in an hour the plateau was overrun.

Ferguson had been killed. He had mounted his horse, blowing commands with a whistle and trying to rally his men. Some accounts have him taking to horseback because he was trying to escape; others, that he was making himself visible to his command.

The next morning, according to James Collins, a Patriot recruit, "the scene became really distressing; the wives and children of the poor Tories came in, in great numbers. Their husbands, fathers and brothers lay dead in heaps, while others lay wounded or dying." Mass burials were dug quickly, because of the concern that British troops from Charlotte were on their way.

Some 700 Loyalists were taken prisoner, of which nine were hanged in retaliation for the deaths of Patriots hanged by the British. The official charge was that they were guilty of hostilities against their neighbors. The citizen soldiers, not being regular army, weren't sure what to do with so many prisoners. Over the course of the next two months, nearly all of the 700 captured escaped from their loosely guarded prison compounds.

The defeat at Kings Mountain left Cornwallis's left flank unprotected, forcing him to retreat to South Carolina. By the time he resumed his offensive in January 1781, he was facing a new general—Nathanael Greene. Greene may not have had Cornwallis's years of experience as a professional and very successful military commander, but he had a gift for strategy. He knew how to defeat Cornwallis.

Visiting the Military Park

Beginning in January 2005, the Visitor Center will be undergoing renovations in preparation for the 225th commemoration of the battle that October. During the renovations, visitors can still view the 27-minute film *Battle for Kings Mountain,* which tells the story of the battle and places it in the context of the Southern Campaign.

A brochure available at the center details events leading up to the battle. It also provides excellent information about Ferguson's rifle design and a comparison of the musket and the long rifle.

The brochure includes a map of the one-and-a-half-mile Battlefield Trail (a walking trail). New wayside markers along the trail, which begins only a few hundred yards from the visitor center, point out the Patriot and Loyalist positions and present highlights of the battle.

The only grave along the trail is that of Patrick Ferguson, though what began as a grave has become the traditional Scottish cairn (a large pile of stones). Whereas in Scotland a cairn is formed by tossing a stone on the grave to honor the individual, at Kings Mountain the tradition began as a way of ensuring Ferguson's "evil" spirit would remain in the grave. Ironically, there's a nearby granite memorial honoring Ferguson.

Three monuments have been erected here. The 28-foot Centennial Monument was unveiled in 1880. In 1889 the local chapter of the Daughters of the American Revolution launched a campaign to restore what had become a neglected battlefield, culminating in the dedication of the 83-foot U.S. Monument in 1909. Finally, in 1930, President Herbert Hoover attended a celebration of the 150th anniversary of the battle, which was commemorated by the Hoover Monument.

Visitor Information

864-936-7921

www.nps.gov/kimo

Hours: The park is open daily from 9 a.m. until 5 p.m., and from Memorial Day to Labor Day it stays open on weekends until 6 p.m.; closed Thanksgiving Day, December 25, and January 1.

Admission: Free.

Accessibility: All buildings are handicapped accessible. The 1.5-mile Battlefield Trail is paved, but there are steep areas where assistance is required.

Special Events: There are evening programs in the summer, including ranger talks and family activities. Each year there are military encampments and demonstrations one weekend each in May, August, September, and October. On October 7 there's a ceremony commemorating the battle.

Getting There: The park is located near Blacksburg, on South Carolina highway 216.

From Greenville, South Carolina, or Charlotte, North Carolina, take I-85 to North Carolina exit 2.

Ninety Six National Historic Site

Nowhere was the determination and bravery of those loyal to the crown more ably demonstrated than in the month-long siege of the Loyalist stronghold Ninety Six in May and June of 1781.

What's thought to be the first land battle south of New England had been fought here between Loyalists and Patriots in November 1775, and in the intervening years, sentiment on both sides became even more fixed.

By the time Nathanael Greene's troops began the siege of Ninety Six's Loyalist fortifications, a bloody Southern Campaign, with major battles lost by both sides, was winding down. In three months, Cornwallis would surrender Yorktown and Britain would be making sounds for peace. But in the late spring of 1781, both sides were still jockeying for territory and power.

Loyalists Take Control

The town of Ninety Six derives its name from the estimated distance between the settlement here in the early 1700s and the nearest trading opportunity, a Cherokee settlement called Keowee.

Ninety Six's first European residents were hunters in the 1730s, followed by cattle drovers and traders a few years later. In 1746 petition was made to the government in Charleston for tax concessions for those who would settle this area. With concessions granted, the next two decades saw a wave of Scots-Irish from Pennsylvania and others from the coastal areas making their way here.

The first permanent European settler, Robert Gouedy, opened a trading post at Ninety Six in 1746, establishing trade with the Indians and a few years later providing goods to the families beginning to settle nearby. By the early 1750s, the encroachment of whites on Native American land caused fighting to break out.

Though peace was eventually achieved, it was not long lived and there was more fighting during the French and Indian War. The British were able to arrange peace with the Cherokees after the war, attracting more families to the area. By the early 1770s, Ninety Six was a major commercial center and the judicial seat for a large section of South Carolina's backcountry.

The history of Ninety Six at this point is similar to that of many communities throughout the colonies where the choice between being a Loyalist and being a Patriot was not cut and dried. Many of the Scots-Irish here were nursing hard feelings toward the British from dealings in their home countries, while many of the more established families saw advantages with remaining part of Great Britain, especially in dealing with the Indians. As elsewhere, the mixture of resentments and expectations was potent.

An attempt at peaceful coexistence was made in September 1775 when a formal peace between the backcountry's Loyalist and Patriot factions was negotiated. Loyalists were guaranteed their "lives, persons and property" and in return promised never to "aid, assist or join" British troops sent to the area. But a few months later, a Loyalist leader was jailed for using "seditious words," and the Patriots tried to preempt any British alliances with the Cherokees by providing 1000 pounds of gunpowder for the Indians' winter hunt.

Loyalists seized the gunpowder and, frightened by rumors of a Patriot-instigated Cherokee attack, prepared to fight. Learning that Patriot forces at Ninety Six had built a ramshackle fort "of old fence rails joined to a barn [and] straw with some beeves' hides," Loyalists immediately laid siege to it.

The siege lasted three days, by which time the Patriots had run out of water and the Loyalists had twice tried unsuccessfully to burn down the fort. A truce was called, the Loyalists retreated, and the Patriots dismantled the fort themselves. Casualties were light on both sides, but James Birmingham became the first South Carolinian to give his life for the Patriot cause. His family was awarded an annual annuity of 100 pounds by the South Carolina General Assembly. (There is a memorial to Birmingham across from the Stockade Fort.)

Although both sides had backed off, feelings ran high. Patriots began sweeping the countryside, rounding up Loyalists to take to Charleston as prisoners. The treaty was forgotten, and there were skirmishes and deaths on both sides.

Although many Loyalists left the area for friendlier parts, many joined the British. By 1780, Ninety Six was a Loyalist stronghold, a source of support and control for the British in South Carolina, and a base for operations into North Carolina and Virginia.

In the summer of 1780, Lord Charles Cornwallis sent Lieutenant Colonel John Harris Cruger, a New York Loyalist, to take command of the post, instructing him that "keeping possession of the backcountry is of utmost importance, indeed the Success of the War in the Southern District depends totally upon it."

Patriots Lay Siege

Cruger set about reinforcing Ninety Six's fortifications, building redoubts, enclosing the town of Ninety Six in a stockade, and having an eight-foot ditch dug around the fort. He also requested the assistance of an engineer to advise him on how best to bolster the defenses. When the engineer, Lieutenant Henry Haldane, arrived in December of 1780, he suggested Cruger build an eight-pointed star fort to the northeast of the town. Though called a fort, this was actually an earthen bunker system, with 14-foot walls protected by a surrounding abatis—a barrier of trees, set at an angle, whose limbs have been sharpened to points. Most of this construction was done by slaves, captured or hired from nearby farms.

Cruger also stockpiled supplies of beef, pork, grain, corn, and other preservables. Unfortunately for his purposes, he couldn't stockpile water. The only water supply was a small stream west of the town. Cruger did have a wooden stockade erected just beyond the stream, which was linked to the stockade fort by a covered walkway. With this final component in place, the British felt prepared to defend this important post. Strictly speaking, however, the British weren't doing the defending. Ninety Six was a Loyalist post, with close to 500 men from New York and New Jersey, plus South Carolina Loyalists under General Robert Cunningham, the man who had been jailed in 1775 for using seditious words.

Opposing them was General Nathanael Greene, with troops from Maryland, Delaware, Virginia, and North Carolina. Greene, commander of the southern forces, had lost a major battle at Guilford Courthouse just two months earlier, but the battle had cost Cornwallis in men and supplies, and Greene was determined to exploit those weaknesses.

Serving with Greene was the Polish general Thaddeus Kosciuszko,

who had proven himself invaluable as an engineer and strategist in the Northern Campaign and now applied himself to dislodging the Loyalists from their fortifications at Ninety Six. Greene and Kosciuszko agreed that if they could take the Star Fort, where the majority of Loyalists were garrisoned, the other two fortifications—the Stockade Fort and the fortified town—would give up.

Not bothering with the usual opening salvo of demanding surrender, Greene instead set a group of sappers (soldiers attached to an engineering detail) to work on a trench not 70 yards from the Star Fort. These were met with a heavy barrage, followed by an attack in which most were killed. Greene pulled back to 400 yards from the fort and began another trench.

The longest siege of the Revolutionary War had begun, with Patriot forces digging around the clock and Loyalists firing on them. To protect construction of the trenches, Greene had a log tower with a cannon on top, built about 30 yards from the Star Fort, from which his men could fire on the Loyalists.

By June 3, a second, parallel trench had been completed, and Greene, confident he was in a position to successfully take the fort called for surrender.

Cruger had lost only eight men and had provisions and arms for a long siege. There was little to encourage him to surrender.

Five days later, Colonel Henry Lee arrived from his victory in Augusta, Georgia, with British prisoners in tow.

Lee set about building trench approaches to the Stockade Fort west of the Star Fort and the town and by June 12 was in range to fire upon the fort from protected positions. Worse for the Loyalists, he was also close enough to prevent them from fetching water without being fired upon.

Water was in short supply at the Star Fort, also. While Loyalists began digging a well in desperation, Greene allowed civilian women within the fort to fetch water from the stream. When it was discovered some of the men were dressing as women to fetch the water, Greene suspended the courtesy.

While the Loyalists futilely dug a well, Kosciuszko was digging a mine the only one known to have been attempted during the war. From the third approach trench, sappers dug a six-foot vertical shaft, tunneling toward the Star Fort. The plan was to blast a hole in the wall of the fort, through which soldiers could attack. First though, Greene needed the powder to effect the explosion, and sufficient quantities wouldn't arrive in time.

The end of the siege came in the middle of June. Greene had received word that Lord Rawdon was marching from Charleston to relieve the Loyalists. Greene decided that since trench warfare hadn't worked, a frontal assault was his only option. At noon on the 18th of June, Lee's troops attacked the Stockade Fort, while Greene's charged the Star Fort. The charge was repulsed by the Loyalists.

The Patriots Withdraw
Following the failed assault, Greene made the decision to withdraw. The Patriots had lost 127 men, killed or wounded, and 20 missing in action. The Loyalists had lost 85, killed or wounded.

On June 19 the Patriots retreated eastward. Greene wrote that he regretted "we were not more successful in this enterprise as the post is of great importance to the enemy and our troops have been exposed to excessive labor and annoyance in the attempt."

In retrospect, Ninety Six was a success. The siege had proved the vulnerability of British posts this far into the interior, and by July the British themselves had retreated to the coast, taking with them Loyalist families seeking refuge from the revenge of their former neighbors.

Visiting Ninety Six
The museum at the Visitor Center displays artifacts discovered during archaeological digs in the park—among these, musket balls and a cannonball from the siege, as well as prehistoric Indian tools and an English salt-glazed stoneware tankard. There's also a 3-pounder cannon similar to those used during the siege. A 10-minute video explains the history of Ninety Six and relates the details of the conflict.

A self-guided mile-long walk of the area (brochure and trail map provided; audio tour for rent) takes visitors to the principal sites of the siege, and also relates aspects of the prewar history of Ninety Six as an important frontier settlement.

Outlines of the Patriot trenches

and of the Star Fort were restored by archaeologists in the early 1970s, and the Stockade Fort has been reconstructed. Coupled with illustrated wayside exhibits, these provide an excellent understanding of the proximity of the two forces and of the difficulties Greene faced in trying to dislodge the Loyalists.

A mile-long loop trail takes visitors to the site of Robert Gouedy's first trading post, to a grave site marked with original fieldstones on the graves, and along a portion of Charleston Road, a sunken road used by Native Americans and traders during the colonial era.

Visitor Information
864-543-4068
www.nps.gov/nisi
Hours: The site is open from 8 a.m. until 5 p.m. daily; closed on Thanksgiving Day, December 25, and January 1.
Admission: Free.
Accessibility: The Visitor Center and museum are accessible. The walking tour of the park is accessible but is steep in places. Those in wheelchairs should use caution.
Special Events: Revolutionary War Days are held the first week in April in odd-numbered years. Costumed interpreters demonstrate the use of period firearms and cannons at the site. In even-numbered years, Lifeways of the Cherokee Indians and Colonial Settlers are held the first week in April, with demonstrations related to life in 18th-century Ninety Six. During the summer months, Living-History Saturdays, one each month, present demonstrations of skills used on the frontier, such as candlemaking and baking in a beehive oven. During the annual autumn candlelight tour every October, costumed storytellers lead visitors along a one-mile historic trail.
Getting There: The town of Ninety Six is located just east of Greenwood, South Carolina, between Augusta, Georgia, and Greenville, South Carolina.

From I-26, take the Newberry exit to state route 34.

From I-20, take U.S. 221 or U.S. 25 north.

From I-85, take U.S. 178 south to state highway 248.

The historic site is 2 miles south of the town of Ninety Six on SC route 248.

Sycamore Shoals State Historic Area

This area in northeastern Tennessee is perhaps best known as the site where the Overmountain Men gathered in September 1780 to march against Major Patrick Ferguson and his Loyalists, subsequently defeating them at Kings Mountain in South Carolina (*see* South Carolina, Kings Mountain National Military Park). Their victory was an important factor in the Southern Campaign that eventually drove General Charles Cornwallis north to Virginia and defeat at Yorktown in 1781.

Equally important, however, were two nonviolent events that took place on this site that were indicative of the country's future rather than its past.

One was the formation of the first majority-rule system of democratic government west of the Appalachian Mountains—the Watauga Association—in 1772. The predominantly Scots-Irish settlers in what was then North Carolina were rugged pioneers given to self-reliance and an independent frame of mind. Nonetheless, they recognized the need for a government, one chosen by and answerable to the governed. Meeting here, they elected five from among themselves to "govern and direct for the common good of all the people."

The other event occurred in 1775, when the Transylvania Company bought 20 million acres of land in present-day Tennessee from the Cherokee Indians. More than 1200 Cherokees met here for several weeks, debating whether to accept the offer. In the end they agreed, in exchange for 2000 pounds sterling and another 8000 pounds worth of comparable goods. Although less than a year later the Cherokee had joined with the British in trying to drive out the pioneers, the purchase established the legitimacy of settlers in the region.

Visiting the Historic Area

A 25-minute film in the park's Visitor Center gives an overview of each of these events, as well as the story of the Overmountain Men. A handsome bronze statue of an Overmountain Man in action stands in front of the center.

The center's south wall is dominated by a large picture window looking toward the wooden Fort Watauga and down to the Watauga River, so that as visitors are walking through the center's museum learning about the Overmountain Men, they can look out at the area where the militia gathered.

The museum also focuses on the lives of the pioneers who established a community here, with exhibits on weaving, spinning, and building.

A pathway from the center leads down to a replica of Fort Watauga, where visitors learn about militia life on the frontier and where there are regularly scheduled demonstrations of frontier cooking and military drilling.

A large amphitheater behind the wooden fort is used for concerts and for the outdoor drama *The Wataugans* every July. On the other side of the amphitheater, visitors can enjoy the quiet pleasures of a nature trail that follows the Watauga River.

Visitor Information

423-543-5808
www.state.tn.us/environment/
   parks/parks/SycamoreShoals/
Hours: The park is open daily from dawn until dusk. The Visitor Center is open Monday through Saturday 8 a.m. until 4:30 p.m.; Sundays 1 p.m. until 4:30 p.m.
Admission: Free.
Accessibility: The site is accessible.
Special Events: The Muster at Fort Watauga, an annual weekend event held every spring, features living-history demonstrations and reenactments of a Revolutionary War battle. The Native American Festival in early June celebrates native culture, with crafts, storytelling, dancing, and demonstrations. The Wataugans, an outdoor drama about the history of the area, is presented on the last three weekends of July. At the Fort Watauga Knap-In held every autumn, visitors learn about the skills of prehistoric Native Americans. The Overmountain Victory Trail Celebration, in late September features a reenactment of the muster. Crafts workshops are held throughout the year.
Getting There: From I-81, exit onto I-181 to Johnson City. Take exit 31 from I-181, and follow state routes 321 and 67 toward Elizabethton for approximately 6 miles.

African Americans in the War

Crispus Attucks was among the five Patriots killed at the Boston Massacre in 1770—the first African American to die in the cause of American liberty. Thousands of African Americans would fight for this cause in the coming war, but many of them would be fighting for their own liberty as members of the British army.

The irony of a country championing the cause of freedom while hundreds of thousands of those living within its borders were enslaved was not lost on America's leaders nor on Britain's. Slavery was a contentious issue in adopting the Declaration of Independence. It remained a bone of contention throughout the war, and would be a major issue in framing the country's constitution. Its existence fed anti-American sentiment in Great Britain, and was a shameful embarrassment to America's diplomats trying to gain European allies for independence.

There were an estimated 500,000 African slaves in the United States in the mid-1700s, all but about 50,000 of them in the southern states. Slaves made up the majority of the populations of Georgia, North Carolina, and South Carolina, half the population in Virginia, and about a third of the population in Maryland.

Southern Patriots opposed the inclusion of any blacks, free or slave, in the Continental Army, for the obvious reason that once armed and empowered, these same people of color might foment rebellion among those still in slavery.

It wasn't until the third year of the war, when the Continental Army was desperate for recruits, that free blacks were encouraged to enlist and those enslaved were offered their freedom in exchange for service.

The British had already made this offer of freedom to American slaves. By the end of the war, some 10,000 African Americans had served in the British army, compared to an estimated 5000 in the Continental Army.

The African Americans who did join the Continental Army fought in many of the major battles of the war, including the Battle of Monmouth in New Jersey, where 700 African Americans were listed among the Patriot combatants.

The most famous group of African Americans who fought on the American side were those of the 1st Rhode Island Regiment, which consisted mostly of blacks, with a few whites and Narragansett Indians, under a white commander, Colonel Christopher Greene.

For the slaves who enlisted in the 1st Rhode Island, their owners were compensated by the state at the going market value. In effect, the state bought them. The 1st Rhode Island fought in several battles, including Yorktown.

In addition to Crispus Attucks, individual African Americans known to have made important contributions to the Patriot cause include James Armistead, who spied for General Lafayette in the months preceding Yorktown; Peter Salem (also known as Salem Middleux), who is credited with fatally shooting British major John Pitcairn at the Battle of Bunker Hill; the renowned preacher Lemuel Haynes, who served with the Massachusetts militia that took Fort Ticonderoga, and the naval innovator and merchant, James Forten, who served on an American privateer during the war.

Following the war, some of the African Americans who fought on the American side were granted their freedom, as promised, but many weren't.

The British government made a more determined effort to keep its promises. As many as 11,000 black men, women, and children were transported on British ships to the West Indies between the surrender of Yorktown in October 1781 and December 1782.

Hessians also numbered African Americans among their troops. In 1783, some 30 of these soldiers with their wives and children arrived in the region of Hessen-Cassel with the troops returning home.

Though she didn't serve in the Continental Army, the poet Phillis Wheatley provided an invaluable service to her country by helping to dispel the notion that slavery could be justified on the basis of the "natural" inferiority of people of color.

Brought to America in 1761 and named Phillis after the ship on which she was transported, Wheatley became the first African American to publish a book in the colonies, and for a while was a celebrity, feted in America and London. During the war she met with George Washington and continued to write—five books in all—but would die destitute at the age of 31 in 1782.

Bennington Museum

The Bennington Museum prides itself on preserving unique items reflective of their times, ensuring to future generations a comprehensive presentation of this region's culture and history. Visitors looking for Revolutionary War artifacts will find the customary and the unusual—such items as a Brown Bess musket and a theodolite.

Though known to the art world as the repository of the largest collection of Grandma Moses paintings in the country, this eclectic museum—the oldest and largest in the region—holds a strong appeal for those interested in Revolutionary War–era history and culture. Artifacts from the Battle of Bennington and from Vermont's colonial and war eras provide a clearer idea of the large contribution this small state made to the Patriot cause.

Visiting the Museum

The majority of Revolutionary War–related items are in the Military Gallery on the first floor. For a basic understanding of Bennington at the time of the 1777 battle, however, visitors are encouraged to begin in the Church Gallery on the second floor.

Located in what was once a church, this space re-creates the museum as it was in 1928, when it opened at its present location. An informative exhibit on the development of the area begins with its earliest days as a hunting ground for the French. The exhibit continues with Vermont's struggle for independence from neighboring states, which led to its becoming a republic in 1777. In 1791, Vermont joined the U.S. as the 14th state.

The Military Gallery on the first floor was reinstalled in 2004. Covering the participation of Vermonters in military actions from the French and Indian War to World War II, the gallery has an impressive collection of items relating to the Revolutionary War. Among the more rare items is one of the cannons used by the Germans in the battle. Very few of this particular type of fieldpiece,

made by the Verbruggen brothers at the foundry in Woolwich, England, survive from that time.

There's also a British officer's gorget. A gorget was a gilt or silver crescent that hung from the neck by a ribbon. A sign of rank among the British, it was engraved with the king's arms and the number of the regiment. Some Patriot officers wore these at the beginning of the war, with an engraved "Don't Tread on Me" replacing the king's arms, but the practice gradually grew out of favor.

Among the firearms is Colonel Moses Nichols's fowling gun, used in peacetime for hunting. Nichols led his men around the Germans' left flank and is thought to have fired the first shot of the battle, signaling that his men were in position. Also displayed are a Brown Bess and a Charleville musket.

A rare piece is a theodolite that was owned by Francis Pfister. Pfister, a Loyalist who lived in the neighboring town of Hoosick Falls, New York, had served in the French and Indian War as an engineer. He probably designed some of the entrenchments used by the Germans in the battle, where he served as a translator for the German commander, Lieutenant Colonel Friedrich Baum.

A theodolite, such as the one displayed here, is a 16th-century surveying instrument used to measure horizontal and vertical angles—a kind of combination compass and sextant. Engineers such as Pfister carried their own instruments with them, priding themselves on how well they maintained them. Displayed here also are some of the instruments Pfister used to draw maps.

Another rarity seen here is a map of the battle fashioned by a Lieutenant Durnford of Burgoyne's engineers. Durnford was not at Bennington, but he drew the map based on the accounts of the few British who escaped. Burgoyne later used this map to defend himself against charges of incompetence. A

number of them were printed and hand colored, such as the one displayed here.

There are a number of swords from the battle, including one with a Ferrara blade and a handle that's been dyed to look like jade, and a German artillery officer's sword. There is also a Scottish basketweave-handled sword. The story is that the man who used it borrowed it from his neighbor who had used it at the Battle of Culloden, where the Scots under Bonnie Prince Charlie were massacred by the British. Swords such as this one were also used by the Scots at Moores Creek (*see* North Carolina, Moores Creek National Battlefield) and one is on display there; but seeing it side by side with other swords, visitors can truly understand what an impressive weapon this is, and how impressive was the man who could wield it. Consider the British cavalry sabers, also deemed heavy swords, whose weight was an advantage in driving them down from the height of the man on horseback. These were thought to be unsuitable for the infantry because of their weight, and yet compared to the heavier and larger Scottish broadsword they look almost puny.

Two different types of canteens carried by the militia are included here. One is a hardwood "water bottle" type with superficial lathe cuts on the outside. The canteen was soaked in water to expand the wood, and the ends were tapped into place; shrinkage when it dried ensured a snug fit. This canteen was attached to a leather shoulder strap and worn on the left side. The other canteen is made of wooden staves held together by wrought-iron straps and was carried by its iron handle. The pouring spout and air vent are made of pewter.

A focal point of the gallery is the 13-foot-long by 10-foot-tall mural

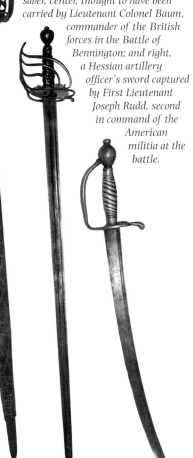

*A **Scottish** basketweave-handled sword, left; a German horseman's saber, center, thought to have been carried by Lieutenant Colonel Baum, commander of the British forces in the Battle of Bennington; and right, a Hessian artillery officer's sword captured by First Lieutenant Joseph Rudd, second in command of the American militia at the battle.*

After the Battle of Bennington, created by WPA artist Leroy Williams in the 1930s. The WPA (Works Progress Administration) hired artists all over the country to paint murals in public buildings during the Depression, and many of these massive works still exist. The artist did a lot of research for this one on the uniforms and on the heroes of the battle, all of whom are included, including the Native Americans who fought at Bennington.

For families in the Bennington area, the Battle of Bennington is a touchstone for connecting with the history of the community. Just about every family whose personal biography dates back to the 1700s has a story about an ancestor who fought in the battle. Bennington Museum

*A **cannon** made by Jan and Peter Verbruggen—one of four captured by General John Stark's troops at the Battle of Bennington. The Verbruggens were employed as master founders of the Royal Brass Foundry at Woolwich, England, from 1770 until 1786.*

The Bennington Battle Monument

The 306-foot-tall Bennington Battle Monument commemorates the courage of the militiamen who took on Burgoyne's troops two miles away in what is now the state of New York. Emotions over the disputed territory that became the state of Vermont were still running so high that a delegation from New York wasn't invited to participate in the dedication of the monument in 1891.

Located on the site where the supplies Burgoyne desperately needed were being stored, the blue-gray limestone monument has an observation area from which visitors can see the surrounding hills and valleys of Vermont, New York, and Massachusetts.

Inside the monument's entrance are a diorama depicting the second engagement of the battle and an immense iron kettle from Burgoyne's camp at Saratoga. On the monument grounds are a number of memorials, including statues of Patriots Seth Warner and John Stark and one in the form of a large granite boulder. On the boulder is a bronze tablet honoring the 1400 New Hampshire men who fought in the battle.

---

has often been the recipient of battle relics that afterward are found to be from a later period, but that represent a family's pride in being part of the fight for independence.

One such piece is the Bennington Flag, which came to the museum from the Fillmore family and which for years was thought to be the oldest Stars and Stripes in existence and possibly the first to fly in battle. Now displayed in the Flag Gallery on the second floor, the flag remains a historic relic, but of a later period. In 1995, as part of a restoration process, a fiber analysis revealed that the fibers used in the flag were machine-spun cotton, not available until after 1800. Curators now think the flag went with the Bennington men to the defense of Plattsburg in the War of 1812. It was probably made as a commemorative piece, which accounts for its use of '76 and the thirteen stars and stripes. Among its unique qualities is the fact that the stripes start and end with white rather than red bars.

For those interested in tracing their New England ancestors, the Genealogy and History Research Library has local, county, and state genealogical materials, census indexes, and Revolutionary War archives, plus thousands of formal and informal genealogies.

Outside, behind the museum is the Bennington Centre Cemetery, where a monument has been raised to honor all who fought in the battle—German, British, and Patriot. The British and German troops who died were buried here in mass graves, without names. The names of many of the Loyalists who died were known and are engraved on the stones.

Visitor Information
802-447-1571
www.benningtonmuseum.org
(for the museum)
www.dhca.state.vt.us/HistoricSites html/bennington.html
(for the monument)

Hours: The museum is open daily November through May 31, 9 a.m. until 5 p.m.; June 1 through October 31, 9 a.m. until 6 p.m.; closed Thanksgiving, December 25, and January 1. The Genealogy and History Research Library is open 11 a.m. until 5 p.m., 6 days a week in the summer and fall, 3 days a week in the winter and spring. Contact the museum for further information. The Bennington Battle Monument is open mid-April through October 31 daily, 9 a.m. until 5 p.m.

Admission: There's a significant fee for adults to visit the Bennington Museum; children under 12 enter free. There's a minimal fee for the Bennington Battle Monument.

Accessibility: Both the museum and the monument are handicapped accessible.

Special Events: The museum has workshops, lectures, craft demonstrations, and special events throughout the year. Information is available on the Web site.

Getting There: To the museum: From the intersection of Vermont route 9 and U.S. 7 in the center of Bennington, take route 9 (West Main Street), one mile west.

To the monument: From the intersection of Vermont route 9 and U.S. 7 in the center of Bennington, take route 9 (West Main Street) up the hill past the Bennington Museum. At the Old First Church, take a sharp right onto Monument Avenue; the Monument is straight ahead.

Hubbardton Battlefield State Historic Site

The Battle of Hubbardton in 1777 was one of the most famous rear-guard actions of the war, and the only battle fought entirely on Vermont soil. Hubbardton remains one of the best-preserved Revolutionary War battlefields in the country.

The Battle of Hubbardton

Following Major General Arthur St. Clair's abandonment of Mount Independence and Fort Ticonderoga, British brigadier general Simon Fraser paused only long enough to assign a small garrison to Independence before heading into the surrounding wooded hills in pursuit of the Patriot army.

The British, German, and American forces all passed a hellish July 6, struggling along a road that was more of a wagon track, interspersed with fallen trees, ponds, and swamps in sweltering heat. Late in the day, St. Clair's forces reached Hubbardton, a tiny hamlet consisting of two houses. Pushing the bulk of his army toward Castleton, St. Clair left Colonel Seth Warner, a Green Mountain Boy from Vermont, to reinforce the rear guard before catching up with the main body. When the rear guard arrived, its commanders, Colonel Ebenezer Francis of Massachusetts and Colonel Nathan Hale of New Hampshire, agreed with Warner that their best position would be an encampment near what is now called Monument Hill.

On the morning of July 7, as the British came into range, the Americans attacked, and then fell back to the top of Monument Hill. Repeatedly the British charged the hill and repeatedly were driven back by merciless gunfire.

When Fraser moved his forces to the American left, Francis's Massachusetts regiment attacked Fraser's now weakened left. The outnumbered British were about to effect a last-ditch bayonet charge when the sounds of fifes, trumpets, and drums signaled the arrival of Baron von Riedesel. These Brunswickers came to Fraser's rescue singing a Lutheran hymn. From Castleton, St. Clair could hear the firing and sent word to two detachments that hadn't yet reached Castleton to turn back and come to the aid of Warner's men. They refused.

Francis was killed in a volley of fire from von Riedesel's Brunswickers, who were charging his troops while a German band played. When an emboldened Fraser ordered a bayonet charge, the Patriot forces retreated.

There were more than 500 casualties—about a fourth of all the men who fought here—and more than 300 Americans were captured.

Though the British held the field, this could still be considered a success for the Americans. They had delayed the British long enough to ensure the escape of the main army, and they had forced a depleted British army to return to Fort Ticonderoga rather than continue in pursuit of St. Clair.

Visiting the Battlefield

Just south of the entrance is the Hubbardton Battle Monument, erected in 1859. Made of Vermont marble, the monument is thought to mark the spot where Colonel Francis was buried by the British. The story is told that von Riedesel was so impressed by the leadership and gallantry shown by Francis that the baron ordered his body to be buried with full military honors.

A brochure available at the Visitor Center and a diorama show the positions of the two sides during the battle. A narrated presentation using a three-dimensional fiber-optic map details various phases of the battle, while a small museum contains exhibits that put Hubbardton in the context of the northern campaign.

Interpretive signage along the battlefield trail provides further explanation.

Visitor Information

802-273-2282 or 802-759-2412
www.historicvermont.org/
hubbardton
Hours: Open Wednesday through Sunday from 9:30 a.m. until 5 p.m., from late May through mid-October.
Admission: Minimal charge for adults, children under 14 free.
Accessibility: The Visitor Center is accessible. Some parts of the battlefield may require assistance.
Special Events: Living-history programs, encampments, and lectures throughout the season, as well as hikes, battlefield tours, and nature programs.
Getting There: The battlefield is northwest of Rutland, on Monument Hill Road in East Hubbardton, 7 miles north of U.S. route 4 coming from Castleton or 6 miles east of state route 30 from Hubbardton.

Lake Champlain Maritime Museum

The Battle of Valcour Island on Lake Champlain is one of the pivotal events of the war, the first falling domino that would eventually seal the British fate.

In defeating Benedict Arnold and his small fleet, the British delayed their invasion of New England, which gave Patriot forces needed time to prepare. This resulted in the surrender of the British at Saratoga the following summer, which convinced the French to enter the war. The French entry brought about the victory at Yorktown, which broke the British will and effectively ended the war.

Exhibits at the Lake Champlain Maritime Museum at Basin Harbor detail the events leading up to the battle, the battle itself, and its aftermath, along with the maritime history of the region. There is also a working replica of a gunboat from the battle, *Philadelphia II,* for visitors to board and explore. New nautical archaeological studies are presented throughout the museum.

A Race to Build Boats

In the spring of 1776, realizing the Canadian invasion would not succeed, Benedict Arnold led his troops on a tortuous retreat to Lake Champlain's southern end. Here the Patriot army prepared to fight for control of the lake, knowing that if the British gained control, they could cut off New England from the other colonies.

John Trumbull, writing to his father, the governor of Connecticut, described Arnold's troops when they arrived at Lake Champlain as "not an army, but a mob, the shattered remains of twelve or fifteen very fine battalions, ruined by sickness [smallpox had hit them hard], fatigue and desertions and void of every idea of discipline or subordination." Besides, few of them had ever been in a boat.

Arnold had. An experienced mariner, he had sailed his own ships to the West Indies and Canada before the war. Now circumstances had placed him in the unfortunate position of having to build the fleet he would command.

His written orders from General Horatio Gates reminded the sometimes overly eager Arnold, "It is a defensive War we are carrying on; therefore, no wanton risque, or unnecessary Display of the Power of the Fleet, is at any Time, to influence your Conduct. . . . A resolute, but

judicious Defence of the Northern Entrance into this Side of the Continent, is the momentous Part, which is committed to your Courage and Abilities. I doubt not you will secure it from further Invasion."

Further invasion was paramount to the British, who viewed the Americans' failed attempt to annex Canada as an opportunity to cleave this fledgling nation in half, dividing to conquer. General Sir Guy Carleton, Canada's governor and commander of the invasion, attempted to use rollers to move 20 or so modified gunboats, 33 to 37 feet long, and a number of smaller boats from the St. Lawrence into Lake Champlain, thereby bypassing the rapids of the Richelieu River. But the rollers got caught in the soft ground, so the vessels had to be disassembled, carried overland, and reassembled. The British settled in at St. Johns at the northern end of the Lake, where Captain John Schank was given a task comparable to Arnold's—building the remainder of the British fleet needed for battle.

Thus began a three-month ship-building competition, with the contestants 120 miles apart but aware of each other's endeavors. It was an extraordinary feat for both sides, marked by determination and ingenuity.

These two qualities were especially true of Arnold, who designed and supervised the construction of

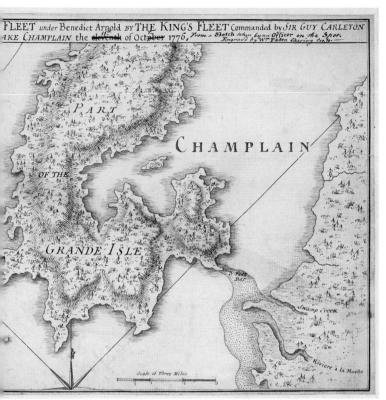

*A **contemporary map** of the battle shows the path of the English fleet to its confrontation with the Americans off Valcour Island.*

12 vessels made from the virgin forest along the lake's shore. He already had three schooners and a sloop captured from the British earlier. Recognizing the lack of sailing experience among the men, he designed his four galleys—*Washington, Congress, Trumbull,* and *Gates*—with short masts and triangular lateen sails, so there would be less canvas for crews to handle. Each of these galleys was 72 feet 4 inches on deck, could hold 80 men, and mounted from 18- to 4-pounder cannons.

Arnold could design the ships, but he needed craftsmen to build them. A bonus system was devised to attract ships' carpenters. Groups of 50 at a time were marched and brought by ship to Whitehall, New York—then called Skenesboro—to work on the ships, after which they returned home (*see* New York, Skenesborough Museum). In requesting supplies for the venture, Arnold listed the need for ironwork such as swivels and anchors, needles, nails, ropes, yarn, pitch and tar, more than 1000 cannonballs, and "Rum, as much as you please. . . . Clothing, for at least [half] the men in the fleet are naked" and "one hundred seamen. No land lubbers." This last request was among several not filled.

The Battle of Valcour Island

On the morning of October 11, 1776, Arnold's hastily constructed fleet had already been on the lake for six weeks when its British counterpart, which now consisted of some 25 vessels, emerged from the northern part to engage the Patriots for control of the strategic lake. The battle lasted from late morning until dark, which, given the superiority of the British forces, says much about the courage and perseverance of the Americans. Arnold, on board *Congress*, at one time was pointing and firing the cannon himself, even as he and his crew were contending with Native American sharpshooters, allied with Britain, who had taken positions on Valcour Island and were shooting at the Americans.

As day ended, the British decided to disengage and wait until daybreak to destroy the remaining vessels in the Continental fleet. The Americans, who had lost the schooner *Royal Savage* and the gunboat *Philadelphia*, slipped past them in a remarkable nighttime maneuver. With oars muffled and a single shrouded lantern in the stern of each vessel, they quietly slipped past the British blockade and escaped.

General Carleton later wrote, "We then Anchored in a line opposite the Rebels within the distance of Cannon shot, expecting in the morning to be able to engage them with our whole fleet, but, to our great mortification we perceived at

225

__Reenactors docking__ the Philadelphia II, *a full-sized replica of a gunboat from the American fleet that confronted the British Royal Navy on Lake Champlain in 1776. The replica is moored at the museum's North Harbor, offering visitors a hands-on encounter with the 18th-century maritime experience.*

day break, that they had found means to escape us unobserved by any of our guard boats or cruisers, thus an opportunity of destroying the whole rebel naval force, at one stroke, was lost . . . by the great diligence used by the enemy in getting away from us."

The British gave chase. Two days later, on October 13, the British fleet caught up with Arnold and his rearmost vessels. The galley *Washington* was forced to surrender as Arnold and his gunboats engaged the British in a two-and-a-half-hour running gun battle. In the end, Arnold realized he could not sustain the engagement and ordered the five rearmost vessels into Ferris's Bay. Here he told his troops to destroy the vessels so that the enemy could not use them. Of the 15 American ships that took part in the three-day engagement, only four made it back to Fort Ticonderoga.

Of the 700 or so Americans involved, about 70 were killed and many more captured. Yet it was a classic Pyrrhic victory for the British. The battle had forced the British to delay their invasion until spring of the following year, and that delay would echo through the remaining years of the war.

Visiting the Museum

Lake Champlain Maritime Museum (LCMM) at Basin Harbor offers exhibits on all aspects of the lake's maritime history, from pre-European eras to modern times. More than a dozen buildings make up the museum complex, which was begun in 1986 in order to preserve the heritage of the Champlain Valley region

while educating the public about its significance.

This mission has developed into a wonderfully entertaining and fascinating combination of exhibits, educational opportunities for children and adults, a conservation laboratory, and an archaeology center.

At the museum's Hoehl Family Education and Visitor Center, which opened in June of 2003, exhibits provide a basic orientation to the museum complex, plus information on the museum's programs, including lectures and special events. The museum also offers courses in traditional crafts such as boat building, blacksmithing, and maritime skills.

In a building just north of the visitor center is LCMM's main Revolutionary War display, the "Key to Liberty" exhibit. Two videos provide background. The 15-minute *Key to Liberty* tells the story of the Battle of Valcour Island, using eyewitness accounts. *A Tale of Three Gunboats* is a 10-minute documentary relating the story of the discovery of two of the original gunboats, *Philadelphia* and *Spitfire*, and the building of the replica, *Philadelphia II*. The original *Philadelphia* was one of the eight gunboats in Arnold's fleet, the others being the *Boston, Connecticut, Jersey, New Haven, New York, Providence*, and *Spitfire*. Each of these small wooden gondolas, or gundalows, was a little more than 53 feet long and 15 feet wide, had three large guns, eight swivel guns, and a crew of 45.

Philadelphia, sunk just after the first day's battle ended, was discovered on the bottom of Lake Champlain by Colonel Lorenzo Hagglund in 1935. Hagglund exhibited the gunboat for the next 25 years, bequeathing it to the Smithsonian Institution upon his death (*see* Washington, D.C., The National Museum of American History, Behring Center). A full-scale working replica, *Philadelphia II*, was built at the Maritime Museum in honor of Vermont's 1991 bicentennial. In 1997, the last unaccounted vessel from Arnold's fleet was located. The *Spitfire* was discovered in deep water on the floor of Lake Champlain, where it remains today.

The "Key to Liberty" exhibit has ship models, including a 9-foot-long scale model of *Philadelphia*, interactive displays showing the disposition of the vessels during battle, artifacts from the battle such as a ship's anchor, and what may have been Benedict Arnold's inkwell and related correspondence. There is also information on the fate of individual vessels in the American and British fleets.

A fascinating part of the exhibit is the display on the Great Bridge that was built by the Americans in 1777 to span the lake between Fort Ticonderoga and Mount Independence (*see* New York, Fort Ticonderoga, and Vermont, Mount Independence State Historic Site). Included here is some of the ordnance matériel thrown into the lake during the British retreat, though the bulk of the matériel recovered is at Mount Independence.

In the Conservation Laboratory, located in the same building as the Nautical Archaeology Center, visitors can observe conservation projects in progress, including recovered Revolutionary War–era artifacts.

"Boat Building in the Champlain Valley" exhibits boat-building tools and includes information on craft used on the lake, including sailing vessels such as those that took part in the battle. There are hands-on learning stations and live demonstrations of boat-building techniques.

Philadelphia II is moored at the north end of the complex. Visitors are welcome to board this 54-foot-long, full-sized working replica and marvel at the fact that 45 men were expected to engage in the rigors of battle while packed into this small boat. The replica cannons onboard evoke the dangers inherent in such powerful armaments on a crowded vessel. One example is a 6-pound cannon found in the lake a few years ago that killed Lieutenant Thomas

Rogers, commanding officer of the gunboat *New York*, when it exploded. It will be on exhibit here beginning in 2004.

Other exhibits include "Steam boats & More," which covers commercial vessels used on the lake, the Schoolhouse Gallery, featuring changing exhibits, the *Champlain Explorer*, a two-man submarine built in 1985, a Coast Guard light tower from the 1930s, and a coast guard buoy tender that visitors can board.

The museum's other site is at the Burlington Shipyard on the historic King Street Ferry Dock in Burlington, Vermont. Exhibits there include a display on the evolution of Burlington's maritime commerce and another on the sailing canal boats of Lake Champlain. The primary exhibit is a work in progress—the construction of the full-sized 88-foot 1862 replica schooner *Lois McClure*, which is expected to be launched in 2004.

Visitor Information
LCMM at Basin Harbor, 802-475-2022; Burlington Shipyard, 802-864-9512 www.lcmm.org for both
Hours: Both locations of the Lake Champlain Maritime Museum are open daily, 10 a.m. until 5 p.m., May 1 through mid-October.
Admission: There is a significant fee for a ticket to the Basin Harbor museum, which is good for two consecutive days. There is no admission charge at the Burlington Shipyard, but donations are welcome.
Accessibility: The buildings are accessible. North Harbor, where *Philadelphia II* is docked, has limited accessibility.
Special Events: There are special events throughout the year, among them the "Rabble in Arms" annual reenactment of the 1777 raid of the Lake Champlain region by British forces from Canada, an annual Kids Maritime and Music Festival, Traditional Maritime Skills Day, and the annual Small Boat Festival.
Getting There: The museum at Basin Harbor is located on the eastern shore of Lake Champlain, 6 miles west of Vergennes.

From state route 22A in Vergennes, turn west on Panton Road. After 1 mile, turn right on Basin Harbor Road. The museum is on the right. Burlington Shipyard is located at the King Street Ferry Dock on the waterfront in Burlington, which is about 15 miles north of Basin Harbor.

Mount Independence State Historic Site

This fortified promontory was the site of one of the war's most impressive engineering feats, a caisson bridge connecting Mount Independence with Fort Ticonderoga. Though the fort at Mount Independence never saw action, its massive size served as a deterrent for General Sir Guy Carleton in his pursuit of Benedict Arnold following the Battle of Valcour Island.

The remains of multiple structures related to the fort's defense works dot the landscape. An even more vivid sense of what was here and why is created through informative displays in the Visitor Center and six outdoor trails with signage. There are also spectacular views from several overlooks atop this 200-foot ridge jutting out into Lake Champlain.

History of Mount Independence

Once Major General Arthur St. Clair made the decision to abandon Fort Ticonderoga (*see* New York, Fort Ticonderoga National Historic Landmark) and retreat across Lake Champlain to the fort on top of Mount Independence, events unfolded rapidly, but not according to plan.

General Philip Schuyler had directed that the two forts provide a combined delaying action against General John Burgoyne and his massive campaign through New York State. To this purpose, soldiers had begun clearing land, building batteries, and planning an eight-pointed star fort in June of 1776. When a copy of the Declaration of Independence was read to the men on July 28, they named the site Mount Independence.

By the fall of 1776, three brigades numbering about 1200 men had completed the batteries and had built hundreds of huts and houses. Work on the picket fort was well under way by this time. With the onslaught of winter, however, many of the men returned to their homes, leaving a force of only about 2500. Harsh weather and lack of supplies that winter resulted in hundreds of deaths from fever and smallpox as well as from freezing.

Working on the design of the fort were the American engineer Jeduthan Baldwin and the Polish patriot Thaddeus Kosciuszko, who arrived in the spring of 1777. Baldwin began working on his seminal accomplishment—a bridge across the lake, linking the forts' shorelines.

The finished 12-foot-wide bridge was a wonder for its day. Twenty-two log caissons filled with rocks were built on the ice. When it melted in the spring, the caissons sank to the bottom. A line of flat-bottomed boats was then stretched from shore to shore, forming a pedestrian bridge. Next, a huge chain was laid along the boats and anchored to the caissons. An enemy ship might have been able to smash through the boat bridge, but it would be stopped by the massive chain.

It was across this bridge that St. Clair and his infantry retreated from Mount Independence on the night of July 5, 1777. The sick and the majority of the artillery and supplies were transported on 200 bateaux and other small craft. St. Clair ordered the troops at Mount Independence to prepare to march southeast to Hubbardton and from there west to Skenesborough.

Leaving was cumbersome. The men had to haul everything by hand from the top of the cliffs down to where the vessels were moored. To mask the sounds of this weary parade, St. Clair ordered cannon fire. The British were lugging artillery up nearby Mount Defiance, which overlooked the fort. For hours on end, they were treated to explosions and no sign of a fight.

At daybreak the British commander, Brigadier General Simon Fraser, was informed by three Patriot deserters that a retreat was under way. The British were a mile and a half from Ticonderoga. Fraser and his troops quick-marched to the bridge, only to find it partially destroyed and artillery on the facing shore trained on it. St. Clair had left four men there to fire on the bridge at the first sign of advancing troops, and then retreat. When the first few British made their way across what was left of the bridge, however, they found the men drunk almost to the point of unconsciousness. Mount Independence was taken.

It would remain in British hands until after Burgoyne's surrender at Saratoga three months hence, after which its buildings and fortifications were burned and its small garrison retreated to Canada, on November 8.

In common with Fort Ticonderoga, this area owes its preservation as a historic site to the Pell family, who bought the northern half of the site and eventually deeded it to the Fort Ticonderoga Association. The rest of

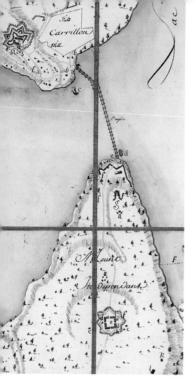

Detail of a contemporary French map showing the proximity of the fort at Mt. Independence to Fort Ticonderoga. The pedestrian bridge can also be seen.

with a capacity for 600 beds. Pictured in this fascinating historical portrait are blockhouses, batteries, barracks, shops for blacksmiths, rope makers, wheelwrights, and other artisans, plus vegetable gardens and the site of a gigantic crane.

A map of the trails is available at the center. Ranging from very short to about two and a half miles, the trails take visitors to the sites of housing units, defensive positions, shops, gardens, the hospital, and the overlooks from which Mount Defiance and Fort Ticonderoga are visible. The topography has changed very little since the time of the war, so walking the trails evokes a strong sense of how formidable a defensive fort Independence was.

The fort's parade ground still forms a neat square, outlined by tall cedars.

A monument, erected on the northern tip of the mount in 1908 by the Hand's Cove Chapter of the Daughters of the American Revolution, commemorates the soldiers who died here. Near the Visitor Center there is a large brass plaque affixed to a huge boulder with a brief history of the mount. A third monument, a large round cairn with a plaque, was erected near the horseshoe battery by the Colonial Dames.

the site was owned by individuals who sold their property to the state over time. Today Mount Independence is jointly owned and administered by the association and the state of Vermont.

Visiting Mount Independence

The Visitor Center is an architectural delight. It is shaped like the bateaux that were used on Lake Champlain, its interior ceiling is made of canvas, and its display areas suggest the fort's stockades.

A brief orientation film about Mount Independence is nicely complemented by a large detailed wall mural of the mount at the time of the war. Artifacts recovered from archaeological digs are displayed, and touch-screen units provide additional information about the men who worked and died here that winter of 1776–1777. The screens are attached to what are called the "talking head" soldiers—four life-size figures representing the English, Hessian, Patriot militia, and Continental personnel. Each is dressed in an authentic uniform and has an interesting history to relate.

Before heading out to the trails that connect the remains of Revolutionary War fortifications on the promontory's nearly 400 acres, visitors are encouraged to take a good look at the mural. Conceived as a bird's-eye view of Mount Independence, it testifies to the fact that this was, in effect, a small city. Independence's hospital was one of the largest in the army when it was built—as long as a football field,

Visitor Information

802-759-2412
www.historicvermont.org/
    mountindependence

Hours: Open daily from 9:30 a.m. until 5 p.m., late May through mid-October.

Admission: There is a moderate charge for adults; children under 15 are free.

Accessibility: The Visitor Center and one trail are accessible. Some parts of the other trails may require assistance.

Special Events: Living-history programs, encampments, and lectures throughout the season, as well as guided hikes, nature walks, and concerts.

Getting There: Follow Vermont route 73 west from Orwell. Take the first left turn off route 73 onto Mount Independence Road. Carefully follow Mount Independence Road for 6 miles, taking a right at the first fork and a sharp left at the second one. The parking lot is on the left at the top of the hill.

Women in the Revolutionary War

Be it known unto Britain, even American daughters are politicians and patriots, and will aid the good work," wrote playwright and historian Mercy Otis Warren at the start of the Revolutionary War.

These sentiments were echoed by Abigail Adams, when she wrote to John in 1775, "If all the American men were to be killed, the women would take up arms and drive out the tyrants!"

Though not all Revolutionary-era women were as fervently involved in the Patriot cause as Adams and Warren, few of them were spared the realities of wartime privations and uncertainties.

While the men fought for independence on the battlefield, America's women dealt with the effects of that war at home. Women from every social class struggled to keep their families economically solvent and physically safe as the war moved through their communities, leaving behind plundered homes and scorched crops.

Colonial women were of necessity an enterprising and self-sufficient group who worked with their husbands to create lives rich in possibilities. Before the war, the roles of men and women were often strictly delineated, with women's work inside the home and men's outside. The war changed that. For months and even years on end, many women became single mothers and their family's only provider.

Many Loyalist women also struggled. As the tides of war shifted, Loyalist families who were grandly entertaining British generals one month could find themselves on the road to Canada the next. Loyalist women were sometimes left behind to protect and provide for their families when their husbands were forced to flee the wrath of their Patriot neighbors. Some lost their homes, businesses, and farms.

Women on both sides and from all classes served as spies during the war. The Loyalist spy Ann Bates, who visited Continental Army camps in Pennsylvania and New Jersey posing as a peddler, reported on "the strength and Situation of each Brigade, & the Numbers of Cannon with their Situation and Weight of Ball each Cannon was charged with."

Benedict Arnold's wife, Margaret Shippen Arnold, worked closely with her husband in his dealings with the British. Her feigned hysteria when his duplicity was discovered allowed Arnold time to escape and convinced George Washington himself of her innocence. Later, however, a letter from Arnold's accomplice, Major John André, proved the opposite.

Female Patriot spies operated in Philadelphia throughout the British occupation, and in New York City Mrs. Elizabeth Burgin provided information as well as an escape route for American prisoners of war until 1779, when she herself had to flee to escape capture.

One of the best known women of the Revolution is seamstress Betsy Ross, who has traditionally been credited with sewing the first American flag. History now views this story is apocryphal, but Ross's role in the war was no less laudable. She lost two husbands to the cause, one in battle, the other in an English prison.

Perhaps the most misunderstood of the war's Patriot women were those labeled camp followers. Though usually characterized as prostitutes by 19th-century historians, they are now known to have served as laundresses, nurses, cooks and blacksmiths. They carried water during battles and loaded muskets. They organized the baggage and cared for the horses.

Many were married to soldiers and officers and traveled with their spouses out of love and out of need. Few families could live on a soldier's pay. Women performing services for the army received a small wage and a half ration. Their children received a quarter ration.

Before the war, women's rights were extremely limited. Laws varied from colony to colony, but generally women were not allowed to be educated past the elementary school level, own property, vote, inherit money or property, obtain a divorce or custody of their children, serve on a jury or testify at a trial, sign a legal document, engage in public speaking, or handle their own money.

Following the war, despite the immeasurable contributions made by women, laws continued to limit women's rights, except those pertaining to education.

Unfortunately, it would be nearly a century and a half before the American government would heed the words of Abigail Adams to her husband, John, and "Remember the Ladies" by granting them the most fundamental rights for which the ladies had fought.

Monticello

The name Monticello means little mountain in Old Italian. It was to this little mountain that the young Tom Jefferson used to retreat, reading his books in the shade of the trees and contemplating the world around him. It served Jefferson this way throughout his life; and even today, standing on the hill in front of the house, looking through the trees into the valley below, one feels a sense of refuge from the realities beyond.

This was an extraordinary residence for its time and place. Visiting Europeans wrote in wonderment of the seemingly effortless amalgam of European classicism and American innovation. The studied balance of elegance and practicality that Jefferson brought together here would be copied many times, but this is the original, and as such it serves as a window on a time when our country was in the process of defining itself.

History of Monticello

The boy's refuge became part of his inheritance of 3000 acres from his father. Eventually, Jefferson's holdings would expand to more than 5000 acres. In May 1768, at the age of 25, Jefferson began to have the mountaintop leveled, in preparation for building a house he had designed. He would be involved in building Monticello for more than 40 years.

Jefferson was a great admirer of ancient—particularly Roman—architecture, especially as interpreted by Italian Renaissance architect and historian Andrea Palladio. From his studies of the architect, Jefferson fashioned a house with two-storied porticoes on the east and west fronts and octagonal bays in several of the rooms. He wanted only the best materials, contracting for specially made mahogany window frames from London, and he hired trained craftsmen to do stonecutting and carving. When he brought his bride to Monticello in 1772, they lived in what is now the South Pavilion as work continued on the rest of the house.

In 1781, two days after Jefferson completed his term as governor of Virginia, Charlottesville was invaded by the British, whose intention was to march on Monticello and capture Jefferson. Sending his family to safety, Jefferson remained behind to gather official documents and hide the family silver and china. Through his telescope he spotted the cavalry approaching, and he just managed to escape. Though Monticello was spared, Cornwallis established his headquarters at one of Jefferson's farms, where the British burned barns and crops, slaughtered sheep and hogs, stole horses, and freed 30 of Jefferson's slaves—to fight on their side—before departing.

After the war, and the death of Martha Jefferson, work continued on the house until Jefferson left for Paris in 1784. During his five-year stay in France, he became enchanted with the modern architecture of new buildings such as the Hôtel de Salm, which was topped by an impressive dome.

Returning to America, Jefferson determined to, in effect, build a second Monticello—modifying what was already there or even rebuilding as necessary. The house was eventually enlarged to include 33 rooms, plus four in the pavilions and six under the South Terrace. Most important, in 1800 the old roof was replaced by Monticello's majestic dome, the first to grace an American home.

Jefferson continued to make modifications to the interior of the house until the last years of his life. The debts that had dogged him throughout his adulthood now forced him to consider selling all his farms, with the hope that he could keep Monticello. His creditors held off until Jefferson's death in 1826. The following year, the family was forced to sell all Jefferson's belongings, which included all his slaves, and in 1830 Monticello too was sold. Four years later, after the interim owner had failed in turning the property into a silk farm, Monticello was bought by Commodore Uriah Phillips Levy of the United States Navy. The Levy family rescued the

estate with the specific intention of preserving it for future generations. As Levy wrote at the time, the houses of America's heroes should be preserved "as monuments to their glory."

Following prolonged litigation after Levy's death, Monticello was bought by his nephew, Jefferson Monroe Levy, a New York Congressman, who restored Monticello and sold it in 1923 to what would become its current owner, the Thomas Jefferson Foundation. So successful has the foundation been in its stewardship that today Monticello is included on the United Nations World Heritage List, along with the Great Wall of China and Egypt's pyramids—two man-made marvels Jefferson probably would have thoroughly enjoyed putting up and improving.

Visiting Monticello

A stop at the Visitor Center is strongly recommended before touring the mansion and grounds. Not only does the center offer the award-winning 38-minute film *Thomas Jefferson: The Pursuit of Liberty*, but its exhibit "Thomas Jefferson at Monticello" gives an excellent grounding in all phases of Jefferson's life to enhance the tour. Displaying nearly 400 artifacts, drawings, and models, the exhibit unfolds chronologically, from "Breaking Ground" in the 1760s to "Return to Domestic Pleasures" in the early 1800s.

Among the treasures on view are architectural books used by Jefferson and a model of his original plan for Monticello, and two of the few remaining samples of Martha Jefferson's handwriting—one a 1777 household account and the other a paper on which both Jeffer-

Monticello's graceful architecture was inspired by the Italian Renaissance architect Andrea Palladio.

son and his wife had written a quote from the novel *Tristran Shandy*. During the last four months of her life, Martha began to copy the passage from the novel, one of Jefferson's favorites: "Time wastes too fast: every letter I trace tells me with what rapidity life follows my pen. The days and hours of it are flying over our heads like clouds of windy day never to return—more everything presses on . . ." The remainder of the passage is in Jefferson's hand: "and every time I kiss thy hand to bid adieu, every absence which follows it, are preludes to that eternal separation which we are shortly to make!"

There are mementoes from Jefferson's years in Paris, including Jefferson's calling card as Minister to the Court of Louis XVI, pages from Jefferson's record books, the design for Jefferson's library in his own hand, his writing equipment, and his green-lensed spectacles to improve vision outdoors—an early version of sunglasses. One particularly charming item is a copy of the 12 "Canons of Conduct in Life" that he wrote for his granddaughter, among them "never trouble another with what you can do yourself" and "when angry, count 10 before you speak; if very angry, 100."

A full-scale model of a plow with Jefferson's moldboard (that part of the plow that lifts and turns the sod) is also on display. Jefferson designed his plow moldboard while serving in France, using mathematics and his knowledge of farming. He never patented it and took pride in the fact that it could be easily duplicated "by the coarsest workman, by a process so exact, that its form shall never be varied by a single hair's breadth."

The center also has an interesting display about the *Getting Word: The Monticello African American Oral History Project*, which over the past four years has been collecting information about the lives of Monticello's slaves from their descendants.

Jefferson's House

There's almost too much to see inside the house on the guided tour, and just about all of it is fascinating. Sixty percent of the objects are original, as is most of the structure.

Above and framing the door of the Entrance Hall is Jefferson's Great Clock, an ingenious mechanism that uses the principles of gravity and cannonball-like weights to mark the hour and the days of the week. A clock of any kind was a novelty in Jefferson's era, when most Americans still told time by the position of the sun. The clock is emblematic of Jefferson's intention for the Entrance Hall, which he meant to serve as a kind of exhibit space.

In the Family Sitting Room there's a copy of the Declaration of Independence that is thought to be one of the original copies printed in England in 1819. There is the drawing table his granddaughter Cornelia used to draw a floor plan of each room, with pieces of furniture included. These floor plans were later used in the restoration of the mansion's interior. There's also an interesting drawing of Jefferson made by the Revolutionary War hero Polish general Thaddeus Kosciuszko.

Very few guests were invited into Jefferson's Library, and that included his own grandchildren. Jefferson's hunger for learning translated into a need for books that resulted in one of the largest libraries in the country, public or private. Jefferson's original collection of nearly 7000 volumes became the nucleus for the Library of Congress, after which he began collecting books again. A number of the books in these cases are from that second collection. Also displayed is Jefferson's design for the University of Virginia campus.

The Greenhouse was used for experimentation and for storing flowers and plants in the winter months. Jefferson, who was "as neat a hand as ever you see to make keys and locks and small chains, iron and brass," according to one of his slaves, may have also kept his tool chest in here.

Jefferson's Cabinet, or study, adjoins his Bedroom. These two rooms are as reflective of the practical man as any rooms in the house. In the Cabinet, Jefferson read, conducted scientific experiments (displayed are his telescope, microscope, and compass), and wrote letters, which task became the bane of his existence in his retirement. "This keeps me at the drudgery of the writing-table all the prime hours of the day. . . . Could I reduce this epistolary corvée within the limits of my friends and affairs, and give the time redeemed from it to reading and reflection, to history, ethics, mathematics, my life would be as happy as the infirmities of age would admit."

The polygraph on display here—one of only two in existence—made the task of correspondence somewhat easier by producing two copies of the letter as one was written. This was accomplished by two pens moving simultaneously by the writer's hand. Though invented by an Englishman, the American rights to the polygraph were assigned to a friend of Jefferson's, who continued to perfect the design, often using Jefferson's suggestions. Also helpful were his revolving chair, the rotating top of his writing table, and the revolving bookstand on which five open volumes could rest at any one time.

Jefferson designed what he called an alcove bed between the walls of his study and the Bedroom, to save space and to give himself more freedom of movement. On a wall shelf at the foot of his bed is the black marble obelisk clock he designed and had made in Paris. Jefferson rose at dawn, "as soon as he can see the hands of his clock," according to guest Daniel Webster. He placed a closet, reachable by ladder, over his bed to store his out-of-season clothes, while his everyday clothes hung on what he called a turning machine, a revolving device with 48 arms.

It was in this room, in this bed, that Jefferson died.

The elegant Parlor was the main gathering place for family and guests. Its draperies and chairs were made in England, France, Philadelphia, and at Monticello. The cittern, a type of guitar, is on display. It was given by Jefferson to his granddaughter. The windows were triple-sashed to allow cross ventilation, and the floors are of the original cherry parquet. Of the 35 portraits that hung on the walls, several originals remain, including those of John Locke and Sir Walter Raleigh. Jefferson felt that "our country should not be without portraits of its discoverers," and so the copies now displayed are likenesses of such as Columbus, Magellan, Cortez, and Raleigh. Grouped with Locke are Isaac Newton and Francis Bacon, the three of them deemed by Jefferson "the three greatest men who have ever lived."

Breakfast was served at nine a.m. and dinner from three until four p.m. in the Dining Room. Cuisine combined the best of Virginia and France, and often included one or more of Jefferson's favorites—peas, macaroni and cheese, and ice cream. Jefferson, as always ahead of his time, brought back a pasta maker from Europe.

The polygonal Tea Room in the alcove off the Dining Room displays ceramics, silver, and glass used by the family. Jefferson lined the walls with engravings, medals, and miniatures of Revolutionary War heroes, and had plaster busts of Benjamin Franklin, John Paul Jones, the Marquis de Lafayette, and George Washington by the French sculptor Jean-Antoine Houdin set on brackets on the walls.

Across from the Dining Room are the Guest Bedrooms, called Mr. (James) Madison's room and Abbé Correia's room by the family in honor of two of their most frequent guests. The Abbé was a Portuguese botanist and statesman.

The bedrooms on the second and third floors were occupied by the family of Jefferson's daughter Martha Jefferson Randolph and are closed to the public. The room directly beneath the dome (also closed) was used as a bedroom and later for storage. Oculi, small circular or oval windows, of hand-blown glass filled the room with light, aided by the bright yellow color of its walls.

The North and South pavilions are attached to the house by walkways. The South Pavilion, the oldest portion of the house, was the first section of the house inhabited by Jefferson and his wife. In later years it was used as a schoolhouse.

The Dependencies, located below the terraces and in the basement of the house, were areas that housed the services upon which the operation of the Monticello house depended. These include the Kitchen, the Cook's Room, the Smokehouse, the Ware Room (where the most valuable stores such as anchovies, sugar, and chocolate were locked up), the Wine Room, the Cellars, and the Ice House.

The Grounds and Gardens

Jefferson was an ardent gardener, taking pleasure in the beauty nature created even as he experimented with her design. "The greatest service which can be rendered any country is to add a useful plant to its culture," Jefferson wrote, and he performed such service, introducing some 250 vegetable and 170 fruit varieties to America. Reproductions of Jefferson's fruit orchard and vegetable garden are to the south of the house.

The roundabout walk bordered by flowers that faces the west front of the house is part of Jefferson's plan that included 20 oval flower beds at the four corners of the house, a plan restored by the Garden Club of Virginia in the 1940s. In gardens, Jefferson observed nature's practical recycling. Describing his garden to his daughter Anne in 1811, Jefferson wrote, "The flowers come forth like the belles of the day, have their short reign of beauty and splendor, and retire like them to the more interesting office of reproducing their like. . . . As your Mama has done to you, my dear Anne . . . and as I shall soon and cheerfully do to you all in wishing you a long, long, good night."

Jefferson planted more than 160 species of trees, creating a grove of trees chosen for their contrasting colors and textures. A few of these original trees survive, including one of the tulip poplars adjacent to the west front. Jefferson also planted a row of mulberry trees along a 1000-foot-long road south of the house. Mulberry Row was the center of plantation activity and of the African American community at Monticello from the 1770s until 1826.

Slavery at Monticello

An excellent brochure provided with the tour leads visitors on a self-guided tour of Mulberry Row, with detailed information about the people who worked here and the 17 buildings they worked in, including a stable, blacksmith shop, and joinery.

Jefferson was the second largest slaveholder in Albemarle County. After inheriting slaves from both his father and his father-in-law, he owned about 200 human beings, almost half of them children under 16. Two thirds of them lived at Monticello and the other one third lived and worked at Jefferson's Poplar Forest estate, also open to the public, in nearby Bedford County.

Of the institution itself Jefferson wrote, "Indeed, I tremble for my country when I reflect that God is just," yet he couldn't break away from the economic stranglehold slavery had upon him. Pronouncing slavery "an abominable crime," Jefferson felt a strong obligation to his slaves. "My opinion has ever been that until more can be done for them, we should endeavor . . . to feed and clothe them well, protect them from ill usage, require such reasonable labor only as is performed voluntarily by freemen, and be led by no repugnancies to abdicate them, and our duties to them."

He nevertheless expected a full day's work. Children as young as 10 years old labored in enterprises such as the nailery, where they, along with older children, produced between 5000 and 10,000 nails a day to be sold in the nearby towns.

The Jefferson Family Graveyard

The site of Jefferson's family graveyard was chosen when Jefferson and his boyhood friend Dabney Carr promised that the first to die would be buried under their favorite oak tree. Carr later married Jefferson's sister and was the first to be interred

here, in 1773.

The obelisk above Jefferson's grave is inscribed as he directed: "Here was buried Thomas Jefferson, Author of the Declaration of American Independence, Of the Statute of Virginia for Religious Freedom, and Father of the University of Virginia." Though history lauds him as a scientist, innovator, and statesman, as the man who oversaw the doubling of the United States and its exploration, these were the three accomplishments of which Jefferson himself was proudest.

Visitor Information

434-984-9822
www.monticello.org

Hours: Monticello is open every day of the year except December 25. Hours are March 1 through October 31, 8 a.m. until 5 p.m.; and November 1 until February 28, 9 a.m. until 4:30 p.m. The Visitor Center is open March 1 through October 31, 9 a.m. until 5:30 p.m.; and November 1 through February 28, 9 a.m. until 5 p.m.

Admission: There is a significant fee for adults, a moderate one for children ages 6 to 11.

Accessibility: The house is wheelchair accessible, as are most of the grounds and gardens. With advance notice, Monticello can accommodate visitors who are sight or hearing impaired.

Special Events: Plantation Community Tours, offered daily in the spring, summer, and fall, focus on the slave community at Monticello and the economic operation of the plantation. Garden tours are offered daily from April 1 through October 31. From June 15 through August 15, there are special tours for children (ages 6 to 11) and their families throughout the day that include hands-on objects. There are celebrations on Jefferson's birthday in April and holiday events in December.

Getting There: Monticello is located on state route 53, approximately 2 miles southeast of Charlottesville, Virginia, near the intersection of state route 20 south and I-64.

Tombstones

The dates on the tombstones have the letters O.S. appearing after them. This stands for "Old Style" and refers to the fact that the Old Style calendar, also called the Julian calendar, was used in the colonies until 1752, when the New Style, or Gregorian, calendar was adopted. Jefferson was born on April 2 under the Old Style calendar, and April 13 according to the New Style, which is when his birthday is celebrated.

Mount Vernon

The Mount Vernon estate, with its mansion, working farm, orchards and gardens, gives human definition to America's first historical icon in ways no words can. The home that Washington designed reflects his eye for grace and beauty encompassed by practicality and balance. The working farm, orchards, and gardens—a microcosm of the five original farms—reflect Washington's keen enthusiasm for refining agricultural principles and his love for verdant open spaces.

"I can truly say I had rather be at home at Mount Vernon with a friend or two about me, than to be attended at the seat of government by the officers of State and the representatives of every power in Europe," wrote Washington in 1790. Standing on the mansion's pillared piazza looking across the Potomac River to the forested shores of Maryland provides a momentary connection to those sentiments and an understanding of why this hilltop home was Washington's anchor, his heart's resting place, and the focus of his life's goals.

A view of the Mansion and the Clerk's Quarters from across the Bowling Green. Right, a 1793 engraving prepared from a "drawing transmitted by the General" showing the extensive series of farms that comprised the Mount Vernon estate.

Early Days

George Washington first came to Mount Vernon in 1735 when he was three years old. The plantation, which was then known as Little Hunting Creek, was part of 5000 acres granted to Washington's great-grandfather in 1674. Washington's family lived here three years before moving to a farm in Fredericksburg, Virginia. When Washington's father died in 1743, Lawrence Washington, George's older half brother, settled on the plantation with his family. He changed the name to Mount Vernon in honor of British Admiral Edward Vernon, under whom Lawrence had served in the war between Spain and Great Britain from 1739 until 1742.

George lived at Mount Vernon off and on over the next five years, until, at age 16, he became a surveyor. Following Lawrence's death, George leased Mount Vernon from his widowed sister-in-law, and he eventually inherited the property upon her death in 1761.

Transforming the Estate

Following their marriage, George and Martha Washington settled at Mount Vernon. This would be their home for the next 40 years of marriage, and Martha's home for the two and a half years following George's death.

Mrs. Washington brought with her a number of slaves, considered part of the property left her by her late husband. At the time of his marriage, George Washington had about 50 slaves, but he would eventually have more than 300 at Mount Vernon. Most of these lived and worked at the four other farms, with only about 90 working at the Mansion House Farm at any one time.

Washington had great plans for the mansion, including adding another story and north and south wings. He culled ideas from architectural texts published in England and studied buildings like the Governor's Palace in Williamsburg, where he served in the House of Burgesses (*see* Virginia, Colonial Williamsburg), adapting these to the tastes and needs of his family. Mount Vernon was always a work in progress. Though Washington occasionally grew impatient with the slow pace of the work—"I am very much engaged in raising one of the additions to my house, which I think (perhaps it is a fancy) goes on better whilst I am present, than in my absence from the workmen"—he

never encouraged speed over crafts-manship, which is probably why most of the buildings here are origi-nal structures. Only the Coach House, Greenhouse, and Slave Quarters are replicas.

Between the time of his appoint-ment as commander in chief in 1775 and the war's end in 1783, Washington would see Mount Vernon only twice—on his way to and from Yorktown. In his absence, a distant relation, Lund Washington, oversaw the five farms and the work on the mansion that continued throughout the war.

Other houses in the area were burned by the British in small skir-mishes, and Mount Vernon itself was threatened in the spring of 1781. When a British sloop-of-war anchored nearby, a number of the plantation's slaves either escaped to the ship or were seized (accounts vary). Amid concern that British marines might attack the main estate, Lund Washington went on board, offering refreshments to the officers and requesting the return of the slaves. When Washington received news of the event, he expressed his displeasure in a letter to Lund. "It would have been a less painful circumstance to me, to have heard, that in consequence of your non-compliance with their request, they had burnt my House, and laid the Plantation in ruins." Washing-ton fully expected that his estate would be lost in the course of the war. "I have no doubt of the enemy's intention to prosecute the plundering plan they have begun. . . . I have as little doubt of its ending in the loss of all my Negroes, and in the destruction of my Houses." Mount Vernon received no further visits from the British, and six of the slaves were returned to the estate.

Washington returned from the war with a determination to make Mount Vernon a thriving example of the emerging agricultural science known as new husbandry—farming that included among its tenets preparing the soil before planting and fertilizing unused fields by planting grasses and clover on which stock could graze. In spite of the fact that Washington lost close to 10,000 pounds sterling during the war, through careful planning and astute management he was able to proceed with his plans for the estate, which eventually encompassed 8000 acres and included five farms, a ferry, carpentry and blacksmith shops, a fishery, a distillery, a gristmill, plus livestock of horses, cattle, sheep, and pigs.

The Presidency and After

Washington's endeavors for transforming his estate continued through his two terms as President, during which time he made 15 visits to Mount Vernon and remained involved in the day-to-day operation of the estate through prodigious correspondence with his managers. In one letter, dated 1793, he covered experimentation with crops (lima beans, Guinea corn from Jamaica, white bent grass), the running of the mill, the price of wheat, bricklaying, the number of nails used in a project, and the correct latch to put on a gate. Little was done at Mount Vernon in which he didn't have a say.

At the end of his presidency, Washington was 65 years old. A year before leaving office, feeling that perhaps five farms were too much for a man of his age to manage, he'd placed newspaper ads offering four of the farms for lease "to real farmers of good reputation, and none others need apply." He hadn't found any "real" farmers, in his estimation, and so once again he threw himself into managing his estate, riding out on horseback each morning, inspecting the farms before breakfast.

On a cold December day, he returned from his morning ride and soon after took to his bed with a cold, which led to his death on December 14, 1799.

The Mount Vernon Ladies' Association

Martha followed him three years later (but not before burning almost every piece of their correspondence), and the property went to Washington's nephew, Bushrod Washington, an associate justice of the Supreme Court. Upon Bushrod's death, the estate passed to his nephew, John Augustine Washington, and eventually to John Augustine's son. John Augustine Washington, Jr., was unable to maintain the estate and tried to interest the federal government and the state of Virginia in buying it. Both declined, and the estate deteriorated.

On a summer's day in 1853, Mrs. Louisa Bird Cunningham of South Carolina was traveling by steamer on the Potomac River. As was the custom, the boat tolled its bell as it passed Mount Vernon, which brought Mrs. Cunningham out on deck to see the historic site. What she saw was a house whose famous piazza was so weakened it was propped up with a sailing mast, and whose grounds were overgrown with weeds. Soon after, she wrote to her daughter that as she viewed the desolation of Washington's once grand house, "the thought passed through my mind: Why was it that the women of his country did not try to keep it in repair, if the men could not do it? It does seem such a blot on our country."

Mrs. Cunningham's daughter, Ann Pamela Cunningham, agreed. In 1853 she founded the Mount Vernon Ladies' Association, which raised the funds necessary to restore the mansion and eventually the grounds, opening 30 acres of the now 500-acre estate to the public in 1860. There is some irony in the fact that the savior of Mount Vernon was the descendant of two notorious South Carolina Loyalists—Patrick Cunningham and "Bloody Bill" Cunningham.

What has developed under the association's stewardship is an evolving and realistic commemoration of Washington—husband, farmer, and slave owner—as well as a thriving example of how a particular class of individuals lived in America's southern colonies.

That Washington himself would have welcomed this scrutiny is evidenced in a letter he wrote in 1794, in which he noted, "I have no objection to any sober or orderly person's gratifying their curiosity in viewing the buildings, Gardens &ct about Mount Vernon."

Visiting Mount Vernon

Mount Vernon is almost entirely a restored original rather than an authentic reproduction, and as such

A new orientation center, museum, and education center is scheduled to open here in 2006. Located just inside the main gate, the complex will feature a state-of-the-art technological introduction to George Washington that will include a biographical film and extensive exhibits from the Mount Vernon collection.

it is an authentic glimpse into 18th-century life. Included here are the mansion, the nearby outbuildings, Washington's tomb, a memorial to the slaves who worked and died here, gardens, orchards, and a working farm.

The Mansion

The two-story Large Dining Room was the last addition made to the house. It was in this room that Washington learned he had been elected President, and it was here that his body lay during the three-day mourning period following his death. This is the largest room in the house, made seemingly larger by its vibrant green color, a favorite of Washington's.

Most evenings, the general and his wife found themselves hosting one or more guests at their table. Some were friends, others were admirers of the general who invited themselves to visit the great man, and still others were travelers who needed a place to stay the night.

Washington delayed finishing the interior of the room until he could find a craftsman to execute his designs exactly as envisioned. The result is an exquisitely graceful room with decorative plaster ornamentation and a palatial mantelpiece, a gift whose opulence had Washington wryly express his fear "for my republican style of living." Two of Mount Vernon's principle crops—wheat and corn—are featured in the ceiling and mantelpiece designs.

From the dining room, guests would often go out onto the Piazza. The idea of the high-pillared colonnade along the length of the mansion was apparently one of Washington's innovations, and it remains the mansion's most distinctive exterior feature.

The oldest part of the house, the Central Passage, is entered off the Piazza. Running the width of the house, this room was where much of the family's socializing took place. On the wall in a small glass-fronted box is a key to the Bastille—a gift from the Marquis de Lafayette, pre-

sented to Washington by Thomas Paine.

Four rooms abut the central hall. In the Little Parlor, guests were entertained by Martha's grand-daughter Nelly Custis on the harpsichord in the corner of the room. The more formal West Parlor is decorated with multiple representations of the Washington family coat of arms. The ornate built-in frame above the mantelpiece is called a neat landskip, landskip being an archaic word for landscape. Ordered from England, its dimensions probably determined the dimensions of the landscape it framed.

In the Small Dining Room is a replica of an English sideboard table, original to Mount Vernon and later given to Martha's great-grand-daughter Mary Randolph Custis, who married Robert E. Lee.

The Downstairs Bedroom, the guest bedroom, was in almost constant use. The Washington family numbered eight—George and Martha, the two Custis grandchildren, Washington's nephew and his wife, and two secretaries—which easily accounted for the upstairs bedrooms.

Washington's Study, on the southern side of the first floor, was his haven. Here were his books (884 bound volumes at the time of his death) and papers, and it was here that he came each morning at sunrise to shave and dress.

On the second floor are six bedrooms. General and Mrs. Washington's Master Bedroom, above his study, and two others are open to the public. Into one of the windows in the yellow bedroom is etched "Eliza P Custis 10 [her age] August 2 1792." Eliza was Martha's grand-daughter.

On the third floor is Mrs. Washington's Room, into which she moved following her husband's death. Displayed here is the trunk used by Mrs. Washington when she traveled to and from the army's winter quarters to be with the general, and a letter written by Eliza describing watching her grandmother pack

After the Revolution, Washington resigned his commission from the army and devoted himself to adapting new agricultural techniques to his farms.

for these trips every year of the war.

The Pantry displays a unique model of the French Bastille made from materials taken from the original and presented to Washington in 1795. Many of the utensils displayed in the nearby Kitchen are from the period, though not original to the house.

Though Washington himself was said to have simple tastes in food, dinners were ample. One, described by a guest, included "a small roasted pigg, boiled leg of lamb, roasted fowls, beef, peas, lettuce, cucumbers, artichokes, puddings, tarts . . ." The general was equally generous with the less fortunate. "Let the Hospitality of the House, with respect to the poor, be kept up," he wrote to Lund Washington. "Let no one go hungry away."

The Archaeology and Restoration Museum

This small museum, located among the outbuildings on the north lane, has a number of interesting items that have been recovered in digs on the property. Among these are pieces of pottery and ceramics, and tools used by blacksmiths and carpenters. The original Dove of Peace weathervane that Washington placed on the roof of the mansion's cupola is displayed here also, as is a hand-sewn replica of Washington's Commander-in-Chief Flag. This replica flew with Senator John Glenn aboard the space shuttle *Discovery* in 1999, in honor of the bicentennial commemoration of Washington's death.

A larger display space will be part of the orientation center.

Outbuildings

The outbuildings along the north and south lanes provide a window into the practical aspects of maintaining an 18th-century plantation, with detailed, realistic displays of implements and equipment, some of which include items from the period.

Most of the work on the five farms was done by slaves. Originally, the Mansion House Farm's slaves lived in brick wings of the Greenhouse, in various outbuildings, and in nearby cabins. The current Slave Quarters were reconstructed using descriptions from that era. Those who lived here were likely skilled workers, such as blacksmiths, carpenters, and seamstresses, rather than fieldworkers. About 90 slaves lived and worked at the Mansion House Farm, almost two thirds of them married. Married couples didn't always live together, especially when the wife and husband worked at different farms.

The Salt House was used to store equipment needed in Washington's fishing business. Washington sold shad, herring, and sturgeon from the Potomac, much of it shipped to markets overseas. Washington insisted on high-quality salt to preserve his meat and fish, so some of the salt was imported from as far away as Portugal. The dried pork, bacon, and ham to be consumed at the Mansion were kept in the Smokehouse.

The Spinning Shop and the Shoemaker's Shop were among Mount Vernon's busiest places. All the fibers used in spinning and knitting were produced on the estate— linen from flax, wool from sheep, and cotton. The clothes produced here were for the slaves, who were issued two sets of clothing each year and one pair of shoes, made by the shoemaker. The shoemaker also worked on saddles and other leather goods.

The Washhouse was also busy, especially when there were guests. Two slave women washed and ironed the clothes, using huge tubs and lye soap. So much laundry passed through here that sometimes the women had to embroider the owners' initials on the clothes in order to ensure the clothes were returned to the right person.

There is also an Overseer's Quarters, and a Storehouse and Clerks Quarters, where Washington's secretary lived and where hammers, nails, leather, thread, powder and shot, blankets, and extra clothes were stored. Paint was kept in the basement. A very expensive commodity, paint was imported from Europe in powder form, then hand mixed with linseed oil. The Ice House was a cover for a brick pit lined with wood where ice cut from the Potomac River was packed in straw.

The Stable contains one of the few surviving coaches of that period, this one originally owned by Samuel Powel, the mayor of Philadelphia and a friend of Washington's. There is also a rare 18th-century riding chair, a two-wheeled conveyance whose light weight and narrowness made it more suitable for country roads than the usual four-wheeled carriage.

Washington was an accomplished rider, the "best horseman of his age," according to Thomas Jefferson.

A French visitor wrote that it was "the General himself who breaks all his horses; and he is a very excellent and bold horseman, leaping the highest fences, and going extremely quick, without standing upon his stirrups, bearing on the bridel, or letting his horse run wild." Fertilizer is made in the nearby Dung Repository. The original was built in 1787. This working reproduction was reconstructed in 2001 on the same site using the original cobblestone floor. This repository is thought to be one of Washington's innovations, a way of fermenting manure until it was ready for use.

The Grounds

Washington designed the grounds adjoining the mansion to be as pleasing to the eye as they were practical to the day-to-day operation of a large estate. From west to east was the domain of a gentleman farmer. From north to south, secluded from the eyes of guests by trees, were the gardens and outbuildings of a working farmer.

Facing the mansion on the west side is the Bowling Green. Along here Washington planted hundreds of young trees, 13 of which survive, brought from other parts of Mount Vernon or bought from neighboring plantations. Trees were a lifelong passion for Washington, fired by research and experimentation to have the most beautiful trees serving the most practical purposes. In his search for the trees he wanted, he

The Seed House sits among spring-flowering tulips and daffodils in the Upper Garden.

even went as far afield as Pennsylvania, where he bought 200 trees from an estate outside Philadelphia.

The Bowling Green served as the entrance for visitors. Its elliptical drive was surveyed by Washington, as was the grassy circle facing the mansion's front door, around which Washington placed 32 posts, corresponding to the points of the compass, with a sundial in the center. The green was "mowed" using scythes and a roller.

Washington's gardens are on both sides of the Bowling Green. The Kitchen Garden is the oldest garden on the estate and an outstanding example of a formal English kitchen garden. Although this was Martha Washington's purview, her husband supervised its design and maintenance. The brick walls enclosing the garden served two purposes: to keep animals out and to increase the temperature enough to extend the growing season. English boxwoods border the entrance to the beds where herbs and vegetables grow and are harvested each year. Along the north wall are espaliered fruit trees. On the other side of the south wall is the Paddock, a common arrangement of the time. The grazing horses here provided dung, which went through a decomposition process and was then used in the garden beds.

The Upper Garden, originally a fruit and nut garden, was converted to flowers in 1785. The correspondence of visitors to Mount Vernon in Washington's time remarks on the charm of this garden and Washington's pride in its creation. Having a purely ornamental garden was unusual for an 18th-century American estate. It reveals much about Washington that a man of such a practical bent would devote this amount of acreage to the simple aesthetic pleasure of beautiful flowers.

The original Greenhouse burned down in 1835; the present one was built in 1951. Washington's greenhouse was his indoor laboratory, where he could experiment with and study the exotic plants sent to him by friends and admirers, such as orange trees from the Carolinas and sago palms from the West Indies. Many of these same types of plants are grown at Mount Vernon today, following Washington's system of sheltering plants in the Greenhouse during the winter months and bringing them out into the courtyard with the arrival of warm weather. East of the Upper Garden, behind the Spinning House, is the Botanical Garden, where Washington himself tended the new plant varieties he was testing.

To enter the Fruit Garden and Nursery, visitors pass through a living hedge fence of honey locusts. Washington frequently planted honey locusts around his gardens as a way to keep animals from foraging. These four acres were restored in 1998, based on archaeological evidence and Washington's written records. This area was originally planted as a vineyard, based on Washington's hopes of producing a fine wine. Unfortunately, the soil wouldn't support that endeavor and so he switched to a fruit garden, which proved more successful, providing fruit to the mansion six months of the year. Cherries, peaches, plums, apples, and pears are planted in the garden. The Nursery was used by Washington both to grow seeds for his farms and as space for his plant experiments.

The Burial Grounds

Washington's will gave instructions that a new tomb be built for himself and Mrs. Washington because the family vault then in use was in disrepair. Inside the tomb are two marble sarcophagi, one inscribed WASHINGTON and the other MARTHA, CONSORT OF WASHINGTON. Each morning, April through October, there's a wreath-laying ceremony here.

Down a short path from the Tomb is the Slave Burial Ground and Memorial. An estimated 75 graves are on the hillside. In 1983, a Slave Memorial was erected—honoring those enslaved at Mount Vernon—across from a smaller memorial dedicated in 1929.

Mount Vernon's approximately 300 slaves on the five farms worked from sunrise until sunset, with two hours off for meals. Their holidays included Sundays, three or four days at Christmas, and the Mondays after Easter and Pentecost. If they had to work on a Sunday, they were either given a day off later or were paid wages for the day. The majority of the women worked in the fields. Washington allowed his slaves to engage in business, and many of them sold food and dry goods at local markets, presumably using the profits to buy personal items, as they were not allowed to buy their freedom.

Washington made it a practice

Washington *was a leader in the development of American agriculture. His passion was his land, and he enjoyed the challenge of cultivating crops and learning what techniques and tools worked best for growing things. His 16-sided threshing barn is one of the main attractions at the Pioneer Farm. Visitors can hitch a ride to see it on a horse-powered wagon, much as the farmhands did in the 18th century.*

never to sell a slave without his or her acquiescence, which became a problem in years when he had financial difficulties and more slaves than he could use. In his will, Washington stipulated that his slaves be freed upon the death of his wife. Mrs. Washington freed them within a year of his death. He also made provision for the support of the older slaves, resulting in his estate paying pensions until 1833, and he provided for the education of the younger ones. His will also stipulated that his slave William Lee be immediately freed "for his faithful services during the Revolutionary War." Lee is buried here.

Pioneer Farm

Near the Wharf, a 19th-century structure restored in 1991 as a drop-off point for excursion boats, is one of the most interesting sites at Mount Vernon—the Pioneer Farm. Shuttle buses run between here and the Crossroads Entrance, April through October. This four-acre site demonstrates the essence of Washington's farming philosophy—a practice that included crop rotation and improved plowing, mandated switching from tobacco—then Virginia's major crop—to crops that nourished instead of depleting the soil, and the creation of the 16-sided threshing barn.

At the time of George Washington's death, Mount Vernon was 16 times as large as it is today and included 8000 acres. The main crops were wheat, corn, grasses, potatoes, and buckwheat, with wheat being the main cash crop. A lot of valuable grain was lost in the primitive threshing process then in use, so Washington invented a 16-sided barn, which many years later was torn down. The current barn was built between 1994 and 1996 using authentic 18th-century methods and tools. For those interested in how this challenging task was accomplished, there's a detailed description on the Mount Vernon Web site, www.mountvernon.org, as well as a film about it shown in a small hut near the barn.

The logic behind Washington's invention seems almost too simple: Horses were trotted around a circular lane on the top floor of the barn, treading out the grain from the straw through floor slats to the floor below, where the grain was gathered and stored until being delivered to the gristmill Washington built three miles away.

Also in the hut are examples of tools used on the farm, such as a beetle maul, a crosscut saw, an auger, and a froe, used to split shingles, oak logs for wheel spokes, and wood for chair legs. Hog Island sheep are penned near a field plowed by costumed interpreters using a reproduction of an 18th-century plow pulled by horses. There are also demonstrations on a variety of activities, such as how linen was made from flax plants.

The Forest Trail

For those who prefer to walk, the Forest Trail connects the Pioneer Farm with the mansion area. Along the path is interesting signage telling visitors about animals, such as black bears and American bison, who used to roam this area, and the Native American tribes who lived here prior to Washington's family.

Less than half of the estate's acres were farmed. The rest, for the most part, were woodlands such as this, from which Washington secured lumber to keep his operation running and to fuel the 13 fireplaces in the Mansion, as well as wild game for his table. Washington's hogs ran freely through these woods. Coming off the trail, visitors pass by the home of another American icon— the wild turkey. Two of them are kept in a small pen at the trail's entrance on Tomb Road.

Other Sites

Washington's Grist Mill, three miles west on Route 235, has been restored to working order. Here visitors learn how this water-powered mill ground corn into meal, and from April through October they can see the mill in operation. Adjacent to the site is a whiskey distillery Washington built in 1797, where an archaeological dig is currently in progress preparatory to restoring the distillery operation.

Visitor Information

703-780-2000
www.mountvernon.org

Hours: Mount Vernon is open every day of the year, including holidays and December 25. Hours are April through August, 8 a.m. until 5 p.m.; March, September, and October, 9 a.m. until 5 p.m.; November through February, 9 a.m. until 4 p.m.

Admission: There's a significant fee, with children age 5 and under free. An annual pass is available. Admission to the Grist Mill can be part of a package admission or a separate fee.

Accessibility: Only the first floor of the Mansion is wheelchair accessible; there is limited accessibility in the Outbuildings area, where the gravel paths can be difficult for the physically challenged. There is limited wheelchair accessibility to the Burial Grounds and at the Pioneer Farm. The Forest Trail is not accessible.

Special Events: Walking tours of the gardens are held three times a day, April through October. A walking tour focusing on the lives of Mount Vernon's slaves is offered four times a day, April through October, and during Black History Month (February) there are special programs. At 10 a.m. each day there is a wreath-laying ceremony at the Tomb. Major celebrations are held for Washington's birthday in February, when visitors are admitted free on the Monday President's Day holiday. Candlelight tours are offered during the holiday season (November–December). From December 1 until January 6, the third floor of the Mansion, where Mrs. Washington lived for two years after the general's death, is open to the public. Special programs for families are held throughout the year, and in summer there is a Hands-On Tent with clothes, toys, and military items. Children are given an adventure map to use on their tour, and Scout and Camp Fire Club member activity booklets are available.

Getting There: Mount Vernon is just south of Washington, D.C., on the Potomac River.

From Washington, D.C.: Cross Memorial Bridge or the 14th Street Bridge and look for the signs for George Washington Memorial Parkway. Stay on the parkway past Reagan National Airport and through downtown Alexandria, to the parkway's end at Mount Vernon.

From Maryland: Take I-270 or I-95 south to I-495, and follow that south to Virginia. Take the exit marked George Washington Memorial Parkway and follow that to Mount Vernon.

From Virginia: Take the George Washington Memorial Parkway to Mount Vernon.

By subway and bus: Take Metro's yellow line to Huntington Station. From there catch the Fairfax Connector Bus No. 101, which runs every hour, to Mount Vernon.

By tour bus: Gray Lines Tours, 202-289-1995.

By boat: Potomac Spirit River Cruise, 866-211-3811.

George Washington

When John Adams nominated George Washington to be commander of the colonial forces, he described Washington as "a gentleman whose skill and experience as an officer, whose independence, great talents and excellent universal character would command the approbation of all Americans and unite the cordial exertions of all the colonies better than any other person in the union."

Though Washington's appointment was a political move to secure the southern colonies' support for the war, there was also genuine regard for this quiet-spoken Virginian. As one Continental Congress delegate wrote of him, "Washington is a gent, highly esteemed by those acquainted with him. . . . He seems discreet and virtuous, no harum scarum ranting fellow but sober, steady and calm."

Sober, steady, and calm is certainly the image succeeding generations would have of the father of his country, though we've also come to know him as a man driven by strong ambition and by the love he had for his wife and family.

Early Life

George Washington was born in 1732 on a Virginia estate about 75 miles from Mount Vernon. George had five brothers and one sister who reached adulthood, and three siblings who died as children. His father died when George was 11 years old. It is generally thought that it was Washington's mother, Mary Ball Washington, who instilled in him the measured and disciplined nature that made Washington an exemplary military commander. One of Washington's childhood friends wrote in later years, "Whoever has seen the awe-inspiring air and manner so characteristic of the son will remember the mother as she appeared as the presiding genius of her well-ordered household, commanding and being obeyed."

A poem composed by Washington as a young man seems to foreshadow the adult. On the theme of things needed "to make a life that's truly blessed," young George wrote, *A good estate on healthy soil/ Not got by vice, nor yet by toil;/ Round a warm fire, a pleasant joke,/ With chimney ever free from smoke;/ A strength entire, a sparkling bowl,/ A quiet wife, a quiet soul.*

Surveyor, Landowner, Soldier

By the time he was 17, Washington was a county surveyor, and at the age of 22 he was appointed commander of the Virginia militia. He also came into possession of his half-brother Lawrence's estate, Mount Vernon.

During the French and Indian War, Washington acquitted himself well as aide to General Edward Braddock, gaining a reputation as one of the ablest military men in the colonies. After the war, he became a member of the Virginia House of Burgesses and, at the age of 26, married a widow, Martha Dandridge Custis. George and Martha settled at Mount Vernon, bringing with them Martha's two children, John Parke and Martha Parke Custis.

Throughout his life, Washington thought of himself as a farmer more than as a soldier; "I think . . . that the life of a Husbandman [farmer] of all others is the most delectable. It is honorable. It is amusing. and, with judicious management, it is profitable." Once married, he anticipated a life as a successful plantation owner.

Commander in Chief

Civic responsibility was an integral part of being a landowner in colonial Virginia, and one that Washington took seriously. Though he never attended college, Washington was a well-read man and well acquainted with the law. He had served as a jus-

tice of the peace and as a member of the county court. Early on, Washington must have realized that as a large and respected landowner and experienced soldier, he and others of his class would be looked to for leadership in the evolving dispute with Great Britain.

As early as 1769, Washington was deliberating the means of dealing with the king and Parliament. In a letter that year to his lifelong friend George Mason, Washington wrote, "At a time when our lordly Masters in Great Britain will be satisfied with nothing less than the deprivation of American freedom, it seems highly necessary that something shou'd be done to avert the stroke and maintain the liberty which we have derived from our Ancestors; but the manner of doing it to answer the purpose effectually is the point in question."

When the First Continental Congress was called in 1774, Washington attended as a representative of Virginia, and he did so again with the second congress in 1775. Washington was not unmindful that in doing so he was putting himself, his family, and their home in jeopardy. In May of 1775, following Lexington and Concord, he wrote to a Loyalist friend who had moved to London, "Unhappy it is though to reflect, that a Brother's Sword has been sheathed in a Brother's breast, and that, the once happy and peaceful plains of America are either to be drenched with Blood, or Inhabited by Slaves. Sad alternative! But can a virtuous Man hesitate in his choice?"

When Congress offered him the position of "General and Commander-in-Chief of the forces raised and to be raised in defence of American Liberty," Washington could not refuse. In his acceptance speech to Congress, Washington said he felt great distress "from a consciousness that my abilities and military experience may not be equal to the extensive and important trust," but he emphasized he would "enter upon the momentous duty, and exert every power I possess in the service, and for the support of the glorious cause." To his confidante, Martha, he again expressed his concern that he wasn't up to the task, but that he had no fear of what lay ahead, and wrote, "I shall feel no pain from the toil or the danger of the campaign; my unhappiness will flow from the uneasiness I know you will feel from being left alone."

In the ensuing eight years of war, while Congress bickered over funds and strategy, while Benjamin Franklin and John Adams courted European powers for alliances and resources, while the course of the fighting swung from great victories to terrible defeats and despair, Washington held together an army that rarely numbered more than 30,000 men and boys but that eventually wore down the most powerful army in the world.

He took no salary, asking only that Congress reimburse his expenses, and did not include in those expenses the seven ships he acquired for use in the war at sea. (His ships captured more than 30 British vessels, bringing needed matériel to the war effort.) By all accounts, he was a dogged campaigner with flashes of brilliance.

When Cornwallis's defeat came at

Yorktown, marking what soon proved to be the determining battle of the war, Washington's communiqué to Congress was typically simple and modest, with no self-aggrandizing descriptions of his strategies. Equally simple was his farewell to his commanders at war's end: "With a heart full of love and gratitude, I now take leave of you. I most devoutly wish that your later days may be as prosperous and happy as your former ones have been glorious and honorable."

In his formal address to Congress resigning his commission, in December 1783, he spoke glowingly of those who had served with him and ended his address with "Having now finished the work assigned me, I retire from the great theatre of Action; and bidding an Affectionate farewell to this August body under whose orders I have so long acted, I here offer my Commission, and take my leave of all the employments of public life."

The First President

A popular song following the war included the sentiment, *Then let's agree, since we are free,/ All needless things to shun;/ And lay aside all pomp and pride,/ Like our great Washington.*

Some at the time felt that Washington, far from laying aside all pomp and pride, was waiting with confidence for the honor of being asked to take charge of the nation he had helped create. This view contradicts his many writings. In June of 1783, he wrote of "a Retirement, for which I have never ceased to sigh through a long and painful absence, and in which (remote from the noise and trouble of the World) I meditate to pass the remainder of life in a state of undisturbed repose."

However, Washington did have strong concerns about how the new nation would evolve. He understood the very real possibility that a union formed to fight a war could devolve into 13 states, each intent on winning every disputatious issue important to its own prosperity. Doing his part to avert this, he rejected an offer to be king, presided over the Constitutional Convention, and accepted the responsibility to be the new nation's first President.

Retirement

George Washington's presidency was defined by its establishment of the federal government. Working with Congress and the judiciary, the first President drew the parameters of power according to the constitutional government he and others had structured.

In 1797, after two terms, Washington returned to Mount Vernon, at the age of 65. Finally, he could concentrate all his energies on his beloved estate. But less than two and a half years later, on December 14, 1799, George Washington died, after contracting a cold that turned into a severe inflammation of the tissues surrounding his tonsils, a condition known today as acute epiglottitis. Washington's will stipulated that "my Corpse be Interred in a private manner, without-parade, or funeral Oration." His funeral was attended by some 200 friends and family members, and he was buried at Mount Vernon.

History has judged Washington to be one of our most complex Founding Fathers. An avid agriculturalist, he repeatedly expressed his desire to spend his life developing innovative farming techniques at Mount Vernon. Yet he spent the majority of his adult life away from his estate, either fighting in wars or serving as President.

An earnest believer in the basic rights of human beings, he was a slave owner all his life; and though he expressed his aversion to slavery, he only made arrangements to free his slaves upon the death of himself and his wife.

An ambitious man who loved the recognition that came with achievement, he turned down the opportunity to be king and worked hard to ensure that the presidency wouldn't take on the trappings of an imperial office.

Dubbed the Father of His Country even during his lifetime, Washington was always mindful of the fact that almost everything he did was setting a precedent. Creating a unified nation was a formidable task he could only begin, and he understood and respected the powers established to achieve that goal. "Government is not reason," he once wrote, "it is not eloquence; it is force! Like fire, it is a dangerous servant, and a fearful master."

Perhaps Washington's most valuable legacy to his country was in trying to draw the fine line between a government strong enough to lead and responsive enough to follow.

Colonial Williamsburg

What began as the joint vision of a country parson and the heir to a great fortune is today the largest and oldest living-history museum in the world. Colonial Williamsburg's 301 acres of restored and reconstructed buildings encompass the grandeur of England's richest colony, as well as the upheaval in its political and economic structure as its citizens tottered on the brink of revolution. Amid this clash of the old and the new are the minutiae of day-to-day existence—buying stamps, getting a horse shod, purchasing a wig.

Through the stewardship of the Colonial Williamsburg Foundation, this microcosm of a 1774 capital continues to expand its forthright exploration of the issues that confronted colonial America, including the economic class system, the evils of slavery, free trade versus protectionism, country versus town, the role of women, and the place of Native Americans in an evolving nation.

History Re-created

In 1774, Williamsburg was the capital of Virginia, the largest of the English colonies. A cosmopolitan center of commerce and politics, Williamsburg bustled with economic and social activity, as wealthy planters, craftspeople, government bureaucrats, tradespeople, servants, and slaves lived and worked here.

Administration of the colony was the charge of the royal governor, appointed by the king; but there was an elective body, called the House of Burgesses, which included such luminaries as George Washington, Thomas Jefferson, and Patrick Henry. By 1774, the time in which Colonial Williamsburg is set, the House of Burgesses had openly defied the wishes of the royal governor over such issues as the Stamp Act and trade restrictions, and had been dissolved on at least three occasions in an effort by the governor to maintain some semblance of control.

It was in early 1774 that Patrick Henry urged getting the Virginia militia into fighting shape, an action that concerned but didn't alarm the governor, Lord Dunmore. However, a year later, following Lexington and Concord, Dunmore was sufficiently alarmed to have the gunpowder that was stored in Williamsburg's magazine transferred in the dead of night to a British schooner anchored nearby.

Reaction among the populace was immediate. In an effort to deter a mob of angry citizens from storming the Governor's Palace, several members of the House of Burgesses presented a written petition to Dunmore that began in the most polite terms ("We, His Majesty's dutiful and loyal subjects") and stated the umbrage of the citizens in having powder they'd paid for stolen—as they saw it—by the English government.

Dunmore, whose first reaction to news of a mob forming had been defiance, soon relented and paid for the powder.

This was the beginning of a rapid progression toward a complete break with England and the diminishing of Dunmore's power. In June 1775, the governor felt threatened enough by events to retreat to the warship *Fowey,* which was anchored in the nearby York River. In November 1775, a desperate Dunmore declared martial law and published a proclamation granting freedom to slaves who would fight for England.

The slaveholders reacted with outrage, as did much of Williamsburg. The Virginia *Gazette* wrote an editorial that implied great harm to the wives and children of slaves who would be left behind "at the mercy of an enraged and injured people" and ended "Be not then, ye Negroes, tempted by this proclamation to ruin yourselves." Nevertheless, about 500 slaves did join Dunmore, who called them Lord Dunmore's Ethiopian Regiment and gave them uniforms with "Liberty to Slaves" printed on them. Dunmore would bring little glory to these soldiers or to himself, as he raided coastal towns, burned Norfolk to the ground, and then returned to England to serve in Parliament.

On May 15, 1776, what was now the government of the colony of Virginia passed a resolution calling for complete independence from Great Britain. By this time, a former member of the House of Burgesses was commander in chief of the Continental Army and another former member soon would be presenting to the Continental Congress in Philadelphia a draft of the Declaration of Independence.

During the war, Thomas Jefferson left the Continental Congress to succeed Patrick Henry as governor of Virginia, living for a time in the Governor's Palace. By June 1781, however, when British general Charles Cornwallis settled on Williamsburg as a good place to rest

The grandeur of the Governor's Palace was intended to instill respect for British power and affluence.

his troops and procure supplies, Williamsburg had already been supplanted by Richmond as Virginia's capital. Richmond was thought to be more centrally located and therefore more easily defended. Williamsburg was well-enough situated for George Washington, however, who met here with his French allies in September 1781 to plan their strategy at Yorktown.

Following the war, Williamsburg—though no longer quite the bustling center of activity it had been—continued as a major market for the surrounding farming community, as well as the site of the College of William and Mary.

The town was once again occupied by soldiers, this time Union ones, during the Civil War. Incredibly, during the late 19th century, given the American inclination for tearing down the old to make way for the new, most of Williamsburg's 18th-century hub was left standing. Former homes and shops were repaired and renovated—some homes continuing to be used as residences, others now used for trade.

Early in the 20th century, inspired by the vision of the Reverend W.A.R. Goodwin, rector of Williamsburg's Bruton Parish Church, John D. Rockefeller, Jr., heir to the Standard Oil fortune, agreed to fund the restoration of the entire 18th-century area of the town.

Research was the foundation of the project, as maps, deeds, plans, and contemporary accounts were studied in order to authentically restore and, in some cases to re-create, the colonial capital. The single most valuable resource was a copper plate, found in the Bodleian Library at Oxford University in England, engraved with a detailed architectural drawing of colonial Williamsburg's main buildings. A copy of the design engraved on the plate and additional information about the plate's origins and use are on display at the Visitor Center. Colonial Williamsburg's first restored building, Raleigh Tavern, opened to the public in 1932.

Today, Williamsburg has a population of almost 12,000, including those Colonial Williamsburg employees who live in many of the restored homes and who daily cross the time line between an era when its residents were leading a new nation toward the future and an era when today's visitors look to the past for inspiration.

Visiting Colonial Williamsburg

As impressive as Colonial Williamsburg's buildings and landscape are, it is the restoration's interpreters who lead visitors through the figurative portal into colonial America. Talking to them provides a wealth of information and a clearer idea of the attitudes and aspirations of 18th-century Americans.

The trade interpreters are not playacting. These are accomplished craftspeople who have served apprenticeships (the wheelwright's apprenticeship, for example, is six years) to learn how to use the tools and techniques of colonial times. The historical interpreters—encountered along Colonial Williamsburg's streets, inside the shops, and as tour guides—and character interpreters, who portray real people, from Virginia's leading citizens to its most humble servants, are playacting, but their words and opinions are based on extensive research.

Throughout the year there is a wealth of opportunities to fully explore the lives of Colonial Williamsburg's residents of all stations in life. Visitors can listen to a debate on independence between neighbors meeting on the street, witness the capture of a runaway slave, and converse with Thomas Jefferson and Martha Washington.

Visitors are encouraged to begin at the Visitor Center, where they can see the 37-minute orientation film *The Story of a Patriot*, buy tickets, and make reservations for walking tours. From here, visitors can walk to the Historic Area or take shuttle buses that stop at various locations.

There are 88 original buildings in the Historic Area, and hundreds of other structures have been reconstructed on their original foundations. Duke of Gloucester, the main street, runs from the Capitol on the east side to the William and Mary campus on the west. From the Gateway Building, east of the Governor's Palace, visitors can take an hour-long orientation walk that provides background and highlights the main buildings.

Some Notable Buildings

The **Governor's Palace** was home to seven royal governors before becoming the official residence of the new commonwealth's governors until 1780. A year later, the building burned to the ground. The reconstruction, built on the original foundations, is based on detailed floor plans made by Thomas Jefferson—no doubt with a thought to making some renovations—while he resided here. At a time when even well-to-do Virginians might live in houses with only a few rooms, the grandeur of the palace and its landscaped gardens made a convincing statement about the power of the ruling government. This power is especially reflected in the entrance hall, where 781 weapons are grouped in wall and ceiling designs. The palace served briefly as a hospital following the siege of Yorktown, before its demise in 1781. A commemorative plaque marks the area behind the palace where 100 soldiers are buried in unmarked graves. Sections of the original foundation are visible in the palace's wine cellar. In the palace's kitchen, there are periodic demonstrations of the ways in which British cooking differed from that of colonial America.

The **Raleigh Tavern** was the site of several important events, as well as a lot of socializing in the days when legislators, farmers, traders, and travelers would gather here to drink, dine, and debate the issues of the day. Following the Stamp Act in 1765, the rebel contingent of the House of Burgesses met here and wrote what came to be known as the Virginia Resolves, which in effect stated that only Virginians could tax Virginians. So incendiary a notion was this that the editor of the Virginia *Gazette* wouldn't even report it. Each time the House of Burgesses was dissolved by a royal governor, the burgesses would meet here, usually in the Apollo Room. In 1769 this resulted in a resolution to boycott British goods, and in 1774 in a resolution calling for a day of prayer and fasting to protest the closing of Boston Harbor.

The **Capitol**, an H-shaped building where the upper and lower houses of government and the General Court of Virginia met, was just a half block walk from the Raleigh Tavern. Note the Union Jack flying atop the building—a reminder that it's 1774. Virginia's upper legislative house, the Council, was composed of 12 leading citizens appointed for life by the king. The lower house, the House of Burgesses, was an elected legislature, with two burgesses from each county and one member each from Jamestown, Williamsburg, Norfolk, and the College of William and Mary.

Only those who were white, male, and property owners could serve in the House of Burgesses. Only their peers could vote for them, and those voters drove a hard bargain. Candidates had to cater to them by offering some kind of libation, preferably alcoholic. The first time George Washington ran, he ignored this tradition and lost. The next time he provided a quart and a half for each of the 361 gentlemen who voted for him.

In the 1760s, as dissatisfaction with British rule began to mount, those burgesses who supported the Crown were called Old Field Nags and those calling for change were labeled High-Blooded Colts. As the final break neared in the early 1770s, few of the old guard were elected to the House. The Council met on one side of the building, the Burgesses on the other. When there was a need to resolve a conflict over an issue, representatives from each met in the Conference Room upstairs, above the piazza that separated the two sides of the building.

In 1774, there were 130 burgesses, among them George Washington, Thomas Jefferson, and Patrick Henry. The burgesses had no assigned seating in their meeting chamber, other than George Wythe (Thomas Jefferson's mentor) at the front table recording events as clerk and Peyton Randolph sitting in the front chair as Speaker of the House. The Speaker's chair here is a reproduction. The original is on display in the nearby DeWitt Wallace Decorative Arts Museum. The Speaker of the House was chosen by the burgesses, but their choice had to be approved by the royal governor. Once this approval was given, the mace of the House, previously placed under the main table, was then placed on top

Patrick Henry

Contrary to common belief, Patrick Henry's "Give me liberty or give me death!" speech in March 1775 was not delivered in the House of Burgesses but in St. John's Church in Richmond. Still, reverberations were felt here and could be credited as being one of the reasons Lord Dunmore removed the powder from Williamsburg's magazine. Henry, once described as "a Quaker in religion but the very devil in politics," was a self-educated lawyer whose hardscrabble exterior played to the common people of Virginia, especially those who felt they had little in common with the plantation families. Though he spent his life in government service, Henry remained an outsider. A devout states'-rights advocate, Henry opposed the U.S. Constitution, declined when George Washington offered him the post of Secretary of State, and again when offered that of envoy to France. He ran for public office once more in 1799 but died before he was able to take his seat in the Virginia legislature.

as a sign that legislative business could commence. Neither the burgesses nor the Council members were paid for their service.

The General Court met in the Capitol, on the ground floor across from the House. An attempt was made to ensure trials were decided relatively quickly. Jurors, who could only be white male property owners, were sequestered with no food, drink, candles, or fire until they'd reached their decision.

The first capitol building on this site was gutted by fire in 1747; the second, completed in 1753, burned down in 1832. This reproduction is based on the first design because of that design's distinctiveness and because there were more architectural records of the first building.

The nearby Secretary's Office, an original building on the Capitol's northwest side, was the repository of some of the colony's most important documents, including land-office records and records of the House of Burgesses. As the keeper of the records, the secretary of the General Court was an extremely influential individual, whose influence was also felt in his appointments of clerks to all the county courts. The building now contains an interesting exhibit called "Choosing Revolution" that includes maps of the area in 1774. Visitors can also buy tickets here for special events.

The **Public Gaol**, north of the Capitol, is where the accused were held until their trial. The grim interior of this partially original building testifies to the harsh treatment meted out to innocent and guilty alike. Unless a prisoner had influential friends and/or money to provide better food and accommodations, she or he was forced to make do with one thin blanket and one meal a day of "salt beef, damaged, and Indian meal." Just as bad was the lack of fresh air and light. Amazingly, abiding with the miserable debtors, runaway slaves, and other prisoners were the gaoler and his family, whose quarters were on the first floor. Visitors can join the family as they go about their daily activities. The gallows out back of the gaol is a reproduction of one that stood just outside town.

Citizens who skipped church on Sunday might find themselves before the justices in the county **Courthouse** on Market Square. Not attending church constituted 35 percent of the crimes brought before

this court in the mid-1770s. Debtors, thieves, and card sharks were also tried here, and in most cases sentences were carried out immediately, often at the pillory out front or at the nearby whipping post. One of Colonial Williamsburg's most popular programs, *Order in the Court!*, presented in this original building, gives visitors an opportunity to become a defendant, a witness, or a justice in a reenactment of an actual 18th-century trial.

In the **Magazine**, facing the Courthouse across Market Square, more than 60,000 pounds of gunpowder, 2000 to 3000 muskets, and other arms were once stored. Visitors will see hundreds of period muskets, many of the variety affectionately called Brown Bess. Why it was given that nickname has been lost in history—some think it's because of the brown color of its walnut stock—but it was the dependable staple of the British and, later, Colonial armies. Rudyard Kipling even wrote a poem in praise of the deadly lady, which ends with the verse, *If you go to Museums— there's one in Whitehall/ Where old weapons are shown with their names writ beneath,/ You will find her, upstanding, her back to the wall,/ As stiff as a ramrod, the flint in her teeth./ And if ever we English had reason to bless/ Any arm save our mothers', that arm is Brown Bess!*

The same might be said of Virginia's colonial militia, which drilled in front of the Magazine on Market Square. A colonial militia wasn't just a citizens' army. It took the place of the fire and police departments, and was considered a major civic duty, required of all men ages 16 to 60. Only one colony, Pennsylvania, didn't require militia service, due to its strong Quaker influence.

The original **Peyton Randolph House**—north of the Courthouse— is interesting for its interiors and furnishings, and for its depiction of the domestic life of one of Williamsburg's wealthiest men. Though little known outside Virginia, Peyton Randolph was one of the major figures of the American Revolution. A member of one of Virginia's leading families, Randolph studied law at the Inns of Court in London, was appointed attorney general of Virginia in 1744, and was elected to the House of Burgesses in 1748.

As Speaker of the House in the 1760s, Randolph was considered

Many original Williamsburg residences have been converted into shops selling typical 18th-century products. At the Ayscough House, left, reproduction flint-lock rifles, pistols, fowling pieces, knives, tomahawks, and powder-horns are made. Below, an interpreter demon-strates the musket drills of Virginia's militiamen.

one of the Old Field Nags because of his moderate views; but he sided with the colonies when it became clear that England had no intention of compromising, and he presided over every important session of the House in the years prior to the war. Interestingly, his brother John remained loyal to the Crown and a confidant of Lord Dunmore's. Peyton chaired both the First and Second Continental Congresses, and worked with his cousin Thomas Jefferson on pushing Virginia toward independence. His sudden death in Philadelphia in October 1775 was considered a great loss to the Congress and to Virginia.

The historical interpreters at the Peyton Randolph House do a partic-ularly fine job in presenting the diffi-culty in the choices made by mem-bers of the household in the prewar years, as well as the contradiction inherent in Randolph's fighting for freedom even as he remained a slaveholder. This is especially true in the story of Eve, Mrs. Randolph's personal maid, who saw her older son sold to another household and determined to keep her younger son with her by running away to the British.

The **George Wythe House,** an even grander home, has been recon-structed, although the kitchen is original. Like Randolph, Wythe (pro-nounced "with") is little known today but was a dominant figure in

the colonies before the war. A profes-sor of law and a judge, a member and clerk of the House of Burgesses, a signer of the Declaration of Independence and one of the framers of the Constitution, Wythe was described by his protégé Jefferson as "the Cato of his coun-try" because of his integrity and his devotion to the cause of liberty. Wythe's death was something of a scandal, as it's thought he was poi-soned by his indolent grandnephew. The grandnephew was brought to trial but went free because the only witness was an African American, and she wasn't allowed to testify against a white person in court.

Cooking demonstrations of the nonpoisonous variety are given in the Wythe kitchen, children's games and hands-on activities are in the backyard, and the stable and laun-dry provide demonstrations of 18th-century transportation and house-hold crafts.

Visitors who'd like information on 18th-century crafts can visit the cabinetmaker, blacksmith, miller, sil-versmith, apothecary, shoemaker, printer, bookbinder, and wigmaker to ask questions of the tradespeople themselves. Booklets on these trades are available at the **Printing Office, Post Office,** and **Bookbindery.** For those interested in 18th-century small arms, gunsmiths at **Ayscough House** fashion iron, steel, brass, and wood into firearms, and they readily answer questions about rifles, fowling pieces, and muskets.

The DeWitt Wallace Decorative Arts Museum, at the southwest corner of the Historic Area, demonstrates the transition from a British culture to an American one in the colonies before, during, and after the war. It is home to a wide-ranging collection of American and British antiques, including furniture, textiles, tools, ceramics, silver, pewter, and clothing from the 17th, 18th, and 19th centuries. There is an extensive display of firearms. Among them is a selection of British military muskets, with the parts labeled and an evaluation of their accuracy. Unique guns displayed include a 1738 Land Service Pistol, a 1784 fowling piece, and a rare 1760 Indian Trade Gun.

Entrance to the museum is through the **Public Hospital,** the first asylum for the insane in the colonies. Proposed by Royal Governor Francis Fauquier to care "for these miserable Objects, who cannot help themselves," the hospital was established by the House of Burgesses in 1773. Though advanced for its day, the hospital employed mechanical restraints, drugs, the ducking chair, and bleeding in treatments. A chillingly realistic re-creation of an inmate's room in the 18th century, complete with chains on the wall, contrasts with the more enlightened treatments of the 19th century, prior to the hospital's burning to the ground in 1885.

Visitor Information
1-800-HISTORY or 757-253-2277
www.colonialwilliamsburg.org
Hours: Colonial Williamsburg is open every day of the year, including holidays and December 25, 9 a.m. until 5 p.m., with seasonal variations. Some of the auxiliary buildings may be temporarily closed on certain days (check the Visitor's Companion), but the main buildings are usually open. Hours for the DeWitt Wallace Decorative Arts Museum change seasonally.
Admission: There are significant fees for visiting Colonial Williamsburg. The Freedom Pass gives visitors 12-month admission to all areas and walking tours, plus 50 percent off evening programs. The General Admission Ticket provides one-day admission to the Historic Area and the museums.
Accessibility: Special accommodations are available, when requested in advance, as are special parking arrangements to provide easier access to the Historic Area. Many of the main buildings are accessible by wheelchair, and there are accessible restrooms located throughout the Historic Area. Some of the 88 original buildings are not accessible, but costumed interpreters on-site provide information and highlights. Hands-on activities are available at certain exhibits, which are particularly informative for the visually impaired, as is the introductory Walking Tour. Escorts are available, with advance notice. The booklet "Colonial Williamsburg: A Guide for Deaf and Hearing Impaired Visitors" and a printed synopsis of the orientation film *Williamsburg: The Story of a Patriot* are available free of charge at the Visitor Center. Headsets with adjustable volume control are available for the orientation film, as well as for lecture programs.
Special Events: There are numerous programs throughout the day highlighting the politics of the time, as well as offerings in the Play Booth Theater, an outdoor venue. Sixty-minute walking tours, available mid-March through mid-December, explore topics such as the Revolution and African American life in colonial Virginia. A wide variety of evening programs, such as "Cry Witch" (a witch trial), "Papa Said; Mama Said" (African American oral histories), and "Colonial Kids on Parade" (colonial life through a child's eyes), greatly enhance the Colonial Williamsburg experience. Schedules are included in the weekly Visitor's Companion.
Getting There: By car: Colonial Williamsburg is midway between Richmond and Norfolk on I-64 (exit 238). After exiting, green and white signs lead the way to the Visitor Center, the only area where parking is allowed. Shuttle buses circle the perimeter of the Historic Area from 8:50 a.m. until 10 p.m.

By train or bus: Amtrak connects to the Williamsburg Transportation Center from Washington, D.C. The center is a few blocks from the Historic Area and has car rentals, cabs, and Greyhound Bus connections.

***Reenactors** representing British troops take part in the annual October 19 celebration of the American and French victory at Yorktown.*

Colonial National Historical Park

"I have the Honor to inform Congress, that a Reduction of the British Army under the Command of Lord Cornwallis, is most happily effected. The unremitting Ardor which actuated every Officer and Soldier in the combined Army in this Occasion, has principally led to this Important Event, at an earlier period than my most sanguine Hope had induced me to expect." With these few words, George Washington presented a new nation to the Continental Congress. Though it was uncertain at the time, Yorktown proved to be the decisive battle of the war.

Prefaced by an incredible military maneuver (moving more than 7000 men 400 miles in a 30-day march) and culminating in relatively few casualties (156 killed, 326 wounded for the British; 75 killed, 200 wounded for the French and Americans), the Battle of Yorktown broke the British will and ensured the eventual victory of the Continental forces.

Today, Yorktown Battlefield is part of the Colonial National Historical Park. Nearby is the Yorktown Victory Center, operated by the Commonwealth of Virginia's Jamestown-Yorktown Foundation.

The British Fleet
Loses the Advantage

As with any major battle, the events leading up to Yorktown may seem scattered and chaotic, yet they form an inevitable course rushing determinedly to conclusion.

In February 1781, Washington sent the Marquis de Lafayette with an army of 1200 New England and New Jersey troops south from New York to defend Virginia from increasing British incursions. The winter of 1781 had been a horrible ordeal for the Continental Army, to the point that a mutiny had barely been averted. The men had signed on for three years or until the end of the war, and they hadn't expected to be still freezing and hungry in another winter camp. They were worried about their families, farms, and businesses, and were questioning whether this war would simply drag on until men and resources were exhausted.

Even their commander in chief was feeling the futility of the American position. "Instead of having the prospect of a glorious offensive campaign before us, we have a bewildered and gloomy defensive one, unless we should receive a powerful aid of ships, land troops, and

The Battle of the Virginia Capes

The Battle of the Virginia Capes was preceded by Admiral Sir Samuel Hood and his fleet of 14 ships' setting out to head off Admiral François Joseph Paul, Comte de Grasse. De Grasse had been successfully harassing the Royal Navy in the West Indies and was supposedly heading north to harass Cornwallis, as well as bring needed troops to Lafayette's contingent in Virginia. Hood arrived in Chesapeake Bay in Maryland, where he expected to confront de Grasse. With de Grasse not in sight, Hood assumed he was the victim of faulty intelligence and that the French were really on their way to New York to attack the British fleet. Hood immediately set sail for New York.

On reaching New York, Hood found no French there, but he did find Admiral Thomas Graves, who was disgruntled at Hood's decision to return. Graves immediately took charge of the fleet. This was unfortunate for the British, as history has judged Graves something of a fool and Hood an exceptional commander. Graves now sailed south because he had reports that the French were heading in that direction from their base in Newport, Rhode Island.

On the morning of September 5, the British fleet sighted de Grasse's fleet in Chesapeake Bay and mistook it for the fleet coming down from Rhode Island. De Grasse, surprised to see the British, didn't want to be cornered in the bay, and undertook to get his ships out to open sea, where they could maneuver better. Unfortunately for de Grasse, he was facing a north-northeasterly wind that, coupled with the flood tide entering the bay, made it a slow pull for his fleet. Graves could have easily picked off the French ships as they exited the bay; but instead he chose to arrange his ships in a formal line of battle. This gave the French time to arrange themselves in a similar configuration. In late afternoon, the fighting began, lasting until dark and ending in a draw.

For the next week, the fleets maneuvered around each other, but did not again engage in any action. On September 11, Graves lost his advantage when the long-expected second French fleet arrived from Newport to support the Americans. Graves was now outnumbered. Yet with the fate of Cornwallis and some 8000 British troops in the balance, Hood and several other commanders strongly felt the fleet should make a fight of it. Graves, ever cautious, decided to turn tail and head back to New York, leaving Cornwallis and his troops trapped.

The significance of the sea battle was immediately apparent. Cornwallis was now unprotected on the York River side, and Washington's army was approaching by land. General George Weedon wrote to General Nathanael Greene, "The business with his Lordship in this State will very soon be at an end, for I suppose you know e'er this that we have got him handsomely in a pudding bag with 5000 land forces and about 60 ships including transports." Cornwallis himself soon felt the drawstrings of the bag pulling tighter.

money from our generous allies, and these, at present, are too contingent to build upon." Discouraged as Washington was, however, he did not despair and wrote to Congress, "The game is yet in our own hands; to play it well is all we have to do. . . . Certain I am that it is in our power to bring the war to a happy conclusion."

Once Lafayette arrived in Virginia, he limited his small force to hit-and-run actions, for, as he wrote Washington, "Were I to fight a battle, I should be cut to pieces. I am therefore determined to skirmish, but not to engage too far." Anthony Wayne and his three regiments of Pennsylvanians joined Lafayette on June 25. Others followed, and soon Lafayette had command of 4500 men, including 3000 Virginia militia.

Meanwhile, Major General Lord Charles Cornwallis was moving down the York Peninsula. Finally, with an eye to naval reinforcements, Cornwallis established his forces at York, a port on the York River.

The British general had been disappointed by the lack of support from the Loyalists in the South, and was feeling rebellious at being sent hither and yon with expectations of that support. "I am quite tired of marching about the country in quest of adventures," he had written his close friend Major General William Phillips months before the current campaign. "If we mean an offensive war in America, we must abandon New York and bring our whole force to Virginia; we then have a stake to fight for and a successful battle may give us America."

Of course, Cornwallis couldn't have known that America would, in effect, be lost because of a sea battle (*see* The Battle of the Virginia Capes, left), that hinged on the questionable judgment of the British naval commander he would be depending on as his backup.

In late September, Cornwallis, holed up in Yorktown, received a letter from Sir Henry Clinton in New York from which Cornwallis understood that Graves would depart with 5000 fresh troops and 23 ships-of-the-line no later than October 5. Whether Cornwallis misinterpreted a hope as a promise is not known; but he determined to wait for reinforcements rather than try to break out of the trap he was in. As Cornwallis wrote in a letter following the surrender, "I thought it would have been wanton and inhuman to the last degree to sacrifice the lives of this small body of gallant soldiers." It truly was a very small body—just 8800—compared to the force of 17,600 that George Washington was assembling to meet them.

Washington's Move South

Washington was in a position to pick his fights. Funded by French generosity—Lieutenant General Jean Baptiste Donatien de Vimeur, Comte de Rochambeau, had given Washington the equivalent of 20,000 dollars in gold from his army's treasury—he'd chosen to attack Clinton in New York first, then move against Cornwallis and thwart Britain's Southern Campaign. While meeting with Rochambeau in Rhode Island in the spring of 1781, however, Washington had learned that the French fleet would be sailing to the West Indies, which meant a change in strategy, since Washington had counted on the fleet to help him in the battle for New York.

In mid-August, Washington and his French allies had begun a grueling march to Yorktown, after ferrying across the Hudson River near New York City. Day after day, longboats and rafts ferried men, horses, guns, and wagons, and yet there was no sign of a British ship nor of any land forces to stop them.

The men were kept in the dark about where they were going and why. In his journal, James Thacher, an army doctor, wrote, "General Washington possesses a capacious mind, full of resources, and he resolves and matures his great plans and designs under an impenetrable veil of secrecy."

This massive Continental Army arrived in Williamsburg, some 15 miles from Yorktown, in mid-September. With this addition to Lafayette's forces already stationed in Williamsburg, they outnumbered Cornwallis more than two to one.

The uniforms of the troops Cornwallis faced were a colorful mixture, representing a new alliance and a very different army. There were the Americans, many in homespun shirts. There were the French, among them the Bourbonnois in crimson and pink, the Royal Deux-Ponts in blue and yellow, and the Soissonois in red, blue, and yellow. There were also Canadians, members of the Second Canadian Regiment, which had been allied with American forces since early in 1776. And there were African Americans, members of the 1st Rhode Island, which had been mustered into service in 1778.

The British Redcoats, on the other side of the fortifications, probably gave little thought to whom they were fighting or how their opponents were dressed. They were more concerned with dwindling ammunition and supplies, even before the battle began. Joining them were Hessians and Loyalist troops.

The Siege of Yorktown

With Cornwallis unprotected on the water side, Washington had ordered Lafayette to cut off any escape by land. From September 28 to October 9, the American army dug trenches and moved up artillery to besiege the British fortifications. The fighting was fierce and unrelenting. The American and French forces pounded Yorktown with shells and the British made counterattacks, fighting for every redoubt, or earthworks fort.

By the second week in October, Cornwallis had learned the British army in New York had had to delay its departure. One possible escape route had been left open, and a desperate Cornwallis, who had by now moved to a cave at the bottom of a garden, tried to use it. The night of October 16, British troops by the thousands readied themselves to be ferried across the York River to Gloucester. But a terrible storm came up, preventing evacuation of the army, and Cornwallis ordered the action stopped.

On October 17, the fourth anniversary of Burgoyne's surrender at Saratoga, the haze from the bom-

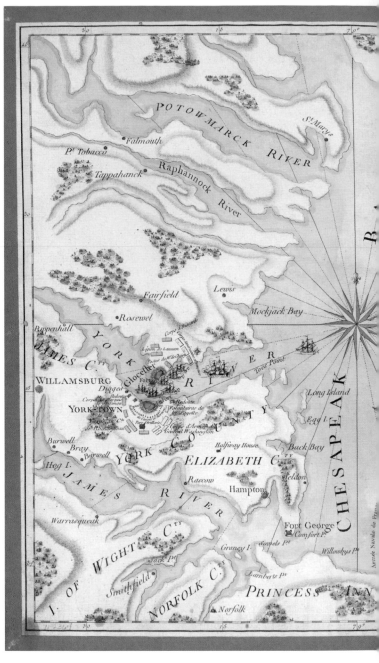

bardment of 52 French and American guns, which had temporarily stopped firing, dissolved long enough for a form to be made out on one of the parapets. It was a British drummer resolutely drumming out a request for a parley. One Pennsylvanian wrote he had "never heard a drum equal to it—the most delightful music to us all." Next an officer with a white cloth appeared, and a quiet settled over the field. The French, nearest the parapet, could easily have sent one of their officers to meet the British, but they were polite enough to send word to the nearest American officer.

A sealed letter was brought to George Washington: "I propose a cessation of hostilities for twenty four hours, and that two officers may be appointed by each side, to meet at Mr. Moore's house to settle terms for the surrender of the posts of York & Gloucester. I have the honor to be Sir Your most obedient and most humble Servant, Cornwallis."

Washington answered, "An Ardent Desire to spare the further Effusion of Blood, will readily incline me to listen to such Terms . . . as are admissible."

Two days later, negotiations for surrender were completed. Before affixing his signature, Washington added the words, "Done in the trenches before Yorktown, in Virginia, October 19, 1781." Washington was the first to sign it.

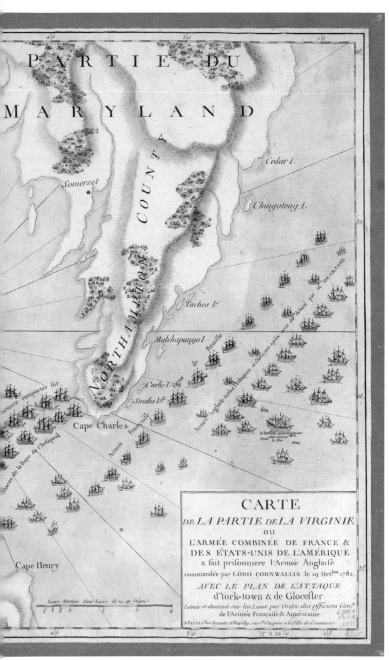

PARTIE DU

MARYLAND

NORTHAMPTON COUNTY

Somerset

Cedar I.

Chingoteag I.

Taches Is.

Malchapungo I.

Curlis I.

Smiths Isn.

Cape Charles

Cape Henry

Lieues Marines d'une heure de 10 au Degré

CARTE
DE *LA PARTIE DE LA VIRGINIE*
OU
L'ARMÉE COMBINÉE DE FRANCE &
DES ÉTATS-UNIS DE L'AMÉRIQUE
a fait prifonniere l'Armée Angloife
commandée par LORD CORNWALLIS le 19 Oct.bre 1781.
AVEC LE PLAN DE L'ATTAQUE
d'York-town & de Glocefter.
Levée et deffinée fur les Lieux par Ordre des Officiers Gen.x
de l'Armée Françoife & Américaine.
A PARIS, Chez Esnauts et Rapilly, rue S.t Jacque a la Fille de Coutances.

A French map drawn by participants depicting the events leading to the surrender at Yorktown. Center, de Grasse's fleet blockades Chesapeake Bay; far right, the Battle of the Capes; left, the deployment of troops at Yorktown on October 19, 1781.

At two p.m. that day, the British quit their defenses, with General Charles O'Hara of the Guards leading them. O'Hara first approached Rochambeau, who indicated the surrender should be made to General Washington. When O'Hara explained Cornwallis could not be there due to illness, Washington said a deputy should accept the surrender from a deputy, and he gave the honor to General Benjamin Lincoln, who had been defeated at Charleston.

The British soldiers laid down their arms, then returned to their works, from whence they would eventually be marched as prisoners of war to Winchester, in Virginia's Shenandoah Valley, or to Frederick,

Maryland.

Lord North, England's Prime Minister, is said to have exclaimed, "Oh, God! It is all over!" upon hearing news of the surrender. Though the British still held New York, Charleston, and Savannah, North recognized the gravity of the defeat. Three months after the news reached England, North resigned and the House of Commons was urging an end to the war, with a view to Britain retaining what territory it still held.

Despite this, peace was not a given. The war would drag on for two more years, and many more would die. But the three-week-long battle for Yorktown was the beginning of the end.

Yorktown Battlefield

The National Park Service's 9000-acre Colonial National Historical Park includes Yorktown Battlefield, Historic Jamestowne—site of the first permanent English settlement in North America (administered jointly with the Association for the Preservation of Virginia Antiquities)—the 17th-century plantation of Green Spring, and Cape Henry Memorial at the approximate landing site of the Jamestown colonists in 1607 and near which the Battle of the Capes was fought. Encompassed within the park are the beginning and the end of British rule in what came to be the United States.

Visitors should begin at the Visitor Center, which features an engaging 15-minute orientation film describing the events leading up to the siege and the battle itself. Just outside the theater is a display of the Lafayette Cannon, so-called because it was recognized by General Lafayette on his 1824 visit to America as one he'd seen in the battle. (He apparently recognized it because of a distinctive dent.) This display provides a close-up look at the implements used to fire the 12-pounder cannon—a rammer, ladle, wormer, and sponge—and explanations of how they were used. An exhibit on the battle includes a 3-pounder grasshopper

cannon, a diorama featuring a detailed depiction of the Battle of the Capes, and a re-creation of below-decks life of a ship at sea that visitors can walk through. Also on display are parts of General Washington's linen office and dining tents, and Lord Cornwallis's campaign table with folding trestle legs that made it portable.

A special exhibit for children is also of interest to adults, as it takes visitors through the battle with the narration of a young soldier barely into his teens. Told from this fictional youth's point of view, the interactive displays, models of the earthworks, and three-dimensional dioramas provide a rudimentary yet fascinating take on the momentous events at Yorktown.

There are two self-guided auto tours. One, a seven-mile battlefield tour that takes about an hour, includes earthworks, siege lines, redoubts 9 and 10, the overlook at Surrender Field, and the Moore House, site of the surrender negotiations. The other is a nine-mile encampment tour that includes Washington's headquarters, French and American artillery parks, the French cemetery, a redoubt, and the French encampment area.

The National Park Service

The World Turned Upside Down

Tradition has long held that the British played "The World Turned Upside Down" as they surrendered. Apparently this was first claimed in a book called *Anecdotes of the American Revolution*, which was published in 1828. Through the years, though, it has been an issue for many historians. Arthur Schrader of the Colonial Music Institute insists there is no tune by that name in any catalogue of 18th-century British tunes or marches. Henry Steele Commager and Richard B. Morris, in their book *The Spirit of 'Seventy-Six*, write that "Light Horse Harry" Lee said that a British march was played, and another spectator reported "a slow march." It's unlikely the issue will be settled anytime soon.

On September 28 the French and American armies began siege operations and started building parallel trenches. To complete the second parallel, Washington ordered the seizure of two British redoubts near the York River. On the evening of October 14, the Americans, with unloaded muskets and fixed bayonets, climbed over and through the obstructing abatis and within 10 minutes the garrison of Redoubt No. 10 was overwhelmed.

(NPS) has excellent audio tours for rent or sale at the Visitor Center that greatly enhance the experience of touring the battlefield. There's also very informative signage at each of the stops.

Visitors interested in artillery will note that there are 13 artillery pieces original to the battle here— 11 cannons mounted in the wall at the Surrender Field Pavilion and the two cannons in the Visitor Center. Each of the four types used at Yorktown is represented: the field cannon, the garrison cannon, the howitzer, and the mortar (used to launch bombs). Estimates number artillery pieces used by both sides during the battle at around 375, with the Americans and French firing an average of 1.2 cannonballs and bombs per minute.

The trench warfare evident at Yorktown reminds visitors of how little war strategies changed in the 135 years following, through the Civil War and World War I. In defending his position, Cornwallis had eight small redoubts dug, with trenches connecting them.

Siege trenches, called approach trenches, were deeply dug at an

Earthworks

Not all of the earthworks at Yorktown are original. Following the siege, Washington had the allied siege lines destroyed, so they couldn't be used against the French who were quartering at Yorktown that winter. The British earthworks were left intact, despite the efforts of Yorktown's citizens, who petitioned Congress for the funds to destroy them.

During the Civil War, Confederate forces did the job for free, modifying remaining British earthworks to their needs. Union forces constructed new earthworks in Washington's encampment areas. In the 1930s, the NPS began reconstructing the French and American siege lines, using archaeological evidence and documents.

The park service asks that visitors be especially mindful of the earthworks, and stick to the designated trails in order to preserve both the original and the reconstructed lines.

angle to the enemy's fortifications. Their purpose was to provide cover for troops and artillery as they inched closer to the enemy lines, ideally forming a crescent that would become smaller as the enemy lines retreated to ever-more-confined space.

The Americans and French dug their trenches 600 yards from the British line and, with their firepower, were able to knock the British guns out of action. A second American-French trench was then begun 400 yards from the British, but it was stopped by the presence of British Redoubts 9 and 10. On the night of October 14, French troops under the command of Lieutenant Colonel Count Guillaume de Deux-Ponts captured Redoubt 9 and Americans under the command of Lieutenant Colonel Alexander Hamilton took Redoubt 10, both in less than 30 minutes.

At the time of the Battle of Yorktown, the Moore House, home of Augustine Moore and his family, stood on a large estate near the town of York. The home was probably chosen for negotiations because it was sufficiently distant from the fighting. The British were represented by Lieutenant Colonel Thomas Dundas, member of a powerful

Scottish family, and Major Alexander Ross; the Americans by Lieutenant Colonel John Laurens; and the French by Louis-Marie, Viscomte de Noailles, Lafayette's brother-in-law.

The negotiations resulting in the Articles of Capitulation took less than a day. The 14 articles covered the disposition of troops, artillery, and arms, and the surrender ceremony. The soldiers would be taken as prisoners, with one field officer for every 50 men providing witness to their treatment. All remaining officers were allowed to keep their side arms and private property and return to Europe or New York, as long as they didn't engage in fighting again until officially exchanged for American prisoners.

On one point General Washington was adamant. It was the custom in such circumstances that the surrendering troops march out of their defenses flying their regimental flags and playing an enemy's tune in honor of the victor. But at the surrender of Charleston in May 1780, the Americans had not been afforded these so-called Honors of War, and Washington would not so honor the British. The British troops, according to the articles, would march out "with shouldered arms, colours cased, and drums beating a British

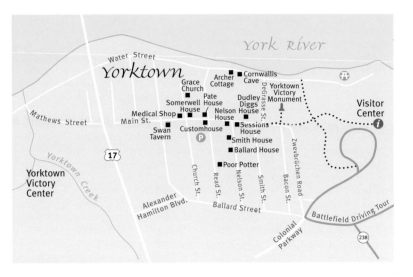

or German march."

The overlook at Surrender Field gives visitors a clear view of what it must have been like that day in mid-October when the British troops by the thousands did just that. Dr. Thacher, writing in his journal that day—"to us a most glorious day"—noted the solemnity of the occasion. "The French troops, in complete uniform, displayed a martial and noble appearance. . . . The Americans, though not all in uniform, nor their dress so neat, yet exhibited an erect, soldierly air. . . . The concourse of spectators from the country was prodigious, in point of numbers was probably equal to the military, but universal silence and order prevailed.

"It was about two o'clock when the captive army advanced through the line formed for their reception. . . . The royal troops, while marching through the line formed by the allied army, exhibited a decent and neat appearance, as respects arms and clothing, for their commander opened his store and directed every soldier to be furnished with a new suit complete, prior to the capitulation. . . .

"But it was in the field, when they came to the last act of the drama, that the spirit and pride of the British soldier was put to the severest test: here their mortification could not be concealed. Some of the platoon officers appeared to be severely chagrined when giving the word 'ground arms,' and I am a witness that they performed this duty in a very unofficer-like manner; and that many of the soldiers manifested a sullen temper, throwing their arms on the pile with violence, as if determined to render them useless."

The Visitor Center exhibit includes a Brown Bess musket whose stock was broken when the British soldier flung it on the pile.

Dr. Thacher also noted the disappointment of those present in not seeing Lord Cornwallis. "[W]hen it is considered that Lord Cornwallis has frequently appeared in splendid triumph at the head of his army, by which he is almost adored, we conceive it incumbent on him cheerfully to participate in their misfortunes and degradations, however humiliating; but it is said he gives himself up entirely to vexation and despair."

Yorktown

Located where the York River empties into Chesapeake Bay, the town of York was established in 1691 by the Virginia General Assembly, one of several port towns created to handle sea traffic and customs. By the early 1700s, the town was one of Virginia's major ports, and by the 1750s it had reached its peak with a population of around 1800 and more than 200 buildings.

The siege of Yorktown decimated the area. By the end of the war, there were fewer than 70 buildings in town and not even 600 residents. During the Civil War, the town was occupied by both sides and further damage was done. Yet the town was never given up for good, and today remains a lovely river town whose buildings reflect its colonial history. Two stops in particular relate to the Revolutionary War—the Nelson House and the Yorktown Victory Monument.

The Nelson House was the home of Thomas Nelson, Jr., an active Patriot throughout the war, who served as a delegate to the Second Continental Congress and as governor of Virginia, was a signer of the Declaration of Independence, and commanded the Virginia militia as a brigadier general at the Battle of Yorktown. His home still bears the scars of artillery shells from that battle.

The Yorktown Victory Monument (officially known as the Monument to the Alliance and Victory) was enthusiastically authorized by Congress in October 1781, just days after the news of the surrender reached Philadelphia. Construction began 100 years later. Completed in 1884, the monument consists of Liberty atop a shaft of Maine granite and stands almost 100 feet high. A nearby plaque commemorates members of the French fleet who died at the Battle of the Capes, and another lists the French officers and their regiments who took part in the Battle of Yorktown.

Visitor Information
757-898-2410
www.nps.gov/colo and
www.nps.gov/colo/Yorktown/
ythome.htm
Hours: The park grounds close at sunset. Yorktown Visitor Center is open daily from 9 a.m. until 5 p.m. The park and Visitor Center are closed on December 25 and January 1.
Admission: There is a moderate charge for adults age 17 and older. Admission is good for 7 days from the date of purchase. A combination ticket to Historic Jamestowne is available for approximately 50 percent more.
Accessibility: The Visitor Center is accessible, as are most areas of the battlefield. Wheelchair accessibility to the Nelson House is usually available with 2 hours' advance notice.
Special Events: Major celebrations are held on the Fourth of July and on Yorktown Day, October 19. Ranger-led walking tours of the British siege lines and the town of York are offered throughout the year. During the summer, rangers give artillery demonstrations, and offer tours of the Nelson House and the Moore House. Families with children 12 and under may take part in the Colonial Junior Ranger program. Sundays and Thursdays during the summer the Fifes and Drums of York Town perform at the Visitor Center.
Getting There: By car: The 23-mile Colonial Parkway that connects Virginia's historic triangle (Williamsburg, Yorktown, and Jamestown) can be reached from I-64 east via route 199, taking exit 242B, and from I-64 west via route 105 east, taking exit 250B to route 17 north.

By bus: There are Greyhound stations in Newport News and Williamsburg, and rental cars and taxi services available.

By train: There are Amtrak stations in Newport News and Williamsburg, and rental cars and taxi services available.

Yorktown Victory Center

The Yorktown Victory Center combines imaginatively devised indoor exhibits and realistic outdoor living-history exhibits to enfold visitors in the experiences of average Americans during the Revolutionary War.

Beginning with an outdoor walkway that details the time line leading up to the war, and continuing through a series of exhibition galleries, re-creations of a Continental Army encampment, and a 1780s Tidewater Virginia farm, the center vividly evokes a time when everyday life demanded difficult decisions that could have devastating effects.

The experience unfolds here along "The Road to Revolution" time line in a series of four pavilions covering the years 1750 to 1776. The time line panels mounted along the walkway chronologically list the events leading up to the Declaration of Independence, with both the British and American point of view represented. The pavilions cover the problems growing out of the 1763 treaty that ended the French and Indian War, cite issues over taxation, display information about trade issues, and, leading indoors, describe the beginnings of armed conflict.

Inside the museum, the entry area includes a large reproduction of a sketch made by a 14-year-old North Carolina girl in her mathematics notebook on "Liberty or Death," evidence of how even children were drawn into the issue of rebellion.

The "Witnesses to Revolution" gallery powerfully presents the struggles of 10 people with very diverse lives. Among these are two African American slaves who have chosen separate sides, a Native American who struggles to remain neutral, a Loyalist, two Continental soldiers, and a woman captured by Indians before the war who must now decide where her loyalties lie. The oral testimony of each character is complemented by life-size cast figures, along with graphics and artifacts from their lives that bring a compelling immediacy to the experience.

In the "Converging on Yorktown" gallery, a neon map highlights British, French, and American troop movements during the battle. Among the artifacts here are two flintlock pistols owned by the Marquis de Lafayette. There's also an 18-minute film, *A Time of Revolution*, that continues the theme of ordinary people in extraordinary circumstances, through the voices of soldiers writing home the night before battle.

"To the Water's Edge: Yorktown's Sunken Fleet" dramatically presents the fascinating story of the British ships sunk offshore in the York River. From the floor above, visitors look down at a re-creation of what divers saw when they first discovered the sunken ship *Betsy*. Proceeding down a ramp takes visitors to cases containing several dozen artifacts from the wreck (excavated between 1982 and 1989), such as a cannon carriage, a window from the captain's cabin, and a pewter spigot. Intriguing is the 1772 copper coin the shipwright placed at the base of the mast to ensure good winds, a common custom of the time. There's also a depiction of life on board the brig, with details of how the ship functioned and how it was constructed, and a model of a similar 18th century English vessel.

"A Soldier's Lot" features exhibits on military life and medicine during the war, with displays of 18th-century surgical instruments used in the field, an apothecary chest, and books listing the rules of military life. There are also arms such as a long rifle circa 1790 and a Brown Bess musket circa 1750.

"The Unfinished Revolution" exhibit highlights the critical transition years of the 1780s, with the end of the war and the adoption of the Constitution and the Bill of Rights. The Yorktown Victory Center also includes a special exhibition gallery offering temporary exhibits related to the war; a children's discovery room where younger visitors can learn about the 18th-century through trying on costumes, playing games, and other activities; and an Adult Resource Room that provides computer stations and reading materials for more in-depth information about topics explored in the museum galleries.

Outdoors is a re-creation of a Continental Army encampment, with historical interpreters on-site to answer questions about camp life and demonstrate military drilling and musket firing, camp cooking techniques, and medical procedures used to treat sick and injured soldiers. Each day, visitors are invited to join the artillery crew in going through the many steps preparatory to firing a cannon.

The re-created Tidewater Virginia farm, which features a farmhouse, kitchen, tobacco barn, outbuildings and gardens, provides an opportunity to explore the life of a typical farming family after the war. Historical interpreters demonstrate open-hearth cooking, farming techniques, and herbal medicine. Visitors can learn such skills as hoeing and breaking flax into fiber.

The foundation's Jamestown Settlement is 20 miles away, off I-64, and includes gallery exhibits and re-creations of James Fort, a Powhatan Indian Village, and life-size replicas of the three English ships that sailed to Virginia in 1607.

Visitor Information

888-593-4682 or 757-253-4838
www.historyisfun.org/

Hours: The Yorktown Victory Center is open daily 9 a.m. until 5 p.m. year-round, and from 9 a.m. until 6 p.m. mid-June through mid-August. Closed December 25 and January 1.

Admission: There is a significant charge for adults, a lower one for children ages 6 through 12.

Accessibility: The Center, its open-air exhibits, and its outdoor living-history exhibits are all accessible. Assistive-listening systems are available for films and outdoor living-history exhibits. Sign-language interpreters are available with a minimum of 2 weeks advance notice.

Special Events: Major celebrations are held on the Fourth of July and on the weekend closest to October 19, Yorktown Victory Day. Other special programs are held throughout the year highlighting aspects of 18th-century life. Check the Web site for schedules.

Getting There: By car: From I-64 take exit 247.

By bus: There are Greyhound stations in Newport News and Williamsburg, and rental cars and taxi services available.

By train: There are Amtrak stations in Newport News and Williamsburg, and rental cars and taxi services available.

Selected Bibliography

Bakeless, John. *Turncoats, Traitors, and Heroes, Espionage in the American Revolution.*
New York, NY: Da Capo Press, 1998.

Boatner, Mark M. III. *Landmarks of the American Revolution.* Harrisburg, PA:
Stackpole Books, 1973.

Buchanan, John. *The Road to Guilford Courthouse, The American Revolution
in the Carolinas.* New York, NY: John Wiley & Sons, Inc., 1997.

Chartrand, René. *The French Army in the American War of Independence.*
Oxford, England: Osprey Publishing, 2002.

Commager, Henry Steele, ed. and Richard B. Morris, ed.
The Spirit of 'Seventy-Six, The Story of the American Revolution As Told By Participants.
New York, NY: Harper & Row, Publishers, 1975.

Debo, Angie. *A History of the Indians of the United States.* Norman, OK:
University of Oklahoma Press, 1970.

DePauw, Linda Grant. *Founding Mothers, Women of America in the Revolutionary Era.*
New York, NY: Houghton Mifflin Company, 1975.

Fischer, David Hackett. *Paul Revere's Ride.* New York, NY:
Oxford University Press, 1994.

Furbee, Mary Rodd. *Outrageous Women of Colonial America.* New York, NY:
John Wiley & Sons, Inc., 2001.

Hagan, Kenneth J. *This People's Navy, The Making of American Sea Power.*
New York: NY, Touchstone Books, 1991.

Harris, Sharon M., ed. *Women's Early American Historical Narratives.*
New York, NY: Penguin Books, 2003.

Harvey, Robert. *A Few Bloody Noses, The Realities and Mythologies of the
American Revolution.* Woodstock, NY: The Overlook Press, 2001.

Haskins, Jim. *Black Stars of Colonial and Revolutionary Times, African Americans
Who Lived Their Dreams.* New York, NY: John Wiley & Sons, Inc., 2002.

Hogg, Ian V. and John H. Batchelor, S. L. Mayer, ed. *Armies of the American Revolution.*
Englewood Cliffs, NJ: Prentice-Hall, Inc., 1975.

Howarth, Steven. *To Shining Sea, A History of the United States Navy,
1885-1998.* Norman, OK: University of Oklahoma Press, 1999.

Lancaster, Bruce. *The American Revolution.* New York, NY: Mariner Books, 2001.

Langguth, A. J. *Patriots, The Men Who Started the American Revolution.*
Touchstone Books, 1989.

Lawrence, Alexander A. *Storm Over Savannah.* Savannah, GA: Tara Press, 1979.

Leckie, Robert. *George Washington's War.* New York, NY: Harper Perennial, 1993.

May, Robin. *The British Army in North America, 1775-83.*
Oxford, England: Osprey Publishing, 2002.

McCullough, David. J*ohn Adams.* New York, NY: Touchstone Books, 2001.

Miller, Nathan. *The U.S. Navy.*
New York, NY: American Heritage Publishing Co.,1977.

Morgan, William James, ed. *Naval Documents of the American Revolution, Volume 6.*
Washington, D.C.: U.S. Government Printing Office, 1972.

Murphy, Jack. *History of the U. S. Marines.* Emmaus, PA: JG Press, 2003.

Neumann, George C. *Battle Weapons of the American Revolution.*
Texarkana, TX: Scurlock Publishing Co., 1998.

Peterson, Harold L. *The Book of the Continental Soldier.*
Harrisburg, PA: Stackpole Books, 1968.

Silverstone, Paul H. *The Sailing Navy, 1775-1854.*
Annapolis, MD: Naval Institute Press, 2001.

Stember, Sol. *The Bicentennial Guide to the American Revolution.*
New York, NY: Saturday Review Press, 1974.

Sweetman, Jack. *The U.S. Naval Academy.*
Annapolis, MD: Naval Institute Press, 1995.

Ward, Christopher. *The War of the Revolution, Volumes One and Two.*
New York, NY: The MacMillan Company, 1952.

Wilbur, Keith C. *The Revolutionary Soldier, 1775-1783.*
Guilford, CT: The Globe Pequot Press, 1993.

Zlatich, Marko. *General Washington's Army, 1775-78.*
Oxford, England: Osprey Publishing, 2001.
———, *General Washington's Army, 1779-83.*
Oxford, England: Osprey Publishing, 2001.

Acknowledgments

In writing this book, I've been fortunate in having the enthusiastic support and assistance of dozens of historians, site managers, and museum curators, among them members of the National Park Service and the park services of individual states. These branches of government are exemplary in protecting and preserving our nation's Revolutionary War heritage and deserve our most sincere gratitude.

I'd like to particularly thank historian John Buchanan in his role as consultant for his invaluable guidance and excellent suggestions, copyeditor Jane Neighbors for catching the mistakes and asking the tough questions, proofreader Dave Hall, and Amy Wilson for her dogged pursuit of elusive site contacts and their even more elusive photographs. Also for her aid in preparing text files for the designer.

Picture Credits

History of the U.S. = Spencer, J. A. *History of the United States of America.*
   New York: Johnson, Wilson & Company, 1874.
Life of Washington = Schroeder, John Frederick. *Life and Times of Washington.*
   New York: Johnson, Fry, and Company, 1857
U.S. Army = courtesy U. S. Army Center of Military History, www.army.mil/cmh-pg

Front cover ©FOLIO/Omni-Photo Communications; **Page 1** courtesy PRC/Picture Research Consultants, Topsfield, MA; Page 6–7 Richard J. Berenson; 9 Drawing courtesy of John Batchelor. Courtesy Chief of Naval Operations, Submarine Warfare Division; 11 courtesy Fort Griswold Battlefield State Park; 12 Library of Congress, Geography and Map Division; 14 courtesy Fort Griswold Battlefield State Park; 17 *History of the U.S.;* 19 National Archives; 21 courtesy National Park Service. Museum Management Program and Valley Forge N.H.P. VAFO 124 Flintlock Musket, VAFO 137, Musket, VAFO 709 Socket Bayonet, VAFO 109 Short Land Service Musket, www.cr.nps.gov/museim/exhibits/revwar/image_gal/vafoimg/vafo1091 24137709. html; 22, 23, 24 Smithsonian Institution's National Museum of American History, Behring Center; 26, 27 courtesy Delaware State Museums; 30 © Bettmann/ CORBIS; 32 U.S. Army; 35, 36–37 courtesy Blue Licks Battlefield State Resort Park; 38-39 © Kevin R. Morris/CORBIS; 40–41 © David Heath, 1daat Media Services; 42, 43, 44 courtesy of the U.S. Naval Academy Museum; 45 © Paul A. Souders/ CORBIS; 46 *History of the U.S.;* 49, 50 *Life of Washington;* 53 *History of the U.S.;* 54 U.S. Army; 57 courtesy Boston National History Park; 61 courtesy Concord Museum, Concord, MA; www.concordmuseum.org; photograph by David Bohl; 62 courtesy Concord Museum, Concord, MA; www.concordmuse um.org; photograph by Chip Fanelli; 63 Collection of the U.S. Senate/Senate Commission on Art; 64 courtesy Concord Museum, Concord, MA; www.concordmuseum.org; and Lexington Historical Society, Lexington, MA; www.lexington history.org; photograph by David Bohl; 65 Courtesy Concord Museum, Concord, MA; www.concordmuseum.org; photograph by David Bohl; 66–67 Courtesy Concord Museum, Concord, MA; www.concordmuseum.org; 68, 69 courtesy Minute Man National Historical Park; 75, 77 courtesy Salem Maritime National Historic Site; 78 courtesy Peabody Essex Museum; 84, 85 courtesy Mackinaw State Historic Parks; 86, 87 courtesy Monmouth Battlefield State Park, photographs by Patricia Robinson; 88 U.S. Army; 89 *History of the U.S.;* 91 courtesy National Park Service. Museum Management Program and Morristown N.H.P. MORR 1892-1893, Ice Creepers; www.cr.nps.gov/museum/exhibits/revwar/image_gal/morrimg/creepersmorr.html; **93 top** courtesy National Park Service. Museum Management Program and Morristown N.H.P. MORR 2022, Canteen, www.cr.nps.gov/museum/exhibits/revwar/image_gal/morrimg/canteenmorr.html; **93 middle** courtesy National Park Service. Museum Management Program and Morristown N.H.P. MORR 3884, Military Cocked Hat, www.cr.nps.gov/museum/exhibits/revwar/image_gal/morrimg/hatcocked.html; **93 bottom** Courtesy National Park Service. Museum Management Program and Morristown N.H.P. MORR 830, Fascine Knife; www.cr.nps.gov/museum/exhibits/revwar/image_gal/morrimg/knifefascine.html; 95 Library of Congress, Prints and Photographs Division; 98-99 *Battle of Princeton* by James Pearle. Princeton University. Courtesy PRC/Picture Research Consultants, Topsfield, MA.; 102–103 Library of Congress, Geography and Map Division; 105 National Archives; 109 Richard J. Berenson; 110–111 *History of the U.S.;* 114 courtesy Old Stone House Historic Interpretive Center; 119, 120 Fraunces Tavern Museum, New York City; 127 Library of Congress, Geography and Map Division; 128–129 courtesy National Park Service, Fort Stanwix N.M.; 131 © Lee Snider/CORBIS; 133 *History of U.S.;* 134 Library of Congress, Geography and Map Division; 136 © Lee Snider/ CORBIS; 139 bottom U.S. Army; 141 courtesy National Park Service. Museum Management Program and Valley Forge NHP; VAFO 172,

Credits *(continued)*

Rifle, www.cr.nps.gov/museums/exhibits/revwar/image_gal/vafoimg/vafo172.html;
142, 143 Angel Art, Ltd./Old Fort Niagara; **146–147** © Bettmann/ CORBIS; **151** courtesy
National Park Service, Saratoga N.H.P.; **152, 153** courtesy West Point Museum Art
Collection, United States Military Academy; **156-157 bottom** Library of Congress,
Geography and Map Division; **158** *History of the U.S.*; **160–161 top** Library of Congress,
Geography and Map Division; **160 bottom** courtesy National Park Service, Museum
Management Program and Guilford Courthouse National Military Park, MORR 4943,
Link of West Point Chain, www.cr.nps.gov/museum/exhibits/revwar/image_ gal/mor-
rimg/linkwestpointchain.html; **162, 163** *History of U.S.*; **164, 165** West Point Museum
Art Collection, United States Military Academy; **168–169** U.S. Army; **170 top** Courtesy
National Park Service, Museum Management Program and Guilford Courthouse
National Military Park; GUCO 30, Light Dragoon Pistol, www.cr.nps.gov/museum/
exhibits/revwar/image_gal/guco30pistol.html; **170 bottom** courtesy National Park
Service, Museum Management Program and Guilford Courthouse National Military
Park, GUCO 349, Drum, www.cr.nps.gov/museum/exhibits/revwar/image_gal/
guco249.drum.html; **171** courtesy National Park Service, Museum Management
Program and Guilford Courthouse National Military Park; GUCO 1999, Powder Horn,
www.cr.nps.gov/museum/exhibits/revwar/ image_gal/guco1999horn.html; **173, 174**
courtesy Moores Creek N.B.; **177** Tryon Palace Historic Site; **178** courtesy Brandywine
Battlefield Park, Matt Mousley, photographer; **181** courtesy National Park Service,
Museum Management Program and Independence N.H.P., www.nps.gov/museum/
exhibits/revwar/image_gal/indeimg/lafayette.html; **180–181** Library of Congress,
Geography and Map Division; **183** *History of the U.S.*; **186** Richard J. Berenson; **188** *Life
of Washington*; **190** Library of Congress; **192** Library of Congress, Geography and Map
Division; **194** courtesy National Park Service; **195** *Life of Washington*; **196** courtesy
National Park Service, Museum Management Program and Independence N.H.P.,

Index

Page numbers in **boldface** refer to illustrations and maps.

www.nps.gov/museum/exhibits/ revwar/image_gal/ indeimg/steuben.html; **197 top** courtesy National Park Service, Museum Management Program and Valley Forge NHP; VAFO 3977, Regulations for the order and discipline..., www.cr.nps.gov/museums/ exhibits/ revwar/image_gal/vafoimg/vafo63977.html; **197 bottom left** courtesy National Park Service, Museum Management Program and Valley Forge NHP; VAFO 1090, Cartridge Box, www.cr.nps.gov/museums/exhibits/revwar/image_gal/vafoimg/vafo1090.html; **197 bottom right** courtesy National Park Service, Museum Management Program and Valley Forge NHP; VAFO 1788, Shot Mold, www.cr.nps.gov/museums/exhibits/revwar/image_gal/vafoimg/vafo1788.html; **198–199** © Bettmann/ CORBIS; **200** courtesy Washington Crossing State Park; **202–203** *History of the U.S.;* **205** courtesy Historic Camden; **207** © National Gallery Collection; By kind permission of the Trustees of the National Gallery, London/CORBIS; **209** U.S. Army; **210 bottom** Cowpens National Battlefield; **210-211 top** *Tartleton's Cavalrymen After the Battle of Cowpens, 1791* by William Ranney. Collection of the State of Carolina, courtesy PRC/ Picture Research Consultants, Topsfield, MA; **212-213** *The Battle of Kings Mountain* by Robert Windsor Wilson. Collection of the state of South Carolina, courtesy PRC/Picture Research Consultants, Topsfield, MA; **220, 221** courtesy The Bennington Museum; **224–225** Library of Congress, Geography and Map Division; **226** courtesy Lake Champlain Museum; **229** Library of Congress, Geography and Map Division; **232** courtesy National Park Service, Museum Management Program and Independence N.H.P., www.nps.gov/museum/exhibits/revwar/image_gal/indeimg/ jefferson.html; **236–237 top** © Tod Gipstein/CORBIS; **237 inset** Library of Congress, Geography and Map Division; **240** © CORBIS; **241, 243** © Paul Franklin; **244, 245** *Life of Washington;* **249** Richard J. Berenson; **251** *History of U.S.;* **253** Richard J. Berenson; **255** © Bob Krist/CORBIS; **258–259** Library of Congress, Geography and Map Division; **260-261** U.S. Army; **262, 263** Richard J. Berenson.